MATH
Connections®

A Secondary Mathematics Core Curriculum

William P. Berlinghoff
Clifford Sloyer
Robert W. Hayden

Published by IT'S ABOUT TIME, Inc. © 2000 MATHconx, LLC

Published in 2000 by
It's About Time, Inc.
84 Business Park Drive
Armonk, NY 10504
Phone (914)273-2233
Fax (914)273-2227
www.ITS-ABOUT-TIME.com
www.mathconnections.com

Publisher
Laurie Kreindler
Design
John Nordland
Production Manager
Barbara Zahm
Studio Manager
Leslie Jander

MATH *Connections*®: *A Secondary Mathematics Core Curriculum* was developed under the National Science Foundation Grant
No. ESI-9255251 awarded to the Connecticut Business and Industry Association.

ISBN 1-891629-83-2   MATH *Connections* Teacher Edition Book 1b   (Soft Cover)
ISBN 1-891629-88-3   MATH *Connections* Teacher Edition Books 1a, 1b Set   (Soft Cover)

ISBN 1-891629-19-0   MATH *Connections* Teacher Edition Book 1b   (3-Ring Binder)
ISBN 1-891629-78-6   MATH *Connections* Teacher Edition Books 1a, 1b Set   (3-Ring Binder)

2 3 4 5 D 02 01 00 99

This project was supported, in part,
by the
National Science Foundation
Opinions expressed are those of the authors
and not necessarily those of the Foundation.

MATH *Connections*: A Secondary Mathematics Core Curriculum

Table of Contents

Chapter 7 Counting Beyond 1-2-3

Chapter 8 Introduction to Probability: What Are
The Chances?

MATH Connections® Team

PRINCIPAL INVESTIGATORS

June G. Ellis, Director

Robert A. Rosenbaum
Wesleyan University

Robert J. Decker
University of Hartford

ADVISORY COUNCIL

James Aiello
Oakton Consulting Group, VA

Laurie Boswell
Profile High School, NH

Glenn Cassis
Connecticut Pre-Engineering Program

Daniel Dolan
Project to Improve Mastery in
Mathematics & Science

John Georges
Trinity College, CT

Renee Henry (retired)
Florida State Department of
Education

James Hogan Jr.
Connecticut Chapter of the National
Technology Association

Lauren Weisberg Kaufman
CBIA Education Foundation

James Landwehr
AT&T Bell Laboratories, NJ

Donald LaSalle
Talcott Mountain Science Center

Daniel Lawler (retired)
Hartford Public Schools

Steven Leinwand
Connecticut Department of Education

Valerie Lewis
Connecticut Department of Higher
Education

William Masalski
ex officio
University of Massachusetts

Gail Nordmoe
Cambridge Public Schools, MA

Thomas Romberg
Wisconsin Center for Educational
Research

Kenneth Sherrick
Berlin High School

Albert Shulte
Oakland Public Schools, MI

Irvin Vance
Michigan State University

Cecilia Welna
University of Hartford

SENIOR WRITERS

William P. Berlinghoff
Colby College, Maine

Clifford Sloyer
University of Delaware

Robert W. Hayden
Plymouth State College,
New Hampshire

STAFF

Robert Gregorski
Associate Director

Lorna Rojan
Program Manager

Carolyn Mitchell
Administrative Assistant

CONTRIBUTORS

Don Hastings (retired)
Stratford Public Schools

Kathleen Bavelas
Manchester Community-
Technical College

George Parker
E. O. Smith High School, Storrs

Linda Raffles
Glastonbury High School

Joanna Shrader Panning
Middletown High School

Frank Corbo
Staples High School, Westport

Thomas Alena
Talcott Mountain Science Center,
Avon

William Casey
Bulkeley High School, Hartford

Sharon Heyman
Bulkeley High School, Hartford

Helen Knudson
Choate Rosemary Hall,
Wallingford

Mary Jo Lane (retired)
Granby Memorial High School

Lori White Moroso
Beth Chana Academy for Girls,
Orange

John Pellino
Talcott Mountain Science Center,
Avon

Pedro Vasquez, Jr.
Multicultural Magnet School,
Bridgeport

Thomas Willmitch
Talcott Mountain Science Center,
Avon

Leslie Paoletti
Greenwich Public Schools

Robert Fallon (retired)
Bristol Eastern High School

Edwin Dudley (retired)
North Haven High School

ASSESSMENT SPECIALIST

Don Hastings (retired)
Stratford Public Schools

Published by IT'S ABOUT TIME, Inc. © 2000 MATHconx, LLC

Welcome to **MATH** *Connections®* *A Secondary Mathematics Core Curriculum*

MATH *Connections* is an exciting, challenging, three-year core curriculum for secondary mathematics! True to its name, this curriculum is built around connections of all sorts:

- between different mathematical areas;
- between mathematics and science;
- between mathematics and other subjects (history, literature, art, etc.);
- between mathematics and the real world of commerce, law, and people.

The following few pages tell you where this program came from, what it is designed to accomplish, and how it is constructed. We hope that reading this will help you, the teacher, become partners with us in making this curriculum come to life for your students.

Published by IT'S ABOUT TIME, Inc. © 2000 MATHconx, LLC

The History

MATH *Connections* began in 1992 when a team of educators associated with the Connecticut Business and Industry Association (CBIA), Wesleyan University, and the University of Hartford collaborated on the development of a new secondary mathematics core curriculum based on the *NCTM Standards*. Funded by a $4.9 million grant from the National Science Foundation awarded to the CBIA Education Foundation, the principal investigators assembled a team of people, including:

1. Senior writers: university mathematics professors with considerable teaching and writing experience who developed and wrote drafts and final copy of all the books.

2. Contributing writers: sixteen high school and community college mathematics teachers and two science specialists who reviewed the chapter drafts and wrote additional problems, projects, and ancillary materials.

3. Advisory Council: twenty respected professionals from the fields of mathematics, science, education and business, who met annually to review the overall direction of the project and to provide advice about various aspects of the emerging materials.

4. Classroom teachers and students: more than 100 field-test teachers and approximately 2500 students from seventeen different inner city, urban, suburban and rural high schools who used preliminary versions of these materials and provided feedback from their classroom experiences.

A many-faceted external evaluation of the MATH *Connections* program was an integral part of the project. External evaluators provided comprehensive reports on student achievement on standardized tests and how well MATH *Connections* met its objectives. Consultants reviewed the materials for gender equity, multicultural equity, and readability.

The Vision and The Mission

The Vision: *All students can learn mathematics, be critical thinkers and be problem solvers.*

The Mission: *The conceptual understanding of the learner.*

The MATH *Connections* team designed the program to meet the following objectives:

MATH *Connections* is for *all* students. It is relevant to students as future citizens, parents, voters, consumers, researchers, employers and employees — people with a healthy curiosity about ideas. It serves well the needs and interests of all high school students, those who will go on to further math-intensive studies and science-related careers, as well as those who choose to pursue other fields of study. In fact, it enchances students' understanding of the interrelatedness of all fields and increases the attractiveness of mathematics and science as it is applied in the real world.

MATH *Connections* is flexible, allowing students with different learning styles equal opportunity to master the ideas and skills presented. This means providing both interactive group work and individual learning experiences, encouraging frequent student-teacher and student-student interaction, in finding answers and in discussing mathematics, relevant student experiences, opinions, and judgments.

The main technological tools of the world of work are an integral part of the material. Students learn to be comfortable with graphing calulators and computers, in order to cope with and profit from the opportunities of our increasingly technological world.

It is reality based. All the mathematical ideas in the curriculum are drawn from and connected to real world situations. Students can immediately see how the mathematics they are learning relates to their own lives and the world around them.

MATH *Connections* focuses on the conceptual aspects of mathematics — reasoning, pattern seeking, problem solving, questioning, and communicating with precision — because those are the features of a mathematical education that are important to lawyers, doctors, business leaders, teachers, politicians, social workers, military officers, entrepreneurs, artists, or writers as they are to scientists or engineers.

Books in Brief

Each of the three years of MATH *Connections* is built around a general theme which serves as a unifying thread for the topics covered. Each year is divided into two half-year books consisting of three or four large chapters. Every chapter has a unifying conceptual theme that connects to the general theme of the year.

Year 1 — Data, Numbers, and Patterns

Book 1a begins and ends with data analysis. It starts with hands-on data gathering, presentation, and analysis, then poses questions about correlating two sets of data. This establishes the goal of the term — that students be able to use the linear regression capabilities of a graphing calculator to do defensible forecasting in real world settings. Students reach this goal by mastering the algebra of first degree equations and the coordinate geometry of straight lines, gaining familiarity with graphing calculators.

Chapter 1. Turning Facts into Ideas
Chapter 2. Welcome to Algebra
Chapter 3. The Algebra of Straight Lines
Chapter 4. Graphical Estimation

Book 1b generalizes and expands the ideas of *Book 1a*. It begins with techniques for solving two linear equations in two unknowns and interpreting such solutions in real world contexts. Functional relationships in everyday life are identified, generalized, brought into mathematical focus, and linked with the algebra and coordinate geometry already developed. These ideas are then linked to an examination of the fundamental counting principle of discrete mathematics and to the basic ideas of probability. Along the way, *Book 1b* poses questions about correlating two sets of data.

Chapter 5. Using Lines and Equations
Chapter 6. How Functions Function
Chapter 7. Counting Beyond 1, 2, 3
Chapter 8. Introduction to Probability: What Are the Chances?

Year 2 — Shapes in Space

Book 2a starts with the most basic ways of measuring length and area. It uses symmetries of planar shapes to ask and answer questions about polygonal figures. Algebraic ideas from Year 1 are elaborated by providing them with geometric interpretations. Scaling opens the door to similarity and then to angular measure, which builds on the concept of slope from Year 1. Extensive work with angles and triangles, of interest in its own right, also lays the groundwork for right angle

MATH *Connections*: A Secondary Mathematics Core Curriculum

trigonometry, the last main topic of this book. Standard principles of congruence and triangulation of polygons are developed and employed in innovative ways to make clear their applicability to real world problems.

Chapter 1. The Building Blocks of Geometry: Making and Measuring Polygons

Chapter 2. Similarity and Scaling: Growing and Shrinking Carefully

Chapter 3. Introduction to Trigonometry: Tangles with Angles

Book 2b begins by exploring the role of circles in the world of spatial relationships. It then generalizes the two dimensional ideas and thought patterns of *Book 2a* to three dimensions, starting with foldup patterns and contour lines on topographical maps. This leads to some fundamental properties of three dimensional shapes. Coordinate geometry connects this spatial world of three dimensions to the powerful tools of algebra. That two way connection is then used to explore systems of equations in three variables, extending the treatment of two variable equations in Year 1. In addition, matrices are shown to be a convenient way to organize, store, and manipulate information.

Chapter 4. Circles and Disks

Chapter 5. Shapes in Space

Chapter 6. Linear Algebra and Matrices

Year 3 — Mathematical Modeling

Book 3a examines mathematical models of real world situations from several viewpoints, providing innovative settings and a unifying theme for the discussion of algebraic, periodic, exponential, and logarithmic functions. These chapters develop many ideas whose seeds were planted in Years 1 and 2. The emphasis throughout this material is the utility of mathematical tools for describing and clarifying what we observe. The modeling theme is then used to revisit and extend the ideas of discrete mathematics and probability that were introduced in Year 1.

Chapter 1. Algebraic Functions
Chapter 2. Exponential Functions and Logarithms
Chapter 3. The Trigonometric Functions
Chapter 4. Counting, Probability, and Statistics

Book 3b begins by extending the modeling theme to Linear Programming, optimization, and topics from graph theory. Then the idea of modeling itself is examined in some depth by considering the purpose of axioms and axiomatic systems, logic, and mathematical proof. Various forms of logical arguments, already used informally throughout Years 1 and 2, are explained and used to explore small axiomatic systems, including the group axioms. These logical tools then provide guidance for a mathematical exploration of infinity, an area in which commonsense intuition is often unreliable. The final chapter explores Euclid's plane geometry, connecting his system with many geometric concepts from Year 2. It culminates in a brief historical explanation of Euclidean and non-Euclidean geometries as alternative models for the spatial structure of our universe.

Chapter 5. Optimization: Math Does It Better
Chapter 6. Playing By the Rules: Logic and Axiomatic Systems
Chapter 7. Infinity — The Final Frontier?
Chapter 8. Axioms, Geometry, and Choice

Appendices

Appendix A. Using a TI-82 (TI-83) Graphing Calculator. This appendix appears in all the books because graphing calculators are important tools for virtually every chapter. It provides a gentle introduction to these machines, and also serves as a convenient student reference for the commonly used elementary procedures.

Appendix B. Using a Spreadsheet. This appendix also appears in all the books. Although a spreadsheet is not explicitly required anywhere in these books, it is very handy for doing many problems or Explorations. It should be considered as a legitimate, optional tool for anyone with access to one.

Appendix C. Programming the TI-82 (TI-83). This appendix also appears in all the books. Students can use it to learn useful general principles of programming, as well as techniques specific to the TI-82 (TI-83).

Appendix D. Linear Programming with Excel. This appendix, which appears in Years 2 and 3, is not primarily a tool for doing problems within the chapters. Rather, it describes a technological approach to ideas that come up from time to time in various chapters. Linear Programming itself is discussed in detail in Chapter 5 of *Book 3b*. This appendix can be used either as a precursor to that discussion, or as an extension of it.

The Features

Here is an overview of the distinctive features that combine to make MATH *Connections* unique.

Standards-based — The NCTM Standards were guiding principles in the development of MATH *Connections*. In particular, various creative devices were employed to implement the four process standards:

- **Problem Solving** — MATH *Connections* demonstrates how mathematics is primarily about asking your own questions and looking for patterns, rather than finding someone else's answers and calculating with numbers. Marginal notes called *Thinking Tips* guide students in specific problem solving strategies. Within sections, many of the *Discuss this* questions and *Explorations* focus students' attention on the problem solving process, while the Problem Sets that conclude virtually all sections further challenge and extend their problem solving skills.

- **Communication** — MATH *Connections*' reading level has been carefully tailored to be, on average, at least one year below grade level. In addition, definitions of all mathematical terms used are clearly identified in the text. The most important ones are displayed as *Words (or Phrases) to Know*. The marginal devices *About Words* and

About Symbols explain fundamental mathematical language and notation. The *Discuss this* and *Write this* questions expect students to talk and write about mathematics in every chapter. The Problem Sets offer many open-ended questions that are suitable for group discussions, or homework writing assignments.

- **Reasoning** — The habit of logical justification is begun in Chapter 1 of *Book 1a* and carried through the entire series. Evaluation of suppositions and arguments occurs throughout all chapters of all books. In Year 1, the reasoning required is largely informal, progressing in Year 2 to more formal justifications. The idea of a counterexample is introduced formally at the beginning of the year and used routinely after that. Expectations of logical justification become more rigorous in Year 3. Also, formal proofs within axiomatic systems (not just in geometry), including mathematical induction, are examined and required.

- **Connections** — This is the defining theme of the entire MATH *Connections* program. The mathematical ideas are connected to the real world by different real life applications — more than 50 professions, 20 job fields and most academic disciplines — within the problems, Explorations and situations of the texts. The most common applications are to science (physics, chemistry, astronomy, biology, archaeology), but there are also applications to theater, music, business and the social sciences, as well as to daily life.

Blended — MATH *Connections* provides a proven approach in which students learn the underlying structure and the skills of mathematics. By presenting mathematics as the subject is used and by blending ideas from traditionally separate fields, students learn not only the topics but also the connections between algebra, geometry, probability, statistics, discrete mathematics, Dynamic and Linear Programming and optimization. By bringing ideas from a wide range of areas to bear on a question, MATH *Connections* presents mathematics as a seamless fabric perhaps with different patterns and colors in different areas, but with no clear boundary lines. Here are some typical examples of the blending of mathematics in MATH *Connections*, one from each year.

- In *Book 1a*, the discussion of carbon dating in Section 4.4 uses first degree equations (algebra), straight line graphs (geometry), least-squares differences (algebra and statistics), and a graphing calculator (technology) to solve a problem in archaeology (natural science). All these tools come together naturally in this context.

- At the end of Section 5.4 in *Book 2b*, algebra, geometry (the volume of a cone) and Cavalieri's Principle (usually in precalculus) are combined to calculate the volume of a sphere.

- In Chapter 6 of *Book 3b*, properties of axiomatic systems (logic) are introduced by examining the rules of a simple card game and the probabilities of certain kinds of outcomes. In Section 6.5 axiomatic systems are related to physics via the Law of the Lever and also to the arithmetic properties of the number systems. The Problem Set for this section includes ideas about population growth, physics, and integer arithmetic.

Accessible — Every major idea in MATH *Connections* is introduced from a commonsense viewpoint using ordinary, nonmathematical examples. For instance, coordinate geometry starts with reading map coordinates, slope follows from building a wheelchair ramp, the concept of function begins with fingerprint files, etc. This helps students see that a mathematical view of the world is not so very different from their view of the world.

Real — This curriculum is firmly grounded in the real world of the students' present and future. The scenarios are realistic, the data sets are drawn from real world sources, the applications are real. Even the whimsical settings use realistic measurements and conditions. Students see for themselves how mathematics is actually used.

Flexible — MATH *Connections* provides for a wide variety of student backgrounds and learning styles. There is plenty of opportunity for student-teacher and student-student interaction in discussing mathematics, students' experiences, opinions, and judgments. Two types of materials are available for each chapter which enhance a teacher's ability to meet the individual needs of all students.

- Supplemental materials for students whose understanding would be strengthened by additional problems or for those who are absent or enter the MATH *Connections* program in midstream

- Extension units for students who want to investigate in greater depth the concepts introduced in a particular section, either individually or in groups

Technological — Your students' future success is likely to depend, at least in part, on their ability to cope with and use the fast-changing tools of electronic technology. We treat the basic technological tools available in the world of work, particularly graphing calculators, as an integral part of the course material. Students are encouraged to use these tools whenever they are appropriate to the work at hand. Students are introduced to the graphing calculator early and are expected to use it routinely as they go along.

The Appendices of every book are filled with simple, illustrative examples of the calculator's basic tasks and functions. In addition, this Teacher Commentary contains many suggestions of where and how you can incorporate other technological tools — spreadsheets, Geometer's Sketchpad, or other geometry software — into your teaching.

Organized — The organization of these books is student friendly:

- Every chapter starts from a point of view that makes sense in the students' world. The expected Learning Outcomes are explicitly stated at the beginning of each section.

- The definitions of all technical terms and the statements of all important facts (theorems) are typographically distinctive, making them easy to find when reviewing.

- Each chapter ends with a retrospective paragraph to help students reflect on their learning.

- Each book contains a glossary, an index, and appendices.

Cooperative Learning

Classes designed around small group and whole class interaction fit the MATH *Connections* curriculum very well. Many of the *Do this now* and *Discuss this* activities are best done in groups. They are particularly useful in traditional and block scheduling situations where there is time for both group work and for direct teacher instruction or discussions involving the entire class. When students work in cooperative settings, they benefit from the interaction and insights of classmates. Student discussions on specific textbook questions often yield surprising and unexpected results. Moreover, working with graphing calculators is greatly enhanced by the group process, as students reinforce their understanding.

MATH *Connection's* classroom experiences reinforce the understanding that learning is a social process and that cooperative learning activities are essential if students are to be able to construct their own knowledge.

Suggested Reading
How to Use Cooperative Learning in the Mathematics Class, Second Edition
By Alice F. Artzt and Claire M. Newman
From the NCTM Educational Materials and Products Catalog
ISBN 0-87353-437-9 #650E1
1-800-235-7566

Elements

About Words are margin paragraphs that explain technical terms and other words that are not part of everyday language, showing how the mathematical use of a word is related to its usage outside of mathematics. This feature facilitates the integration of mathematics with English, especially with English as a second language.

About Symbols are margin paragraphs that point out how specific symbolic conventions are reasonable shorthand ways of writing and communicating the ideas they represent.

Thinking Tips are margin paragraphs that highlight the use of specific problem solving techniques.

A Word to Know and **A Phrase to Know** signal particularly important definitions. Some words appear in boldface where they are defined or first described.

A Fact to Know signals an important mathematical result. In mathematicians' terms, they are significant theorems.

Do this now identifies questions that students should deal with before moving ahead. Often, these questions are answered within the few pages that follow. If the students don't wrestle with the question when it appears, its value as a learning experience may be lost.

Discuss this identifies questions intended to provoke interchange among students, open-ended Explorations, and/or a variety of opinions. They can be done as soon as they appear in the text, but you might want to delay some and omit others, depending on your sense of how they might work best with your students.

Write this identifies student writing exercises and requires students to gather information or reflect upon a topic. These exercises are suitable for group work and reporting, and can be assigned individually as homework or completed in class.

Pacing

Each school district will need to evaluate the pacing of the curriculum according to the needs of their students and schedule it has adopted. The two models shown here are examples of how school systems have adapted MATH *Connections* to fit their needs. Each semester assumes 16 weeks of class time, allowing two weeks per semester for other activities such as projects, statewide testing, etc.

3-YEAR PACING MODEL

Year 1:

Book 1a	Chapter 1	4 weeks including assessments
	Chapter 2	5 weeks including assessments
	Chapter 3	4 weeks including assessments
	Chapter 4	3 weeks including assessments
Book 1b	Chapter 5	4 weeks including assessments
	Chapter 6	6 weeks including assessments
	Chapter 7	3 weeks including assessments
	Chapter 8	3 weeks including assessments

Year 2:

Book 2a	Chapter 1	5 weeks including assessments
	Chapter 2	6 weeks including assessments
	Chapter 3	5 weeks including assessments
Book 2b	Chapter 4	5 weeks including assessments
	Chapter 5	6 weeks including assessments
	Chapter 6	5 weeks including assessments

Year 3:

Book 3a	Chapter 1	6 weeks including assessments
	Chapter 2	5 weeks including assessments
	Chapter 3	4 weeks including assessments
	Chapter 4	3 weeks including assessments
Book 3b	Chapter 5	3 weeks including assessments
	Chapter 6	3 weeks including assessments
	Chapter 7	4 weeks including assessments
	Chapter 8	4 weeks including assessments

(Teachers sometimes assign Chapter 8 as independent study resulting in student projects and research papers.)

MATH *Connections*: A Secondary Mathematics Core Curriculum

The sections within each chapter vary in length and each is built around a major idea. Several sections might take only one class period; others may take two, three or four class periods. MATH *Connections* gives you the flexibility to successfully match the capabilities of your students with the program. Higher level classes complete the *a* and *b* books in one year, making this a 3-year program. In other situations, however, MATH *Connections* can be taught over $3\frac{1}{2}$ to 4 years.

$3\frac{1}{2}$ - YEAR PACING MODEL

Year 1:

Book 1a	Chapter 1	5 weeks including assessments
	Chapter 2	6 weeks including assessments
	Chapter 3	6 weeks including assessments
	Chapter 4	4 weeks including assessments
Book 1b	Chapter 5	5 weeks including assessments
	Chapter 6	6 weeks including assessments

Year 2:

Book 1b	Chapter 7	3 weeks including assessments
	Chapter 8	2 weeks including assessments
Book 2a	Chapter 1	9 weeks including assessments
	Chapter 2	8 weeks including assessments
	Chapter 3	3 weeks including assessments
Book 2b	Chapter 4	4 weeks including assessments
	Chapter 5	3 weeks including assessments (up to section 5.5)

Year 3:

Book 2b	Chapter 5	3 weeks including assessments (start at section 5.6)
	Chapter 6	4 weeks including assessments
Book 3a	Chapter 1	7 weeks including assessments
	Chapter 2	6 weeks including assessments
	Chapter 3	5 weeks including assessments
	Chapter 4	7 weeks including assessments

Year 4:

Book 3b	Chapter 5	4 weeks including assessments
	Chapter 6	4 weeks including assessments
	Chapter 7	5 weeks including assessments
	Chapter 8	5 weeks including assessments

Materials Included With Teacher Edition

MATH *Connections* provides a full range of support materials. In addition to the Teacher Edition, each year includes:

Assessments Form A — Allows students to use a variety of formats to demonstrate their knowledge of mathematical concepts and skills. Assessments are tied to specific mathematics objectives and are linked to the Learning Outcomes for each section of the chapter. Form A was developed for each quiz and chapter test.

The Solution Key and Scoring Guide for each quiz and chapter test contains solutions to all questions as well as suggestions for scoring based on a 100 point scale.

Blackline Masters — Contain spreadsheets, graphs, tables and forms which can be copied and distributed to students in the class or used as transparencies.

Ancillary Materials

Assessments Form B — Provides teachers with an alternative but equivalent assessment for each quiz and chapter test along with corresponding Solution Keys. They can be used as alternate assessments or makeup tests, etc.

Supplements — Complement the MATH *Connections* curriculum for students whose understanding of mathematics would be strengthened by additional work or for those who have been absent or enter the MATH *Connections* program in midstream.

Extensions — Enable students to investigate in greater depth the concepts and activities introduced in a particular section.

Test Banks — Allow teachers to prepare tests such as Midterms and Final Exams that are specifically tailored to the particular needs of their students. They include sample formats and test questions, along with the corresponding Solution Keys.

Professional Development Videos — It is always preferable to attend Professional Development Workshops. But sometimes schedules and budgets make attendance difficult. We developed these videos to support the professional development of teachers as they implement MATH *Connections* in their classrooms.

NCTM 9-12 Standards Correlation

Integrated into all three years of MATH *Connections* are the four process standards:

1. **Mathematics as Problem Solving:** **Explorations, Projects, Simulations and Problem Solving**

2. **Mathematics as Communication:** *Do this now, Discuss this, Write this, About Words, About Symbols, Justify Opinions*

3. **Mathematics as Reasoning:** **A thematic thread in all three years**

4. **Mathematics as Connections:** **Connections with more than 50 professions, 20 job fields and all academic disciplines**

	Year 1	Year 2	Year 3
5. Algebra	**Chap. 2, 3, 4, 5**	**Chap. 1, 2, 6**	**Chap. 1, 5**
6. Functions	**Chap. 5, 6**	**Chap. 1**	**Chap. 1, 2, 3**
7. Geometry from a Synthetic Perspective	**Chap. 5, 6**	**Chap. 1, 2, 4, 5**	**Chap. 1, 5, 6, 8**
8. Geometry from an Algebraic Perspective	**Chap. 3**	**Chap. 1, 4, 5**	**Chap. 1**
9. Trigonometry		**Chap. 3, 4, 5**	**Chap. 3**
10. Statistics	**Chap. 1, 4, 5, 8**		**Chap. 4**
11. Probability	**Chap. 7, 8**		**Chap. 4**
12. Discrete Mathematics	**Chap. 1, 2, 4, 5, 7, 8**	**Chap. 2, 5, 6**	**Chap. 4, 5, 6**
13. Conceptual Underpinnings of the Calculus	**Chap. 2, 5, 6**	**Chap. 2, 5, 6**	**Chap. 1, 7**
14. Mathematical Structure	**Chap. 2, 4**	**Chap. 2**	**Chap. 6, 7, 8**

Published by IT'S ABOUT TIME, Inc. © 2000 MATHconx, LLC

Planning Guide Book 1b

This book generalizes and expands ideas begun in *Book 1a*. It begins with techniques for solving linear equations in two unknowns and interpreting such solutions in real world contexts. Functional relationships in everyday life are identified, generalized, brought into mathematical focus, and linked with the algebra and coordinate geometry already developed. These ideas are then linked to an examination of the fundamental counting principles of discrete mathematics and to the basic ideas of probability.

Chapter Objectives	*Pacing Range	Assessments Form A (A)	Blackline Masters
Chapter 5 Using Lines and Equations In the context of comparing utility rate schedules, Chapter 5 uses the mathematical concepts of Chapters 2 and 3 to solve linear equations in two unknowns. These ideas are then extended and linked with Chapters 1 and 4 in discussing how to compare relationships for two sets of data, including data for exponential growth.	4-5 weeks including Assessments	Quiz 5.1-5.3(A) Quiz 5.4-5.5(A) Quiz 5.6-5.7(A) Chapter Test(A)	Student pp. 278, 283
Chapter 6 How Functions Function Starting with fingerprints and postal rates, Chapter 6 presents discrete, step, linear and growth functions. It draws on Chapters 2, 3 and 5 to describe functions algebraically and graphically, and applies function composition to real world situations. This lays the groundwork for in-depth treatment of polynomial, exponential, and periodic functions also found in great depth and breadth in Chapters 1-3 of Year 3.	6 weeks including Assessments	Quiz 6.1-6.2(A) Quiz 6.3-6.4(A) Quiz 6.5(A) Quiz 6.6(A) Chapter Test(A)	Student pp. 375, 376, 388, 391-392
Chapter 7 Counting Beyond 1, 2, 3 Chapter 7 focuses on counting. It summarizes basic ideas, language, and notation for sets, introduces Venn diagrams and tree diagrams, and establishes the Fundamental Counting Principle, all in concrete, commonsense contexts. This lays the groundwork for the topics of discrete mathematics that appear in later chapters.	3 weeks including Assessments	Quiz 7.1-7.2(A) Quiz 7.3(A) Quiz 7.4-7.5(A) Chapter Test(A)	No Blackline Masters for this chapter
Chapter 8 Introduction to Probability: What Are the Chances? Chapter 8 makes immediate use of Chapter 7. Combining counting with chance, it presents the probability function for events of equally likely outcomes. Later sections describe how to simulate uncertain situations by using random number tables or by calculator programs.	2-3 weeks including Assessments	Quiz 8.1-8.2(A) Quiz 8.3(A) Project 8.4-8.5(A) Chapter Test(A)	Student pp. 455-456, 477, 489-490

*Pacing Range   Teachers will need to adjust this guide to suit the needs of their own students. Not all classes will complete each chapter at the same pace. Flexibility — which accommodates different teaching styles, school schedules and school standards — is built into the curriculum.

Ancillary Materials

Assessments Form B (B)	Supplements for Chapter Sections	Extensions	Test Banks
Quiz 5.1-5.3(B) Quiz 5.4-5.5(B) Quiz 5.6-5.7(B) Chapter Test(B)	5.1 A Guessing Game — 2 Supplements 5.2 Organizing Trial and Error — 1 Supplement 5.4 Pictures on Your Calculator — 1 Supplement 5.6 Precise Answers to Real Life Situations — 4 Supplements 5.7 Using Algebra to Solve Systems of Equations — 1 Supplement	No Extensions for this chapter	To be released
Quiz 6.1-6.2(B) Quiz 6.3-6.4(B)) Quiz 6.5(B) Quiz 6.6(B) Chapter Test(B)	6.1 It All Depends — 3 Supplements 6.3 Between the Dots — 1 Supplement 6.4 Describing Functions With Algebra — 1 Supplement 6.5 Growth Functions — 1 Supplement 6.6 Links in a Chain: Composition of Functions — 2 Supplements	Following 6.6 Recursive Relations	To be released
Quiz 7.1-7.2(B) Quiz 7.3(B) Quiz 7.4-7.5(B) Chapter Test(B)	7.2 Sets: What to Count — 1 Supplement 7.3 Venn Diagrams: Counting With Pictures — 1 Supplement 7.5 The Fundamental Counting Principle — 1 Supplement	7.5 The Genetic Code Following 7.5 Counting Jeans	To be released
Quiz 8.1-8.2(B)) Quiz 8.3(B) Chapter Test(B))	8.1 Basic Ideas of Probability — 1 Supplement 8.2 Intuition and Probability — 1 Supplement	8.3 What Are the Odds?	To be released

Published by IT'S ABOUT TIME, Inc. © 2000 MATHconx, LLC

Published by IT'S ABOUT TIME, Inc. © 2000 MATHconx, LLC

Chapter 5 Planning Guide

Chapter 5 Using Lines and Equations

In the context of comparing utility rate schedules, Chapter 5 uses the mathematical concepts of Chapters 2 and 3 to solve linear equations in two unknowns. These ideas are then extended and linked with Chapters 1 and 4 in discussing how to compare relationships for two sets of data, including data for exponential growth.

Assessments Form A (A)	Assessments Form B (B)	Blackline Masters
Quiz 5.1-5.3(A) Quiz 5.4-5.5(A) Quiz 5.6-5.7(A) Chapter Test(A)	Quiz 5.1-5.3(B) Quiz 5.4-5.5(B) Quiz 5.6-5.7(B) Chapter Test(B)	Student pp. 278, 283

Extensions	Supplements for Chapter Sections	Test Banks
No Extensions for this chapter.	5.1 A Guessing Game — 2 Supplements 5.2 Organizing Trial and Error — 1 Supplement 5.4 Pictures on Your Calculator — 1 Supplement 5.6 Precise Answers to Real Life Situations — 4 Supplements 5.7 Using Algebra to Solve Systems of Equations — 1 Supplement	To be released

Pacing Range 4-5 weeks including Assessments

Teachers will need to adjust this guide to suit the needs of their own students. Not all classes will complete each chapter at the same pace. Flexibility — which accommodates different teaching styles, school schedules and school standards — is built into the curriculum.

Teacher Commentary is indexed to the student text by the numbers in the margins (under the icons or in circles). The first digit indicates the chapter — the numbers after the decimal indicate the sequential numbering of the comments within that unit. Example:

5.9

5.37

Student Pages in Teacher Edition

5.9

5.37

Teacher Commentary Page

Observations

Bryan Morgan, Teacher
Oxford Hills Comprehensive
High School, ME

"MATH *Connections* presents the problems first, then helps the students find the skills necessary to solving the problems. The traditional method of teaching algebra was to teach kids how to solve systems of equations even when they didn't understand why they'd ever need them. Then later, they may have been given examples of real world applications. MATH *Connections* is just the opposite — first it poses a real world problem that they see some value of solving, then it guides the students towards some trial and error methods for solving it. The next step is to introduce the algebraic technique as a final component to show a better way to arrive at a solution. You demonstrate to the students a need to use the tool before you show them the tool. It's called guided discovery. Kids really appreciate this approach and have a much greater understanding and retention."

Rosalie Griffin, Teacher
Crosby High School, CT

"In this chapter I recommend that students work through all the charts and tables that are presented in the text. It is very helpful to have them put these charts into their notebooks and complete them for several values. This technique enables them to become excellent 'record-keepers' and to continually search for patterns and trends. I found that this helped to develop excellent critical thinking and problem solving skills. The problems in general for this chapter are excellent in that they directed students towards the understanding that certain 'plans' or 'offers' are better than others under certain circumstances. This enables them to be more discerning in real life situations and makes them more aware that solutions can sometimes depend on the parameters and constraints of a situation."

The Profiles are where students will meet people in various careers and professions who use mathematics in their everyday work.

The Profiles point out to students how many different and diverse professions utilize mathematics as a key building block. This is an excellent opportunity to open up class discussions and will lead to an increased knowledge of the value of mathematics in the real world. Students come to realize the importance of mathematics in many more of the professions, occupations and careers than they might have previously thought.

Deirdre Lord
Reducing Electricity Costs

Deirdre Lord works for Citizens Energy Corporation in Boston, Massachusetts. Joe Kennedy founded this nonprofit energy company. Its goal is to use industry to provide low-income communities with energy education and assistance programs.

As a project manager, Deirdre helps people understand and take advantage of new utility regulations. "Deregulation is very confusing," she explains. "It means that utilities can now compete with each other, just like any other business. My big challenge is to get low-income customers to join an energy pool. As a pool, they can get better rates from the electric companies."

Deirdre has a Masters Degree from the University of Delaware. As a student, she saw the need for mathematics, so she studied statistics as well as economics.

"I now use these tools all the time," she says. "They are very important to my work."

Deirdre often uses bar charts and graphs to show her clients why they should join an energy pool. "I put the mathematics of the utility bills into something visual. This helps my clients understand what they can save. There are a number of dependent and independent variables in these calculations. I use estimation techniques to explain the savings.

"By putting our group with other groups, say large community centers or public housing complexes, we can do even better," Deirdre adds. "I'd like to see this program expand and become an example for the entire country."

274

Chapter 5 Using Lines and Equations

There are several parallel strands throughout this chapter. One strand is the *comparison* of relationships. There are usually just two relationships to compare, and the relationships are usually linear, but there are exceptions to both of these generalizations.

A less obvious strand is a deeper study of **algorithms**. In today's college curriculum, this would normally be taught in a discrete mathematics or numerical analysis course. Algorithms would also come up in many computer science classes. At this level we want students to realize that things can be done in many ways, and each way usually has its own strengths and weaknesses.

A third strand is a **review** and an **extension** of material from past chapters. The comparison of two relationships is done for empirical data such as we studied in Chapters 1 and 4, and for equations such as the ones we studied in Chapter 2. A major tool for our comparisons is the type of graph we developed in Chapter 3. There are no explicit review sections here. The problems that arise in real life are rarely limited to the section students read for homework last night, and we want to send students the message that they are responsible for material covered earlier in the course. Of course, you may have to help them review previous material, if needed.

Using Lines and Equations

CHAPTER

5

5.1 A Guessing Game

Learning Outcomes

After studying this section you will be able to:

Use mathematics to develop strategies for a simple guessing game;

Read a tree diagram using an algorithm;

Compare different algorithms for the same real life problem.

In this course, you have already learned how to solve many mathematical problems. In Chapter 1 you learned how to display and interpret data. In Chapter 2, you learned how to set up and solve equations. In Chapter 3, you learned how to graph equations. In Chapter 4, you learned how to find a line to fit some data, and then found an equation of the line. In this chapter we will tie these ideas together and learn to solve many types of new problems.

For some of the problems you have solved, you used a definite algorithm. There was a sequence of steps you went through that always led to an answer. In other cases you used techniques like guessing, estimating, or trial and error. In this chapter, you will learn algorithms to solve problems you previously solved using other techniques.

Mathematicians have always been interested in algorithms but the study of algorithms became even more important after the invention of computers. Before you can write a program to make a computer do something, you must have a particular algorithm in

Published by IT'S ABOUT TIME, Inc. © 2000 MATHconx, LLC

275

5.1 A Guessing Game

5.1

We begin this chapter with a game activity (see student page 276 on T-8) we hope your students will find engaging. They may be surprised that mathematics can be applied to games. They may not feel this has much practical importance, but the line between games and such serious activities as war or business is a fine one indeed. Actually, they may not immediately recognize what happens here as mathematics at all, since there are no formulas and no arithmetic. There is, however, a lot of reasoning about numbers and a more explicit analysis of an algorithm than we have made previously.

Chapter 5

Additional Support Materials:

Assessments	Qty
Form (A)	1
Form (B)	1

Blackline Masters	Qty
Student p.278	1

Extensions	Qty

Supplements	Qty
A Guessing Game	2

mind. In some cases, several algorithms must be analyzed to determine which is best.

As an example, we will develop an algorithm for playing a simple game. The game works like this. One person picks a whole number from 1 to 100. Another person tries to guess the number by asking only questions that can be answered "Yes" or "No." He can make a simple guess like "Is it 53?" or ask questions like "Is it more than 9?" or "Is it less than 88?"

5.1 Pair off with one of your classmates and play the game four times. Take turns being the guesser. Record the number of questions the guesser asks before he or she guesses the number.

After playing this game, you and your partner should have four pieces of data. If either of you guessed the number with 8 or fewer questions, you did a very good job! How did your classmates do?

a
5.2 Gather data from the entire class. Use some data analysis techniques to summarize and display the data.

When you were guessing, did you have a strategy or did you just guess at random? What about your classmates?

b
5.3 Examine the data from the entire class. Did any students find the number after asking very few questions? Did they have a strategy or were they just lucky? You can check this out by having the good guessers repeat the game with several different partners. Did you find anyone who consistently was a good guesser? If so, try to find out their strategy. Discuss possible strategies with your classmates and try to find a good strategy. See if you can predict the minimum number of questions needed to guess the number.

Here is a simple algorithm for playing this game. The guesser asks the questions,

1. Is the number 1?
2. Is the number 2?
3. Is the number 3?
4. Is the number 4?

and so forth.

5.2

5.3

Most sections of this chapter start with material suitable for you to use with the class as a whole. Each section could probably be finished by the students on their own or working in small groups.

NOTES

Chapter 5

Does this algorithm work? That is, if you are the guesser will you eventually find the number if you use this algorithm?

5.4

Pretend you have a partner and you are the guesser. How many questions will you have to ask if the number picked is 25? What if it is 95? What would be the *least* number of questions that you might have to ask? What would be the *most* number of questions that you might have to ask? Can your partner make you ask a lot of questions?

This algorithm is not very efficient. We will now look at an algorithm that is slightly more complicated, but more efficient.

We will start with an algorithm for guessing a number from 1 to 8. Then we will see if we can apply the algorithm to guessing a number from 1 to 100. First, to be sure that we understand the problem clearly, we will write it in mathematical language.

The guesser must guess the value of a whole number x where $1 \leq x \leq 8$. (Earlier you learned that $1 \leq x \leq 8$ means "x is between 1 and 8, inclusive.") Also, can be read "1 is less than or equal to x and x is less than or equal to 8."

Thinking Tip

Sometimes when trying to solve a problem it is helpful to try a simpler version of the problem first.

The basic idea of our new algorithm is to reduce the number of possibilities (roughly) in half with each question. For example, if $1 \leq x \leq 8$, the first question to ask is, "Is x more than four?" If the answer is, "Yes," then x must be 5, 6, 7, or 8. If the answer is, "No," then x must be 1, 2, 3, or 4. In either case, you have reduced the problem to one of guessing one of four numbers, a much shorter problem.

If your partner says x is greater than four, the next question would be "Is it greater than 6?" This again divides the possibilities in two.

What is the next question if your partner says x is *not* bigger than 6?

5.5

If your partner had answered your *first* question by saying that x was *not* less than four, what would be your next question?

5.6

277

5.4

We hope your students will think that this is an inefficient algorithm. If they do, try to draw out *why* they think it is. We want them to realize that there are usually many different ways to solve a problem. Once they realize this, it makes sense to start evaluating the different ways. This first algorithm is not a great one, but it does actually get the job done, is easy to understand, and provides a basis of comparison for other possible algorithms.

Some points you might watch for in the discussion are the facts that the algorithm does work, but the number of guesses needed is highly variable and tends to be rather large, averaging around 50 if the player who chooses the number is not biased. If your class is highly motivated, you might ask it to devise a better algorithm before going on in the text.

These questions are here to check that the students understand the new algorithm.

5.5

In 5.5, the possibilities are now (5, 6). Continuing the algorithm, the next question is, "Is x more than five?" Students may want to diverge from the algorithm and ask, "Is x five?" or "Is x six?" Depending on exactly what rules we adopt for the game (see below), this might be a good strategy. However if we want to analyze an algorithm, we need to be consistent in applying it. Whichever of these two questions we ask, it always takes three questions to uniquely determine x.

5.6

In 5.6, the next question is, "is x more than two" or "is x more than 6?". After further branching in a tree diagram, the second question leads to testing for 5, 6, 7 and 8; the first question tests for the number 4.

As a word of caution, please note that students may get off to an unproductive start on this problem if they begin with $x \geq 4$ and then branch, unbalanced to 1, 2, 3 and 4, 5, 6, 7, 8. The starting inequality is $x > 4$, with the equality $x = 4$ spinning off the first "No" branch.

This algorithm is represented by the **tree diagrams** in Display 5.1. (You will learn more about tree diagrams in Chapter 7.) Read this tree starting from the left, where it says "Is $x > 4$?" If the answer is "Yes," then follow the line going up to a next question ("Is $x > 6$?") If the answer is "No," then follow the line going *down* to the next question ("Is $x > 2$?") Then start again with the new question and continue as before. Tree diagrams help us to map out all the possibilities. Often, we call these diagrams trees.

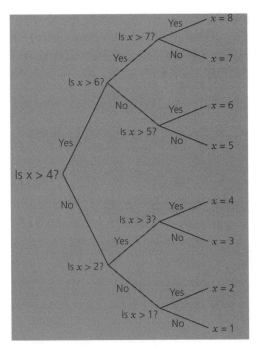

Display 5.1

5.7 Try the game of guessing a whole number x with $1 \leq x \leq 8$ a few times with your partner. Use the algorithm in the tree diagram.

5.8 Does this algorithm work? That is, will a guesser eventually find x if you use this algorithm?

Pretend that you are the guesser. How many questions will you have to ask if your partner picked the number 2? What if your partner picked 5?

278

5.7 A tree is one way to express this algorithm. Trees are studied more formally in Chapter 7. If this one helps some visually oriented students to understand the algorithm, it will have served its purpose. If other students find the tree mystifying, we would not pursue it at this time.

You may need to reach a consensus on how questions are to be counted. If you have narrowed the possibilities down to (7, 8) and are told the number is greater than seven, do you stop there or do you have to go on to ask "Is it eight?" We don't care what your students decide, but it is important to realize that any counting problem must begin with a clear identification of what we are counting. Subsequent answers are based on the assumption that a final redundant question is not necessary and will not be counted.

5.8 Some points you might watch for in the discussion are the facts that the algorithm does work, and the number of guesses needed is constant at three. Contrast this with the earlier algorithm, in which the number of guesses was highly variable. When numbers are chosen without bias, this algorithm would need an average of more than four questions when guessing numbers from one to eight.

NOTES

What would be the *least* number of questions you might have to ask? What would be the *greatest* number of questions you might have to ask? Can your partner make you ask a lot of questions?

Create an algorithm similar to the one just described for guessing a whole number x with $1 \leq x \leq 16$. How many questions are needed to guess x? Make a tree similar to Display 5.1. (Ask your teacher for a copy of Display 5.1. Expand that tree to fit your algorithm.)

5.9

Create a similar algorithm for guessing a whole number, x, with $1 \leq x \leq 4$. How many questions are needed to guess x? Make a tree. (*Hint:* Save a tree by covering up a part of the one you already have.)

5.10

Create a similar algorithm for guessing a whole number, x, with $1 \leq x \leq 2$. Of course, almost any algorithm will be quick in this case. How many questions are needed to guess x? Make a tree. (*Hint:* Save a tree by covering up a part of the one you already have.)

5.11

Copy and complete Display 5.2. Look for a pattern.

5.12

Thinking Tip

In looking for a pattern, it is often important to consider extreme cases. Here we look at guessing numbers from a very short list. When we studied exponents, we found x^2, x^3, and x^4 were easy, but x^1 and x^0 required special cases to comprehend.

Guess a Number from 1 to...	Number of Questions Needed
2	
4	
8	
16	

Display 5.2

In the examples we have looked at so far, we could always divide the possibilities exactly in half. We cannot do that if we want to guess numbers from one to five. In cases like this, we come as close as we can. We might ask if x is greater than 2 and divide the possibilities into {1, 2} and {3, 4, 5}, or we might ask if x is greater than 3 and divide the possibilities into {1, 2, 3} and {4, 5}. In any case, the goal is to divide the set of possibilities into two sets in such a way that *both* of the new sets are as large as possible. That way, no matter what our partner answers, we eliminate nearly half of the possibilities.

Published by IT'S ABOUT TIME, Inc. © 2000 MATHconx, LLC

279

5.9 The tree can be recycled by relabeling it and adding another choice at the end of each existing branch. If this does not seem like a neat idea to the students, we would not pursue it. We *would* like to see them find some way to adapt their algorithm for (1 to 8) to (1 to 16), rather than see (1 to 16) as an entirely new problem.

5.10 Now we'd like them to see that an algorithm for (1 to 4) is embedded in the algorithm for (1 to 8), whether or not they see that via the tree. This is the key to extending the algorithm to large numbers arbitrarily. The tree below left follows the pattern of Display 5.1. Below right is the alternative $<$ pattern.

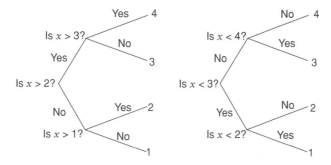

5.11 If your students can hear the sound of one hand clapping, they may want to consider the case of guessing a number from 1 to 1.

5.12 The numbers of questions needed are 1, 2, 3, 4.

NOTES

_____

5.13 Try playing the guessing game for $1 \leq x \leq 10$. If you use an algorithm similar to the one we have been describing, how many guesses are needed to find x? Is the number of guesses you need always the same?

5.14 Pair off with a classmate and play the guessing game four times for $1 \leq x \leq 100$. Apply the algorithm you learned in this section. Take turns being the guesser. Record the number of questions the guesser has to ask before guessing x. Pool data from the entire class. Use data analysis techniques to summarize and display the data. Are the results better than the first time you played the game?

If your class did better the second time, the time you spent using guessing or estimating techniques was not wasted. Using algorithms are important skills to practice and learn! No matter how much you know about mathematics, there will be problems for which you do not know an algorithm. In such cases, it is important to be good at guessing, estimating, and trial and error.

Problem Set: 5.1

1. Continue the table you began in Display 5.2. Add four more rows continuing the pattern in the left column of the table. Use your completed table to estimate the number of questions needed to guess a whole number x, when $1 \leq x \leq 100$. Look at the data you compiled when your class played this game. How well did your class do?

2. Suppose that you are guessing a whole number x where $101 \leq x \leq 200$. If you used an algorithm similar to the one described in this section, what question would you ask first? What if you were guessing a whole number between 368 and 593, inclusive?

Published by IT'S ABOUT TIME, Inc. © 2000 MATHconx, LLC

5.13

We don't want to get bogged down in the particular ways in which things do not work out as neatly when the number of numbers to choose from is not a power of two. Some of your students may want to look into this. The point is, that with obvious adjustments, the algorithm still works. Make sure the students are making the necessary adjustments by having them try 1 to 10.

5.14

Now we get to do 1 to 100 and compare the results to whatever algorithm your students used initially. You should also compare the results with the algorithm of just guessing each number from 1 to 100 in turn. Back-to-back stem-and-leaf plots, or parallel boxplots, would be good tools for these comparisons. The important point is that different algorithms may behave very differently. In practical situations it is often important to choose an appropriate algorithm. In Chapter 7 students will learn about a real situation in which failing to analyze an algorithm caused scientists to ask a computer to carry out an impossible task.

Problem Set: 5.1

1. The pattern is 2^n and n is the number of guesses. Guessing a number from 1 to 100 should take 6 or 7 guesses where $2^6 < 100 < 2^7$. You might want to discuss with your students the fact that there is now some variability in the number of guesses needed, though not so much as for the earlier algorithm. You might also raise the question of whether the number of guesses needed should be "a number *between* 6 and 7". In Chapter 6 we will look at situations in which such interpolation makes sense and others, like this one, where it does not though here the *average* number of guesses would be between 6 and 7.

2. Well, you could use the median of the boundary numbers, or if you prefer, you could use the mean. If you don't like fractions, you could round them off. We would encourage finding something simple and intuitive that works and discourage trying to find a formula that exactly agrees with what was done in every example in the chapter.

Chapter 5

3. A dealer in rare coins has a bag of 100 silver dollars. She knows that there is one counterfeit coin that was mixed in with the good ones by mistake. It is hard to tell a real coin from a fake one by looking at them. She does know that the fake coin weighs less than a real one. The coin dealer asked a nearby laboratory if she could use their accurate balance scale. They will let her use it, but they charge for each weighing. She could weigh each coin one by one, but this method might take 100 weighings to find the fake coin. She cannot afford to pay for a lot of weighings. She has figured out a way to find the fake coin with less than ten weighings.

    (a) How do you think she did it?

    (b) Would your method change if you knew that the fake coin does not weigh the same as a real one, but you do not know if it weighs more or less? Explain your answer.

Published by IT'S ABOUT TIME, Inc. © 2000 MATHconx, LLC

3. We assume the noncounterfeit coins all weigh the same.
    (a) Divide the coins equally into two stacks. Place one stack on each side
        of the balance. The counterfeit coin is in the lighter stack. Repeat the
        procedure with the lighter stack.
    (b) There are many ways to do this. Encourage your students to try to find
        as many as they can. Here's one in case they can't find any, but don't
        feel compelled to explain this one to them if they find others. Divide the
        coins into three groups of 33 and weigh the groups by pairs, one on
        each side of the balance. If each group weighs the same, the leftover coin
        is the counterfeit. If they do not weigh the same, two groups will agree
        and the counterfeit coin is in the odd group. Whether the weight of the
        odd group is high or low will tell you whether the counterfeit coin is over
        or under weight, reducing this problem to the previous one.

NOTES

5.2 Organizing Trial and Error

Learning Outcomes

After studying this section you will be able to:

Use the guessing game algorithm to solve applied problems.

In the previous section we looked at an old guessing game and found an algorithm for playing it. In other mathematics classes you usually had algorithms for all the problems you tried to solve. However, in real life problems we do not always have an algorithm. Sometimes we have to guess. You may recall that earlier in **MATH** *Connections* we were comparing two rate schedules for the Central Connecticut Electric Company. That was one place where you had to guess. The electric company had been charging a monthly customer service charge of $8.50 plus 9 cents per kiloWatt-hour (kWh). Then, the electric company asked the Public Utility Commission (PUC) for an increase to 10 cents per kWh. The PUC agreed to the rate increase provided that the customer service charge was reduced to $6.00.

a
5.15

Write equations that express the total charge (T) in terms of the number of kiloWatt-hours used (u), for each of the two rate schedules.

b
5.16

In comparing the electric company's rate schedules, you were asked to see if you could find a usage for which the two rate schedules charge the same amount. Were you able to solve this problem? If so, how did you do it?

One algorithm for solving this problem would be to try successive values of u, such as 0, 1, 2, 3, ... until we find a solution.

5.17

Does this algorithm work, that is, will you eventually find the answer if you use this algorithm? How long do you think it will take? What will happen if there *is* no value of u for which the two schedules give the same bill?

We will start with this algorithm even though it is not very efficient. Then we will try to improve it.

Published by IT'S ABOUT TIME, Inc. © 2000 MATHconx, LLC

5.2 Organizing Trial and Error

This section gives the numerical (table) version of solving systems of equations. The algorithm used here for solving a system of equations may be unfamiliar, but it is representative of a kind of numerical algorithm that has become important with the advent of computers. It is a close cousin to the algorithm developed for the guessing game in the previous section. Another related algorithm is used by graphing calculators to find zeros of functions. A key aspect of all these algorithms is that you must start with an interval in which you seek a solution. Coming up with such an interval may require some understanding of the application involved, along with good estimating skills. These are the same skills that go into setting an appropriate WINDOW when graphing with a graphing calculator.

The table approach is the most concrete approach to solving equations. Later in the section we supplement it with a visual approach. The symbolic approach of a traditional algebra course is the most abstract. It is also the most limited in that you need special techniques for each different type of equation. For example, there are many methods for *linear* equations that do not work for nonlinear equations. The numerical and graphical techniques can be used with *any* type of equation.

Old, $T = 0.09u + 8.5$ and   New, $T = 0.10u + 6$

5.15

If anyone was able to solve this problem back in Chapter 2, and they remember how they did it, this might be a chance to have them explain to the class what they did. If no one did, or no one remembers, you can just move on saying, "Now we'll learn how."

5.16

The method will work if there is a nonnegative integer solution, but it may take a long time. If there is no solution, this method will go on forever.

5.17

Assessments   Blackline Masters   Extensions   Supplements
For Additional Support Materials see page T-23

Make a table like Display 5.3. We have done the first two lines for you. Leave lots of extra space so you can add additional rows later.

a
5.18

Usage, u (kWh)	Old Rate Schedule Total Charge, T (dollars)	New Rate Schedule Total Charge, T (dollars)
0	8.50	6.00
1	8.59	6.10
2		
3		

Display 5.3

One difference between this problem and the guessing game problem is that we knew there was an answer to the guessing game problem.

Which rate schedule gave the larger bills for the usages you have in your table? Based on your table, do you think there will be a usage for which the other rate schedule gives larger bills? Explain. Do you think the two rates will ever give the same bill?

5.19

The next four values in the table would be for $u = 4$, 5, and 6 kWh. From the table we have so far, it does not look like we are very close to a solution. Maybe we should try some larger values for u.

b
5.20

Add rows for $u = 100$, 200, 300 and 400 kWh to your table. We will be adding more values of u later, so leave a blank row between each pair of new rows. Do you find any values of u for which the new rate schedule gives a larger bill? If not, what do you need to do next?

We are now going to adapt our guessing game algorithm to solve the usage rate problem. Eventually, we would like to see how this algorithm may be applied to many different problems. If you solved this problem earlier, you should compare your solution then to the algorithm we will develop.

Based on the table you completed, we will make certain assumptions. Because they are assumptions, we cannot be sure that they are true, but they are reasonable guesses that will

Published by IT'S ABOUT TIME, Inc. © 2000 MATHconx, LLC

283

5.18

kWh	Old	New
0	$8.50	$6.00
1	$8.59	$6.10
2	$8.68	$6.20
3	$8.77	$6.30

5.19

For the usages we have so far, the old rate schedule gives higher bills. We don't know whether your students will see that the new one will eventually catch up because it goes up by 10 cents each time while the old goes up by 9 cents. In fact, this observation can be used to solve the problem. The new rate schedule "catches up" by a penny for each kWh. It starts at $2.50 lower, so it will take 250 kWh for it to catch up. We would prefer you *not* mention this to your students at this time, but welcome such a solution if offered by a student.

5.20

kWh	Old	New
100	$17.50	$16.00
200	$26.50	$26.00
300	$35.50	$36.00
400	$44.50	$46.00

The new rates are higher for 300 and 400 kWh. Had they not been, we would have tried larger kWh values.

Additional Support Materials:

Assessments	Qty
Form (A)	1
Form (B)	1

Blackline Masters	Qty
Student p.283	1

Extensions	Qty

Supplements	Qty
Organizing Trial and Error	1

allow us to get started. Later, if we do not find a usage at which both rate schedules charge the same amount, we will come back and recheck our assumptions.

After you completed your table, you should have found that the new rate schedule is less expensive for usages of 100 and 200 kWh. Therefore, our first assumption will be that the new rate schedule is less expensive for usages of 200 kWh or less. We can express this assumption in mathematical language by saying that the new rate schedule is less expensive when $u \leq 200$.

Looking at the table you made, it appears that if there is a usage for which both rate schedules have the same total charge, it will probably be one that is between 200 and 300 kWh. We could go ahead and guess any number in the range 200 to 300, but we want to use a more systematic method that allows us to apply the guessing game algorithm. The idea is to use a guess *halfway* between 200 kWh and 300 kWh, just as you did in the guessing game. You may remember that when you studied data analysis that the mean of two values will always be halfway between the two numbers.

5.21

1. What number is halfway between 200 and 300?

2. Add a new row for the usage that is halfway between. What did you find?

The algorithm we have been using is another version of the one we used for the guessing game. At each step, we cut the interval in half between two previous guesses. Before we could do this, we had to have a value of u for which the old rate schedule costs more than the new rate and a value of u for which the new rate schedule costs more than the old rate schedule. Then we had to look in between those two values.

In the electric utility example, our algorithm found the correct answer ($u = 250$ kWh) very quickly. It was certainly a big improvement over trying $u = 1, 2, 3, ...$ up to $u = 250$! In other situations, we may not be so lucky.

You may recall that in a problem you solved earlier about simple and compound interest, Alfredo was saving money for a trip to Central America. He had a gift of $1,000 and needed a total of $2,400. We wanted to know how long he would have

284

5.21

1. 250   2. The charges are the same $31.00 for old and new rates.

NOTES

to save before he had $2,400. You solved the problem for compound interest given by

$$T = 1000 * (1.07) \wedge n$$

See how much money Alfredo would have after 0, 8 and 16 years at 7% annual compound interest rate. Apply the methods of this section to find out when he has $2,400.

a
5.22

You solved this same problem by trial and error back in Chapter 2. That algorithm took a long time and a lot of work.

If Alfredo's aunt paid him simple interest instead of compound interest, the total amount, T, that he would have after n years at 7% interest would be given by

$$T = 1000 + 1000 * (0.07) * n$$

so, by the Distributive Law

$$T = 1000 (1 + 0.07n)$$

Apply the methods of this section to find out when Alfredo will have $2,400 using a simple interest of 7%.

b
5.23

There are some practical problems that may come up when we use the algorithm for compound interest. One is that there may not be an exact answer. However, we can find out when he goes over $2,400, and that is good enough.

Here is a slightly different example where we never get an exact answer. In the beginning of **MATH** *Connections*, you found standard deviations by taking the square root of the variance. You probably did that with a square root key on your calculator. Here is a way to find a square root using the algorithm we have been studying in this section.

What is the square root of three? We know 1 is too small because $1^2 = 1$, and we know that 2 is too large because $2^2 = 4$. Guess halfway between. Keep on going and see how accurate a value you can get. Use the square root key on your calculator to check your accuracy.

c
5.24

Take our word for it, you will *never* get an exact value for the square root of 3 using this (or any other) algorithm. However, you can get answers that are as accurate as you want.

Published by IT'S ABOUT TIME, Inc. © 2000 MATHconx, LLC

285

5.22

The answers are included in the full table that follows. You can apply the algorithm if you interpret it generally. Alfredo does not have enough money after 8 years but he has more than enough after 16. Following the algorithm, you would try 12, 14 and 13 years in turn. You would then stop because fractions of a year are not appropriate here.

We chose guesses that were powers of 2 for two reasons. First, they increase rapidly, so we have a better chance of finding a number of years that gives more than $2,400 (if there is one). Also, it helps to avoid fractions when we go halfway between two values of year.

NOTES

Years	Simple	Compound	Goal
0	1000	1000.00	2400
1	1070	1070.00	2400
2	1140	1144.90	2400
3	1210	1225.04	2400
4	1280	1310.80	2400
5	1350	1402.55	2400
6	1420	1500.73	2400
7	1490	1605.78	2400
8	1560	1718.19	2400
9	1630	1838.46	2400
10	1700	1967.15	2400
11	1770	2104.85	2400
12	1840	2252.19	2400
13	1910	2409.85	2400
14	1980	2578.53	2400
15	2050	2759.03	2400
16	2120	2952.16	2400
17	2190	3158.82	2400
18	2260	3379.93	2400
19	2330	3616.53	2400
20	2400	3869.68	2400
21	2470	4140.56	2400
22	2540	4430.40	2400
23	2610	4740.53	2400
24	2680	5072.37	2400
25	2750	5427.43	2400
26	2820	5807.35	2400
27	2890	6213.87	2400
28	2960	6648.84	2400
29	3030	7114.26	2400
30	3100	7612.26	2400
31	3170	8145.11	2400
32	3240	8715.27	2400
33	3310	9325.34	2400
34	3380	9978.11	2400
35	3450	10676.58	2400

→

5.23

The algorithm can still be used. This time we give students a little more freedom of choice. We know that using simple interest will take longer than using compound interest, so we would try 16 as the next power of 2. This gives 2120, so we would try 32 next. This gives 3240, more than enough, so we would try 24 and then 20. We find 20 is a solution.

These first examples are somewhat loaded in the student's favor in that the equations actually do have a solution for a reasonably small value of the independent variable and natural choices of values to try to avoid fractions and lead to rapid convergence. If some of your students make other choices, they may run into difficulty. The one bit of advice we can give is to use only whole number guesses in a situation where fractional values are inappropriate. Hence, a student who decides the answer must be between 16 and 29 years should try 22 or 23 next, not 22.5.

We do not want to get bogged down in all the things that could possibly go wrong with this numerical algorithm. In practice, someone trained to worry about such things would write a program or design a calculator to carry out the arithmetic. One of the important things that students *should* notice and carry over to technology is the need to specify a range of values of the independent variable between which we expect to find a solution. This is often a surprise to people who have worked only with symbolic approaches. It applies to graphical approaches as well; to find a solution graphically you have to set a graphing WINDOW that contains a solution! This choice is also important when there is more than one solution. Specifying an appropriate range helps us to get the one we want! On the other hand, it may cause us to miss other possible solutions.

5.24

Here are the first six steps. A computer scientist would not consider our method an algorithm because there is no definite procedure for knowing when to stop. If we want to implement this on a machine, we would have to tell the machine when to stop, or it would go on calculating forever!

Step	Number	Square
0	1	1
1	1.5	2.25
3	1.625	2.640625
4	1.6875	2.847656
5	1.71875	2.954102
6	1.734375	3.008057
2	1.75	3.0625
0	2	4

Our spreadsheet gave 1.732051 as the square root of 3.

In trying to find the square root of 3, you may have found that going halfway between two numbers was not always convenient. For example, halfway between 1.75 and 1.625 is 1.6875. In the guessing game, you need not go *exactly* halfway between the two numbers. You may take any number in between. In picking a number, notice whether one of the earlier guesses is closer than the other. At one point in finding the square root of 3, you wanted to go between 1.5 and 1.75. You can compute that $1.5^2 = 2.25$ and $1.75^2 = 3.0625$. It looks like 1.75^2 is *much* closer to 3 than 1.5^2. You might make your task easier *and* quicker by guessing 1.7 next rather than using the number that is exactly halfway between 1.5 and 1.75.

5.25 Try to find the square root of 3 using our algorithm, but pick convenient in-between values. At each step, discuss with your classmates what the next step should be. When you agree, try the guess. See if this is faster or easier than what you did before.

Of course, this algorithm may not be too impressive if your calculator has a square root key, so let's try fifth roots. We say x is a **fifth root** of y if

$$x^5 = y$$

For example, 2 is a fifth root of 32 because $2^5 = 32$

5.26 Find a fifth root of 3.

Problem Set: 5.2

1. Find the following roots.

   (a) $\sqrt{2}$

   (b) $\sqrt[3]{3}$

   (c) $\sqrt[4]{4}$

   (d) $\sqrt[5]{5}$

   (e) $\sqrt[5]{1000}$

Published by IT'S ABOUT TIME, Inc. © 2000 MATHconx, LLC

Chapter 5

5.25

What we want to bring out here is that humans are good at making clever choices. Machines are good at carrying out calculations quickly. Hence, it is best to leave the calculations to the machine, while the role of humans is to decide what to tell the machine to do and check the reasonableness of its answers.

5.26

Number	Fifth Power
1	1
1.125	1.802032
1.1875	2.361392
1.21875	2.688891
1.234375	2.865732
1.242188	2.957575
1.246094	3.004374
1.25	3.051758
1.5	7.59375
2	32

Our spreadsheet gave 1.245731 for the fifth root of 3.

Problem Set: 5.2

1. (a) 1.41421356   (b) 1.44224957
   (c) 1.41421356   (d) 1.37972966
   (e) 3.98107171

2. (a) $S = 100 - 9t$

   (b)

Hours	% Surviving
0	100
1	91
2	82
3	73
8	28
10	10
12	−8
15	−35

2. You saw the following data set in Chapter 2.

   A bacterial culture is being treated with ultraviolet rays in an attempt to kill the bacteria. The following table shows the percentage of bacteria surviving after t hours of treatment.

Length of Treatment (t hours)	% Surviving (S)
0	100
1	91
2	82
3	73

   (a) Write an equation that gives the percentage of bacteria surviving (S) in terms of the number of hours of treatment (t).

   (b) Copy the table and add rows for 8, 10, 12 and 15 hours of treatment.

   (c) Suppose that we wanted to know when all of the bacteria will be dead. Use the algorithm you studied in this section to estimate how long it will take for all of the bacteria to be killed.

3. Sonia just began working for the Chesapeake Company. She is earning $18,000 a year right now. She has been told that each year she will get a raise equal to 5% of her previous year's salary.

   (a) How much will she be earning next year?

   (b) How much will she be earning after 16 years?

   (c) Use the algorithm studied in this section to estimate how long it will take before she earns $30,000 per year.

287

Published by IT'S ABOUT TIME, Inc. © 2000 MATHconx, LLC

(c)

Hours	% Surviving
0	100
1	91
2	82
3	73
8	28
10	10
11	1
11.125	−0.125
11.25	−1.25
11.5	−3.5
12	−8

This one does not come out a whole number of hours and thereby illustrates a weakness of numerical methods. We will see later that the last bacterium dies at 11.11111111111111... hours.

3. This problem presupposes that students have done the original problem (problem 6 in Problem Set 2.5) and have the results at hand. You may wish to review that problem with them before you have them tackle this extension. In particular, we begin with the initial condition of $18,000 after 0 years (i.e., at the beginning) and a result for what happens after 16 years. Since that gives more than $30,000, we seek a solution between 0 and 16 years.

Years	Salary	
0	$18,000.00	Given
8	$26,594.20	Step 1
10	$29,459.81	Step 3
11	$30,892.61	Step 4
12	$32,325.41	Step 2
16	$39,291.74	From original problem

(a) $18,900   (b) $39,291.74

(c) Since Sonia gets this raise once a year, it does not make sense to pursue fractional values. She does not make $30,000 until the end of her 11th year, at which time she actually earns somewhat more than that.

5.3 A Picture Is Worth...

Learning Outcomes

After studying this section you will be able to:

Use graphs to solve systems of equations.

Earlier in **MATH** *Connections* you learned how to make graphs of equations and how to make graphs of data. One use of such graphs is to visualize a situation. A graph of some data often helped you to visualize the relationship between two variables. In the previous section, you used tables to compare two electric utility rates. When we want to determine the relationship of two variables, we have to decide which method to use. Let's look at the two methods.

Some of the values you calculated for your table in Display 5.3 are shown in Display 5.4.

Usage, u (kWh)	Old Rate Schedule Total Charge, T (dollars)	New Rate Schedule Total Charge, T (dollars)
0	$8.50	$6.00
100	$17.50	$16.00
200	$26.50	$26.00
300	$35.50	$36.00
400	$44.50	$46.00

Display 5.4

In Display 5.5, we have graphed the information from the old rate schedule.

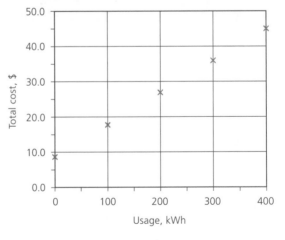

Display 5.5

Published by IT'S ABOUT TIME, Inc. © 2000 MATHconx, LLC

288

5.3 A Picture Is Worth...

This section looks at the idea of plotting two mathematical relationships on the same graph. There is a lot of review embedded here as in other sections of this chapter.

We want students to be able to make accurate, readable graphs by hand. This is especially important if you plan to have them make graphs with a graphing calculator. Students often have trouble choosing a WINDOW for a calculator graph, and we have heard students declare that a graph of $y = 2x + 3$ is "not a line, it's a zigzag" because of the low screen resolution of their calculator. The process of WINDOW selection is the same whether you make the graph with paper, a spreadsheet or a graphing calculator. We think it is best if students master making graphs *before* turning to the calculator. Students need to know what a variety of graphs look like on paper in order to interpret the approximations they will see on a calculator screen.

Once students have mastered graphing on paper, we want them to use technology to make routine graphs and to explore graphs. Our graphs were made with a spreadsheet. After working through the material in the text, you may want to have your students reproduce our graphs with whatever technology you plan to use. They should compare their graphs to ours as an aid in learning to interpret the output of their own graphing device.

Additional Support Materials:

Assessments	Qty
Form (A)	1
Form (B)	1

Blackline Masters	Qty

Extensions	Qty

Supplements	Qty

Notice that we chose scales on the axes that matched our table. We have usages from 0 to 400 kWh in the table and on the graph. For the cost axis, we rounded and let the scale go from 0 to 50. (It is convenient to include the origin (0, 0) if it is not too far from the rest of the graph.) We put tick marks every 50 units on the usage axis and every 5 units on the cost axis. Alternate tick marks are labeled with numerals.

Put a ruler on Display 5.5 and see if the points fall close to a straight line. Do they? Recall that equations in the form $y = ax + b$, where a and b are constants, form a straight line. Is the equation $T = 0.09 * u + 8.50$ in this form?

5.27

In Display 5.6, we have added the line that fits the old rate schedule data.

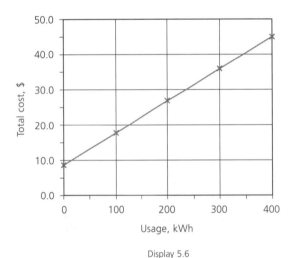

Display 5.6

We are going to use this graph to compare the two rate schedules. We can do this by putting the information for the new rate schedule on the same graph.

When we graph data, we usually want the individual points to stand out. When we graph a straight line, we usually want the line to stand out. Once we have the line for the old rate schedule, we do not need to keep the points we used to get the line. Display 5.7 shows the line for the old rate schedule and the points for the new rate schedule.

Published by IT'S ABOUT TIME, Inc. © 2000 MATHconx, LLC

289

5.27 The points fall *exactly* on a straight line because $T = 0.09u + 8.5$ is a form of the equation $y = mx + b$.

NOTES

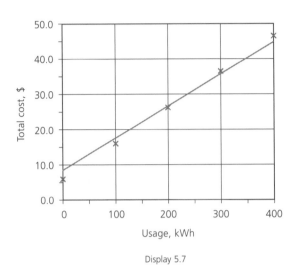

Display 5.7

5.28 How can you tell from the graph when the new rate schedule gives a higher cost than the old rate schedule?

Now we can put in the line for the new rate schedule and eliminate the points we used to get the line. The result is shown in Display 5.8.

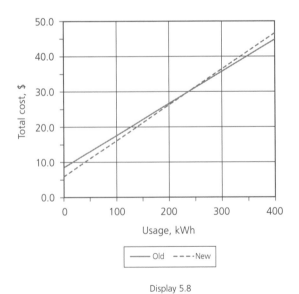

Display 5.8

290

Published by IT'S ABOUT TIME, Inc. © 2000 MATHconx, LLC

5.28 The new rate schedule gives a higher cost than the old when the points fall above the line for the old rate schedule.

NOTES

Here we have used a dashed line for the new rate schedule to make it easier to distinguish it from the old. You can look at the graphs for the two rate schedules and compare them. Comparison is easier if you graph both lines on the same scale, and even easier if you put them both on the same graph.

Look at your graph and answer the following questions.

5.29

a) **Which rate schedule charges more for usages less than 200 kWh? How did the graph help you to reach your conclusion?**

b) **Which rate schedule charges more for usages greater than 300 kWh? How did the graph help you to reach your conclusion?**

c) **Where do the two lines seem to intersect? What does this point of intersection tell you about the two rate schedules? How does this compare to the solution to the problem you solved in the last section?**

In Section 5.2, we guessed at the answers to questions (a) and (b) above when we made our assumptions before we started the algorithm. The graph supports our assumptions and shows us that they are true.

The two straight lines intersect exactly once and will never intersect again. In particular, to the left of the point of intersection one rate schedule will *always* charge more, and to the right of the point of intersection the *other* rate schedule will *always* charge more. Since usage can never be negative, we can see all the points to the left of the point of intersection in Display 5.8. We cannot see past 400 kWh to the right. However, we can see that the lines are getting further apart, so they will not intersect again.

The coordinates of the intersection point are the usage and total cost at which the two rate schedules are the same. In the last section we used a modification of the guessing game algorithm to find this point. We can also use a graph.

291

5.29

a) The old rate schedule charges more for 200 kWh or less. The old rate schedule line is above the new rate schedule line.

b) The new rate schedule charges more for 300 kWh or more. The new rate schedule line is above the old rate schedule line.

c) The lines intersect at exactly (250, 31). This means the two rate schedules charge the same ($31) when the usage is 250 kWh. This agrees with what we found using a table to solve the same problem in the previous section. Student estimates of the intersection point coordinates will vary considerably. Displays 5.10 and 5.11 zoom in on the intersection to permit better estimates to be made.

NOTES

5.30

Make a graph of Alfredo's interest earning. Use a full sheet of graph paper and draw lines with a ruler, since you will need to read your graph accurately. We suggest you include years from 0 to 30 along the horizontal axis and savings from $1,000 (what Alfredo started with) to $3,000 along the vertical line. Draw a line to represent his goal of $2,400. Then graph his earnings at 7% simple interest

$$T = 1000 \,(1 + 0.07n)$$

and at 7% compound interest

$$T = 1000 * 1.07 \,\hat{}\, n$$

In the graph in Display 5.8, the solid line shows all the points that satisfy the old rate schedule,

$$T = 0.09 * u + 8.50$$

The dashed line shows all the points that satisfy the new rate schedule,

$$T = 0.10 * u + 6.00$$

Any points that the graphs have in common satisfy *both* equations. When we have two or more equations, and we find numbers that satisfy all of them, we say we have a **system of equations.** Finding values of the variables that satisfy *all* the equations is called **solving the system.**

You can solve some equations using your graph of Alfredo's interest earnings.

5.31

Find all solutions of the following systems of equations.

1. $T = 1000 \,(1 + 0.07n)$ and $T = 2400$

2. $T = 1000 * 1.07 \,\hat{}\, n$ and $T = 2400$

3. $T = 1000 \,(1 + 0.07n)$ and $T = 1000 * 1.07 \,\hat{}\, n$

4. $T = 1000 \,(1 + 0.07n)$ and $T = 1000 * 1.07 \,\hat{}\, n$ and $T = 2400$

Published by IT'S ABOUT TIME, Inc. © 2000 MATHconx, LLC

5.30

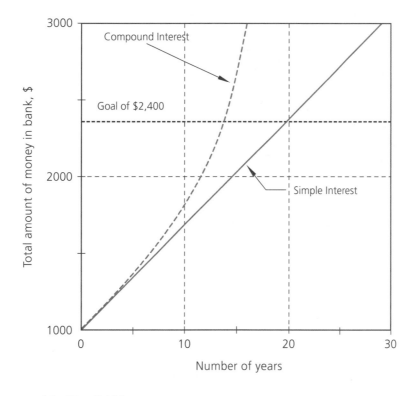

5.31

1. $n = 20$; $T = 2400$

2. $n = 12.93949491$; $T = 2400$. Obviously you cannot read the value of n this accurately off the graph, which is one of the disadvantages of the graphical approach. It does not matter much here for two reasons. First, we are only interested in an integer answer. Second, we can check the solution with a simple calculation.

3. $n = 1$; $T = 1070$ and, of course, $n = 0$ and $T = 1000$.

4. There is no point where all three graphs intersect.

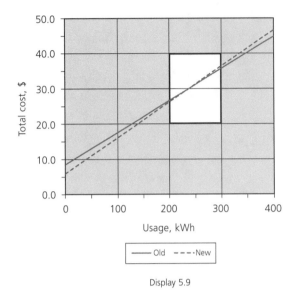

Display 5.9

Display 5.8 gives us only a rough idea of where the lines intersect. We can get a better idea by magnifying the area around the intersection. We do this by making a new graph that shows only a region closer to where the lines cross. We have chosen a Window of $200 \le u \le 300$ and $20 \le T \le 40$, as shown in Display 5.9.

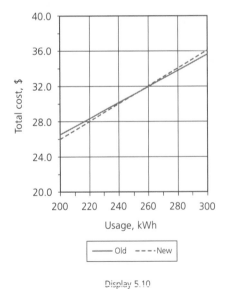

Display 5.10

Published by IT'S ABOUT TIME, Inc. © 2000 MATHconx, LLC

Chapter 5

NOTES

Display 5.10 should look about the same as Display 5.8, until you look at the scale. You should be able to read the intersection point more accurately from the new graph.

We can keep zooming in like this and find the coordinates of the point of intersection as accurately as we want.

Display 5.11 has another scale.

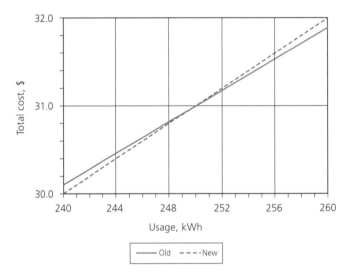

Display 5.11

5.32

1. (a) What is the Window in Display 5.11?

    (b) What is the Window in Display 5.10?

    (c) Where is Display 5.11 located in Display 5.10?

2. Use the Display 5.10 to estimate the coordinates of the intersection point. Interpret the values of T and u that you find. Do they agree with the values you found in the previous section? Which method do you prefer for solving this problem?

A disadvantage of the graphical method is that it takes a great deal of time to draw all of the graphs by hand. The graphs must be made carefully to have accurate results. We can make accurate graphs very quickly with a spreadsheet program. Using a spreadsheet program, these graphs can be made professional looking for use in a presentation. If we need to find the intersection point only, we can use a graphing

294

Published by IT'S ABOUT TIME, Inc. © 2000 MATHconx, LLC

5.32

1. a) $240 \leq u \leq 260;\quad 30 \leq T \leq 32$
    b) $200 \leq u \leq 300;\quad 20 \leq T \leq 40$
    c) Display 5.11 is located in the "center" rectangle of Display 5.10.

2. Students' answers will vary. The point of intersection is (250, 31).

NOTES

Chapter 5

calculator. The graphs will not be as attractive, but the calculator can zoom much more quickly.

Problem Set: 5.3

In problems 1 through 4, use a graph to determine the coordinates of the point where each pair of lines intersects.

1. $y = 0.5x + 1$ $y = 1.0x + 4$

2. $m = 2p + 3.5$ $m = 1.8p + 5$

3. $y = 2x + 7$ $y = 2(x + 7)$

4. $y = 2x + 8$ $y = 2(x + 4)$

5. All new appliances have an Energy Cost sticker. This sticker displays the average cost of using the appliance for one year. Its purpose is to help the consumer consider the cost of using an appliance as well as the initial cost of buying the appliance.

    Kara is looking at refrigerators at the Huge Appliance Store. She finds two models that are the size she needs and have the features that she wants. Kara wants to keep this refrigerator for a long time, and she is concerned about how much it will cost to use the refrigerator once she brings it home. She decides that she will try to calculate the total cost of owning each model (the initial price of the model *plus* the cost for energy) and then use this information to decide which one is more economical. She has compiled the data in Display 5.12:

Model	Cost	Average Yearly Energy Cost
Cool Air	$575	$47
Arctic Blast	$500	$55

Display 5.12

(a) For each model, write an equation that gives the average total cost, T dollars, after y years.

(b) The average life of a refrigerator is 15 years. Draw a graph of each equation on the same coordinate axes to display at least 15 years of use.

(c) If Kara plans to keep her refrigerator for less than 4 years, which model should she buy?

Published by IT'S ABOUT TIME, Inc. © 2000 MATHconx, LLC

295

Problem Set: 5.3

You might encourage your students to put together what they learned in Sections 2 and 3 of this chapter as they try to solve these problems. They can first use a table to get some points on the graph. They will want to find at least one point on each side of the intersection of the two lines, just as they did in Section 2. This will help them to choose an appropriate scale for the graph they make, so the intersection is actually on the graph! They will need to do this sort of thing again when they solve such equations with a graphing calculator and have to set an appropriate WINDOW.

1. $(-6, -2)$

2. $(p, m) = (7.5, 18.5)$

3. This one has no solutions. A look at the graph should show that the lines appear to be parallel. Trying to solve this one with a table could be highly frustrating! Any students who have only one line on their graph need to review the Distributive Property.

4. This is really just one line, along with another review of the Distributive Property.

5. (a) *Cool Air:* $T = 47y + 575$; *Arctic Blast* $T = 55y + 500$
   (c) She should buy the *Arctic Blast* if she keeps the refrigerator for less than 4 years. It will cost less money to own over this time period.

NOTES

(d) If Kara plans to keep her refrigerator for more than 13 years, which model should she buy?

(e) Use the method described in this section to determine the coordinates of the point where the two lines intersect. How are the coordinates of this point related to the total cost of owning a refrigerator?

(f) If you were Kara, which refrigerator would you buy? Explain your answer.

6. Insulin is a drug that allows your body to use the sugar that you eat. Many people have a condition called diabetes mellitus. Their pancreas doesn't produce enough insulin, so their body must get it from other sources. In the past, insulin has been harvested from animals processed for meat.

Scientists are now looking at faster and better ways of harvesting insulin. One way that they do this is to splice the appropriate human gene to the gene of common yeast and then grow the yeast in a culture. As the yeast makes the chemicals it needs to live, it also manufactures insulin based on instructions from the "hitchhiking" gene. Then the yeast and all of the other compounds can be filtered away leaving a solution of human insulin.

Different strains of yeast will produce the insulin at different rates. Display 5.13 is a table of expected results for two strains. For each strain, the table shows the number of hours the yeast was cultured and the amount of insulin harvested.

Insulin Yield (in grams)		
Hours	Strain 1	Strain 2
4	19.44	10.2
8	23.88	19.4
12	28.32	28.6
16	32.76	37.8
20	37.20	47.0
24	41.64	56.2
28	46.08	65.4
32	50.52	74.6
36	54.96	83.8
40	59.40	93.0
48	68.28	111.4

Display 5.13

(d) She should buy the *Cool Air* if she keeps the refrigerator for more than 13 years. It will cost less money to own over this time period.
(e) The exact coordinates of the intersection point are (9.375, 1015.625).
(f) Answers will vary.

6. This is a nice example about a real world scientific event. The data, however, is made up so that straight lines fit the data perfectly and nothing surprising happens.

NOTES

(a) On the same set of axes make a graph for both sets of data. Do the relationships appear to be linear? If they are, draw a straight line for each strain of yeast.

(b) Which strain would be best if you have to harvest the yeast after eight hours? After 10 hours? After 30 hours? Which of these questions are best answered from the graph and which are best answered from the table?

(c) In determining which strain of yeast to use, a scientist must consider various other factors such as the cost and size of equipment. As a first step, one needs to find the point at which the production of insulin is the same no matter which strain is used. Estimate this from your graph.

7. The Rent & Roll car rental agency charges $100 per week and 25¢ per mile for its small cars.

(a) What would be the cost to rent a small car from Rent & Roll for a week, if you drove it 150 miles?

(b) Write an equation to find the total cost, C dollars, of renting a small car from Rent & Roll for a week and driving it m miles.

(c) What kind of equation did you write in part (b)?

(d) What is the slope of the equation you found in part (b)?

(e) What is the y-intercept of the equation you found in part (b)?

(f) Graph the equation you found in part (b).

8. The Save-A-Buck car rental agency charges $50 per week and 50¢ per mile for its small cars.

(a) What would be the cost to rent a small car for a week from Save-A-Buck if you drove it 150 miles?

(b) Write an equation to find the total cost, T dollars, of renting a small car from Save-A-Buck for a week and driving it m miles.

(c) What is the slope of the equation you found in part (b)?

(d) What is the y-intercept of the equation you found in part (b)?

(e) Graph the equation you found in part (b) of this problem and the equation you found in problem 7(b).

Published by IT'S ABOUT TIME, Inc. © 2000 MATHconx, LLC

(a) Yes, the relationships are perfectly linear.

(b) Strain 1 is best after 8 or 10 hours and Strain 2 is better after 30. Since 10 is not in the table, it might be easier to deal with via the graph. However, it is clear even from the table that strain 2 is better after 30 hours.

(c) (11.7647..., 28.0588...)

Note that problems 7–9 should be done as a set.

7. (a) $137.50   (b) $C = 100 + 0.25m$ (c) Linear
    (d) Slope is 0.25   (e) y-intercept (C-intercept) is 100   (f) Students may have difficulty selecting scales that will produce a useful picture for this problem. If this happens, it should lead to comparison and discussion of students' graphs.

8. (a) $125   (b) $T = 50 + 0.50m$
    (c) Slope is 0.50.   (d) y-intercept (C-intercept) is 50   (e) See (f) above.

NOTES

9. Use your results from problems 7 and 8 to answer the following questions.

   (a) Graph the equation you found in problem 7(b) along with the equation you found in problem 8(b) on one set of axes.

   (b) Look at a graph you drew in part (a). Would it cost more to rent a small car from the Rent & Roll agency (problem 7) than from the Save-A-Buck agency (problem 8)? Would it ever be the same? Less? Do the lines intersect?

   (c) What does the point where the lines intersect represent?

   (d) Find the coordinates of the intersection point.

   (e) Mr. Washington wants to rent a small car for a week-long trip. Under what conditions should he rent from Rent & Roll? Under what conditions would it be better to rent from Save-A-Buck?

10. Mary's house is 5 miles from Juan's.

   (a) If Mary begins bicycling toward Juan's house at 3 o'clock, and she bicycles at an average of 6 mph, how many miles will she go in 2 hours? In 15 minutes? Explain how you figured this out.

   (b) Let t be the number of hours since 3 o'clock. Write an equation for the distance, M miles, Mary is from her house in t hours. What is the slope of this line?

   (c) At the same time Mary leaves her house, Juan begins bicycling from his house toward Mary's. Juan bicycles at an average rate of 4 mph. Draw a diagram representing the situation.

   (d) How far from Mary's house will Juan be $\frac{1}{2}$ hour after he leaves his house?

   (e) Again let t be the number of hours since 3 o'clock. Write an equation for the distance, J miles, Juan is from Mary's house in t hours. What is the slope of this line?

   (f) Graph the two equations on one set of axes that represents Mary's and Juan's trip. Do the two lines intersect? At that point, Mary and Juan are both the same distance from Mary's house. What is that distance? At what time does that happen?

Published by IT'S ABOUT TIME, Inc. © 2000 MATHconx, LLC

9. The two agencies will charge exactly $150 if you drive 200 miles. The Rent-and-Roll agency charges less if you drive more than 200 miles and the Save-A-Buck agency charges less if you drive less than 200 miles. If you drive more than 200 miles rent from Rent-and-Roll.

10. (a) Mary will travel $6 \cdot 2 = 12$ miles in 2 hours and $6 \cdot (0.25) = 1.5$ miles in 15 minutes.
    (b) $M = 6t$, the slope is 6.
    (d) Juan will have traveled $4 \cdot (0.5) = 2$ miles in half an hour, so he will be $5 - 2 = 3$ miles from Mary's house.
    (e) $J = 5 - 4t$, the slope is -4.
    (f) Mary and Juan meet after riding for half an hour. At that time, they are 3 miles from Mary's house.

NOTES

11. Tommy Kaye's Video charges a $10.00 membership fee and $3.00 per video rental.

    (a) What is the total cost for renting 16 videos (including the membership fee) at Tommy Kaye's?

    (b) Write an equation that gives the total cost T for r rentals at Tommy Kaye's. Is this equation linear?

    (c) Graph the equation you found in part (b) on your graphing calculator. Is the graph a line?

12. The Shop Quick video store has no membership fee but charges $3.25 per video rental.

    (a) What is the total cost for renting 16 videos at Shop Quick?

    (b) Write an equation that gives the total cost S for r rentals at Shop Quick. Is this equation linear?

    (c) Graph the equation you found in part (b).

13. This problem refers to problems 11 and 12.

    (a) Graph the equations you found for the total cost of rentals at Tommy Kaye's and Shop Quick on one set of axes.

    (b) Should the two graphs intersect? (*Hint:* Think about the slopes of the graphs.) If they should, find the point of intersection. What would this point represent?

    (c) Under what conditions will the total cost at Tommy Kaye's be the same as the total cost at Shop Quick? Under what conditions will it be less? More? Use your graph to explain your answers.

Published by IT'S ABOUT TIME, Inc. © 2000 MATHconx, LLC

Chapter 5

Note that problems 11–13 should be done as a set.

11. (a) $58   (b) $T = 10 + 3r$ (c) Yes

12. (a) $52   (b) $S = 3.25r$

13. Since the two lines have different slopes, they will intersect at
     exactly one point. The two stores will charge exactly $130 to rent
     40 videos. Shop Quick is less expensive if you rent fewer than 40 videos.
     Tommy Kaye's is less expensive if you rent more than 40 videos.

NOTES

5.4 Pictures on Your Calculator

Learning Outcomes

After studying this section you will be able to:

Solve a linear equation for one of its variables;

Use a graphing calculator to solve a system of equations.

You can use a graphing calculator or spreadsheet to draw the graphs of the Electric Company data from Section 5.3. This technology can make our work easier in some ways, but harder in others. Most computers and calculators have a particular way to enter the equations and may limit your variables to x and y.

Recall that the old rate schedule is described by the equation $T = 0.09u + 8.5$. The new rate schedule is described by the equation $T = 0.10u + 6$. Because we graphed T on the vertical axis, it is acting like y. Because we graphed u on the horizontal axis, it is acting like x. We say that T is the *dependent variable* because the total charge for the electricity is dependent on the number of kiloWatt-hours used. Like y, the dependent variable is usually graphed on the vertical axis. The other variable here, u, is called the *independent variable*. It is plotted on the horizontal axis like x. Mathematically, it does not matter whether we call our variables x and y or u and T. The graph of the pair

$$T = 0.09u + 8.5$$
$$T = 0.10u + 6$$

with u as the horizontal axis and T as the vertical axis, looks exactly like the graph of the pair

$$y = 0.09x + 8.5$$
$$y = 0.10x + 6$$

with x as the horizontal axis and y as the vertical axis.

Using u and T as our variables has the advantage of reminding us that they are abbreviations for the Usage and the Total Charge, while x and y have the advantage that they are the labels used on many graphing calculators.

Another problem we may have in using technology is that we may need to input our equations in a particular form. For example, the equation

$$8h + 32v = 160,000$$

is a perfectly good one, but it cannot be put into most spreadsheets or graphing calculators in that form. We will look

300

5.4 Pictures on Your Calculator

You may already have your students using graphing calculators in this chapter. This section deals with the algebra needed to use the calculator with an equation that is not already solved for *y*.

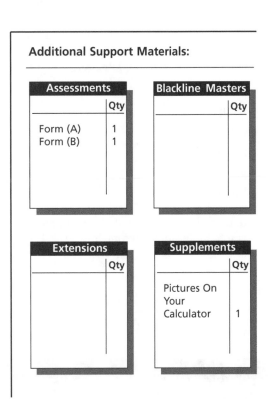

Additional Support Materials:

Assessments	Qty
Form (A)	1
Form (B)	1

Blackline Masters	Qty

Extensions	Qty

Supplements	Qty
Pictures On Your Calculator	1

at an example that illustrates where such an equation might appear in real life. We will see how to graph the equation by hand and how to put it into a form that a spreadsheet or graphing calculator can use.

WebFoot, Inc. sells Internet access and helps its customers set up home pages on the World Wide Web. They offer two kinds of accounts. The less expensive one, HotFoot, provides the customer with 8 megabytes (Mb) of disk space. The more expensive *Very*HotFoot account provides 32 Mb. WebFoot has 160 gigabytes (or 160,000 Mb) of space available on the Internet.

WebFoot needs your help in analyzing their options.

5.33

1. **If WebFoot sells, h, HotFoot accounts, how much space will that take up? Write an expression in terms of h.**

2. **If WebFoot sells, v, *Very*HotFoot accounts, how much space will that take up? Write an expression in terms of v.**

3. **Write an expression for the *total* space used up by both types of accounts.**

4. **WebFoot would like to have enough customers to fill up *all* of its space on the Internet. Write an equation to describe a situation in which this happens.**

This equation describes all the various ways WebFoot could use up its space. For example, if it sells 10,000 HotFoot accounts and 2500 *Very*HotFoot accounts, they will use up

$$8 * 10{,}000 + 32 * 2500 = 160{,}000 \text{ Mb}$$

or all of its storage space.

Most of the equations we have studied so far have been linear equations of the form $y = mx + b$. The equation $8h + 32v = 160{,}000$ is not in that form, so it might not be a line. Let's try to graph it and see if it is a line or a curve. We know that $h = 10{,}000$ and $v = 2500$ are the coordinates of one of the points on the graph. Let's find some more points on the graph. For example, we might try $v = 1000$. Substituting this into $8h + 32v = 160{,}000$, we have

$$8h + 32 * 1000 = 8h + 32{,}000 = 160{,}000$$

5.33

1. $8h$

2. $32v$

3. $8h + 32v$

4. $8h + 32v = 160{,}000$

NOTES

Recall that you learned how to solve equations like this earlier.

a

Solve 8*h* + 32,000 = 160,000.

5.34   Now we have two points on the graph. We could also pick a value of *h* and find *v*.

b

Find the value of *v* when *h* = 8000.

5.35   We can put the points we have found that must be on the graph into Display 5.14.

h	*v*
10,000	2500
16,000	1000
8000	3000

Display 5.14

Let's add a few more points to the table, before graphing the equation 8*h* + 32*v* = 160,000.

c

5.36

Copy and complete Display 5.15, so that each point is on the graph of 8*h* + 32*v* = 160,000.

h	*v*
	0
0	
10,000	
30,000	
	2000
	4000
	6000

Display 5.15

302

5.34

$b = 16,000$

5.35

$v = 3000$

5.36

b	v
20,000	0
0	5000
10,000	2500
30,000	−2500
12,000	2000
4000	4000
−4000	6000

NOTES

Notice that not all of the values in your table make sense for the problem. Practically speaking, the number of accounts of each type cannot be negative, so we must have $v \geq 0$ and $h \geq 0$. In addition, we cannot have a fraction of an account.

You now have the coordinates of several points on the graph of $8h + 32v = 160{,}000$. Plot these on graph paper. Just so everyone's graph looks the same, put the v scale on the vertical axis and the h scale on the horizontal axis. Let both scales go from 0 to 20,000. What do you think the graph of this equation looks like? Draw it as best you can.

a
5.37

You should notice two special points on your graph. The point with coordinates $h = 20{,}000$ and $v = 0$ is called the *h-intercept*. The point with coordinates $h = 0$ and $v = 5000$ is called the *v-intercept*.

Find these two points on the graph. Do you think they are appropriately named? Explain.

b
5.38

In the past, when we had an equation like $y = mx + b$, it was easy to find the y-intercept—we just had to look at b! Since our equation is not in that form, we must work a little more. Remember that we found the x-intercept of $y = mx + b$ by substituting 0 for y and solving for x. We use this method to find *both* intercepts of $8h + 32v = 160{,}000$. The intercepts are important for a variety of reasons. We already know that the y-intercept may have a useful interpretation. The intercepts are often the easiest two points to find on a graph. If we replace v with 0 in

$$8h + 32v = 160{,}000$$

we have an equation that is easy to solve for h. In fact, you have already done it.

What are the dependent and independent variables in $8h + 32v = 160{,}000$? Does h depend on v? Does v depend on h? Explain.

5.39

Published by IT'S ABOUT TIME, Inc. © 2000 MATHconx, LLC

303

5.4 Pictures on Your Calculator

5.37

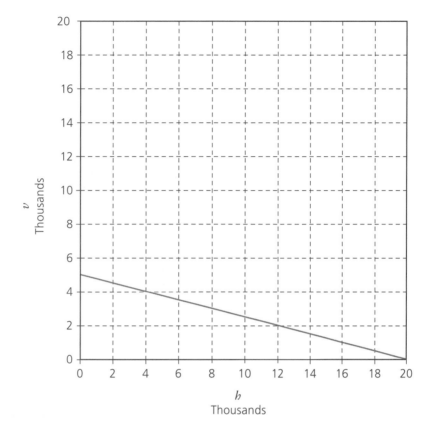

5.38

This is here to emphasize that the meaning and geometrical interpretation of the intercepts remains the same no matter how we calculate them.

5.39

Neither depends on the other, so neither is a dependent variable.

When we have an equation with a definite independent and dependent variable, usually the equation is *solved for* the dependent variable. If the dependent variable is y, this means we have the equation in the form $y =$ something. If we replace all the variables in the "something" with numbers, we can calculate y and see how it depends on the other variables. A graphing calculator or spreadsheet may require you to enter things in the "$y =$" form. When we put an equation in this form, the variable y should not appear in the "something." After all, if we already had a value for y, we would not need to calculate it. When you cannot determine the type of the variables, the equation may be solved for either variable. This is the case with our equation involving h and v.

Here is how we can solve this $8h + 32v = 160,000$ for v. (We could use the same method we used to solve the equation for h for any value of v.)

Since the steps are the same, why not do them once? Starting with

$$8h + 32v = 160,000$$

you probably found 8 times your value of h, then subtracted that value from both of the equal quantities $8h + 32v$ and $160,000$. If we do not have a specific value of h, we can still subtract $8h$.

$$\begin{array}{r} 8h + 32v = 160,000 \\ -\ 8h = \ -\ 8h \\ \hline \end{array}$$

The result is
$$32v = 160,000 - 8h$$

When you had a value for h, you probably divided by 32 next. We can still do that. The result is

$$\frac{32v}{32} = \frac{160,000}{32} - \frac{8h}{32}$$

so

$$v = 5000 - 0.25h$$

5.40 Where did the 0.25 come from? Is there a form of the Distributive Law involved here? Is the graph of this equation a straight line? If so, what are the slope and intercept? Check the equation by using it to calculate v when $h = 0$, 10,000 and 30,000. You can check your results because you already did these (see Display 5.15).

Published by IT'S ABOUT TIME, Inc. © 2000 MATHconx, LLC

5.40

$0.25 = \dfrac{8}{32}$

Yes, $\dfrac{160,000 - 8h}{32} = 5000 - 0.25h$.

Yes, this is a straight line with $m = -0.25$ and $b = 5000$.

Note that in addition to facilitating calculator entry, solving the equation for one of the variables helps us identify whether its graph is a straight line.

NOTES

Chapter 5

You can think of the process of solving for v as "undoing." Why is $8h + 32v = 160,000$ not solved for v? Because v is multiplied by 32 and has $8h$ added to it. We undid the addition with subtraction. Then we undid the multiplication with division.

Here are some more examples of undoing for you to try.

5.41

1. To solve $y - 7 = 3x$ for y, undo the subtraction by adding 7. What do you get?

2. To solve $y - 7 = 3x$ for x, undo the multiplication by dividing by 3. What do you get?

3. To solve $P = 2l + 2w$ for l, undo the addition and then undo the multiplication. What do you get?

4. To solve $P = 2l + 2w$ for w, undo the addition and then undo the multiplication. What do you get?

Now, you try solving some equations for the indicated variable.

5.42

1. $2x + 3y = 6$; solve for x.

2. $6x + 2y = 10$; solve for y.

3. $-7x + 4y = 28$; solve for x.

4. $C = 2\pi r$; solve for r.

5. $S = 30 + 2r$; solve for r.

Problem Set: 5.4

For each of the following pairs, use your calculator to graph both equations and find the coordinates of the point(s) where they intersect.

1. $y = 0.5x + 1$
   $y = 1.0x + 4$

2. $y = 2x + 8$
   $y = -1x + 4$

3. $y = 2x + 8$
   $y = 2(x + 4)$

Published by IT'S ABOUT TIME, Inc. © 2000 MATHconx, LLC

305

5.41

1. $y = 3x + 7$

2. $x = \dfrac{y - 7}{3}$ We prefer $x = (y - 7)/3$ form for calculator entry. Dividing through by 3 gives a coefficient and decimal number that must be rounded. Let the calculator carry out the division.

3. $l = \dfrac{P - 2w}{2} = 0.5P - w$

4. $w = \dfrac{P - 2l}{2} = 0.5P - l$. Note the symmetry in the roles of l and w.

5.42

1. $x = \dfrac{6 - 3y}{2} = 3 - \dfrac{3}{2}y$

2. $y = 5 - 3x$

3. $x = \dfrac{28 - 4y}{-7} = 4 + \dfrac{4}{7}y$

4. $r = \dfrac{C}{2\pi}$

5. $r = \dfrac{S - 30}{2} = \dfrac{S}{2} - 15$

Problem Set: 5.4

The first four problems only involve linear equations. We find that the biggest problem students have is selecting an appropriate WINDOW.
Note that *this is not a peculiarity of using a calculat*or—you would have to set a "window" if you made a graph on graph paper. Students can use the skills they learned in this section to find the intercepts of the linear equations and select a WINDOW that includes them. This should reduce the number of people with blank calculator screens! Then, if no intersection is visible on the screen, students should examine the pattern in what they *do* see, and estimate where there might be an intersection. Then they can change the WINDOW setting accordingly. Finally, note that nonlinear graphs are more difficult in two ways. First, there may be more than one point of intersection. Second, it will be more difficult to estimate what the rest of the graph might look like from looking at part of the graph.

1. $(-6, -2)$

2. $(-1.3333..., 5.3333...)$

3. This is just one line, along with another review of the Distributive Property.

4. $y = 2x + 5$
   $y = 1.8x + 5$

5. $y = 3x^2 + 5$
   $y = 8x + 1$

6. $y = 2x^2$
   $y = 5x + 3$

7. $y = 2x^3$
   $y = 8x$

8. $y = 1.49x + 11.34$
   $2x + 3y = 7$

9. $x - 4y = 12$
   $2x + y = 13$

10. $100a - 470b = 1600$
    $50a + 15b = 500$

Solve each equation for the indicated variable.

11. $A = \frac{1}{2}bh$; solve for h.

12. $P = a + b + c$; solve for a.

13. $L + 2 = 5m$; solve for m.

14. $LA = 2\pi rh$; solve for r.

15. $E = mc^2$; solve for m.

16. $V = lwh$; solve for w.

17. $P = 2l + 2w$; solve for l.

18. $SA = \frac{1}{2}pl + B$; solve for p.

19. $P = IE$; solve for I.

20. $I = Prt$; solve for t.

Published by IT'S ABOUT TIME, Inc. © 2000 MATHconx, LLC

4. $(0, 5)$

5. Make sure your students find *both* intersections: $(2, 17)$ and $(0.66666..., 6.33333...)$. Notice that once we understand what a solution to a system of equations means in terms of an intersection on a graph, the introduction of a quadratic is easier. Contrast this method with trying to solve these equations algebraically!

6. Make sure your students find *both* intersections: $(3, 18)$ and $(-0.5, 0.5)$.

7. Make sure your students find *these* intersections: $(2, 16)$, $(-2, -16)$ and $(0, 0)$.

8. $x = -4.176$ and $y = 5.117$ approximately. We do not want students to get the impression that coefficients and solutions are always whole numbers!

9. $x = \frac{64}{9}$ or about 7.111 and $y = \frac{-11}{9}$ or about -1.222.

10. $a = 10.36$ and $b = -1.2$. Students will have to decide which variable to treat as x and which to treat as y. The choice will affect the appearance of the graph but not the solution.

Solve each equation for the indicated variable.

11. $h = \dfrac{2A}{b}$

12. $a = P - b - c$

13. $m = \dfrac{L + 2}{5}$

14. $r = \dfrac{LA}{2\pi h}$

15. $m = \dfrac{E}{c^2}$

16. $w = \dfrac{V}{lh}$

17. $l = \dfrac{p - 2w}{2}$

18. $p = \dfrac{2(SA - B)}{l}$

19. $I = \dfrac{P}{E}$

20. $t = \dfrac{I}{Pr}$

5.5 Pictures for Data

In previous chapters we compared data using linear graphs. In this section we will compare two sets of data using graphs that are not linear.

Display 5.16 gives population figures for two states, Indiana and North Carolina, for the beginning of each decade of this century.

Learning Outcomes

After studying this section you will be able to:

Use nonlinear graphs to compare two sets of data.

Year	Indiana	North Carolina
1900	2,516,462	1,893,810
1910	2,700,876	2,206,287
1920	2,930,390	2,559,123
1930	3,238,503	3,170,276
1940	3,427,796	3,571,623
1950	3,934,224	4,061,929
1960	4,662,498	4,556,155
1970	5,195,392	5,084,411
1980	5,490,214	5,880,095
1990	5,544,159	6,628,637

Display 5.16

5.43

1. Why would an economist or a business person be interested in how the population of Indiana and North Carolina varied over the years?

2. Why would they be interested in comparing the population of Indiana with that of North Carolina? Explain.

3. Why do you think the table gives data for every ten years?

Published by IT'S ABOUT TIME, Inc. © 2000 MATHconx, LLC

307

5.5 Pictures for Data

Sections 2–4 of this chapter have carried on the work of Chapters 2 and 3 with exact mathematical relationships and their graphs. Now we turn to the analogous case for empirical data, which continues from Chapter 4, Graphical Estimation. Throughout all these previous sections we have been concerned with comparing two relationships, e.g., the usage cost for two rate schedules of the electric company, or the year population relationship for two states.

5.43

1. Answers will vary. Companies base expansion of their business when populations increase is one answer.

2. Answers will vary. Shifts in population are one indicator of housing and business trends.

3. The Constitution of the United States mandates that a census be done every ten years.

Additional Support Materials:

Assessments	Qty
Form (A)	1
Form (B)	1

Blackline Masters	Qty

Extensions	Qty

Supplements	Qty

We can see that for some decades these two states have had similar populations. The table provides accurate data but it may be more difficult to determine a pattern from it. A graph may make an overall pattern easier to see. As you see on the legend in Display 5.17, we use different symbols for the two populations we want to compare.

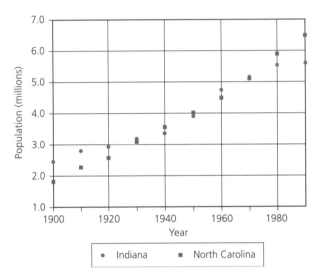

Display 5.17

5.44 In which years did Indiana have a larger population than North Carolina? In which years did Indiana have a smaller population than North Carolina? Is it easier to see this from the graph or the table?

5.45 Find the least-squares line for each state. Is each line a good fit?

If the points are on a straight line exactly, then connecting the points gives us the line. That is not true here. We could draw the least-squares line or we could connect the points. Let's compare the two methods. In Display 5.18, we connect the points.

Published by IT'S ABOUT TIME, Inc. © 2000 MATHconx, LLC

Chapter 5

5.44

Indiana had more in 1900, 1910, 1920, 1930, 1960 and 1970, fewer in 1940, 1950, 1980 and 1990. Students answers may vary; they find the graph or the table easier to interpret here. If the populations differed by one, that could be seen in the table but not on the graph. Note that the census data do not tell us which state had the greater population during the years between censuses, though they enable us to make plausible inferences.

5.45

The data fall approximately on a straight line. We used Minitab to analyze this data and Quattro Pro to make better graphs. For Indiana, Minitab gives

```
The regression equation is
IN population  =  −70155848  +  38108 Year
s = 230120        R-squared  =  96.6%
```

The correlation is 0.98. The value of *s* is a typical value for the residuals, i.e., for how far points are from the line (*y*-fitted–*y*-actual). Although the correlation is close to one, a typical error of about one quarter million people suggests limited accuracy.

For North Carolina,

```
The regression equation is
NC population  =  −96948288 + 51882 Year
s = 197998        R-sq  = 98.6%
```

The correlation is 0.99.

We can better understand the lack of fit if we plot the residuals against year for each state.

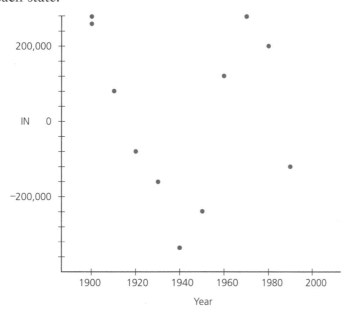

Ideally, if our model captures the systematic patterns in the data, the residual plot should show a residue that is random and unsystematic. The residual plot for Indiana suggests an S-shape that is also evident (but less so) in the plot of the raw data that "connects the dots"—a good reason for connecting them! A line is not a good fit for this data. We might prefer a graph of a cubic equation. The lack of fit can also be made more evident by plotting the data and the least-squares line on the same graph.

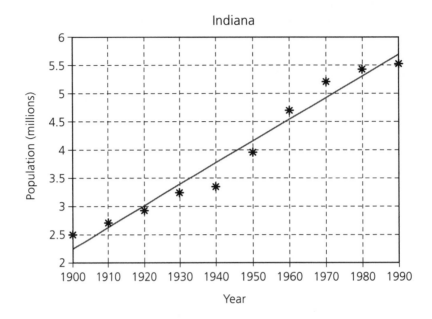

The residual plot for North Carolina also looks rather like the graph of a cubic, but this time we see just one nonsymmetric hump.

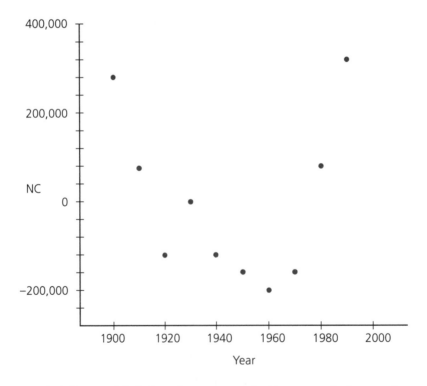

We might also model this with two straight lines, one before and one after about 1960—perhaps the time people began to discover North Carolina as a retirement location! This behavior is very similar to that shown in the main problem on the first Advanced Placement Test in Statistics (May 1997). For our data, the residual plot is especially revealing for North Carolina. The dramatic shift around 1960 does not stand out in any of the other displays.

Chapter 5

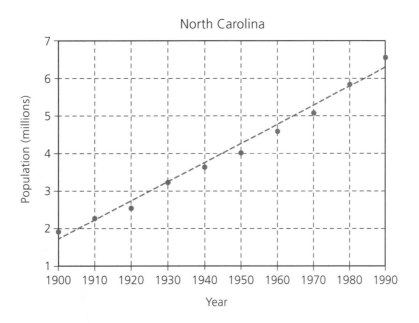

North Carolina

We leave it to you how much you want to get into analyzing the lack of fit with your students. The one point you do need to make is that the least-squares line would not be good for answering the discussion questions that follow because it leaves out too much detail.

NOTES

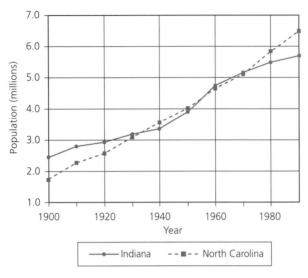

Display 5.18

5.5 Pictures for Data

(As you can see on the legend on Displays 5.17 and 5.18, we use different marks to help us see which mark represents Indiana and which represents North Carolina.)

Connecting the marks helps the eye to follow the trend in each state. It also makes it easier to interpolate or extrapolate from the data.

Which state do you think had the larger population in 1975? In 1965? In 1955? Predict the population of each state for the year 2000. Is it easier to do these tasks from the graph or the table? Explain.

a
5.46

Were there any times in this century that Indiana and North Carolina had the same population? If so, state the year(s).

b
5.47

You may wonder when you should use the table and when you should use the graph. Which one you choose will depend on the situation.

5.46

1975	North Carolina
1965	Indiana
1955	too close to call

You can quickly eyeball a rough prediction for the year 2000 from the graph. You can use the table to get a very precise estimate if you assume the increase during 1990–2000 will be the same as it was in 1980–1990. This gives for the year 2000

Indiana	$5544159 + (5544159 - 5490214) = 5598104$
North Carolina	$6628637 + (6628637 - 5880095) = 7377179$

This can be compared to regression predictions.

	Linear Extrapolation	Regression
Indiana	5598104	6060152
North Carolina	7377179	6815722

The regression equation predicts a dramatic population increase for Indiana and a much smaller increase for North Carolina—just the opposite of what the raw data suggest.

The population data is an example of time series data, i.e., data for which time is the independent variable, and we have single measurements of the dependent variable at regular time intervals. Simple linear regression is generally not appropriate for such data. One reason is that it gives equal weight to all the points. In predicting the future from time series data, we should probably give more weight to the most *recent* data.

5.47

From the graph showing the data for both states with dots connected, it appears the two states had about the same population three times in this century: first in about 1934-1935, then in 1955-1956, and again in 1971-1972.

5.48

You may wonder why we didn't simply find the intersection point of the least-square lines that fit our data sets. Let's try this method and see what happens.

a) Use your calculator or a spreadsheet to find an equation for a line that is close to the population data for Indiana. What is the slope of the line? What is your interpretation of the slope in this situation? If your calculator gives a value for r or r^2, what is the value and what does it mean?

b) Use your calculator or a spreadsheet to find an equation for a line that is close to the population data for North Carolina. What is the slope of the line? What is your interpretation of the slope in this situation? If your calculator gives a value for r or r^2, what is the value and what does it mean?

c) Use your calculator or a spreadsheet to graph the two least-squares lines. Do the lines appear to intersect near the coordinates you found when you looked at Display 5.18?

d) Use your calculator or a spreadsheet to estimate the coordinates of the point where the two least-squares lines intersect. (Be careful! Because the lines are very close together, this will be difficult.)

e) In this situation, do you think that it is better to look at a graph of the least-squares lines or at a graph like Display 5.18? Explain your answer.

310

Published by IT'S ABOUT TIME, Inc. © 2000 MATHconx, LLC

5.5 Pictures for Data

5.48

This exercise is meant to show students the perils of using linear regression in inappropriate situations.

(a) $y = 38108x - 70155848$; $r = 0.98$
(b) $y = 51882x - 96948288$; $r = 0.99$
(c) They shouldn't.
(d) The point of intersection is about 1945, 4 million. Students should note that this does not approximate the points of intersection they observed from Display 5.18 in the text.

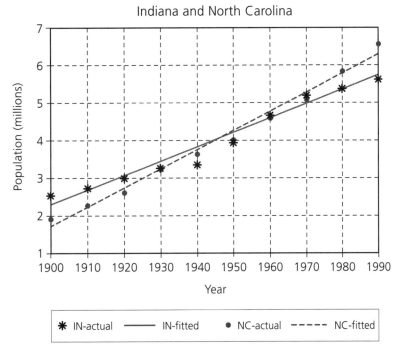

Indiana and North Carolina

IN-actual — IN-fitted • NC-actual ----- NC-fitted

(e) The least-squares lines do *not* give a reasonable answer.

Published by IT'S ABOUT TIME, Inc. © 2000 MATHconx, LLC

Chapter 5

Problem Set: 5.5

1. Display 5.19 gives the populations of Hawaii and Nevada for each census of the United States during this century.

    (a) Compare the populations at the start of the century. What do you notice?

    (b) Compare the populations in 1990. What do you notice?

    (c) Do the graphs of the populations and time for the two states intersect somewhere? Why?

    (d) Graph the data for Hawaii. Are the points close to forming a straight line?

    (e) Graph the data for Nevada. Are the points close to forming a straight line?

    (f) Make an appropriate graph to compare how the two populations grew during the century. Write a statement expressing your comparison.

    (g) Give the year(s) in which the populations of the two states were the same.

Year	Hawaii	Nevada
1900	154,001	42,335
1910	191,874	81,875
1920	255,881	77,407
1930	368,300	91,058
1940	422,770	110,247
1950	499,794	160,083
1960	632,772	285,278
1970	769,913	488,738
1980	964,691	800,508
1990	1,108,229	1,201,833

Display 5.19

Published by IT'S ABOUT TIME, Inc. © 2000 MATHconx, LLC

Chapter 5

Problem Set: 5.5

1. (a), (b) Hawaii had nearly four times the population of Nevada at the start of the century but a slightly smaller population at the end of the century.

    (c) They should intersect, because Hawaii starts higher and ends lower.

    (d) The points for Hawaii are pretty close to a straight line $r = 0.98$, but we also see some evidence of curvature. A line that fits the second half of the century well would not fit the first half of the century.

    (e) The points for Nevada shows a much more pronounced curvature. It would not be reasonable to fit a straight line to this data.

    (f) We give a rough graph provided by Minitab. It could be improved by connecting the dots.

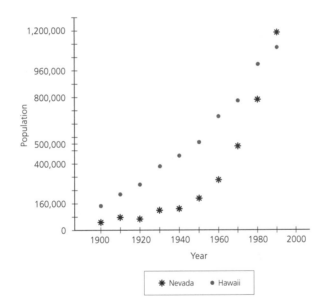

    The population of Hawaii grew steadily, with the rate of growth increasing over the years. The population of Nevada grew very slowly until after World War II, after that it grew very rapidly.

    (g) The population of Nevada passed the population of Hawaii in about 1986.

2. Display 5.20 shows some data on how homes in the United States have been heated over the years.

Percent of Homes in U.S. Heating With		
Year	Electricity	Oil
1950	22.1	0.6
1960	32.4	1.8
1970	26.0	7.7
1980	18.1	17.7
1983	14.9	18.5
1985	14.1	20.8
1987	14.0	22.7
1989	13.3	24.6
1991	12.3	25.5

Display 5.20

(a) On one set of axes make graphs for each set of data. Do these graphs appear to be linear?

(b) From your graphs, estimate when the number of U.S. homes heating with oil was equal to the number of U.S. homes heating with electricity.

(c) Enter the data into your calculator or spreadsheet and find the equations of the lines that best represent the data.

(d) Graph these lines and use your graph to estimate when the number of U.S. homes heating with oil was equal to the number of U.S. homes heating with electricity.

(e) Which estimate is more accurate—the one found in part (b) or in part (d)? Explain your answer.

Published by IT'S ABOUT TIME, Inc. © 2000 MATHconx, LLC

2. (a) Relationships do not appear to be linear.
   (b) Point of intersection looks to be (1981, 18).
   (c) The line for electricity is $y = -0.395130674x + 799.8389271$;
       $r = -0.8141065498$
       The line for oil use is $y = 0.6672077029x - 1303.673453$;
       $r = 0.9811422687$
   (d) The lines intersect at (1980.0776, 17.449547).
   (e) Both estimates are pretty good. This method works better on this
       example than it did on the population example since the two lines are
       closer to being perpendicular to one another.

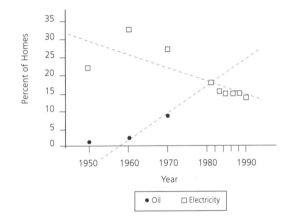

NOTES

5.6 Precise Answers to Real Life Situations

Earlier in this chapter, you solved the following problem using the guessing game algorithm.

A bacterial culture is being treated with ultraviolet rays in an attempt to kill the bacteria.

Length of Treatment (t hours)	% Surviving (S)
0	100
1	91
2	82
3	73

Display 5.21

Determine the amount of time it will take to kill all the bacteria.

We can also solve this problem using a graph (Display 5.22).

Place a ruler on the data points on the graph in Display 5.22. Do they seem to fall on a straight line? Draw the best line you can. Use your graph to determine how long it will take to kill all the bacteria. Did everyone in your class get the same result?

5.49

Learning Outcomes

After studying this section, you will be able to:

Solve a system of two linear equations by using tools of algebra (graphing, intercepts, substitution and solving equations);

Recognize systems of equations that can be solved graphically.

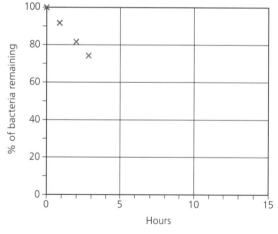

Display 5.22

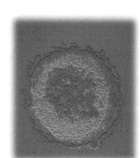

313

5.6 Precise Answers to Real Life Situations

This section is fairly traditional material. Note that the compound interest problem would normally be solved using logarithms. In real life an approximate and general method that can be used on a wide variety of problems is often more useful than an exact but highly specialized method.

5.49

The last bacterium dies after 11.1111... hours. If all your students report answers like "a little more than 11" there will not be much variability in their answers. However, if they report specific numbers that do show some variability, you might want to apply some of the techniques of Chapter 1 to explore the data they provide.

Chapter 5

Additional Support Materials:

Assessments	Qty
Form (A)	1
Form (B)	1

Blackline Masters	Qty

Extensions	Qty

Supplements	Qty
Precise Answers to Real Life Situations	4

Graphical techniques give only approximate answers, generally. Different people may get different answers depending on the accuracy with which they drew their graphs and lines. There are other techniques for solving problems like this that will often lead to exact answers. These techniques are based on equation solving skills.

To use these methods, we must first translate the given information into equations. We know that a straight line may have an equation of the form $y = mx + b$ where m is the slope and b is the **y-intercept**. Recall that the y-intercept is the y-coordinate of the point where the line intersects the y-axis. We can see from the graph that this happens at the point where $y = 100$. Notice in Display 5.22 that $x = 0$ for all points on the y-axis (where % of bacteria remaining equals 100).

a
5.50

Look at all of the information you have on the bacterial culture. Is there a way to determine the y-intercept without looking at the graph?

Now that we know the value of the y-intercept, substitute it for b in $y = mx + b$, and get $y = mx + 100$. This is a step toward finding the equation for this line. Now we need to find the slope.

Recall that the slope of a line is

$$\frac{\text{change in } y}{\text{change in } x}$$

To find the slope of the line, let's work with the first and last points in the table in Display 5.21.

The change in x as we go from (0, 100) to (3, 73) is $3 - 0 = 3$.

The change in y as we go from (0, 100) to (3, 73) is $73 - 100 = -27$. (Note that the change is *negative*. As time increases, the percent of surviving bacteria *decreases*.)

So, the slope is $\frac{-27}{3} = -9$. If you substitute $m = -9$ into $y = mx + 100$, you get $y = -9x + 100$. This is the equation of the line through the two data points.

b
5.51

Could you use another pair of points from the table to find the slope? Would you get the same slope? Why?

314

5.50

We want students to notice that the y-intercept (0, 100) can be read from the first line of the table.

5.51

It is important that the students understand that the rate of decrease, the slope, is constant.

NOTES

Now that you have the equation, you can find out how long it will be until all the bacteria are dead. This will happen at the time corresponding to 0% of the bacteria left alive. By looking at the graph, you can see that this will be the point where $y = 0$ and the line intersects the x-axis. This point is called the **x-intercept** of the line. Also, notice that all along the x-axis, $y = 0$.

To find out when all the bacteria will be dead, you must find the coordinates of the point where the line $y = -9x + 100$ intersects the line that is the x-axis. You can use the graph (Display 5.23) to get an approximate answer.

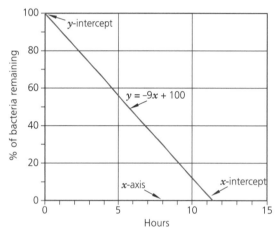

Display 5.23

It looks as though the x-intercept is a little more than 11. This may be close enough for our purpose, but sometimes we will need a more precise answer. You can get it by working with the equation of the line. If you have an equation in the form $y = mx + b$, and you know the values of m, x and b, you can plug them into the equation and find the value of y.

In this case, you have a value for y, and you want to find the corresponding value for x. We can think of this as solving the system of equations $y = 0$ and $y = -9x + 100$. To solve these two equations, substitute the value for y (which is $y = 0$) into the other equation,

$$y = -9x + 100$$

substituting $y = 0$

$$0 = -9x + 100$$

Then solve this equation for x.

Published by IT'S ABOUT TIME, Inc. © 2000 MATHconx, LLC

315

NOTES

As a guide to solving this equation, keep your goal in mind. You would like to end up with something that looks like "$x = ?$", where the "?" is a particular number. If you add $9x$ to each side the equation you have

$$0 = -9x + 100$$
$$9x = 9x$$
$$\overline{9x = 100}$$

$$\frac{9x}{9} = \frac{100}{9} = 11.111$$

a
5.52

Check the value $x = \frac{100}{9}$ in the original equation. Do you get an equality? Explain.

5.53

Check the value $x = 11.111$ in the original equation. Do you get an equality? Explain.

Now try solving this next real life problem. We will help you.

b
5.54

How long will it take to drain a completely filled 1500 gallon septic tank with a pump that can remove 5 gallons per minute?

1. Choose appropriate variables, and use them to set up an equation that describes this situation.

2. Solve the equation to find out how long it will be before the tank is empty. (*Hint:* Which variable equals zero?)

3. What are the units of your answer? Change your units to hours.

So far we have been trying to solve a system of two equations in which one equation has the form $y = mx + b$ and the other is $y = 0$. However, the second equation could have y equal to some other number.

For example, you may recall that Alfredo was saving money for a trip to Central America. His Aunt Mercedes had offered him a gift of $1,000 and he needed $2,400 total for the

316

Published by IT'S ABOUT TIME, Inc. © 2000 MATHconx, LLC

This is a good opportunity to discuss roundoff error.

5.52

5.53

5.54

If g = # of gallons remaining in the tank, and m = # of minutes the tank has drained, then $g = 1500 - 5m$ models this problem. Solving $0 = 1500 - 5m$, we get $m = 300$ *minutes* or $\frac{300}{60} = 5$ *hours*.

NOTES

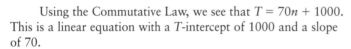

trip. Recall that if he put his gift in a bank account paying 7% simple interest the total amount due equals the principal plus the interest.

$$T = P + P * i * n$$

The total amount T dollars that he would have after n years would be given by

$$T = P(1 + i * n)$$

or

$$T = 1000(1 + 0.07n)$$

If we use the Distributive Law, we see that

$$T = 1000(1 + 0.07n) = 1000 + 70n$$

Using the Commutative Law, we see that $T = 70n + 1000$. This is a linear equation with a T-intercept of 1000 and a slope of 70.

What does the slope of 70 represent here?

a
5.55

Suppose the bank paid 8% simple interest. Find and interpret the slope and T-intercept.

b
5.56

Remember, Alfredo wanted to see how long it would be before $T = 2400$, so this is the second equation in our system. To solve the system, substitute $T = 2400$ into $T = 1000 + 70n$ to get $2400 = 1000 + 70n$. This last equation has only one variable. We can solve it using the tools of algebra that we learned earlier.

Find the value of n in the equation $2400 = 1000 + 70n$. Do you think Alfredo will want to wait this long?

5.57

You solved this same problem by trial and error earlier. That method took a long time and a great deal of work. You could also solve this problem by making a graph, but that method would take more time and be inaccurate. Using algebra to solve an equation is quick and exact. Right now the only trouble is that we've been dealing only with systems of two linear equations.

Published by IT'S ABOUT TIME, Inc. © 2000 MATHconx, LLC

317

5.55

Alfredo earns 70 dollars a year in simple interest.

5.56

If the bank pays 8% interest, we have the equation
$T = 1000(1 + 0.08n) = 1000 + 80n$. The slope is 80 and the T-intercept is
$T = 1000$.

5.57

$70n = 1400$, so $n = 20$

NOTES

Published by IT'S ABOUT TIME, Inc. © 2000 MATHconx, LLC

Originally, Aunt Mercedes was going to hold the $1,000 and eventually pay Alfredo the $1,000 and 7% compound interest. The total amount he was due was given by

$$T = 1000(1.07)^n$$

The compound interest curve is not a straight line. And we have not studied how to use algebra to find where the curve intersects the goal (represented by the line $T = 2400$). However, we can use the graph in Display 5.24 to make a good estimate.

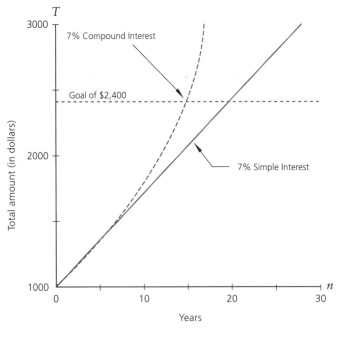

Display 5.24

5.58   Use the graph in Display 5.24 to estimate the number of years it will take Alfredo to get $2,400 if he is paid 7% compound interest. How accurate is your answer? How could you make it more accurate?

5.58 It will take Alfredo about 13 years. This is probably accurate to plus or minus one year. We could get better accuracy with a larger graph, with a graph that showed just a neighborhood of the intersection.

NOTES

Problem Set: 5.6

1. Find the point where each pair of lines intersect.

   (a) $y = 0$ and $y = 5x - 10$

   (b) $y = 5$ and $y = 3x - 1$

   (c) $y = -4$ and $y = -2x + 3$

2. Find the x-intercept of $y = -2x + 10$.

3. Of course, x and y are not the only variables we can use. Find the p-and q-intercepts of $p = -3q + 15$.

4. The outside air temperature drops by about one degree Celsius for each 100 meters an airplane flies skyward. Suppose the ground temperature is 20° Celsius.

   (a) Write an equation that can be used to determine the outside air temperature, T degrees, at a height of h meters.

   (b) What is the T-intercept of your equation? Interpret this.

   (c) Use your equation to predict how much the temperature will drop if you go to the top of the Empire State Building in New York City. (You may need to go to the library and look up the height of the Empire State Building.)

   (d) A pilot realizes that the deicers on her airplane's wings are not working. Use your equation and the method of this section to find out how high she can fly before there is danger of ice forming on the wings.

5. Sonia is earning $18,000 a year. Each year, she expects to get a raise that is 5% of the previous year's salary.

   (a) Write an equation that determines her salary, s dollars for y years.

   (b) What is the s-intercept of your equation? Interpret this.

   (c) Sonia wants to know how long it will be before she is earning $30,000 per year. Do you think she should use the equation or make a graph to answer this question? Explain.

   (d) How many years will it be before Sonia's salary is $30,000 a year?

Published by IT'S ABOUT TIME, Inc. © 2000 MATHconx, LLC

Chapter 5

| Problem Set: 5.6 |

1. (a) (2, 0)   (b) (2, 5)   (c) (3.5, –4)

Although the problem is stated in terms of lines, we want students to find solutions using the algebraic method of this section rather than a graphical method.

2. (5, 0)

3. The *p*-intercept is 15 and the *q*-intercept is 5.

4. By this time your students have learned many ways to find the equation. You might suggest they use a method you would like them to review.

   (a) $T = 20 - 0.01h$
   (b) The *T*-intercept is the ground temperature.
   (c) It should drop 3.81 degrees if you don't climb the TV tower too. This one may require a library expedition and a conversion from feet to meters.
   (d) Assuming that water freezes at 0° Celsius at the altitude in question, we can solve $0 = 20 - 0.01h$ to get 2000 meters.

5. This is a nonlinear compound interest problem.

   (a) $s = 18,000 \, (1.05^y)$
   (b) When $y = 0$, $s = \$18,000$, her current salary.
   (c) Because the equation is nonlinear, it's better to make a graph.
   (d) The calculator gives 10.469848 years, but the raise is probably given annually, so she will have to wait 11 years.

5.7 Using Algebra to Solve Systems of Equations

Learning Outcomes

After studying this section, you will be able to:

Use algebra to solve a system of two equations both of the form $y = mx + b$;

Identify the independent and dependent variable;

Determine if a pair of values is a solution to a system of two equations in two variables.

Thinking Tip

Sometimes when we are trying to solve a problem it is helpful to reduce it to a problem we already know how to solve.

In Section 5.6 we used algebra to solve problems in which a line intersected a horizontal line. Earlier in the chapter we worked on a problem involving the Electric Company and two rate schedules. When we solved that problem graphically, we were looking for a point where two lines intersected. Neither of those lines was horizontal or vertical. Can we solve such problems with algebra? We can and it's just a little more work.

Recall that the Electric Company's old rate schedule is described by the equation

$$T = 0.09u + 8.5$$

and the new rate schedule is described by the equation

$$T = 0.10u + 6$$

Since we are interested in the point where the values of T and u are the same for both rate schedules, we substitute $0.10u + 6$ for T into the equation $T = 0.09u + 8.5$. From this substitution we get the equation

$$0.10u + 6 = 0.09u + 8.5$$

Now we have a situation that is a little more complicated than the ones we encountered earlier in the chapter—each of the two expressions contains a variable. As usual, the key is to reduce this new situation to a type of problem we already know how to solve (having all the terms with u on one side of the equation). One way to do this is by subtracting $0.09u$ from both sides.

Subtract $0.09u$ from the equation $0.10u + 6 = 0.09u + 8.5$.

$$0.10u + 6 = 0.09u + 8.5$$
$$\underline{0.09u \quad\quad = 0.09u}$$
$$0.01u + 6 = \quad\quad\quad 8.5$$

Now we have reduced our problem to solving the equation $0.01u + 6 = 8.5$. This is a type of equation we already know how to solve.

320

Published by IT'S ABOUT TIME, Inc. © 2000 MATHconx, LLC

5.7 Using Algebra to Solve Systems of Equations

This section covers the traditional topic of using algebra to solve a system of two equations in two unknowns. Note that the equations are in the form $y = mx + b$ rather than $Ax + By = C$. Most people who work in technology prefer the form $y = mx + b$. This use leads to the function concept that will be developed in the next chapter.

Chapter 5

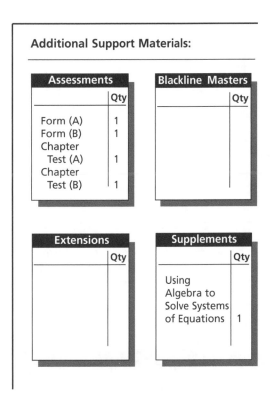

Additional Support Materials:

Assessments	Qty
Form (A)	1
Form (B)	1
Chapter Test (A)	1
Chapter Test (B)	1

Blackline Masters	Qty

Extensions	Qty

Supplements	Qty
Using Algebra to Solve Systems of Equations	1

Now undo addition by subtracting 6 from both sides of the equation.

a
5.59

There is just one step left. Do it.

b
5.60

Once you have a value for *u*, you can find the corresponding value of *T*.

5.61

Substitute your value of *u* into the old rate schedule equation to find the value of *T*. Then substitute your value of *u* into the equation for the new rate schedule to find the value of *T*. How do your two answers compare? Did you expect this result? Explain.

In Display 5.25, we have drawn a graph of the situation.

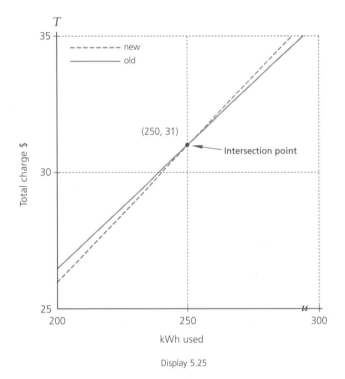

Display 5.25

We say that *T* is the *dependent variable* because the total charge for electricity depends on the usage. Like *y*, the dependent variable is usually graphed on the vertical axis.

Published by IT'S ABOUT TIME, Inc. © 2000 MATHconx, LLC

5.59

$$0.01\ u = 2.5$$

5.60

$$u = 250\ \text{kWh}$$

5.61

Both equations should give \$31.00 as the total charge. We should not be surprised that these values agree because 250 was supposed to be the value of u that *made* them agree! What we have done here is to check our solution.

Chapter 5

NOTES

The other variable here, u, is called the *independent variable*. It is plotted on the horizontal axis like x.

Suppose that we have a system of two (or more) equations involving two variables, such as the system

$$T = 0.09u + 8.5$$
$$T = 0.10u + 6$$

that we worked with in this section. A **solution** to the system is a list of two values, one for each variable, that make *all* of the equations in the system true. You can check whether a pair of values is a solution by substituting the two values into all of the equations in the system. All of the resulting equations will be true if the pair of values is a solution.

Use algebra to solve the system

5.62
$$y = 3x + 14$$
$$y = 2x + 11$$

In the case where you have only two variables, such as the Electric Company problem, solutions are often given in ordered pairs. The first value in the pair is normally a value for the independent variable. In the Electric Company problem, the solution is written as (250, 31). These are the coordinates of the point where the two lines intersect. They are labeled on the graph in Display 5.25.

Regardless of the method you use, when you solve a system of equations you should:

Always check your results in the original equations in the system to see that they are solutions. This way you will be certain that you have made no mistakes.

Check the three ordered pairs (2, 20), (4, 19) and (−3, 5) to see if they are solutions of

5.63
$$y = 3x + 14$$
$$y = 2x + 11$$

Published by IT'S ABOUT TIME, Inc. © 2000 MATHconx, LLC

5.62

$x = -3, y = 5$

5.63

(2, 20) satisfies $y = 3x + 14$ but not $y = 2x + 11$.
(4, 19) satisfies $y = 2x + 11$ but not $y = 3x + 14$.
(-3, 5) satisfies both equations, so it is the only solution of the three. Most errors lead to a solution that satisfies just one equation, so it is important to always check a possible solution in *both* equations.

Chapter 5

NOTES

REFLECT

In Chapter 1 you summarized data on a single variable with a mean or median. In Chapter 2 you learned how to use equations to express exact relationships between variables, and in Chapter 3 you learned how to graph these relationships. In Chapter 4, you used a line and its equation to summarize the relationship between data for *two* variables. In this chapter, we looked at situations where there were two *relationships*, and we wanted to compare them. For example, we compared two electric utility rates using both graphs and equations. We did the same in comparing simple and compound interest. These were all relationships expressed by equations. Often the points where the graphs of the equations intersected were important. For example, the intersection might tell us when one rate schedule would be higher than another. We can find these important points from a table, from a graph, or (sometimes) by manipulating algebraic symbols. We also used graphs and tables to compare relationships for two sets of *data*, such as the relationship between populations and time for two different states. We found that equations may give a good overall picture of the data, but graphs and tables are more useful for seeing the details.

Problem Set: 5.7

1. For the system of equations
$$y = 2x + 7$$
$$y = 3x - 5$$

   decide whether each of the following ordered pairs are solutions.

   (a) $(10, 27)$

   (b) $(11, 28)$

   (c) $(12, 31)$

2. Use the method of this section to solve each system of equations or explain why the method cannot be used. In that case, is there another method that could be used instead?

   (a) $y = 2x$
   $y = 5x + 3$

   (b) $y = 0.5x + 1$
   $y = 1.0x + 4$

Published by IT'S ABOUT TIME, Inc. © 2000 MATHconx, LLC

323

Problem Set: 5.7

1. All three points satisfy at least *one* of the equations, but only the last one satisfies both, so it is the only solution.

2. By now students should be able to recognize the equation of a line when given in $y = mx + b$ form. Probably, they do not have many skills at this stage to decide whether or not other equations are lines in disguise. We suggest that they simply try the techniques of this section on each system of equations and make a graph, if students have difficulty.
   If the difficulty is real, the graph will show the cause. Then the graph can be used to find approximate solutions, if there are any.

   (a) $x = -1, y = -2$
   (b) $x = -6, y = -2$

NOTES

(c) $y = 2x + 8$
$y = 2(x + 4)$

(d) $y = 2x + 7$
$y = 2(x + 7)$

(e) $y = 3x^2 + 5$
$y = 8x + 1$

(f) $y = 8x$
$y = 2x\char`\^3$

(g) $y = \dfrac{2x + 8}{2}$
$y = 2x + 7$

(h) $y = \dfrac{2x + 8}{x}$
$y = 2x + 7$

Published by IT'S ABOUT TIME, Inc. © 2000 MATHconx, LLC

(c) There are infinitely many solutions. Examining a graph is enlightening.

(d) There are no solutions. Examining a graph is enlightening.

(e) The algebraic manipulation techniques we have studied so far will not handle this because of the x^2 term, but we can solve this graphically or numerically. $x = \frac{2}{3}$ and $y = \frac{19}{3}$ or $x = 2$ and $y = 17$ are the solutions.

(f) The algebraic manipulation techniques we have studied so far will not handle this system because of the x^3 term, but we can solve this graphically or numerically. $x = 0$ and $y = 0$ or $x = 2$ and $y = 16$ or $x = -2$ and $y = -16$ are the solutions.

(g) $x = -3, y = 1$

(h) The algebraic manipulation techniques we have studied so far will not handle this because we divided by a variable, x. Compare this with the previous system of equations where we divided by a constant. We can still solve this system graphically or numerically (but only approximately): $x = 1.1085$ and $y = 9.217$ or $x = -3.608$ and $y = -0.217$ are the solutions.

3. We already know that a graph of the data is very close to being a straight

NOTES

3. Earlier in the chapter, you used a graph to find the number of hours in which two yeast cultures would produce the same amount of insulin. Now find this point as precisely as you can. We have reproduced the data here. For each strain, Display 5.26 shows the number of hours the yeast were cultured and the amount of insulin that could be harvested from each culture.

	Insulin Yield (in grams)	
Hours	Strain 1	Strain 2
4	19.44	10.2
8	23.88	19.4
12	28.32	28.6
16	32.76	37.8
20	37.20	47.0
24	41.64	56.2
28	46.08	65.4
32	50.52	74.6
36	54.96	83.8
40	59.40	93.0
48	68.28	111.4

Display 5.26

(a) Designate some variables and find an equation for each strain of yeast.

(b) Solve this system of equations to find the number of hours the yeast should be cultured so that both strains yield the same amount of insulin.

(c) Compare your solution to part (b) to the results you found graphically in Section 5.5. Which method is more accurate? Which method would you prefer to use if you had to solve problems like this every day in your job?

4. The students at White Mountain School want to have a soda machine in their school. The principal agrees to install one, provided that the students agree to maintain it. Rudy, the president of the student government, is in charge of the project. He found an old machine that the school can buy for $120. Also he found a supplier from whom he can buy soda for 45 cents a can. The student government has decided to sell the soda for 75 cents a can.

Published by IT'S ABOUT TIME, Inc. © 2000 MATHconx, LLC

line. We could use the calculator to fit a line to each strain and verify that we do get an exact fit.

(a) $y = 1.11x + 15$ for Strain 1 and $y = 2.3x + 1$ for Strain 2.
(b) $x = 11.7647$
(c) Did everybody check their answer? Solution of the problem by graph is less accurate, so when accuracy is sought, solution by systems of equations is preferable. When accuracy is not at a premium, and quick approximate answers will suffice, graphs may sometimes be preferable.

4. Finding a break-even point is a common business application of finding the intersection of two graphs.

(a) $A = 120 + 0.45c$

NOTES

(a) Write an equation for the amount of money, A dollars, that Rudy will spend if he buys the machine and c cans of soda.

(b) Write an equation for the amount of money, M dollars, the machine will collect, if c cans of soda are sold.

(c) How much money will Rudy spend if he buys the machine and 150 cans of soda? How much money will the machine collect if all 150 cans are sold? Will the student government make a profit in this case? If so, how much?

(d) How much money will Rudy spend if he buys the machine and 500 cans of soda? How much money will the machine collect if all 500 cans are sold? Will the student government make a profit in this case? If so, how much?

(e) Solve your equations to determine the number of sodas Rudy will have to sell in order for the expenses to exactly equal the income.

(f) On one set of axes, draw a graph of your equations and mark the point on your graph that corresponds to the solution you found in part (e). This point is called the **break-even point** (when the expenses exactly equal the income). It helps a business to estimate the amount of a product it needs to sell before it starts to make a profit. Why is the break-even value important to everyone in business?

Published by IT'S ABOUT TIME, Inc. © 2000 MATHconx, LLC

(b) $M = 0.75c$

(c) He collects \$112.50 and spends \$187.50 for a *loss* of \$75.

(d) He collects \$375 and spends \$345 for a *profit* of \$30.

(e) We solve $0.75c = 120 + 0.45c$; $c = 400$.

(f) The break-even value tells business people when they will begin making a profit if income exceeds expenses or when they will begin taking a loss if expenses exceed income.

NOTES

NOTES

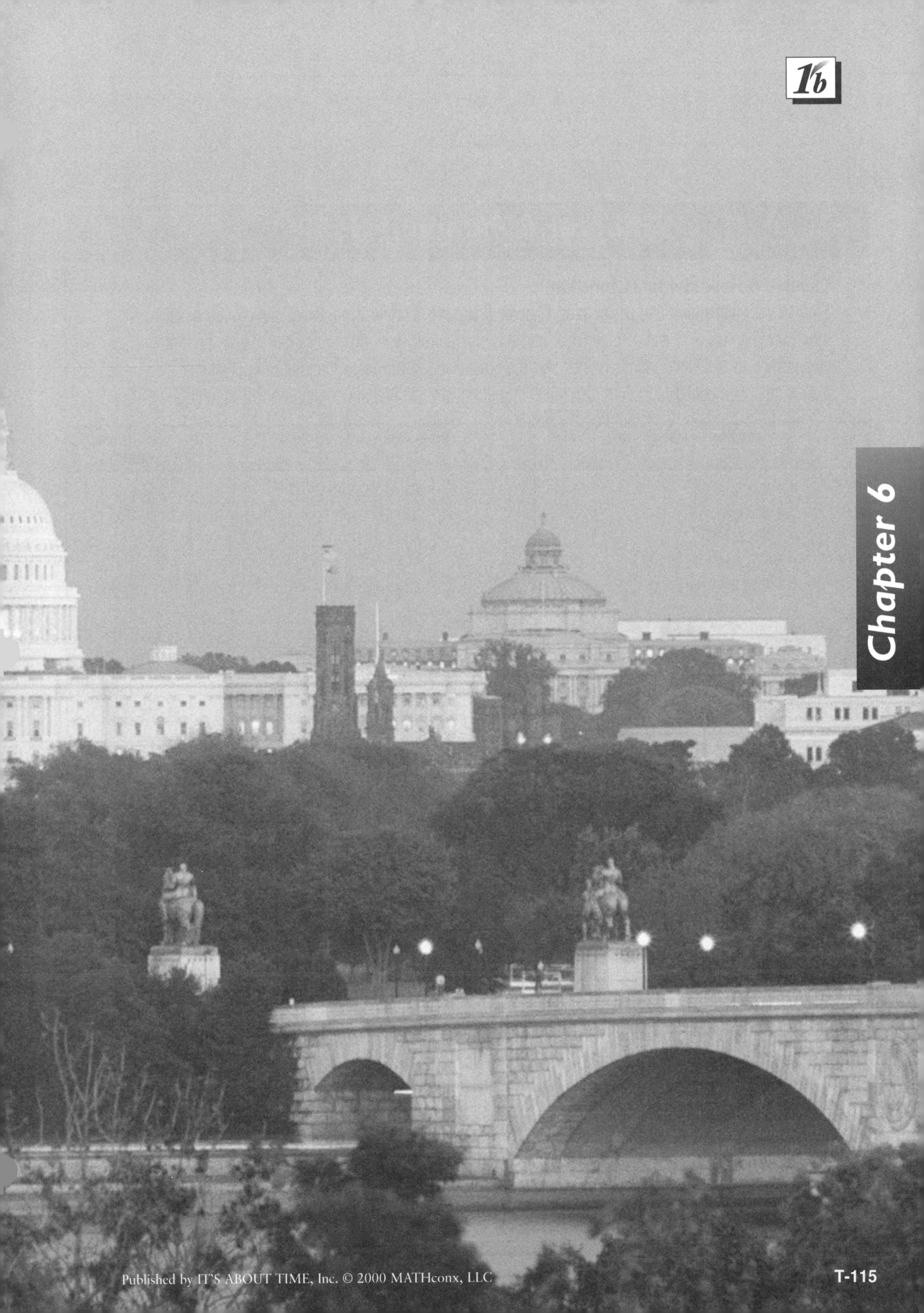

Chapter 6

Chapter 6 Planning Guide

Chapter 6 How Functions Function

Starting with fingerprints and postal rates, Chapter 6 presents discrete, step, linear and growth functions. It draws on Chapters 2, 3 and 5 to describe functions algebraically and graphically, and applies function composition to real world situations. This lays the groundwork for in-depth treatment of polynomial, exponential, and periodic functions also found in great depth and breadth in Chapters 1-3 of Year 3.

Assessments Form A (A)	Assessments Form B (B)	Blackline Masters
Quiz 6.1-6.2(A) Quiz 6.3-6.4(A) Quiz 6.5(A) Quiz 6.6(A) Chapter Test(A)	Quiz 6.1-6.2(B) Quiz 6.3-6.4(B) Quiz 6.5(B) Quiz 6.6(B) Chapter Test(B)	Student pp. 375, 376, 388, 391-392

Extensions	Supplements for Chapter Sections	Test Banks
Following 6.6 Recursive Relations	6.1 It All Depends — 3 Supplements 6.3 Between the Dots — 1 Supplement 6.4 Describing Functions With Algebra — 1 Supplement 6.5 Growth Functions — 1 Supplement 6.6 Links in a Chain: Composition of Functions — 2 Supplements	To be released

Pacing Range 6 weeks including Assessments

Teachers will need to adjust this guide to suit the needs of their own students. Not all classes will complete each chapter at the same pace. Flexibility — which accommodates different teaching styles, school schedules and school standards — is built into the curriculum.

Teacher Commentary is indexed to the student text by the numbers in the margins (under the icons or in circles). The first digit indicates the chapter — the numbers after the decimal indicate the sequential numbering of the comments within that unit. Example:

6.9

6.9

Student Pages in Teacher Edition   **Teacher Commentary Page**

Observations

Bryan Morgan, Teacher
Oxford Hills Comprehensive High School, ME

"Chapter 6, in a sense, is the culminating chapter for the first year. The foundation for its basic formal approach has already been laid down by all the informal work the students have done in the earlier chapters. It is about Functions and is so central and well done that it deserves all the time that a teacher can give it. Up here at Oxford Hills, we finish our first year with this chapter – and I really advise not to hurry it along. Many of the problems in this chapter are 2 or 3 daylong projects that lend themselves to great discussions and group side-talks. Section 6.3, to me, is MATH *Connections* in a nutshell. In this one section they learn about dotplots, different domains and step functions. In most traditional mathematics courses, these three types of graphs are usually separated into different sections. But here, the students see and learn about all three together which helps them integrate and conceptualize the abstract concepts."

Chapter 6

Xiaolong Zhang
Unlocking the Mysteries of Disease

Xiaolong Zhang is a researcher at the National Institutes of Health. He studies diseases such as cancer. What interests him a lot is the behavior of genes that may cause cancer.

"A gene is a 'blueprint' for all the building blocks in a cell," explains Xiaolong. "If you can manipulate a gene, you can change the blueprint.

"We don't even know when we're using math," he states, "because we use it all the time. For example, if we grow a bacterial culture, we start with a certain number of cells. Then, after a certain number of hours, we want to see how many cells have grown. What we are seeing is the exponential growth of that bacteria. From these experiments, we have developed mathematical calculations and algebraic formulas to represent those growth rates."

Xiaolong also uses math in DNA research. He explains that scientists use various techniques to make enough DNA to study. One technique Xiaolong uses is called a polymerase chain reaction.

Polymerase is an enzyme that speeds up the DNA production. "Each time you have a reaction, the number of DNA strands doubles. The growth rate is also exponential. Say you start with one double strand of DNA. If you do a reaction, you get 2 double strands. If you do two reactions, you get 4 double strands. After three reactions, you've got 8. If you do 20 reactions, you get 2 to the power of 20 double strands, and so on."

Learning which genes are linked to various diseases can lead to better treatments and cures. "It's very exciting to find something new in science," states Xiaolong. What motivates him, he adds, is 'pure curiosity.' "It's very difficult work and you just have to keep at it. Perhaps someday you'll hit something important and achieve something that in scientific terms is durable."

Published by IT'S ABOUT TIME, Inc. © 2000 MATHconx, LLC

Chapter 6 How Functions Function

The basic idea of *function* is a seminal concept. If we can get students to understand and be comfortable with it at a commonsense level before we dump a lot of algebraic notation and terminology on them, we shall have gone a long way toward making lots of different mathematical instances of functions understandable and useful. The critical first steps in Section 6.1 may not have learning outcomes that are as specific or as activity oriented as some would like, but it would be a real pity if we slid past this material lightly in our hurry to get to something for students to do.

Chapter 6

Published by IT'S ABOUT TIME, Inc. © 2000 MATHconx, LLC

How Functions Function

6.1 It All Depends

Learning Outcomes

After studying this section, you will be able to:

Identify and explain functions in real world situations;

Describe real world relationships using the language of functions;

Find images for particular domain elements when given a function described in words, by a pattern, or with a table.

In Washington, DC, the Identification Division of the FBI has a huge file of fingerprints—almost 203,000,000 of them! This file has one purpose: to identify people from their fingerprints. Its use depends on the fact that no two people have the same fingerprint. Each fingerprint on file leads to one, and only one, person. Of course, a person may have as many as ten fingers, so several different fingerprints may belong to the same person. However, no print can belong to two different people. The fingerprints in the file identify more than 68,000,000 people. When police investigators get a fingerprint from a crime scene, they can send it to the FBI for identification. If the print is in the FBI's file, then the investigators will know exactly which person was at the crime scene.

A fingerprint

Display 6.1

Published by IT'S ABOUT TIME, Inc. © 2000 MATHconx, LLC

329

6.1 It All Depends

As the title of this section suggests, the important idea to get across in this first section on functions is the fact that the "output" (dependent variable) of a function depends totally on its "input" (independent variable). That is, the power of the function concept is embodied in the fact that a function connects domain elements with range elements in a dependably predictable way. Recognition of this kind of linkage between two sets of things, rather than any algebraic formulation, is the main focus of the section. In fact, we have deliberately avoided using algebraic formulas to describe functions until the very end of this opening section.

Chapter 6

Additional Support Materials:

Assessments	Qty
Form (A)	1
Form (B)	1

Blackline Masters	Qty

Extensions	Qty

Supplements	Qty
It All Depends	3

About Words

In the title of this chapter, *function* is used as a noun and as a verb. The verb *function* means do something in a predictable or expected way. The noun *function*, then, means a process that does something predictable.

The FBI's fingerprint file is an example of a **function**, a process that relates each thing in some first set to exactly one thing in a second set. The first set is called the *domain* of the function; the second set (in this case) is called the *range*. In this example, the set of fingerprints on file is the **domain**, and the set of people on file is the **range**.

In everyday English, we say that something's "function" is what it has been designed to do or is supposed to do. For instance, the function of a lawn mower is to cut grass. In some sense, the cutting of the grass depends on the proper *functioning* of the lawn mower. We say that something *functions* if it works properly.

Other uses of *function* in everyday English say that one thing depends on another.

- When your teacher says, "In this course, the amount you learn is a function of how much studying you do," you are being told that how much you learn depends on how much you study.

- If your boating partner says that the amount of water inside your leaky rowboat is a function of how fast you bail, you are being told that the faster you bail, the less water will be left in the boat.

This notion of dependence—especially of one quantity depending on another—is the basic idea of a function.

ZIP codes form another common example of a function. Each piece of mail with a ZIP code in its address is sent to exactly one post office location. The location to which the postal service delivers an item depends on its ZIP code. For instance,

a letter marked 06417 is sent to Deep River, Connecticut;
a letter marked 37379 is sent to Soddy Daisy, Tennessee;
a letter marked 59011 is sent to Big Timber, Montana;
a letter marked 75668 is sent to Lone Star, Texas;

and so on. The set of all pieces of mail *with ZIP codes in their addresses* is the domain of this function. The set of all post office locations is the range.

330

Published by IT'S ABOUT TIME, Inc. © 2000 MATHconx, LLC

NOTES

What is your ZIP code? Which post office is assigned to it? Does any other post office in the United States have the same ZIP code as yours?

6.1

Do the white pages of your local telephone directory form a function?

6.2

- If they do, how does the function work? What is its domain? What is its range?

- If they don't, explain why not. What adjustments might make them form a function?

Functions occur throughout the physical sciences, the social sciences, economics, manufacturing, business, and daily life. Here are a few examples.

- The volume of a quantity of gas is a function of the pressure put on it.

- The size of a colony of bacteria is a function of the time it has been growing.

- The amount of pressure that a steel bolt can stand before it breaks is a function of its diameter.

- The profit made by a Burger King franchise is a function of how much food it sells.

- The pay of a cook at Burger King is a function of the number of hours he or she works.

- The cost of a particular style of wall-to-wall carpeting is a function of the area to be covered.

We could go on for pages listing examples like this—but we won't, because you get the point: The idea of *function* is a fundamental building block for just about anything that can be described mathematically. It occurs so often in so many different settings that it is essential for you to have the basic meaning of the term firmly and clearly in your mind. Here it is again:

Words to Know: A **function** is any process or rule that assigns to each element of a first set exactly one element from a second set. The first set is called the **domain** of the function. The thing that is assigned to a domain element is called the **image** of that domain element. The set of all the images is called the **range** of the function.

About Words

In everyday English, a *domain* is a territory ruled by a single person or government. In mathematics, it is a set ruled by a function in the sense that each of its elements is used by the function in the matching process.

331

Published by IT'S ABOUT TIME, Inc. © 2000 MATHconx, LLC

6.1

Some quick questions to get students actively involved in this example.

6.2

This discussion has two purposes: (1) to get students comfortable with the idea of a function as a matching or assignment process, and (2) to emphasize that each domain element must have *exactly* one image. The white pages of a telephone book *almost* form a function that matches names with phone numbers. If the domain is taken to be the set of all people with listed phone numbers, the only difficulty is that some people may have two different phone numbers under the same name. If no one has two phone numbers, or if you agree to use only the first listing for each person, then this matching is a function. On the other hand, if you want the domain to be the set of phone numbers listed, then the difficulty is that the same number might be listed with two different names for two people living in the same household. This can be fixed by using only the name of one of the persons who is listed, for example.

Chapter 6

NOTES

....

....

....

....

....

....

....

....

....

....

....

In the FBI example, the image of a fingerprint is the person whose finger made the print. In the ZIP code example, the image of a letter is the post office to which it is sent.

6.3 Each motor vehicle that travels on public roads must be registered with the Motor Vehicle Department of some state. License plates show the registration number of each vehicle.

1. Describe this situation as a function.
2. What is its domain?
3. What is its range?
4. Pick out a particular domain element; what is its image?

6.4 Look up the many everyday English meanings of *range* in the dictionary. Pick the one that you think is most closely related to the mathematical meaning of *range*. Write a short paragraph explaining your choice. Do the same thing for the word *image*.

6.5 As you saw earlier in **MATH** *Connections*, mathematical notation is used to write ideas in precise ways and to abbreviate long expressions. Here is how the language of functions is abbreviated.

The assignment of a grade to each student in a class is a function. Its domain is the set of all students in the class. If Alvin gets a grade of B, we might say,

The grading function assigns B to Alvin.

That's a long, stuffy way to express a simple idea. We can shorten it a little by using a letter to stand for the grading function; let's use *g*. Then we can say or write,

The image of Alvin under *g* is B.

Better, but not great. The phrase "The image of Alvin under *g*" contains two important facts,

(1) the function being used is *g*, and
(2) it is being applied to the domain element Alvin.

We abbreviate this information by writing the name of the function outside of parentheses and the particular domain element inside the parentheses.

$g(\text{Alvin})$ is B   or $g(\text{Alvin}) = \text{B}$

332

6.3

A quick class discussion of these questions should solidify the meanings of the function related words. In this situation, there is a one-to-one correspondence between license plate *numbers* (not necessarily *plates,* depending on the state you're in) and registered vehicles. If the students choose "registered vehicles" as the domain, then the range is the set of all license plate numbers in use. If they choose the set of license plates or of license numbers as the domain (they can do either), then the image of a plate or number is the vehicle that displays it. The range, then, is the set of all registered motor vehicles.

6.4

This question has no "best" answer for everyone. Its purpose is to help students keep straight the domain/range and the range/image distinctions by getting them actively involved in thinking about the words and their meanings. A model for the kind of answers we have in mind is the analogous marginal note about *domain.*

6.5

The purpose of this somewhat long-winded discussion of function notation is to nip in the bud an all too common confusion—students often translate $f(x)$ as "f times x," treating f and x as if they were numbers of some sort. This profound misunderstanding often is not detected until long after function notation has been introduced and used repeatedly in class. By that time, the mismatch between what the teacher has been saying and what the student has been hearing has caused so much bewilderment that the damage is virtually irreparable. The fact that function notation is used throughout all of mathematics and in many other areas that use mathematics makes this a particularly serious problem. Please take great care to make sure that all your students are reading and using this notation properly right from the start.

Chapter 6

NOTES

....

....

....

....

....

....

....

which is read as "*g* of Alvin equals B."

Similarly, if we used *F* to stand for the FBI's fingerprint file function, we could represent the matching of a particular fingerprint with a person by

$$F\left(\; \text{} \; \right) = \text{John Doe}$$

(We probably wouldn't write it this way, but we *could*. All the necessary information is contained in this one line.)

Functions occur in many different forms. Sometimes they can be recognized from real world situations, as in the previous examples. Sometimes they are described by a table or diagram. The diagrams in Display 6.2 define three different functions, *f*, *g*, and *h*. Each arrow points from a domain element to its image. All three functions match the numbers 1, 2, 3, and 4 with letters in the set {*a*, *b*, *c*, *d*}, but each function differs from the other two in some important ways.

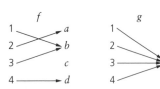

Three functions

Display 6.2

These questions refer to the three functions shown in Display 6.2.

6.6

1. **Find each of these images.**

    $f(1) = \underline{\ \ }$; $g(1) = \underline{\ \ }$; $h(1) = \underline{\ \ }$; $f(2) = \underline{\ \ }$;

    $g(2) = \underline{\ \ }$; $h(2) = \underline{\ \ }$; $f(3) = \underline{\ \ }$; $g(4) = \underline{\ \ }$

2. **What is the range of each function?**

3. **For each function, describe one property that you think makes it different from the other two in some important or interesting way.**

You might think that functions like the ones in Display 6.2 have nothing to do with real world situations, but they are actually just small versions of a familiar school event: the multiple choice test. If you were answering a four question

333

6.6

These questions serve to give students a picture of various kinds of function correspondence. Students who learn well from pictures or visual patterns might find these simple diagrams particularly helpful. The first two parts are straightforward.

1. $f(1) = b$ $g(1) = c$ $h(1) = a$ $f(2) = a$
    $g(2) = c$ $h(2) = c$ $f(3) = b$ $g(4) = c$

2. The range of f is $\{a, b, d\}$. The range of g is $\{c\}$. The range of h is $\{a, b, c, d\}$.

3. This question is more challenging than the other two. It is also open-ended; there is not a unique set of right answers. We hope that students will notice these features and describe them in some way.

    g takes all its domain elements to the same image. Later in the chapter, they will see that this is called a *constant function*.

    h always takes different domain elements to different images. Later in the chapter, they will see that this is called a *one-to-one correspondence*.

    f is neither a constant function nor a one-to-one correspondence. Its range is a smaller set than its domain, but it contains more than a single element.

    In these problems the word "process" in the text's definition of function takes on meaning. The process is matching shown in each table, whether or not there is a rule of great interest visible.

NOTES

_____

Chapter 6

multiple choice test, with possible answers *a*, *b*, *c*, *d*, you would assign exactly one of those letters to each question number, right? Of course, you wouldn't make an arrow diagram; you'd just list the choices, maybe like this.

$$1.\ b \qquad 2.\ a \qquad 3.\ b \qquad 4.\ d$$

Well, this listing *is* the function *f* of Display 6.2! The only real difference between this kind of function and answer sheets for most multiple choice tests is that the tests usually have more than four questions. That is, the domain of the function is larger.

6.7

Suppose your class takes a ten question multiple choice quiz. Each question has four possible answers—a, b, c, or d—and only one is correct.

1. The answer sheet of one of your classmates looks like this.

1. c	6. d
2. a	7. c
3. a	8. d
4. b	9. a
5. b	10. c

Copy Display 6.3 and draw in arrows to represent these answers. Is this a function?

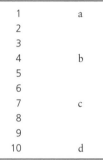

Display 6.3

2. The diagram for another person's answer sheet is shown in Display 6.4. List the ten answers it represents. Is this a function?

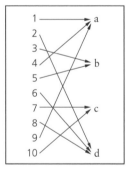

Display 6.4

3. Make your own answer sheet by copying Display 6.5. Fill in the answers any way you want, then make an arrow diagram for it. Is it a function? Why or why not?

1. ___	6. ___
2. ___	7. ___
3. ___	8. ___
4. ___	9. ___
5. ___	10. ___

Display 6.5

334

6.7

These questions are completely routine. Their purpose is to get students comfortable with the domain to range assignment idea, to give all students an initial sense of success in this chapter, and to provide students who are more visually inclined with a way to picture what kinds of correspondence patterns represent functions.

1. See Display 6.1T.

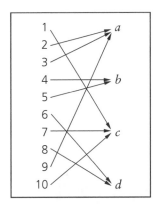

Display 6.3, filled in

Display 6.1T

The display defines a function.

2. 1. *a*   6. *d*
    2. *d*   7. *c*
    3. *b*   8. *d*
    4. *a*   9. *a*
    5. *b*   10. *c*

The display defines a function.

3. There will/should be wide variations in these answers.

NOTES

4. When filling in your own answer sheet, what two things might you do to make sure that it's *not* a function? When you do these things on a real exam, what kind of credit do you get?

Many of the tables in Chapter 4 describe functions. For instance, the table in Display 4.10—shown again here in Display 6.6—is a function from the set of Olympic years from 1904 through 1992 (the domain) to the set of running times listed in the right column (the range). Using function notation, if we called this function *t*, we could write

$$t(1904) = 116.0$$
$$t(1908) = 112.8$$
$$t(1912) = 111.9$$
$$t(1920) = 113.4$$
$$\vdots$$

Years and Times for Olympic 800-meter Finishes	
Year	Running Time (in seconds)
1904	116.0
1908	112.8
1912	111.9
1920	113.4
1924	112.4
1928	111.8
1932	109.8
1936	112.9
1948	109.2
1952	109.2
1956	107.7
1960	106.3
1964	105.1
1968	104.3
1972	105.9
1976	103.5
1980	105.4
1984	103.0
1988	103.45
1992	103.66

Display 6.6

335

4. The two things that would make the answer sheet *not* a function are (i) leaving an answer blank, or (ii) putting more than one letter in an answer slot. Such answers usually get no credit. Sometimes they even get negative credit!

NOTES

Sometimes functions are described by algebraic formulas. This method is particularly useful when the domain is a large set of numbers. For instance, the process that finds the area of a square from the length of one side is a function. Since we can make a square with a side length as large or as small as we please, the domain of this function is the set of all positive numbers. (That's a *very* large set of numbers!) As you know, the area is found by squaring the side length—that is, by multiplying it by itself. If *s* stands for the side length and *A* stands for the area, then this process is represented by the formula

$$A = s^2$$

Both *A* and *s* are *variables* here; each one can represent many, many different numbers. We are free to choose any domain element for *s*, so it is called an *independent variable*. However, once we have chosen a particular side length *s*, the value of the area *A* is determined. For this reason, the area *A* is called a *dependent variable*. We can show that its value depends on the choice of *s* by writing it as *A(s)*. That is, the area function *A* can be written as

$$A(s) = s^2$$

For instance, if we choose a side length *s* of 7 cm, then the area of this square is

$$A(7) = 7^2 = 49 \text{ cm}^2$$

6.8

Assume that *A* is the area function for squares, as described.

1. Write in function notation: "The area of a square 5 miles on a side is 25 square miles."

2. Evaluate *A*(3.2 ft.). Then explain what it means.

3. Choose *s* to be any number you want. Find *A(s)* and explain what it means.

4. If $A(s) = 36 \text{ cm}^2$, what is *s*? Explain your answer in terms of a square.

When a function is defined by a formula, the symbol that stands for the domain element is the **independent variable**, and the symbol that stands for its image is the **dependent variable**.

336

6.8

These are routine reinforcement questions for interpreting function notation and also for handling decimals and units of measure.

1. A(5 mi.) = 25 sq. mi.

2. A(3.2 ft.) = 10.24 sq. ft. The area of a square 3.2 ft. on a side equals 10.24 sq. ft.

3. This question underscores the independence of s. $A(s)$ is the area of a square s units on a side for whatever the student chooses as s.

4. This foreshadows inverses and recalls square roots. In this case, $s = 6$ cm. The expression $A(s)$ stands for the area of a square, so the side length must be positive.

NOTES

Chapter 6

6.1 It All Depends

Think of a function as a tool, a process that you use to get a particular result, and think about independent and dependent variables like this,

- you control the independent variable;

- the function controls the dependent variable.

Here is another example: As you may already know, the area inside a circle is found by the formula

$$A(r) = \pi r^2$$

where r is the radius of the circle and π is a specific number (about 3.14). If you want to use this formula, *you* supply the radius of the circle, so r is the independent variable. Once you have told the function the value for r, your choosing is done. The function takes control and gives you a number for $A(r)$, so $A(r)$ is the dependent variable. (You or a machine do the arithmetic, of course, but the function tells you how to do it.)

Two standard sizes of round pizza are 10 inch and 14 inch.

a
6.9

1. To what do these measurements refer?

2. About how much more pizza is in the 14 inch size than in the 10 inch size?

3. If a 10 inch pizza costs $5 and a 14 inch pizza costs $9, are you getting your money's worth?

4. Generalize your work on questions 1–3 to write a formula for the area inside a circle as a function of its diameter.

Explain your answers.

What formula describes the perimeter of a square in terms of its side length? Express it as a function called P. What is the independent variable in your formula? What is the dependent variable? Find $P(7\ cm)$.

b
6.10

The dependence of one variable on another is a way of looking at predictability in science. In an experiment, you change some condition, and note any changes observed in the thing you're studying.

337

Published by IT'S ABOUT TIME, Inc. © 2000 MATHconx, LLC

6.9

Besides discussing variables and algebraic notation, this material provides a review of and practice with some basic geometric formulas in a new context. Depending on your students' abilities, you might have to lead them through these questions in some detail.

1. The measurements refer to the diameter of each pizza, not to the radius.

2. The function $A(r) = \pi r^2$ is the appropriate tool here. If students are using a calculator, they can leave π as it is, letting the machine do the approximation. Otherwise, they should rewrite the function as $A(r) = 3.14r^2$. The numerical result will be an approximation in either case.

   The students get to control the variable r, the radius. They need to recall that the radius is half the diameter, and to see that they should put in 5 for the small size and 7 for the large size. Once these substitutions are made, the function takes over.

   $$A(5) = 78.54 \text{ sq. in.} \qquad A(7) = 153.94 \text{ sq. in.}$$

   Thus, the large size has 75.4 sq. in. more pizza than the small size—very nearly twice as much! Students who have written their answers first in terms of π can see this directly, since 49π is almost double 25π.

3. The important thing here is to reinforce the fact that the large size contains almost twice as much pizza as the small size. Students being what they are, you might get a No answer to this question for other reasons such as "The place down the street only charges $8." That's OK, as long as the students recognize that the $9 size costs less per square inch of pizza than does the $5 size. The price difference is about half a cent per sq. in.

4. $A(d) = \pi \left(\dfrac{d}{2} \right)^2$

6.10

This is a routine practice exercise. It can be skipped if you are pressed for time and/or think that your students are comfortable with the idea of functions as formulas. $P(s) = 4s$, where s is the independent variable and $P(s)$ is the dependent variable. $P(7 \text{ cm}) = 28 \text{ cm}$.

Chapter 6

Dorsal fin

For instance, suppose you have a question like this.

> Does feeding marshmallows to sharks change the length of their dorsal fins?

Silly, but easy to picture in your mind. The best way to state this as a hypothesis is

> Feeding marshmallows to sharks will have no significant effect on the length of their dorsal fins.

Why be negative? Because it's much easier to explain finding "nothing" than it is to explain finding "something." Also, if you assume that you're going to find something, you can fool yourself into believing it much more easily.

Notice that we've stayed away from the words *cause* and *effect*. You see them a lot in science, but when you are first testing a hypothesis, you don't really know what causes what. For instance, no matter how many marshmallows you use, there are a thousand other things that happen to a shark. Its fin length might change for any number of reasons. And any good research question will generate a whole new set of questions. Scientists do try to find causes eventually, but only after a lot of analysis.

Let's get back to the sharks and the marshmallows.
- You carry out this experiment by taking a sample of sharks from the population of sharks in the ocean—not too many (they are a bit rough to work with), but not just one (with your luck, you might get the one shark that is allergic to marshmallows).

- Next you apply the independent variable—in this example, the marshmallows. Why is it called independent? Because it is not determined by anything else. You decide when, where, and how the marshmallows will be fed.

- Then, from a safe distance, you measure the dependent variable—fin length. Why is fin length the dependent variable? Because you are trying to see whether or not its value depends on what else has been done to the subject.

NOTES

Chapter 6

The labels *independent variable* and *dependent variable* depend on the question you ask (the hypothesis), not on the answer you get (the result of the experiment).

The independent variable is what you control.
The dependent variable is what you observe.

When you want to identify the independent variable and the dependent variable in a hypothesis, just think of the marshmallows and the sharks.

Problem Set: 6.1

1. For each part, decide whether or not the statement describes a function. Explain your answer. For each one that is a function, what is its range? (In each case, the elements mentioned first are in the first set.)

    (a) Each word in this sentence is matched with its first letter.
    (b) Each word in this sentence is matched with its last letter.
    (c) The first letter of each word in this sentence is matched with the last letter of that word.
    (d) Each word in this sentence is matched with the number of letters it contains.
    (e) Each of the numbers 1, 2, 3, 4, 5, 6, 7, 8, 9, 10 is matched with every word in this sentence having that number of letters.

2. For each of the six diagrams in Display 6.7, state whether or not it describes a function with domain {1, 2, 3, 4}. If it does, give the image of 2; then list all the elements of the range. If it does not, explain why not.

Display 6.7

Problem Set: 6.1

1. (a) Yes. The range is {e, f, i, l, m, s, t, w}.
   (b) Yes. The range is {d, e, h, n, r, s, t}.
   (c) No. Some first letters are paired with more than one last letter; e.g., *l* with *r* (in *letter*) and with *t* (in *last*).
   (d) Yes. The range is {2, 3, 4, 6, 7, 8}.
   (e) No. Some numbers are matched with more than one word, e.g., 2 with *of, is,* and *in*; some numbers are not matched with any words e.g., 1.

2. (a) function; image of 2 is *a*; range is {*a, c, d*}.
   (b) not a function; 2 is matched with more than one thing (as is 3).
   (c) not a function; 4 is not matched with anything.
   (d) function; image of 2 is *b*; range is {*b*}.
   (e) not a function; 2 is matched with more than one thing; no other domain element is matched with anything.
   (f) function; image of 2 is *c*; range is {*a, c*}.

NOTES

Chapter 6

3. Display 6.8 shows part of the 6% Sales Tax table that is used by retail stores in Maine. It describes a function, which we'll call T, that matches each price from $0.01 to $40.00 with a specific tax amount. Use this table to answer these questions.
   (a) Find $T(\$5.00)$.
   (b) Find $T(\$0.67)$.
   (c) Find $T(\$5.67)$.
   (d) Find $T(\$.45)$.
   (e) Find $T(\$12.45)$.
   (f) Find $T(\$36.79)$.
   (g) Find $T(\$19.98)$.
   (h) Find $T(\$20.05)$.
   (i) What is the domain of T?
   (j) What is the range of T?
   (k) Suppose a customer buys an item costing $95.48. Explain how this table can be used to find the proper amount of sales tax.

4. Which of these situations can be viewed as functions? For each one that can, describe the domain and the range, and explain how the function works. For each one that cannot, explain what "goes wrong" with the idea of function.
   (a) Every taxpayer has a Social Security Number.
   (b) Every child has a mother.
   (c) Every mother has a child.
   (d) Every licensed driver in a state has a numbered driver's license.
   (e) McDonald's has a cash register with icons (pictures) on the keys.
   (f) Every football player on the team has a number.

5. A switch that controls a 60 Watt light bulb can be thought of as a function in this way: Its two positions, *on* and *off*, form the domain. The image of *on* is 60 Watts, the amount of power being used by the bulb; the image of *off* is 0 Watts.
   (a) If the bulb burns out, is this situation still a function? Why or why not?
   (b) Describe a lamp that has a 3 way bulb (50-100-150 Watts) as a function. What is its domain? What is the image of each domain element?
   (c) Some lights (such as stage lights) have a rheostat control, a knob or lever that can be used to vary the light intensity gradually from totally dark to very bright. Can this be viewed as a function? If you think so, describe its domain and explain how the function works. If you don't think so, explain what goes wrong with the function idea in this situation.

Published by IT'S ABOUT TIME, Inc. © 2000 MATHconx, LLC

340

3. Besides reinforcing the function idea and its terminology and notation, this exercise gives students practical experience in reading a real sales tax table, something that many of them will have to do if they ever get part-time work in a retail store. The parts increase in order of difficulty, from direct table reading to interpretation, in several easy steps.

   (a) 0.30   (b) 0.05   (c) 0.35   (d) 0.03   (e) 0.75   (f) 2.21   (g) 1.20
   (h) 1.20
   (i) Actually, this table implicitly contains enough information to extend to any sale price; see part (k). However, the explicit domain is all amounts between $0.01 and $40.00 (or $41.00).
   (j) Explicitly, $0.00 to $2.40 (or $2.46).
   (k) Tax on each $40.00 amount is $2.40. Subtracting $80.00 from the given price leaves $15.48, on which the table says the tax is $0.93. Thus, the total tax is $2 \times \$2.40 + \$0.93$, which is $5.73.

4. (a) This can be viewed as a function on the domain of all taxpayers. Each one is assigned a unique number; all the *assigned* numbers form the range. It can also be viewed as a function from the set of all assigned numbers to the set of all taxpayers and former taxpayers.

   (b) This part and the next should be considered at the same time. If the domain is the set of all children, then this is a function because each child has exactly one mother.

   (c) If the domain is the set of all mothers, then this is not a function. Many mothers have more than one child.

   (d) This is very much like part (a). The correspondence between drivers and drivers' license numbers is a function from the set of all licensed drivers (domain) to the set of all numbers used on the licenses (range). It is also a function the other way around, provided that the domain is restricted to the numbers that are actually assigned to drivers.

   (e) The McDonald's cash register is a function from the domain of all McDonald's products to the set of all their prices. Each time an icon button is pushed, the price for that item appears on the register tape.

   (f) This is a function from the set of players (domain) to the set of numbers. The numbers actually assigned to players form the range. As in parts (a) and (d), it can also be viewed as a function the other way around, provided that the domain is restricted to the numbers actually assigned to players. It might be argued legitimately that this is not a function if you allow that a player might change numbers temporarily to reflect his eligibility in a certain formation. However, normal procedure is for each player to have a single assigned number on the team roster.

6.1 It All Depends

6% Sales Tax Schedule

Sale		Tax
From	To	
$0.01	$0.09	$0.00
0.10	0.16	0.01
0.17	0.33	0.02
0.34	0.50	0.03
0.51	0.66	0.04
0.67	0.83	0.05
0.84	1.00	0.06

The tax to be collected is the amount indicated below for each dollar of the sale price plus the amount indicated above for any fraction of a dollar.

Sale	Tax	Sale	Tax
$1.00	$0.06	$21.00	$1.26
2.00	0.12	22.00	1.32
3.00	0.18	23.00	1.38
4.00	0.24	24.00	1.44
5.00	0.30	25.00	1.50
6.00	0.36	26.00	1.56
7.00	0.42	27.00	1.62
8.00	0.48	28.00	1.68
9.00	0.54	29.00	1.74
10.00	0.60	30.00	1.80
11.00	0.66	31.00	1.86
12.00	0.72	32.00	1.92
13.00	0.78	33.00	1.98
14.00	0.84	34.00	2.04
15.00	0.90	35.00	2.10
16.00	0.96	36.00	2.16
17.00	1.02	37.00	2.22
18.00	1.08	38.00	2.28
19.00	1.14	39.00	2.34
20.00	1.20	40.00	2.40

Display 6.8

341

5. The purpose of these questions is to underscore, in a fairly simple setting, the input-output idea of a function.

   (a) Yes, but not a very interesting one. It's the constant function 0. That is, the value "0 Watts" is the range element assigned to both domain elements in this case.

   (b) Its domain is the set of the four switch positions, {*off, low, medium, high*}. The respective images of each of these domain elements are 0 Watts, 50 Watts, 100 Watts, 150 Watts.

   (c) You might want to decide whether your students are ready, at this time, to ponder the idea of continuous change. This is a function. In theory, its domain is the continuous interval from *off* to the highest position of the rheostat. In practice, because of the way many rheostats are made, this may really be just a lot of discrete positions that are very close together. Each position allows a specific amount of power to flow to the lights, so the image of each position can be described either as a specific amount of power (measured in Watts, for example) or a specific amount of light perhaps measured in lumens.

Chapter 6

NOTES

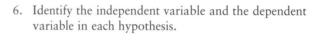

6. Identify the independent variable and the dependent variable in each hypothesis.

   (a) Hours of sunlight will have no effect on the flowering of poinsettias.
   (b) The length of the work week will have no effect on the rate of unemployment.
   (c) There will be no difference in food sales with respect to the color of the decor in fast food restaurants.
   (d) The use of CFC plastic foam will have no effect on the concentration of ozone over the south polar region.
   (e) There will be no significant difference in mathematical ability between boys and girls.

7. Here is a true story. As a special promotion, a pizza restaurant made 36 inch pizzas. A person who called in to order one was told that they were no longer available, but he could have two 18 inch pizzas for the same price. The customer agreed, but later wondered if this was fair. He wrote a letter to the consumer advocate column of the local newspaper asking whether or not this was a fair deal.

   (a) If you were the newspaper columnist, how would you answer this letter? Explain.
   (b) If f is a function, is it always true that $f(2x) = 2 \cdot f(x)$? Use part (a) to explain your answer to this question.

8. The use of "DNA fingerprinting" depends on the assumption that it can be viewed as a function. Write a paragraph explaining this statement. (You might start by reading about DNA fingerprinting in an encyclopedia.) Then explain why DNA fingerprinting might *not* be a function.

9. Describe two situations from your everyday life that can be viewed as functions. For each one, specify its domain and its range, and explain how the function works.

10. (a) How can a piano keyboard be viewed as a function?
    (b) Pick any other musical instrument that you know and explain either (i) how it can be viewed as a function, or (ii) why it can't be viewed as a function.

Published by IT'S ABOUT TIME, Inc. © 2000 MATHconx, LLC

6. Each of these hypotheses has been the subject of serious scientific study at one time or another.

   (a) *Independent:* hours of sunlight; *dependent:* flowering
   (b) *Independent:* length of work week; *dependent:* unemployment rate
   (c) *Independent:* decor color; *dependent:* food sales
   (d) *Independent:* use of CFC foam; *dependent:* ozone concentration
   (e) *Independent:* gender; *dependent:* mathematical ability

7. (a) No, it's not a fair deal. The amount of pizza is determined by the area. For a 36 in. pizza, this is
$$A(18) = \pi \cdot 18^2 \approx 1018 \text{ sq. in.}$$
For two 18 in. pizzas, this is
$$2 \cdot A(9) = 2 \cdot \pi \cdot 9^2 \approx 509 \text{ sq. in.}$$
Therefore, the two 18 in. pizzas cost the customer twice as much as one 36 in. pizza.

   (b) This part links abstract function notation with the real world of pizzas. No. Part (a) provides a counterexample to this statement. Using the area function, A, we have
$$A(2 \cdot 9) = A(18) \neq 2 \cdot A(9)$$

8. This is similar to the FBI fingerprint file example. Because of the huge number of possible DNA patterns, it is believed that each person's pattern is unique. *If* that's true, then the DNA pattern can be used to match the pattern of any cell from a person's body (fingernail, hair, etc.) with the person, and hence the process is a function. However, there are two difficulties here. First, although no two people's DNA patterns have been shown to be the same, there is nothing in our knowledge of DNA that says it could never happen. Second, even if no two people can ever have the same DNA pattern, the pattern chain is so long that comparisons have to be done by sampling parts of it, and this process might indicate a match when there really are differences in other parts of the chain.

9. Not much can be said about this in advance; the answers will be quite varied. The critical idea, regardless of the setting, is uniqueness of images. Each domain element must have one and only one thing assigned to it.

10. This might make a better discussion question than a homework assignment. If given for homework, it is a writing exercise.

   (a) Each key (domain element), when struck, produces a single sound (image). Thus, a function is defined. The exception is the out-of-tune piano. For example, the key for middle C on the piano causes three strings to be struck; if one of them is loose, it will sound a lower note, along with the two that are tuned properly.
   (b) Answers to this part can be highly variable. Few instruments exhibit the function structure as clearly as a keyboard, but, in some sense, any instrument that produces a controlled pitch can be viewed as a function. The trick is to describe the input elements carefully enough so that each input element produces one and only one pitch. If that can't be done, then the instrument cannot be viewed as a function.

Chapter 6

6.2 Functions Step by Step

Ms. Terius is giving a ten question, multiple choice quiz to her three science classes. Each question has five possible answers, labeled (a) through (e), with only one correct answer. She can label the correct answer with any of these five letters.

6.11

1. Help Ms. Terius make up an answer key to the quiz for her first class. For each question, choose a letter to label the correct answer. List your ten choices.

2. Ms. Terius wants to give the same questions to the second class, but she wants the correct answers to be labeled differently in the two classes. (For example, if the correct answer for question 1 is (a) in the first class, it should be (b), (c), (d), or (e) in the second class.) Make up an answer key to the quiz for her second class.

3. Is your first answer key a function? If you say Yes, describe its domain, its range, and the image of 7. If you say No, explain how it doesn't fit the definition of a function.

4. Is your second answer key a function? If you say Yes, describe its domain, its range, and the image of 7. If you say No, explain how it doesn't fit the definition of a function.

5. She wants to change the quiz form for her third class. The first eight questions will be the same, but questions 9 and 10 will say "Choose as many as apply" and there will be three correct choices for each of these questions. Make up an answer key to this quiz.

6. Is your third answer key a function? If you say Yes, describe its domain, its range, and the image of 9. If you say No, explain how it doesn't fit the definition of a function.

Functions are all around us, just waiting to be recognized. For instance, every restaurant menu is a function. It assigns a price to each item the restaurant sells. In the same way, every price list or catalog describes a function. In each case, the

Learning Outcomes

After studying this section, you will be able to:

Construct examples of functions on finite sets using diagrams and tables;

Describe a sequence recursively and use that description to list its terms with a graphing calculator;

Describe a sequence algebraically and use that description to find specific terms;

Determine whether or not two functions are equal (in some cases).

343

6.2 Functions Step by Step

The main purpose of this section is to introduce algebraic formulas as a convenient way of describing *some* functions. While it is true that most functions that students will see and use in mathematics and science are usually defined algebraically, it is critically important that students continue to realize that there is a difference between the generic idea of a function and the algebraic descriptions of some of them: A function is *not* a formula, but formulas are sometimes useful for describing functions.

The section begins with a simple exercise to remind students of the basic idea of a function as a process that assigns values to a set of elements, to get them actively involved, and to give them a chance to be successful early in the section. That exercise and the McDonald's example that follows it establish the idea of representing a function as a set (a list) of ordered pairs. This idea is important for two reasons:

One, it begins to move students to a more algebraic way of representing functions; and two, it builds the foundation for graphing functions on coordinate axes.

The three examples that come next serve three distinct, but related, purposes.
- The first example reestablishes "$f(x)$" notation as something distinct from multiplication and from traditional algebraic formulas, relating it, instead, to ordered pairs and to the idea of a function as a matching process.

- The second example uses a commonplace setting involving money to illustrate the idea of using variables and algebra in general function notation. This function points out the usefulness of having a formula; its domain is inconveniently large to handle by assigning values to each element "by hand."

- The third example extends the second to a more abstract mathematical setting in which the domain (the natural numbers) is infinite. In this case, it is essential to have a general formula of some sort to define the function; it is impossible to handle this domain by hand. This example leads to the definition of a *sequence* as a function on **N**.

The final concept of this section is equality of functions. The main idea is that the equality or inequality of two functions is determined by comparing their *results* (images), not by comparing their definitions. It doesn't matter whether the definitions of two functions look similar or different. If they apply to the same domain and if they both assign the same image to each domain element, then the two functions are equal (on that domain). If *any* element of their common domain is assigned different images by the two functions, then *the functions* are not equal.

Assessments   Blackline Masters   Extensions   Supplements

For Additional Support Materials see page T-151

6.11

This opening exercise provides two student generated examples of functions on a finite set, along with one counterexample. It gives the students some practice with the language of functions in a setting that is not formally algebraic. The critical fact in the description of the quiz is that each question has only one correct answer.

1. This is a free choice question for the students. The only constraint is the each question should have exactly one answer. A typical, correct student response might look like this.

| 1. (b) | 2. (d) | 3. (a) | 4. (a) | 5. (e) |
| 6. (d) | 7. (b) | 8. (b) | 9. (a) | 10. (d) |

   Any letter choice for each question is OK, even if the student chooses the same letter as the correct answer for each question. You might get an interesting discussion here about whether certain patterns are "sneakier" than others, from the students' point of view.

2. This is an almost free choice question. Any list of ten letters is correct, provided that none of the ten answers are the same as in the student's first list.

3. Yes, the first list is a function, no matter what the choices are, as long as there is exactly one letter for each question number. Its domain is the set of questions (or the numbers 1–10). Its range is the set of correct answers (or the set of letters actually used to label the correct answers); in our "typical" case, it is the set {(a), (b), (d), (e)}. The image of 7 is the correct answer for question 7 or the letter for that answer in the student's list. In our typical case, the image of 7 is (b).

4. Yes, the second list is also a function, for the same reason, and its domain is the same as that of the first function. The range may be different, depending on which letters the student uses. This second image of 7 should not be the same as the first one.

5. Again, this is a free choice question, except that the answers to questions 9 and 10 must each have three letter choices.

6. No, the third list is not a function (assuming that images must be single letters) because 9 and 10 each would have more than one image. Any student who answers Yes will have to confront the multiple image issue directly when deciding the image of 9.

→

A subtle distinction may arise here if there is class discussion of these questions. If the domain elements are considered to be the *questions* themselves, rather than their numbers, and the images are considered to be the *correct answers* rather than their answers, then the first two quizzes are *exactly the same function*. However, if the domain elements are considered to be the numbers 1–10 and their images are the corresponding letters, then the first two answer keys represent different functions. This point probably is too sophisticated to inject into the discussion if it is not raised by the students.

Chapter 6

Additional Support Materials:

Assessments	Qty
Form (A)	1
Form (B)	1

Blackline Masters	Qty

Extensions	Qty

Supplements	Qty

domain is the set of all things being offered for sale, and the range is the set of all prices charged. The image of each item is its price. If we wanted to treat the McDonald's menu as a function in a very formal way, we might call it m and write the prices as

$$m(\text{hamburger}) \ = 0.85$$
$$m(\text{cheeseburger}) = 0.95$$
$$\vdots$$

Of course, it's pretty silly to do that when a simple listing of items and prices gives you the same information.

$$\text{hamburger} \quad 0.85$$
$$\text{cheeseburger} \quad 0.95$$
$$\vdots$$

And that's the point of this paragraph.

You get exactly the same information about a function f from the ordered pair (a, b) as you do from the expression f(a) = b.

Both expressions tell you that f assigns the range element b to the domain element a.

So why bother with all this function notation? The reason is that the interesting, useful functions in mathematics, science, and business usually don't have a domain as small as a restaurant menu. Most of them have domains that are too large to count, let alone list. In order to deal with these functions, we need some way of describing the matchups between domain and range elements without having to list each pairing.

Example 1: Suppose that you want to make up a simple letter-substitution code for sending secret messages, and you want to give the code to a friend who will read the messages. One easy way to make a code is to turn each letter into the letter two places further along in the alphabet, starting over when you get to the end. (This is a function, which we shall call c. What is its domain? What is its range?) This verbal description is good enough to understand how the code works, but a listing of the letter matchups probably would be easier to use for decoding a message. We could write this listing of c in the three different ways shown in Display 6.9; they all provide exactly the same information.

344

(6.12) This example could be a time trap, if you're not careful. The topic has a natural appeal for many (but not all) students and, of course, it is wise to capitalize on whatever enthusiasm appears. However, as stated above, this is only the first of three examples that are designed to lead, step-by-step, to the main ideas of the section. Of course, this example is only one of many, many possible alphabet codes, whose variety is limited only by the creativity of their designers.

For your information, the code given in this example is a function, and because it is actually a one-to-one correspondence, its inverse—the decoding process—is also a function. In general, a coding process might not be a function; a given letter might be disguised in several different ways. However, it is essential that the *decoding* process be a function, so that there is no ambiguity in translating the message. Discussion of such things would be useful if we were aiming at developing the theory of inverse functions, but in this context it probably would be too distracting for the students.

NOTES

....

....

....

....

....

....

....

....

....

....

....

....

....

Chapter 6

A ——→ C	(A, C)	$c(A) = C$
B ——→ D	(B, D)	$c(B) = D$
C ——→ E	(C, E)	$c(C) = E$
D ——→ F	(D, F)	$c(D) = F$
E ——→ G	(E, G)	$c(E) = G$
F ——→ H	(F, H)	$c(F) = H$
G ——→ I	(G, I)	$c(G) = I$
H ——→ J	(H, J)	$c(H) = J$
I ——→ K	(I, K)	$c(I) = K$
⋮	⋮	⋮
X ——→ Z	(X, Z)	$c(X) = Z$
Y ——→ A	(Y, A)	$c(Y) = A$
Z ——→ B	(Z, B)	$c(Z) = B$

Display 6.9

6.13

1. What is the code letter for N? Write this matching in the three different ways shown in Display 6.9.

2. What is the code letter for V? Write this matching in the three different ways shown in Display 6.9.

3. Write your full name (first and last) using the code function c. Of the four ways in which this coding function was described (words and three different lists), which did you use?

4. Decode the message "JCXG C PKEG FCA." Of the four ways in which this coding function was described, which did you use?

Example 2: Pre-holiday business has been good at the Fuzzy Friends Toy Co. Management tells the Payroll Office to give each of the company's 150 employees a holiday bonus of $100. In order to print the paychecks, the Payroll Office has to add $100 to each employee's regular salary for the last week of December. Listing the new amount for each of the 150 employees would be a long, tedious job. Instead, they put into the computer a "holiday check" function, h, defined by

$$h(s) = s + 100$$

where s is an employee's regular salary for the week.

6.13

These questions bring home the point of Example 1, that listing ordered pairs is a perfectly good way of describing a function with a relatively small domain. Questions 1 and 2 check the students' understanding of how the code pattern is represented by the lists. They also provide the extra matchups beyond those in Display 6.9 needed to answer question 4. The message is "HAVE A NICE DAY".

NOTES

6.14

1. What is the domain of *h* (the holiday check function in Example 2)?

2. What is the independent variable for the holiday check function *h*? What is its dependent variable?

3. Calculate *h*(450). Then interpret its meaning in Example 2.

4. Business at Fuzzy Friends continues to be very good, so the management decides to give every employee a 4% raise. Write a "raise function" *r* that will compute each employee's new salary from his/her old one. (Note: The old salary does *not* include the holiday bonus, which was a one time gift.)

5. What is the domain of *r*? What is its range?

6. If you were earning a weekly salary of $300 before the raise, what will you be earning after the raise? Write this statement in function notation.

In Example 2, it was more convenient to write a formula for the function than to list all the pairings of old salaries with new ones, but it would have been possible to list the pairs. In the next example, listing all the pairs for the function is absolutely impossible. We *must* use a formula.

Example 3: Let's match each natural number with its double. That's an easy enough idea, right? We list the first few pairs of this matching:

But, no matter how long a list we make, we can *never* list all the matchings for this function. The only way to describe *all* the images of *all* the natural numbers is by some rule, either in words or in symbols. In this case, the words describe a function, which we'll call *d*, that can by symbolized like this.

$$d(n) = 2n$$

The independent variable is *n*; it stands for any natural number. The domain of this function is the set of all natural numbers,

Published by IT'S ABOUT TIME, Inc. © 2000 MATHconx, LLC

6.14

Example 2 shows a situation in which defining a function by a formula is much more convenient than listing all the matchings. These questions serve to reinforce the language and notation of functions in the context of that example.

1. The domain of h is the set of all regular weekly salaries.

2. The independent variable is s. The dependent variable is $h(s)$ (not just h, which is the function).

3. $h(450) = 550$. It is the salary with bonus for an employee whose regular weekly salary is $450.

4. $r(s) = s + 0.04s$ or $r(s) = 1.04s$, where s is an employee's salary before the raise. It would be helpful to make sure that your students see how to rewrite $s + 0.04s$ as $1.04s$. This device is used later in the chapter, particularly in Section 6.5.

5. The domain of r is the set of all preraise salaries; its range is the set of all postraise salaries.

6. $312 \quad r(300) = 1.04 \cdot 300 = 312$

NOTES

Chapter 6

which is abbreviated as *N*. Its range is the set of all even natural numbers (because every even number is the double of some number).

The first three questions refer to the "doubling" function of Example 3.

6.15

1. What is $d(5)$? What is $d(20)$? What is $d(351)$?

2. If $d(n) = 12$, what is n? If $d(n) = 454$, what is n?

3. Why does the statement $d(n) = 35$ not make sense?

4. Define in words another function—call it f—on the domain *N* of all natural numbers. Then write a formula for f, if possible. If you cannot write a formula for f, explain why it can't be done.

5. Use the function f you defined in the previous question to find $f(3)$, $f(25)$, and $f(100)$. If you can't find one or more of these values, what makes you believe that f is a function with domain *N*? Explain.

Example 3 illustrates a very important kind of function called a *sequence*.

A Word to Know: A sequence is a function that has the set of all natural numbers as its domain.

....

Does this definition surprise you? Do you think of a sequence as a list that has a first element, then a second, then a third, and so on? Do you think

4, 7, 10, 13, 16, ...: is a sequence?

If you said Yes, you're right! This is just another way of writing a function that has the natural numbers as its domain. Each of the numbers listed in a sequence is called a **term**. If we call this sequence *s*, then

the first term is the image of 1 (that is, $s(1) = 4$);
the second term is the image of 2 (that is, $s(2) = 7$);
the third term is the image of 3 (that is, $s(3) = 10$);
and so on.

Published by IT'S ABOUT TIME, Inc. © 2000 MATHconx, LLC

347

6.2 Functions Step by Step

6.15

Example 3 is an introduction to sequences, which are functions with domain N. Sequences are defined more formally and discussed immediately after this set of questions.

1. 10   40   702

2. 6   227   This is an informal taste of the inverse of a function.

3. Because all images under *d* must be even.

4. The answers to this question can vary widely. Note that the difference in phrasing the two parts of the last sentence is deliberate. A student who cannot write a formula to describe his/her own function should try to explain why *nobody* could write a formula for that function.

5. These images depend on the student's answer to the previous question. If any one of them can't be found, then *f* is not a function on the domain N because every domain element must have an image.

NOTES

Chapter 6

Sometimes the "..." can be troublesome. This symbol, ..., called an **ellipsis**, indicates that the pattern set up by the first few terms continues. There are two problems with this.
- The pattern of a particular sequence may not be obvious to everybody (or to anybody).
- Even if it is clear how to get from each term to the next, finding out what value corresponds to a large natural number can be a long, tedious job.

a
6.17

1. In the sequence 4, 7, 10, 13, 16, ..., how can you find each term (after the first) from the term just before it? Use this process to find *s*(6) and *s*(17).

2. Can you use this process to find *s*(99)? What about *s*(567)? (Don't actually do this.) What is the problem with defining a sequence just by saying how to get from each term to the next one?

About Words

In English, saying that something *recurs* means that it happens again. (Think of *recur* as a short form of *recurrence*.)

When a sequence is described by saying how to get each term from the one before it, we say that it is **recursively defined**. Finding the first few terms of a recursively defined sequence is usually pretty easy, but finding terms farther along can get tedious. As you just saw, it's easy to find *s*(6), but it's not so easy to find *s*(17), and it's really annoying to find *s*(99) or *s*(567).

Once you recognize how to get from each term to the next, a spreadsheet program or a calculator can get you many terms in a hurry. They make finding *s*(17) and *s*(99) almost as easy as finding *s*(6). But what about *s*(1000) or *s*(1,000,000) or *s*(1,000,000,000)? Even the best spreadsheets and calculators have their limitations, but the natural numbers go on forever. If a sequence really is a function on N, then we must be able to find the image of *any* natural number, no matter how large it is. That is, we need a rule that will supply *s*(*n*) for any natural number *n*. Finding such a rule begins with looking for a pattern.

b
6.18

Let us use calculator power to help find a pattern for this sequence.

1. Enter 4, 7, 10, 13, 16, ... into your calculator *as a recursively defined sequence*. Then store the first 99 terms of this sequence in one of your calculator's lists. (Your teacher will explain how to do this.)

348

6.16

The painstaking discussion of the sequence 4, 7, 10, 13,... serves several purposes.

- It explores the distinction between a pattern that is recursively defined and one that can be used to find any sequence value without knowing explicitly the one just before it. In so doing, it gives students who have difficulty recognizing patterns several different strategies to use in similar situations.

- The spreadsheet or calculator setting makes clear the power of using variables to describe patterns, and also illustrates the essential limitation of a recursively defined pattern.

- This example of a function described in two different ways which always yield the same image either way sets up the formal definition of *equal functions*, which follows immediately.

It would be a mistake to view this merely as a long way to get the formula. Recursively defined functions will play a significant role in Section 6.5.

6.17

These questions start to set up the contrast between defining a sequence recursively and defining it directly with an algebraic function on N.

1. Each term is 3 more than the previous one. $s(6) = 19$ and $s(17) = 52$. Finding $s(17)$ this way involves the tedium of finding all the terms before it. This annoyance is deliberate! Please do not show the students a shortcut here; it would undermine a major part of this discussion.

2. Yes, you can, but it's very tedious. The problem is that finding a term by this process requires finding all the terms before it. For terms such as the 99th or the 567th, this can be an annoyingly long chore.

6.18

This calculator exercise is essential to the material that follows. Plan enough time for it so that you can get beyond the details of handling the machines to look at the ideas it illustrates. Different calculators handle recursively defined sequences in different ways. Here are detailed instructions for the TI-82 (TI-83). For other calculators, consult their instruction manuals. Note that spreadsheets do this sort of thing much more easily. If your students have access to computers with spreadsheet software, you can easily adapt this discussion to that technology.

1. TI-82.

   - Choose Seq in line 4 of the MODE menu.

   - Define Un, the nth term of the sequence, recursively in terms of Un-1, the preceding term, as follows: In Y=, set Un= Un-1 + 3, using 2nd 7 for Un-1.

   - In the WINDOW menu, set UnStart to 1 because the first term of our sequence is obtained by adding 3 to this value.

Published by IT'S ABOUT TIME, Inc. © 2000 MATHconx, LLC

2. Look at the list of terms you just made. These are the images of the numbers 1 to 99. Do you see a pattern in the way each image is related to its domain element? If so, describe it in words and then in symbols. If you don't see it right away, try focusing on the images of

   10, 20, 30, 40, 50, ...

   Now do you see the relationship? Describe it.

3. Use your answer to part 2 to find $s(1000)$, $s(567)$, and $s(1,000,000)$.

4. Define another sequence in your calculator using the algebraic form of your answer to part 2. Then store the first 99 terms of this sequence in a different list. How is this list related to the first one? Is that surprising? Why or why not?

Did you get two copies of the same 99 terms in your two lists? Good! That's what was supposed to happen.

"So what?" we hear you say. "If I just get what I already had, why bother putting in another formula?"

We bother because the formula can do something that the recursive definition can't do. Try this: Pick your favorite four-digit number and suppose that's n. In order to find its image in this sequence using the recursive definition, you'd have to list more than a thousand terms, right? But if you put your number into the algebraic formula, the calculator will give you that term right away! (Try it.) That's the power of defining a function in terms of its independent variable (the variable that you control).

Look back at the two ways in which the pattern of the sequence 4, 7, 10, 13, 16, ... was described—first as a process that goes from each term to the next, then as an algebraic formula. Using the book's development to guide you, do the same thing for the sequence

6.19

   3, 8, 13, 18, 23, ...

(Call this new sequence s during this discussion.) Make sure you answer these questions along the way.

1. Find $s(4)$, $s(6)$, and $s(10)$.

Published by IT'S ABOUT TIME, Inc. © 2000 MATHconx, LLC

- To store the first 99 terms in list L1, say, choose 4:Sequence in the Y-VARS menu, then choose 1:Un. Next to it, type (1,99). The 1 tells the calculator to start at the first term of the sequence and the 99 tells it to print out 99 terms. Store in L1. That is, Un(1,99) →L1 should appear on your screen. When you press ENTER, you should get {4 7 10 13 16 1...}. If you check L1, you should find all 99 terms there.

TI-83.

- Choose Seq in line 4 of the MODE menu.

- In the Y= display, set u(n)=u($n-1$)+3 by typing in the individual characters. Be sure to use the variable key for n. Then set u(nMin)=4. This is the first term of the sequence.

- To store the first 99 terms in L1, say, go back to the main display and type in u(1,99)→L1. The pair (1,99) tells the calculator to start with the first term and print out 99 terms.) When you press ENTER, you should get {4 7 10 13 16 1...}. If you check L1, you should find all 99 terms there.

2. The image of a number is 3 times that number plus 1. That is, $s(n) = 3n + 1$.

3. $s(1000) = 3001$; $s(567) = 1702$; $s(1,000,000) = 3,000,001$

4. This part gives students a chance to use algebraic notation and also sets up the idea of equality of functions. You may have to help with calculator mechanics. Here are detailed instructions for the TI-82 (TI-83).

    TI-82. In the Y= screen, define Vn=3*n+1. Quit that, go to the main screen, and use the Y-VARS Sequence choice to enter Vn, followed by (1,99), and store that in L2 (to put the terms in L2). The operative line should look like this: Vn(1,99) →L2

    TI-83. In the Y= display, set v(n)=3*n+3, using the variable key for n. Quit that, go to the main screen, and type in v(1,99) →L2 to store the first 99 terms in L2. The two lists should be identical. This should not be a surprise because we are looking at two different ways (recursive and nonrecursive) to define the same sequence.

6.19

This is an exercise in mimicry, which may be suitable for small group work. It reinforces, but does not add to, the ideas and methods developed in the preceding several pages. Each term after the first is 5 more than the one before it. The general formula is $s(n) = 5n - 2$. Therefore, $s(4) = 18$; $s(6) = 28$; $s(10) = 48$; $s(25) = 123$; $s(1,000,000) = 4,999,998$.

2. Describe in words the pattern you see.

3. Use the pattern to find $s(25)$.

4. Describe how each term of the sequence is related to the one before it.

5. Describe how each term of the sequence is related to its corresponding domain element. Write this correspondence as an algebraic formula for $s(n)$.

6. Find $s(1,000,000)$.

The work you have just done shows that you can describe a function in two different ways and get the same results. This suggests an important question. What does it mean to say that two functions are the same?

6.20

Two functions, f and g, on the domain of natural numbers, are defined by these formulas.

$$f(n) = n + n \qquad g(n) = 2n$$

In what way(s) are these two functions the same? In what way(s) are they different?

When you look at the formulas defining the two functions f and g in the question above, you can see that any number n is matched with the same thing by both f and g. That is, $f(n) = g(n)$ because adding any number to itself gives the same answer as multiplying it by 2. But f and g are not *identical*; they are defined by different arithmetic operations. That might not seem very important to you, but in some situations it could make a big difference. For example, a very simple adding machine— one that can't multiply or can't store a constant number (in this case, 2)—would be able to deal with f, but not with g.

To clarify which sense of sameness we are using, we talk about functions being *equal*, rather than *the same*, and we define *equal* like this.

350

6.20

This discussion question should be done right at this point because it is answered by the text material that follows. You can skip over class discussion by treating it as a rhetorical question, if you prefer. However, students should at least look at the two functions because the subsequent text refers to them.

NOTES

Chapter 6

A Word to Know: Two functions are **equal** if they have the same domain and if each domain element is paired with the same image by both functions. That is, two functions f and g with the same domain are equal if

$$f(x) = g(x)$$

for *every* element x of the domain.

Before ending this section, we should tie up one loose end. We have been dealing with sequences in function notation, to emphasize that a sequence is a function on the domain of all natural numbers. In function notation, the terms of a sequence s are listed like this:

$$s(1), s(2), s(3), ..., s(n), ...$$

where n is the independent variable and $s(n)$ is the dependent variable. Once you know this (which you do now), there is no need to keep reminding yourself of it by using clumsy notation and language. Most books list the terms of a sequence like this:

$$s_1, s_2, s_3, ..., s_n, ...$$

The subscript numbers are the domain elements; they indicate the position of each term in the list. The general rule for finding a term is represented by s_n, which is called the "nth term" of the sequence. Both ways of writing sequences give you exactly the same information.

This sequence, s, lists the "perfect squares"

$$1, 4, 9, 16, ..., n^2, ...$$

6.21

1. Copy the following list and fill in the values.

   (a) $s_2 =$; $s(2) =$

   (b) $s_3 =$; $s(3) =$

   (c) $s_5 =$; $s(5) =$

   (d) $s_{10} =$; $s(10) =$

   (e) $s_n =$; $s(n) =$

2. In what way does s_n represent a rule? In what way does it represent a number? Explain.

351

Published by IT'S ABOUT TIME, Inc. © 2000 MATHconx, LLC

6.21

These questions reinforce the sameness of the two notations for sequences.

1. The fill-in questions are routine; the two answers in each part should be identical.

    (a) $s_2 = s(2) = 4$ (b) $s_3 = s(3) = 9$
    (c) $s_5 = s(5) = 25$ (d) $s_{10} = s(10) = 100$
    (e) $s_n = s(n) = n^2$

2. It might be best to handle this as a discussion question in class. You could even arrange a mini debate about it! The point here is fairly subtle, but it is important for a proper understanding of the notation. The issue may arise from your students, if not, you might want to decide whether this is appropriate for your students at this time.

    If n is considered as a variable, an unknown quantity, then s_n is the rule that tells you how to find the appropriate sequence term when you are given or choose a value for n. On the other hand, if n is considered to be a fixed number, known but unspecified, then s_n represents the corresponding known but unspecified number in the sequence.

Chapter 6

NOTES

Problem Set: 6.2

1. Find the Index at the back of your textbook. Is it a function? If you answer Yes, describe its domain, its range, and the image of one particular domain element. If you answer No, explain how it doesn't fit the definition of a function.

2. This problem is similar to Example 1 presented earlier in this section. Make a letter substitution code by listing the letters of the alphabet in order, then listing the letters in reverse order and directly matching the two lists. For example, A is matched with Z, B with Y, C with X, and so on. This is a function; call it r.

   (a) What is the domain of r? What is its range?

   (b) Find these values

   $$r(D) = \underline{\quad} \quad r(J) = \underline{\quad} \quad r(M) = \underline{\quad} \quad r(T) = \underline{\quad}$$

   (c) Write this sentence in code.

   (d) Write your answer to part (c) in code.

   (e) Parts (c) and (d) suggest that this code has a peculiar property. What is it? Do you think that every letter-substitution code has this property? Check your thinking by trying an example using the code in Example 1.

3. (a) Make up a letter substitution code that is different from the one in Example 1 and from the one described in problem 2 above. Describe your code in words, then write it in one of the list forms shown in Display 6.9. Use it to encode the message

   THIS IS A MESSAGE

   Which list form did you choose? Why?

   (b) Are some letter substitution codes easier to describe by a list than in words? Explain your answer briefly.

4. Sleeping Giant Mattress Co. and the union representing its 275 workers are starting contract negotiations. The current total annual payroll for these workers is $7,150,000.

   (a) The union proposed a 12% annual salary raise. By how much would this increase the company's annual payroll?

Published by IT'S ABOUT TIME, Inc. © 2000 MATHconx, LLC

Problem Set: 6.2

1. It's probably not a function because it is likely that at least one entry has more than one page reference. If each listing has only one page reference, then it would be a function. Its domain would be all of the words, names, and phrases listed; its range would be all of the page numbers listed.

2. (a) The domain is the set of letters of the alphabet, which is also its range.
   (b) $r(D) = W$; $r(J) = Q$; $r(M) = N$; $r(T) = G$
   (c) "Dirgv gsrh hvmgvmxv rm xlwv."
   (d) "Write this sentence in code."
   (e) This code decodes itself. That is, the image of the image of a letter is the original letter. No; most codes don't have this property. The code in Example 1, for instance, turns A into C, then turns C into E.

3. (a) This question should lead students to prefer either arrows or ordered pairs to the more cumbersome function-notation list. If we're lucky, they'll pick ordered pairs over arrows, but it doesn't really matter. This lays the groundwork for graphs of functions.
   (b) This question can be used to point out that sometimes the *only* way to specify a function is by listing all its ordered pairs. Codes without regular patterns are much harder to break than codes with neat correspondence rules.

4. This problem is somewhat like Example 2. It asks the students to construct and use several simple functions in a realistic business setting. Besides reinforcing the process of expressing functions algebraically, this problem provides practice in dealing with percents, decimals, and reading comprehension. You may have to help some students with this reading task. The benefit of this extra effort is that students see a real world situation in which calculators and simple functions are actually used to help make important decisions.

   (a) $0.12 \cdot \$7,150,000$, which is $858,000$

(b) Management knows that many changes to this percent figure will be discussed during the bargaining. Members of its bargaining team want to have a function in their calculators that computes the increase in the annual payroll for any percentage of raise. Write this function for them; call it m (for "management").

(c) Use the function m to find out how much the company's annual payroll would increase if it agreed to a 10% raise; a 7% raise; a 5% raise; a 3% raise; a 1.5% raise. Write each of these payroll increases in function notation.

(d) Management proposes a total annual payroll increase of $100,000, to be distributed equally to all the workers. How much more money would each worker earn in a year?

(e) The union knows that many changes to this total increase amount will be discussed during the bargaining. Members of its bargaining team have a function in their calculators that computes the salary increase per worker from any total payroll increase. Write this function for them; call it u (for "union").

(f) Use the function u to find out each worker's annual salary increase if the total payroll increase is $150,000; $200,000; $275,000; $350,000. Write each of these payroll increases in function notation.

(g) After several days, the bargaining teams finally agree on this salary settlement: Each worker will get a 4% raise plus an additional $350 for the year. How much will this increase the company's total payroll?

(h) The Payroll Office needs a function that will compute each worker's new annual salary from his/her old annual salary. Write one for them; call it p (for "payroll").

(i) Use the function p to compute the new annual salary for a worker whose old annual salary was $19,000; $22,500; $26,150; $31,233. Write each of these salary increases in function notation.

5. The game of chess probably originated in India many centuries ago. It is said, that when the inventor of chess presented the game to his king, the king was so pleased that he said to the inventor, "You can have anything in my kingdom! Just tell me what you want."

Published by IT'S ABOUT TIME, Inc. © 2000 MATHconx, LLC

353

(b) $m(x) = \$7{,}150{,}000x$

(c) $m(10\%) = \$715{,}000$; $m(7\%) = \$500{,}500$; $m(5\%) = \$357{,}500$;
  $m(3\%) = \$214{,}500$; $m(1.5\%) = \$107{,}250$

(d) $\$100{,}000 \div 275$, which is $\$363.64$

(e) $u(x) = x \div 275$

(f) $u(\$150{,}000) = \$545.45$; $u(\$200{,}000) = \$727.27$;
  $u(\$275{,}000) = \$1000.00$; $u(\$350{,}000) = \$1{,}272.73$

(g) The 4% raise increases the payroll by $0.04 \cdot \$7{,}150{,}000$, which is $\$286{,}000$. The $350 per worker raise increases the payroll by $\$350 \cdot 275$, which is $\$96{,}250$. The total payroll increase is the sum of these two amounts: $\$382{,}250$.

(h) $p(x) = x + 0.04x + \$350$ or $p(x) = 1.04x + \$350$. Notice that the question asks for the new annual salary, not just the increase.

(i) $p(\$19{,}000) = \$20{,}110$; $p(\$22{,}500) = \$23{,}750$;
  $p(\$26{,}150) = \$27{,}546$; $p(\$31{,}233) = \$32{,}832.32$

5. This problem uses the recursive definition process to define a power of two function on a finite set. It also gives students practice with scientific notation, estimating large numbers, and visualizing large quantities in meaningful ways. Later parts move away from the idea of function. You will have to decide, based on your knowledge of your own class, how much of this problem will be interesting and informative for them.

NOTES

6.2 Functions Step by Step

And the inventor said, "I only want some wheat. Give me one grain of wheat for the first square on my chessboard, two for the second, four for the third, and keep on doubling the number of grains for each square, until the last one [the 64th]. I want just that much wheat, nothing more."

Was this a foolish choice by the inventor of such a clever game, or was it smart? Let's analyze this situation. Think of the 64 chessboard squares as the numbers 1 through 64. Then the inventor is describing a function that has {1, 2, 3, ..., 64} as its domain; call this function g (for "grains").

(a) What are the values for $g(4)$, $g(5)$, $g(6)$, and $g(10)$?

(b) If you know a value for a square, how do you find the value for the next square? What formula can you use to list all 64 values recursively?

(c) What formula can you use to compute $g(n)$ for a particular square n without first finding the values for all the squares before it? Explain how you got this formula.

(d) Use your formula to find $g(10)$, $g(25)$, $g(31)$, $g(40)$, and $g(64)$. (Do the computations with a calculator.)

(e) How much space would be filled by $g(64)$ grains of wheat—a bushel? A barrel? A boxcar? A barn? How could you estimate the approximate number of cubic meters in this much wheat? Do it, if you can.

(f) Of course, $g(64)$ is not the total amount of wheat the inventor requested; it's only the amount for the last square. The total amount is

$$g(1) + g(2) + g(3) + ... + g(64)$$

which is just about twice as much as $g(64)$. In fact, it's 1 grain less than twice as much. Can you figure out why this last statement is true?

(g) Compute the total amount of wheat the inventor requested (in grains); then estimate its volume in cubic meters. Estimate the size of this amount of wheat by relating it to the size of some well known object (anything you choose).

(h) Was the inventor's request smart or foolish? What do you think? Explain your answer.

354

Published by IT'S ABOUT TIME, Inc. © 2000 MATHconx, LLC

(a) $g(4) = 8$; $g(5) = 16$; $g(6) = 32$; $g(10) = 512$

(b) Multiply by 2. $g(n) = 2 \cdot g(n - 1)$

(c) $g(n) = 2^{n-1}$

(d) $g(10) = 512$ (a check to see that the formula gives the same result as earlier methods), $g(25) = 16,777,216$; $g(31) = 1,073,741,824$; $g(40) = 5.497558139 \times 10^{11}$; $g(64) = 9.223372037 \times 10^{18}$. Of course, the numbers in scientific notation are approximations.

(e) This part is good for small group work. Here's one way to get a rough estimate. Make a cubic centimeter cup by cutting, folding, and taping a piece of paper. Fill this tiny cup with wheat grains (if you have them in your kitchen) or rice grains (which are a little smaller than wheat, but close to the same size). Count how many grains were needed to fill the little cup—about 30–40 grains.

This is the weak link in the estimation process. Each variation of 1 grain per cc here changes the overall estimate by about 3%. This difficulty can be eased, though not completely cured, by counting grains from a larger initial measure and or by taking the average of several students' counts. Since the problem is somewhat fanciful to begin with, precision here is not central to the point of this question, which is to get students to manipulate a very large measurement until they get an intuitive picture of its size relative to something they can visualize. Any reasonable estimate will allow for this.

Now, there are 100^3 cubic centimeters in a cubic meter, so divide $g(64)$ by 35,000,000. The result is about 260,000,000,000 cubic meters, or 260 cubic kilometers! Since a kilometer is about $\frac{5}{8}$ of a mile, that's *much* bigger than any of the containers listed in the question.

(f) This part is quite challenging. For some students willing to accept the statement without justification it might be best to move on. One way to see why it is true is to look at the pattern of sums of powers of 2.
$1 + 2 = 3$, which is 1 less than 4;
$1 + 2 + 4 = 7$, which is 1 less than 8;
$1 + 2 + 4 + 8 = 15$, which is 1 less than 16;
$1 + 2 + 4 + 8 + 16 = 31$, which is 1 less than 32;
and so on.

(g) Double $g(64)$, then follow the method of part (e). The result is about 527,000,000,000 cubic meters, or 527 cubic kilometers. That's about 128.5 cubic miles—enough to cover the entire state of Kansas with a layer of wheat more than 8 feet deep!

(h) This is, of course, an opinion question without a unique "right" answer. In this author's opinion, the inventor's request was clever, but not smart. He tried to make his request look smaller than it was, thereby leading the king to agree to a bad deal. But even the inventor probably did not realize that the amount requested was much too large for the king to pay. Given the customs of the time, one might guess that, once the king found out how much he had agreed to, he simply "liquidated" his debt by executing the too clever inventor!

6. In each part, list the first five terms and the tenth term of the sequence defined by the formula.

   (a) $s(n) = 3 + n$ (b) $s(n) = 3n$

   (c) $s(n) = 2n + 5$ (d) $s(n) = 4(n - 1)$

   (e) $s(n) = n^2 + 1$ (f) $s(n) = 2^n + 1$

   (g) $s(n) = n^2 - 3n + 2$ (h) $s(n) = \dfrac{1}{n}$

   (i) $s(n) = \dfrac{n}{2}$ (j) $s(n) = \dfrac{n}{n + 1}$

7. A sequence s begins 13, 23, 33, 43, 53, ...

   (a) What are the next two terms of this sequence? How did you find them?
   (b) Define this sequence recursively.
   (c) Write a formula for $s(n)$.
   (d) Use your formula to find $s(200)$.

8. A sequence t begins 4, 11, 18, 25, 32, ...

   (a) What are the next two terms of this sequence? How did you find them?
   (b) Define this sequence recursively.
   (c) Write a formula for $t(n)$.
   (d) Use your formula to find $t(200)$.

9. Which of these pairs of functions are equal on the domain of natural numbers? For those that are not, find at least one number n for which $f(n) \neq g(n)$.

   (a) $f(n) = 3(n - 2)$; $g(n) = 3n - 2$

   (b) $f(n) = 3(n - 2)$; $g(n) = 3n - 6$

   (c) $f(n) = 3n - 2$; $g(n) = 2 - 3n$

   (d) $f(n) = 3n - 2$; $g(n) = {}^-2 + 3n$

   (e) $f(n) = n^2$; $g(n) = 2^n$

   (f) $f(n) = n^2$; $g(n) = n + n$

   (g) $f(n) = n^2$; $g(n) = n \cdot n$

   (h) $f(n) = n^2 + n$; $g(n) = n(n + 1)$

355

6. These routine exercises provide practice in interpreting algebraic notation and in the process of finding images. You need not assign all of them.

(a) 4, 5, 6, 7, 8; 13

(b) 3, 6, 9, 12, 15; 30

(c) 7, 9, 11, 13, 15; 25

(d) 0, 4, 8, 12, 16; 36

(e) 2, 5, 10, 17, 26; 101

(f) 3, 5, 9, 17, 33; 1025

(g) 0, 0, 2, 6, 12; 72

(h) $1, \frac{1}{2}, \frac{1}{3}, \frac{1}{4}, \frac{1}{5}; \frac{1}{10}$

(i) $\frac{1}{2}, 1, \frac{3}{2}, 2, \frac{5}{2}; 5$

(j) $\frac{1}{2}, \frac{2}{3}, \frac{3}{4}, \frac{4}{5}, \frac{5}{6}; \frac{10}{11}$

7. (a) 63, 73
   (b) Start with 13 and add 10 each time: $s(1) = 13$; $s(n) = s(n - 1) + 10$
   (c) $s(n) = 10n + 3$
   (d) $s(200) = 2003$

8. (a) 39, 46
   (b) Start with 4 and add 7 each time: $t(1) = 4$; $t(n) = t(n - 1) + 7$,
   $t(1) = 4$, $t(2) = t(2 - 1) + 7$, $t(2) = t(1) + 7 = 4 + 7 = 11$,
   $t(3) = t(2) + 7 = 11 + 7 = 18$
   (c) $t(n) = 7n - 3 \; (= 7(n - 1) + 4)$
   (d) $t(200) = 1397$

9. Besides reminding students about equality of functions, these questions reinforce some of the basic laws of algebra from Chapter 2. They give students a strategy for deciding by substitution when they are uncertain whether or not two algebraic expressions are equal.

(a) Not equal   (b) Equal   (c) Not equal   (d) Equal
(e) Not equal   (f) Not equal   (g) Equal   (h) Equal

NOTES

Chapter 6

6.3 Between the Dots

Learning Outcomes

After studying this section, you will be able to:

Identify and describe real world examples of step functions;

Explain some common-sense restrictions on the domains of functions;

Use graphs to represent functions and to find images of domain elements;

Interpret graphs of step functions in real world situations.

In Sections 6.1 and 6.2 we saw that a function can be represented in different ways—in a table, by a diagram, as a set of ordered pairs, and sometimes by a formula. If a function matches numbers with numbers, it can also be pictured on a coordinate plane.

Here's an example. Suppose that we want to match each even digit in the set

$$\{0, 1, 2, 3, 4, 5, 6, 7, 8, 9\}$$

with the odd digit that comes right after it, like this.

$$0 \longrightarrow 1$$
$$2 \longrightarrow 3$$
$$4 \longrightarrow 5$$
$$6 \longrightarrow 7$$
$$8 \longrightarrow 9$$

We could represent this function by marking the digit points on a horizontal axis and on a vertical axis, then draw a point for each ordered pair of digits in the matching, as shown in Display 6.10. This is called making a **graph** of the function.

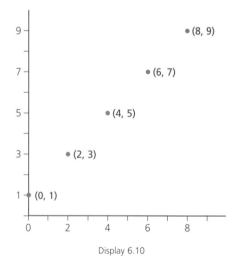

Display 6.10

6.3 Between the Dots

This section bridges the gap between discrete and continuous functions by discussing step functions and some simple linear functions. It explores everyday settings in which functions with domains beyond the integers occur naturally and it examines the difference between step by step change and continuous change in some simple situations. Some of the examples in this section provide a review of the main ideas about the equations and graphs of straight lines.

Chapter 6

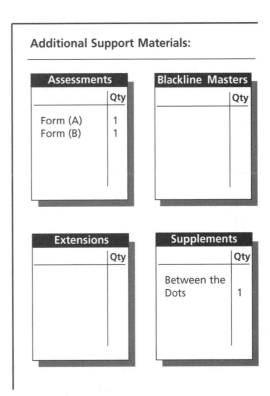

Additional Support Materials:

Assessments	Qty
Form (A)	1
Form (B)	1

Blackline Masters	Qty

Extensions	Qty

Supplements	Qty
Between the Dots	1

What is the domain of the function pictured in Display 6.10? What is its range?

a

6.22

Of course, not all functions have such a nice, simple pattern or such a small domain. Here is an example of a function on the domain *N* of all natural numbers that has a more scattered graph. (What is a function with domain *N* called?)

Let *f* match 1 with itself and match any natural number greater than 1 with its smallest positive factor other than 1. (Remember: A *factor* of a number divides that number without leaving any remainder.)

For instance, $f(2) = 2$, $f(6) = 2$, $f(9) = 3$, and so on. The graph of the first 25 ordered pairs of this function is shown in Display 6.11.

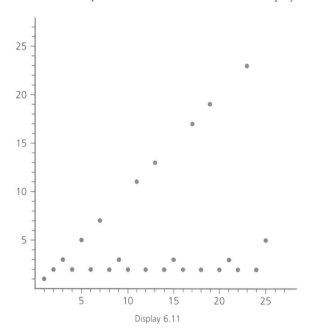

Display 6.11

These questions refer to the function *f* in Display 6.11.

b

6.23

1. Find $f(26)$ and $f(27)$. What ordered pairs do you get from these images? Where are these points in Display 6.11?

2. Find $f(77)$ and explain why your answer is correct.

3. Find a number *n* larger than 25 such that $f(n) = 11$. What is the smallest such number? Explain.

357

6.22

The domain is the set {2, 4, 6, 8, 0}, *not* the entire set of digits. Note that this reminds students, in passing, that 0 is an even number (digit). If there is any confusion about this, help them to recall that a number is even if it can be divided by 2 with no remainder. The range is {1, 3, 5, 7, 9}.

6.23

These questions serve to get the students comfortable with how f works and how the graph in Display 6.11 represents it. Expect to take quite a bit of time with this example. The function may be a little confusing at first, but the idea is not difficult. It appears here as an example of a function on the natural numbers that has no natural extension to nonintegers. In a few pages, it will be contrasted with the doubling function, which does extend naturally. Time spent clearing up confusion in this setting should pay dividends later, not only with a better understanding of functions, but also with a deeper insight into factors of whole numbers.

The patterns in the graph of this function provide a rich source of questions about the prime factorization of natural numbers, but focusing on them would distract us from our main objective, which is to see how graphs of functions work. If any students become interested in exploring this function further, they might start by extending the graph another 25 or 50 points and then write about the patterns they see.

1. $f(26) = 2$ and $f(27) = 3$;   (26, 2) and (27, 3)

2. $f(77) = 7$ because $77 = 7 \cdot 11$

3. 121, which is 11^2, is the smallest such number. The others are of the form 11 times any prime(s) greater than 11.

NOTES

_____

....

....

....

....

....

....

....

....

Chapter 6

4. Give an example of a natural number that is not the image of any number. Explain your answer.

5. What is the range of *f*?

6. How would the graph of the function look if we dropped the phrase "other than 1" from the end of its definition? Why?

6.24

Near the bottom of Display 6.11, there seems to be a regular pattern, starting with the point (2, 2).

Do you think that this pattern continues forever? Explain your answer. (*Hint:* What are the domain elements for the points in this pattern?)

Often the graph of a function can help you to see patterns that are not obvious from a list or a table. However, because coordinate axes usually represent the entire number line, a graph may not show clearly the domain and range of the function. Look again at Displays 6.10 and 6.11 for example. In Display 6.10, the entire domain of the function is the set of five numbers listed below the horizontal axis {0, 2, 4, 6, 8} and the range is the set of five numbers listed next to the vertical axis {1, 3, 5, 7, 9}. But in Display 6.11 the numbers listed below the horizontal axis are only a very small part of the domain; the range of this function contains only some of the numbers listed next to the vertical axis (but many others, too).

For a function to be clearly defined, it is not enough just to know its rule for assigning images. We must also know its domain and what kinds of things can be images. That is, since every function matches the things from some domain with images in some set, we need to know what these sets are, too. You might picture a function *f* as "going from" a domain set *A* and "going to" a set *B* that contains all the images (and maybe other things), as in Display 6.12.

6.25

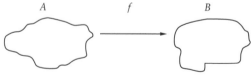

Display 6.12

358

4. Any composite number, such as 4, 6, 9, etc.

5. This is a relatively sophisticated question, requiring students to know that every natural number greater than 1 has prime factors. The range is the set consisting of 1 and all the primes.

6. It would be just a horizontal row of dots 1 unit above the horizontal axis because 1 is the smallest positive divisor of every number.

6.24

Yes, the pattern continues "forever." The domain elements of the lower dots are all the even numbers, which means that the image of each one is 2. They occur regularly, 2 units apart, forever. The domain elements of the upper dots are all the odd multiples of 3, which means that the image of each one is 3. They occur regularly, 6 units apart from 3 on, forever.

6.25

Notice that the set *B* is *not* necessarily the range of the function; it simply *contains* the range. Many mathematicians refer to this set as the *codomain* of the function, for reasons that lie far beyond students' needs, now. We suggest that you do *not* teach this potentially confusing terminology to your students.

NOTES

Chapter 6

The function in Display 6.11 goes from and goes to the same set, the counting numbers. Another example like this is the "doubling" function d, defined by the rule $d(n) = 2n$. Its graph is shown in Display 6.13.

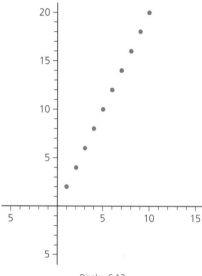

Display 6.13

"Wait a minute!" you say. "A coordinate axis has a number for every point on it, not just for the counting-number points. What about them?"

You're right, of course. A coordinate axis does have a number for each point on it, and these numbers form a much bigger set than the counting numbers. That set is called the **real numbers**; it is denoted by R.

"What happens to those other numbers? The dots don't tell us that. What happens between the dots?"

It depends.

"On what?"

On the domain of the function and on the rule for finding images. If the function only makes sense on the set of counting numbers, then nothing at all happens between the dots—only the counting numbers have images. The smallest factor function f of Display 6.11 is like that. The idea of *factor* that is used to define f only applies to integers; it doesn't make sense to try to apply it to numbers like $\frac{2}{3}$ or 23.856 or any of the other numbers between the counting numbers.

NOTES

On the other hand, the rule that defines the doubling function *d* of Display 6.13 makes sense for *all* numbers. Any number can be doubled. The function *d* was defined only on the natural numbers. However, the rule makes sense for every real number, so we can extend its domain to include all real numbers. Formally, we define a "new" function *D* that applies to every real number *x* using the same rule: $D(x) = 2x$. This new function *D* agrees with the old function *d* on every natural number, but it fills in the picture between the dots, as Display 6.14 shows. (Compare Displays 6.13 and 6.14 to see how *D* connects the dots of *d*.)

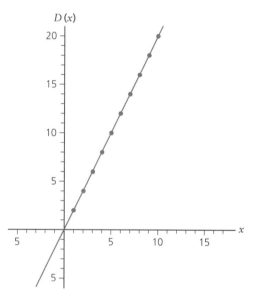

Display 6.14

6.26

Display 6.6 describes a function *t* that matches the set of Olympic years 1904 through 1992 with the set of running times for the men's 800-meter race in that year's Olympic Games. Its graph is shown in Display 6.15. Does it make sense to extend this function to the domain of all times between 1904 and 1992?

- If you answer Yes, then explain what $t(1911)$ and $t(1953.47)$ mean.

- If you answer No, explain why it doesn't make sense.

360

6.26

6.27

These two discussion questions are a complementary pair. They ought to be done together. Their main purpose is to get students to think about reasonable interpretations of the mathematical ideas and procedures they are learning. The two questions present similar tables and graphs; the domain in both cases is a span of years. However, in 6.26 it makes little sense to talk about the image of any time between the given Olympic years (because no Olympic races were run at any other times), whereas the population function in 6.27 can reasonably be extended to any point in time between the census data points (because the population is changing virtually continuously). In this case, although we can't tell from the graph the exact values of $p(1911)$ and $p(1953.47)$, they can be interpreted as representing the population of the U.S. at each of those points in time. We might even get reasonable approximations of their values by sketching in a rough curve connecting the dots, but that's another story to be told shortly.

NOTES

Chapter 6

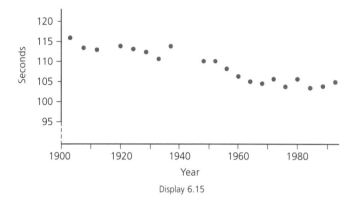

Display 6.15

The table in Display 6.16 and the graph in Display 6.17 describe a population function p . The points on the graph represent the population of the United States in each of the census years 1790 through 1970. Does it make sense to extend this function to the domain of all times between 1790 and 1970?

6.27

- If you answer Yes, then explain what $p(1911)$ and $p(1953.47)$ mean.

- If you answer No, explain why it doesn't make sense.

Year	Population (in millions)
1790	3.929
1800	5.308
1810	7.240
1820	9.638
1830	12.866
1840	17.069
1850	23.192
1860	31.443
1870	38.558
1880	50.156
1890	62.948
1900	75.995
1910	91.972
1920	105.711
1930	122.775
1940	131.669
1950	150.697
1960	179.323
1970	203.185

Display 6.16

Published by IT'S ABOUT TIME, Inc. © 2000 MATHconx, LLC

361

6.3 Between the Dots

NOTES

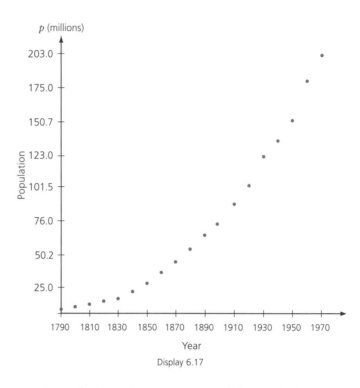

Display 6.17

Even when it makes sense to extend the graph of a function from a few known points to a much larger domain, there may be more than one sensible way to do it. Here is an example, based on a function used in everyday life.

A few years ago, the state of Maine had a 5% sales tax; that is, the tax was 1 cent for every 20 cents. Every taxable item sold had a certain amount of tax added to its price. This means that the 5% sales tax process is a function that assigns a tax amount to each price. If we think in pennies, this tax function sets up the pairings shown in Display 6.18. Thus, the graph of this function, which we'll call f, contains the points

$$(20, 1)\ \ (40, 2)\ \ (60, 3)\ \ (80, 4)\ \ (100, 5)$$

These five points are shown in Display 6.19.

How can we extend the graph in Display 6.19 to show how this tax function f works on *all* possible prices; that is, on all positive real numbers?

362

NOTES

Price (¢)	Tax (¢)
20	1
40	2
60	3
80	4
100	5
⋮	⋮

Display 6.18

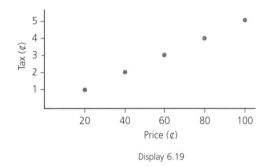

Display 6.19

The process of taking 5% of a number is simple enough—just multiply the number by 0.05. Thus, the 5% tax function can be described by the formula

$$f(x) = 0.05x$$

Now, when we graph a function, the y-axis is the $f(x)$-axis. In other words, the images of the domain numbers are found on the vertical axis. Therefore, the graph of this function is the graph of

$$y = 0.05x$$

This is a straight line with slope 0.05 and y-intercept 0. It is shown in Display 6.20.

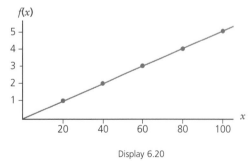

Display 6.20

363

NOTES

Chapter 6

The graph in Display 6.20 shows how this tax function can be extended in a neat, simple way from the five points we know to a function defined on the set of all positive real numbers. (Saying that a function is **defined on** a particular set means that this set is within the domain of the function.)

Unfortunately, real life is not always so neat and simple. Display 6.20 is *not* an accurate picture of how this tax function really worked in Maine! Display 6.21 shows part of the table used to describe the actual tax function, which we'll call *t*. As you can see from this table, *t* agrees with *f* on the five points we have been using as examples, but behaves differently between them. Both functions assign exactly one tax amount to each purchase amount, but they don't always agree.

6.28

1. Find $f(25)$ and $t(25)$. (Here the number 25 means 25 cents.)

2. Find $f(462)$ and $t(462)$.

3. Find two prices higher than $5.00 for which these two tax functions agree. Use them to copy and complete parts (a) and (b).

   (a) $f(\ \ ) = t(\ \ ) =$ ___

   (b) $f(\ \ ) = t(\ \ ) =$ ___

4. Find two prices higher than $5.00 for which these two tax functions disagree. Use them to copy and complete parts (a) and (b).

   (a) $f(\ \ ) =$ ___ $t(\ \ ) =$ ___

   (b) $f(\ \ ) =$ ___ $t(\ \ ) =$ ___

Published by IT'S ABOUT TIME, Inc. © 2000 MATHconx, LLC

6.3 Between the Dots

6.28

This is partly a routine exercise in understanding how to read the tax schedule in Display 6.21. It is also an illustration of how step functions and linear functions differ. The only discussion issue that might arise is the question of rounding. Notice that, even if the images under f are rounded to the nearest cent, f and t disagree in many places. This is because t rounds every fractional tax amount *up* to the nearest cent, *except* for prices between an even dollar amount and 10 cents above the dollar amount. It's sufficiently weird to make the exercise more interesting than just a matter of rounding one way or the other.

1. $f(25) = 1.25¢ = 1¢$ or $2¢$
   $t(25) = 2¢$

2. $f(462) = 23.1¢ = 23¢$ or $24¢$

3. The functions will agree for all whole dollar amounts and other numbers divisible by $20¢$.

4. Answers will vary. Examples include
   $f(641) = 32.05¢ = 32¢$ or $33¢$
   $t(641) = 33¢$
   $f(682) = 34.1¢ = 34¢$ or $35¢$
   $t(682) = 35¢$

NOTES

Chapter 6

5% SALES TAX SCHEDULE
ALL SALES EXCEPT
AUTO AND LODGING RENTALS

For sales of $1.00 or less, the tax shall be added as indicated below:

Sale		Tax (cents)
From	To	
$0.01	$0.10	0
0.11	0.20	1
0.21	0.40	2
0.41	0.60	3
0.61	0.80	4
0.81	1.00	5

This table shows tax to $100 by units of $1.00. For fractional parts of one dollar, add amount appearing above. For example, tax on a sale of $59.50 would be $2.95 from table below plus $0.03 from table above or a total tax of $2.98.

Sale	Tax		Sale	Tax
$1.00	$0.05		$51.00	$2.55
2.00	0.10		52.00	2.60
3.00	0.15		53.00	2.65
4.00	0.20		54.00	2.70
5.00	0.25		55.00	2.75
6.00	0.30		56.00	2.80
7.00	0.35		57.00	2.85
8.00	0.40		58.00	2.90
9.00	0.45		59.00	2.95
10.00	0.50		60.00	3.00
⋮	⋮		⋮	⋮

Display 6.21

NOTES

Chapter 6

The graph of the function *t* appears in Display 6.22. It shows that the tax doesn't increase gradually as the price increases, but moves up in steps, 1 cent at a time (as you would expect). Each time it takes a step, it stays at that level for a while before moving up again. A function that changes in this way—jumping from one value to another in a fairly regular pattern and staying at each value level for a span of domain numbers—is called a **step function**.

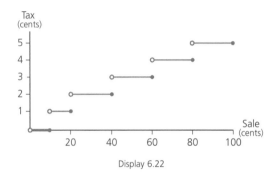

Display 6.22

Display 6.22 illustrates a common custom used in drawing graphs. Notice that the left end of each horizontal segment is an open dot, while the right end is a solid dot. The graph "jumps" at each of these places, and it is important to know which level shows the image of the point where the jump occurs. The solid dot signals that the image is determined by that point; the new level is to be used right after the open dot. For instance, the image of 20 is 1, but the image of 21 (or of 20.5 or of 20.001) is 2. An open dot at the end of a line segment means that the segment includes all the points up to the endpoint, but not the endpoint itself. A solid dot at the end means that the segment includes the endpoint, as well.

Published by IT'S ABOUT TIME, Inc. © 2000 MATHconx, LLC

NOTES

Chapter 6

Part of a U.S. Postal Service rate sheet appears in Display 6.23. It shows the postage rates for standard size, first-class letters. This table defines a function, which we shall call *p*.

6.29

1. What is the domain of *p*?

2. Find *p*(4), *p*(4.2), and *p*(8.75).

3. Make a graph of the function *p*.

4. Draw the straight line determined by the pattern of the whole ounce rates, then answer these questions about it.

   (a) Write an equation for this line, treating it as a function called *s*. That is, write an equation in the form "*s*(*x*) = ..."
   (b) If *s* were the postage function, what would it cost to send something that weighed absolutely nothing (if such a thing existed)?

FIRST-CLASS MAIL	
SINGLE-PIECE RATES:	
1st ounce...$0.32	
Each additional ounce......................................0.23	

Weight not over (oz.)

1...............$0.32*	7................$1.70
2.................0.55	8.................1.93
3.................0.78	9.................2.16
4.................1.01	10................2.39
5.................1.24	11................2.62
6.................1.47	

OVER 11 OUNCES, SEE PRIORITY MAIL

*Nonstandard Size: An additional $0.11 is required if 1 ounce or less and (a) over any of these dimensions: 11½" long, 6 ⅛" high, ¼" thick; or (b) the length divided by the height is less than 1.3 or more than 2.5.

Display 6.23

Published by IT'S ABOUT TIME, Inc. © 2000 MATHconx, LLC

367

6.29

This function better exemplifies the continuous domain of positive real numbers. It could be argued that the sales tax function applies to prices stated in whole cents, and hence it actually has only the positive integers as its domain. However, postage rates are computed by weight, which varies continuously over the positive reals. Moreover, this function has two interesting peculiarities: (1) Its first step is larger than the subsequent steps, and (2) it is not applicable beyond 11 oz. These restrictions remind students that real world restrictions must be accommodated by any mathematical solution of a real world problem.

1. The domain is the set of all weights, in ounces, from 0 through 11 oz.

2. $p(4) = \$1.01$; $p(4.2) = \$1.24$; $p(4.9) = \$1.24$; $p(8.75) = \$2.16$

3. See Display 6.2T, which shows both the step function p and the linear function s of the next question.

4. (a) $s(x) = 0.23x + 0.09$ (b) $s(0) = \$0.09$ (the y-intercept)

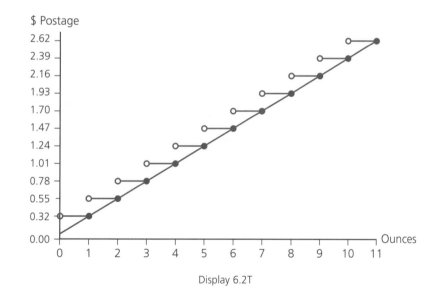

Display 6.2T

Chapter 6

6.30

Display 6.24 shows a bank advertisement for a Certificate of Deposit (CD), exactly as it appeared in the bank's flyer. The outside of the flyer says

Our 5 year CD is only good for one year.
Then it gets better.

Is the graph they have drawn an accurate representation of the interest rate arrangement they are offering? Discuss.

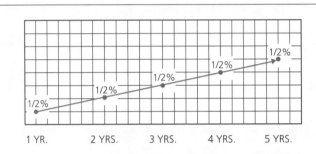

1 YR.   2 YRS.   3 YRS.   4 YRS.   5 YRS.

Introducing the
Peoples Heritage Rising Rate CD

With a Rising Rate CD from Peoples Heritage Bank, you know you're getting ahead. Your interest rate increases 1/2% every year until maturity, guaranteed. And we allow you to withdraw all or part of the certificate at the end of any 12 month period, without penalty. When you want a good interest rate now, and a guaranteed better interest rate later, ask about Rising Rate.

From *"Rising CD Rates"* advertising flyer by Peoples Heritage Bank. Copyright © by Peoples Heritage Bank. Reprinted by permission.

Display 6.24

A particular step function is built into many calculators. It is called the **greatest integer function,** which is shortened to "int" in the calculator's language. This function matches each real number with the largest (greatest) integer that is less than or equal to that real number. For instance,

$$\text{int}(4.9) = 4 \qquad \text{int}(6) = 6 \qquad \text{int}(-2.1) = -3$$

6.30

It appears from the text on the outside of the flyer that the answer probably is No. Saying that the CD is "good for 1 year" seems to imply that the interest rate is fixed for the first year, then jumps a half percent for the second year, jumps another half percent for the third year, and so on. By extension from the first year, one would suppose that *during* each of these years the rate of interest remains fixed. For the graph to represent accurately the rate of interest paid, it would have to be a step function.

NOTES

Chapter 6

1. Use your graphing calculator to find int(3.2), int(7.0338), int(5), and int(-3.2).

6.31

2. On a piece of graph paper, draw the graph of int over the domain of all real numbers between -4 and 4, inclusive. Be sure to mark each endpoint of each segment in your graph with a filled in or an open circle, depending on whether or not that point represents a pair of numbers that are matched by the function.

3. Use your graphing calculator to draw the graph of int over the domain of all real numbers between -4 and 4, inclusive. Once you have the graph, use **TRACE** to find int(2.7), int(0.685), int(-0.685), and int(-2.7).

4. Compare the calculator graph of part 3 with the graph you drew in part 2. How are they alike? How are they different? Which do you think is easier to make? Which do you think is easier to use? Give reasons for your answers.

Problem Set: 6.3

1. A function on the set {0, 1, 2, 3, 4, 5, 6, 7, 8, 9} of single digits matches each digit with the next one in the list, up to 9, and it matches 9 with 5. Make a graph of this function.

2. A function f on the set {0, 1, 2, 3, 4, 5, 6, 7, 8, 9} of single digits is defined by

$$f(d) = 4 \text{ if } d \text{ is an even digit}$$
$$f(d) = 7 \text{ if } d \text{ is an odd digit}$$

Find $f(1)$, $f(2)$, and $f(3)$. Then make a graph of this function.

3. An airport parking lot has these rates posted for short-term parking,

   $2.00 for first hour or fraction thereof;

   $1.00 for each additional hour or fraction thereof, up to a maximum of $10.00 for any 24 hour period.

(a) Make a table that the parking lot attendants can use to find the total charge from the number of hours shown on a customer's time ticket. (Make the table for a 24 hour period.)

(b) Draw a graph of this parking fee function for a 24 hour period.

Published by IT'S ABOUT TIME, Inc. © 2000 MATHconx, LLC

369

6.3 Between the Dots

6.31

The main purpose of these questions is to get students familiar with the int function on their calculators, particularly with its visual characteristics.

1. On the TI-82 (TI-83) calculators, the int function is found by pressing MATH, then choosing int from the NUM menu.) int(3.2) = 3; int(7.0338) = 7; int(5) = 5; int(-3.2) = -4.

2. See Display 6.3T.

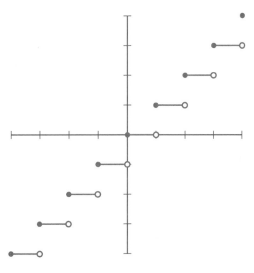

Display 6.3T

3. To do this on the TI-82 (TI-83) calculators, students who have been using the calculator in Seq mode will first have to reset to Func mode. Then they can enter Y₁ = int X in the Y= function list. The int function is found in the NUM menu of MATH. Set WINDOW to go from -4 to 4 on each axis. The TRACE exercise gets students to focus on the visual pattern of the greatest integer function. This is particularly useful for clearing up any confusion about how it works for negative numbers. int(2.7) = 2; int(0.685) = 0; int(-0.685) = -1; int(-2.7) = -3.

4. This part is good for a short class discussion.

1. See Display 6.4T.

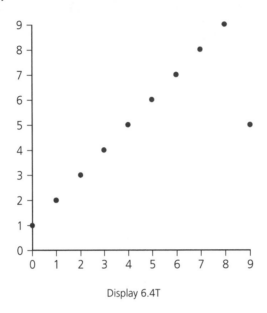

Display 6.4T

2. $f(1) = 7$; $f(2) = 4$; $f(3) = 7$ See Display 6.5T.

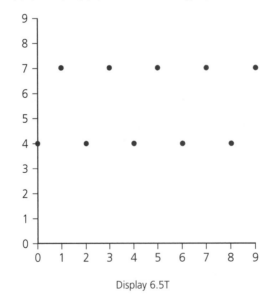

Display 6.5T

3. (a) See Display 6.6T.

Time		Amount
From	To	
0:00:01	1:00:00	$ 2.00
1:00:01	2:00:00	3.00
2:00:01	3:00:00	4.00
3:00:01	4:00:00	5.00
4:00:01	5:00:00	6.00
5:00:01	6:00:00	7.00
6:00:01	7:00:00	8.00
7:00:01	8:00:00	9.00
8:00:01	24:00:00	10.00

Display 6.6T

(b)

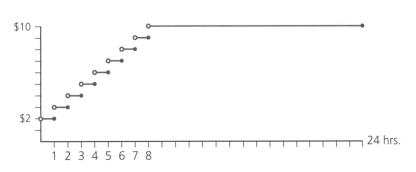

Display 6.7T

NOTES

Chapter 6

4. Draw a graph of the tax function t that extends Display 6.22 to the domain of all sale prices up to $2.00.

5. Suppose the State of Maine had decided to set up its 5% sales tax table by rounding the tax amount to the nearest cent, with halves always rounded up. Then the top part of the table in Display 6.21 would have to be changed.

   (a) Copy and complete the table in Display 6.25 to show how this tax applies to sales less than $1.00. Assume that the rest of the table in Display 6.21 applies to this new tax function, which we shall call r.

Sale		Tax (cents)
From	To	
$0.01		0
		1
		2
		3
		4
	1.00	5

Display 6.25

   (b) Find $r(\$0.25)$, $r(\$0.98)$, $r(\$2.87)$ and $r(\$3.99)$. Then compute the tax on these same amounts by using the function t.

      (i) Which sale amounts have the same tax amounts under r and t? Which have different tax amounts?
      (ii) Are r and t equal functions? Why or why not?

   (c) Does the function t ever result in a smaller tax amount than the function r? If so, in what case(s)? If not, explain how you know this.

370

Published by IT'S ABOUT TIME, Inc. © 2000 MATHconx, LLC

4. See Display 6.8T.

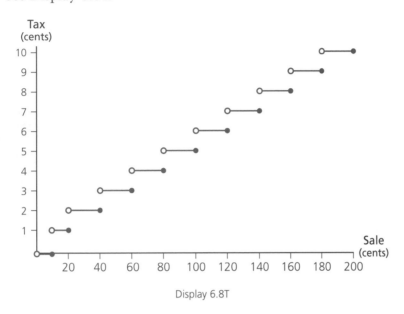

Display 6.8T

5. (a) See Display 6.9T.

Sale		Tax (cents)
From	To	
$0.01	$0.09	0
.10	.29	1
.30	.49	2
.50	.69	3
.70	.89	4
.90	1.00	5

Display 6.9T

(b) $r(\$0.25) = \$0.01$; $r(\$0.98) = \$0.05$; $r(\$2.87) = \$0.14$; $r(\$3.99) = \$0.20$; $t(\$0.25) = \$0.02$; $t(\$0.98) = \$0.05$; $t(\$2.87) = \$0.15$; $t(\$3.99) = \$0.20$

The functions r and t are *not* equal because some images are different. The purpose of this question is to remind the students that two functions are equal only if they *always* produce the same images.

(c) Because of the way the $0.10 sale amount is handled by the two functions, t produces a smaller tax amount than r for all sales that are exactly 10 cents more than an even dollar amount.

$$\$0.10, \$1.10, \$2.10, \$3.10,...$$

These are the only cases.

6. The Fuzzy Friends Toy Co. marketed a new product in Maine right at the start of football season—plush, purple, potato shaped pillows, which they advertised as couch potatoes. They sold 8000 pillows in the first two weeks, at a special introductory price of $3.89 each.

   (a) How much tax did the State of Maine collect on these sales, assuming that the tax function *t* of Display 6.21 was being used at the time? How much less tax would they have collected using the rounding off tax function *r* of Display 6.25?

   (b) Draw a graph of *r*, similar to the one in Display 6.22. Then, on the same coordinate system, draw the straight line $y = 0.05x$ that represents the "pure" 5% function.

7. Telephone numbers beginning with the area codes 900, 976, 940, or 550 connect to information or entertainment services that charge at a fairly high rate per minute of connection time. One such service recently advertised on TV said, at the end of its commercial, "Calls cost $2.95 per minute or fraction thereof."

   (a) What is the cost of a 2 minute call?

   (b) What is the cost of a 2 minute, 10 second (2:10) call?

   (c) What is the cost of a 2 minute, 55 second (2:55) call?

   (d) Make a graph of the cost function for calls of up to 10 minutes in length. Call your function *c* (for "cost").

   (e) Mark your graph to show your answers to parts (a), (b), and (c).

   (f) Use the function int to define a new function by

   $$f(x) = \$2.95 \cdot \text{int}(x)$$

   For which times do *c* and *f* give you the same value?

   (g) Use the function int to define a new function by

   $$g(x) = \$2.95 \cdot \text{int}(x + 1)$$

   For which times do *c* and *g* give you the same value? Are these *c* and *g* equal over this domain? Why or why not?

Published by IT'S ABOUT TIME, Inc. © 2000 MATHconx, LLC

371

6. (a) This is mostly an exercise in reading, arithmetic, and common sense. $t(\$3.89) = 20$ cents, so the total tax collected was $8000 \times 0.20 = \$1,600.00$.
However, $r(\$3.89) = 19$ cents, a penny less per pillow, so the total tax under r would have been $80.00 less.

(b) See Display 6.10T. Note that the function int can be used to get the graphing calculator to produce this graph. $Y_1 = int(.05*(X+10))$ will produce the graph of r, and $Y_2 = .05X$ will produce the graph of the 5% function. WINDOW should be set for X from 0 to 100 and Y from 0 to 5. This is probably too complicated to be assigned as an exercise, particularly since it uses int as part of a composite function. However, if you have students who are really interested in the graphics capabilities of the TI-82 (TI-83), you might show them this as a "trick" and ask them to explore why it works, how it can be adapted to similar tasks, etc.

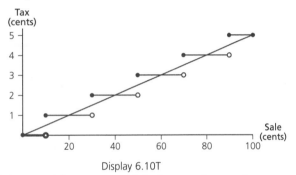

Display 6.10T

7. Parts (a)–(e) of this problem are straightforward questions—parts (f) and (g) are a bit more challenging.

(a) $5.90   (b) $8.85   (c) $8.85
(d) and (e) See Display 6.11T.

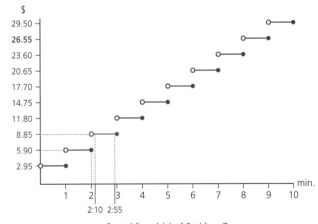

Parts (d) and (e) of Problem 7

Display 6.11T

(f) c and f give the same value only at the exact-minute times: 1:00, 2:00, 3:00, etc.

(g) c and g agree everywhere *except* at the exact-minute times, at which g jumps to the next higher price (but c doesn't). Since c and g give different images at some points of the domain, they are not equal functions.

6.4 Describing Functions With Algebra

Learning Outcomes

After studying this section, you will be able to:

Use any first degree equation of the form $y = ax + b$ as a function;

Find images of real numbers using linear functions and some functions of higher degree;

Use a graphing calculator to find images for linear functions and some functions of higher degree;

Use a graphing calculator to draw graphs of linear functions and some functions of higher degree.

Sometimes people describe a function as a "machine" or a "mystery box" like the one in Display 6.26—you put a thing in, something happens to it, and some (related) thing comes out.

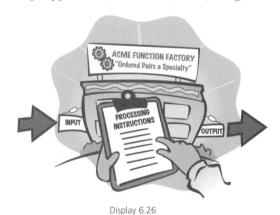

Display 6.26

The point of this picture is not that a function is magic or mysterious, but that *it's an "automatic" routine*. Whenever you put a domain element into a function, the process automatically gives you one, and only one, image. It might take some (brain) power to run the machine, but there is no puzzle or uncertainty in the process. Once a thing is put in, exactly one result can come out.

Viewed in this way, functions show you the power of using symbols for numbers. We work through a process once, mapping out what happens to a "typical" input (domain element) that is represented by a symbol. Then all we have to do is plug any number we want into the place of the input symbol, and we get the corresponding output without any further hard work. It becomes just a matter of routine, something that can be done over and over again in exactly the same way, without having to think much about it.

The following example illustrates the power and efficiency of using algebra to describe a process in function form.

372

6.4 Describing Functions With Algebra

This section has two major purposes.

• To make the connection between a function and a formula without blurring the distinction between the two ideas, and

• To get students comfortable with treating linear equations as functions.

The first half of the section discusses the power of using an algebraic formula as the "mystery box" that turns input into output. The second half extends this to a discussion of graphing functions (either with pencil and paper or with a graphing calculator) and to an implicit (but not explicit) awareness that first degree and some higher degree algebraic expressions describe continuous functions over the real line.

The extended example about Fahrenheit–Celsius conversion serves several purposes here. It is a good vehicle for talking about linear functions, it explains an everyday measurement scale that students need to understand, and it typifies the connection between the graphical interpretation of a linear equation discussed in Chapter 3 and its functional interpretation. The exercises provide similar examples in various realistic settings.

Chapter 6

Additional Support Materials:

Assessments	Qty
Form (A)	1
Form (B)	1

Blackline Masters	Qty
Student p.375	1
Student p.376	1

Extensions	Qty

Supplements	Qty
Describing Functions With Algebra	1

You are an assistant to the weather forecaster for a large TV network in the U.S. During each broadcast, the forecaster presents the latest temperatures from around the world. Your job is to get the latest temperatures as they come into the studio from 25 different foreign cities and put them onto a list to be read during the show.

The difficulty is that most countries measure and report temperature in degrees Celsius, but the U.S. measures it in degrees Fahrenheit. Ten minutes before the start of each broadcast, you have to prepare the list for the U.S. audience by converting each temperature from Celsius to Fahrenheit.

As soon as you get this job, you look up the Celsius and Fahrenheit scales of temperature measurement. The first thing you find out is that 9 Fahrenheit degrees measures the same change in temperature as 5 Celsius degrees. You jot this down in abbreviated form.

$$9f = 5c$$

You also know that water freezes at 32°F and 0°C, and it boils at 212°F and 100°C. You jot down these facts, too.

$$32°F = 0°C \qquad 212°F = 100°C$$

You can use the first of these equations, $9f = 5c$, to find out what 1 degree of either type is "worth" in the other system. Both sides of the equation represent the same amount (of temperature change). If you divide both sides by a particular number, both sides will represent that portion of the same amount. So, dividing both sides by 9,

$$\frac{9}{9}f = \frac{5}{9}c$$

we see that 1 Fahrenheit degree is the same as $\frac{5}{9}$ of a Celsius degree. That is, a Fahrenheit degree is a little larger than half of a Celsius degree.

1. If you divide both sides of the equation $9f = 5c$ by 5, what information do you get?

6.32

2. Since 1 Fahrenheit degree equals $\frac{5}{9}$ of a Celsius degree, do we convert Celsius temperatures to Fahrenheit just by multiplying the Celsius temperature by $\frac{5}{9}$? In particular, if the temperature outside is 18 Celsius, is it 10° Fahrenheit? Why or why not?

6.32

These are in class discussion questions that should be done right at this point because their answers appear in the material that follows immediately.

1. This tells you that 1 Celsius degree is the same as $\frac{9}{5}$ of a Fahrenheit degree. That is, 1 Celsius degree is almost, but not quite, twice as large as a Fahrenheit degree. This answer is used in the statement of question 3.

2. This question draws students' attention to which of the two ratios is the appropriate one to use. This one is not. To convert Celsius to Fahrenheit by multiplying, you need to know the value of a single Celsius degree, measured in Fahrenheit. That is, the answer to question 1 is needed. However, even if you use that ratio, you don't get the answer you seek; see the next question.

NOTES

Chapter 6

3. Question 1 implies that 1 Celsius degree equals $\frac{9}{5}$ of a Fahrenheit degree. Do we convert Celsius temperatures to Fahrenheit just by multiplying the Celsius temperature by $\frac{9}{5}$? In particular, if the temperature outside is 20° Celsius, is it 36° Fahrenheit? Why or why not?

Now pull together the ideas from these three questions. Suppose the report from Buenos Aires says that their current temperature is 30°C. This means that their temperature is 30° Celsius degrees above the freezing point of water. Now, each Celsius degree is "worth" $\frac{9}{5}$ Fahrenheit degrees, so this temperature is $\frac{9}{5} \cdot 30°$ Fahrenheit degrees above the freezing point of water. But water freezes at 32°F, so the Fahrenheit temperature must be

$$\frac{9}{5} \cdot 30 + 32$$

That is, the current temperature in Buenos Aires must be 86°F.

6.33

A report from Calgary says that their current temperature is 5°C. Rewrite the preceding paragraph, substituting Calgary for Buenos Aires and 5°C for 30°C and finding the current temperature in Calgary.

6.34

1. Where is Buenos Aires? Do you think that 30°C is a likely temperature for that city? At what time of year?

2. Where is Calgary? Do you think that the temperature could be 5°C in Calgary at the same time that it is 30°C in Buenos Aires? Explain.

By doing the exercise about Calgary you can see that the process of converting temperatures from Celsius to Fahrenheit is the same, no matter what Celsius temperature you are given. If we let x represent any given Celsius temperature, we can summarize this process by the formula

$$\text{Fahrenheit temperature} = \frac{9}{5}x + 32$$

This formula gives us exactly one Fahrenheit temperature for each Celsius temperature, so it is a function. (What is its domain?) If we call this function F, we can write the formula as

$$F(x) = \frac{9}{5}x + 32$$

374

3. This question reminds students that the difference in the meaning of 0° in the two systems affects the conversion process. Multiplying a Celsius amount by $\frac{9}{5}$ gives you the corresponding Fahrenheit amount *as a measurement of change* in temperature. That is, if the temperature has *changed* by 20°C, then it has *changed* by 36°F. A Celsius thermometer reading of 20° measures the change from 0°C and a Fahrenheit thermometer reading of 36° measures the change from 0°F. The *change* is the same, but *it is being measured from different starting points!* 0°C corresponds to 32°F, the temperature at which water freezes. Therefore, the temperature change conversion has to be adjusted by adding 32°, as is discussed in the material that follows.

6.33

The relevant computation is $\frac{9}{5} \cdot 5 + 32 = 41°F$.

6.34

These questions provide a short lesson in Western hemisphere geography. Students might find this interesting as it adds to the realism of the problem set.

1. Buenos Aires is on the east coast of Argentina, at a southern hemisphere latitude roughly equivalent to that of Cape Hatteras, North Carolina. Thus, a temperature of 30°C is likely for a day in their late spring to early fall, which corresponds to our seasons of late fall to early spring.

2. Calgary is in the province of Alberta, in western Canada, about 150 miles north of the Montana border. It could easily be 5°C there at the same time that it is 30°C in Buenos Aires in November or March, for example.

    Students may recall that the domain of $F(x) = \frac{9}{5}x + 32$ has the constraint that x be greater than absolute zero, -272.2°C.

NOTES

_____

....

....

....

....

....

Now that you have a formula, converting Celsius temperatures to Fahrenheit becomes automatic, a routine that you can do without thinking about anything except the arithmetic involved.

Copy and complete the chart in Display 6.27 for your boss. Round your entries to the nearest Fahrenheit degree. Can you name the country for each of these major cities?

6.35

City	° C	° F
Berlin	2	
Buenos Aires	30	86
Calgary	5	
London	10	
Moscow	−5	
Nairobi	32	
Rome	19	
Sydney	18	
Tokyo	14	

Display 6.27

Unfortunately, the table you just completed is only part of the 25 city list that your boss needs. Worse yet, the entire list has to be updated three times a day! Doing all that arithmetic can get pretty boring. Let's get a calculator to do it. We have already done the difficult part—writing the conversion function as an algebraic formula. The algebra tells the calculator exactly what it needs to do its work.

The calculator ought to do three things.

1. It ought to ask you for the Celsius temperatures that you want to convert. (These are the domain elements you want to use.)

2. It ought to compute the corresponding Fahrenheit temperature. (This is the function step.)

3. It ought to tell you its answers. (These are the images in the range of the function.)

A graphing calculator can do this chore in several different ways. Perhaps the simplest way uses its built-in, spreadsheet style lists. Make one of those lists—call it L1—the "input" (the domain of the function) and another—call it L2—the "output" (the range). You'll have to fill in the domain list by hand, but the

Published by IT'S ABOUT TIME, Inc. © 2000 MATHconx, LLC

375

6.35

Most of these are actual temperatures from a day in November. The chart in Display 6.12T supplies the required information.

City (Country)	° C	° F
Berlin (Germany)	2	36
Buenos Aires (Argentina)	30	86
Calgary (Canada)	5	41
London (Great Britain)	10	50
Moscow (Russia)	–5	23
Nairobi (Kenya)	32	90
Rome (Italy)	19	66
Sydney (Australia)	18	64
Tokyo (Japan)	14	57

Display 6.27, filled in

Display 6.12T

NOTES

Chapter 6

list of images (the range) can be calculated automatically. Just treat L2 as the dependent variable and define it by the formula we found, using L1 as the independent variable. That is, define

$$L_2 = (9/5) * L_1 + 32$$

(This is usually done at the top of the range column.) Try it. Enter the Celsius temperatures of Display 6.27 into the L1 column. Then define L2 by the formula and enter it. You should get all the Fahrenheit temperatures automatically!

6.36 The latest Celsius temperatures for the other sixteen cities your boss needs are listed in Display 6.28. Copy the chart and use your calculator to find the corresponding Fahrenheit temperatures. Round your entries to the nearest Fahrenheit degree. Can you name the country for each of these major cities?

City	°C	°F
Athens	21	
Bangkok	28	
Barcelona	13	
Beijing	7	
Cairo	19	
Calcutta	27	
Havana	25	
Istanbul	12	
Melbourne	7	
Mexico City	20	
Paris	9	
Quebec	−8	
Reykjavik	−15	
Rio de Janeiro	23	
Singapore	33	
Stockholm	1	

Display 6.28

The algebraic form of the Celsius to Fahrenheit conversion function,

$$F(x) = \frac{9}{5}x + 32$$

says something important about the way the Celsius temperatures are related to their Fahrenheit images. Recall your work with linear equations earlier in **MATH** *Connections* and think of $F(x)$

PuPublished by IT'S ABOUT TIME, Inc. © 2000 MATHconx, LLC

376

6.36

Display 6.13T supplies the required information. Please advise your students about one potential source of annoyance in this process. They *must* enter the domain column (the Celsius temperatures) *before* they enter the formula for the function. Unlike spreadsheets, the TI-82 (TI-83) calculators (and perhaps others) *do not store the formula* as the column heading. They simply use the formula to calculate the column entries and then store the entries. If you go back and change a domain temperature later, the "image" in the next column will *not* change automatically.

City (Country)	° C	° F
Athens (Greece)	21	70
Bangkok (Thailand)	28	82
Barcelona (Spain)	13	55
Beijing (China)	7	45
Cairo (Egypt)	19	66
Calcutta (India)	27	81
Havana (Cuba)	25	77
Istanbul (Turkey)	12	54
Melbourne (Australia)	7	45
Mexico City (Mexico)	20	68
Paris (France)	9	48
Quebec (Canada)	–8	18
Reykjavik (Iceland)	–15	5
Rio de Janeiro (Brazil)	23	73
Singapore (Singapore)	33	91
Stockholm (Sweden)	1	34

Display 6.13T

Chapter 6

as the dependent variable in this first degree equation. If you graph this equation, using the y-axis for the $F(x)$ values, you get a straight line.

1. What is the slope of the straight line $F(x) = \frac{9}{5}x + 32$? What is its y-intercept? What does the y-intercept represent?

6.37

2. Copy Display 6.29; then draw the graph of this function, F, on your coordinate axes. What part of this picture represents the range of F?

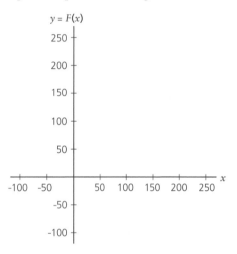

Display 6.29

The graph of F is an example of an important idea. Earlier we saw that any straight line graph (except for the vertical ones) has an equation of the form

$$y = ax + b$$

where a is its slope and b is its y-intercept. Each point on the line corresponds to an ordered pair (x, y) of numbers for which the equation becomes a true statement. For instance, $(5, 4)$ is on the line

$$y = 0.6x + 1$$

because $4 = 0.6(5) + 1$ is true.

How would you find another point on this line? One way is to pick a number for x and then compute the y that makes the equation true.

If $x = 2$, then $y = 0.6 \cdot 2 + 1 = 2.2$

377

6.37

This example is an important steppingstone to the general idea of linear function. It connects the graphical ideas of Chapter 3 with the language and notation of functions.

1. The slope is $\frac{9}{5}$; the y-intercept is 32. The y-intercept is the place at which x is 0. Since x is Celsius temperature, the y-intercept is the Fahrenheit temperature at which water freezes.

2. See Display 6.14T. The range of F is the vertical axis, except numbers below absolute zero, -459.7°F.

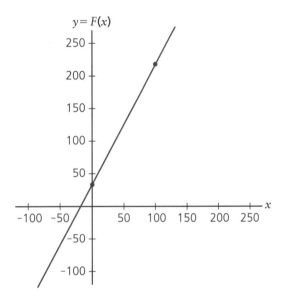

Display 6.14T

NOTES

6.4 Describing Functions With Algebra

which means that (2, 2.2) is on the line. Notice that, each time you pick a value for x, the equation gives you exactly one correct value for y. In other words, the equation

$$y = 0.6x + 1$$

describes a *function* on the domain of all real numbers. For each number x you choose, the y value for that equation is the image of x. The equation

$$f(x) = 0.6x + 1$$

is the rule that describes this function.

Of course, there's nothing special about this particular slope or y-intercept. The equation of *any* nonvertical straight line, in the form

$$f(x) = ax + b$$

describes a function that assigns real numbers to real numbers.

These functions are particularly nice because it is easy to draw a picture of how they work. The function $f(x) = 0.6x + 1$, for instance, is shown in Display 6.30. To find the image of a number on the x-axis, just move vertically (up or down) until you hit the line. Then move horizontally (left or right) until you hit the y-axis; that y-axis number is the image you want.

Display 6.30

1. Why don't vertical lines represent functions?

6.38

2. Are the functions represented by horizontal lines special in any way? Explain.

Published by IT'S ABOUT TIME, Inc. © 2000 MATHconx, LLC

6.38

These are simple, but important ideas to get across. The discussion should not take very long if the students are grasping the connection between the graphs and their functions. If these questions are not answered fairly quickly, it's a danger signal that your students might be missing the main idea.

1. A vertical line matches a single x value with *all* y values, so that particular domain element does not have exactly one image. No other x-value (domain element) has any image at all.

2. A horizontal line represents a function that takes all the domain elements to the same image. Such functions are called *constant functions*.

NOTES

Chapter 6

So far we have focused on one kind of function that can be described with algebra—the linear functions. Many other kinds of functions can be written algebraically. You have seen a few of them already, and you will see many others soon. Various kinds of functions occur throughout mathematics and science, as well as in economics, business, psychology, and many other fields. But you do not need to see all these different kinds now to understand the basic message of this section.

A function that can be expressed as an algebraic equation usually can be handled much more easily than a function expressed only in words.

Algebra is the key that unlocks the toolbox of coordinate systems, graphing calculators, and many mathematical techniques that turn difficult questions into routine exercises.

We end this section with a simple illustration of this message. Here is a function that is not linear, but that can be handled with many of the same tools used for linear functions.

The area enclosed by a circle is equal to pi (π) times the square of the radius (r^2).

If we call this statement function A and the radius of the circle r, then we have a familiar formula.

$$A(r) = \pi r^2$$

We can use either this formula or the description in words to compute the area inside a circle "by hand," of course. For instance, if the circle has a radius of 5 meters, then the area inside is given by $\pi \cdot 5^2$, which is 25π square meters. Since π is approximately 3.14, this area is approximately 78.54 square meters.

However, if we need to compute the area for many circles, or if the answer has to be precise, a calculator comes in handy. And the calculator's language is algebra. For instance, we can just enter the formula in the calculator's function list and let the machine do the rest of the work.

Try it. Enter the formula into your calculator as a function. To speak the calculator's language, you'll probably have to treat the image symbol, $A(x)$, as Y and use X (the variable key) in place of r in the formula. That is, you should enter

$$Y = \pi * X^{\wedge}2$$

in some Y= line. Now your work is pretty much done. To find

Published by IT'S ABOUT TIME, Inc. © 2000 MATHconx, LLC

NOTES

areas, you can use **TRACE** with the graph of this function. You may have to change the WINDOW settings to get close enough to the answer you want, but the calculator will do all the computations for you.

6.39

1. Set your calculator's WINDOW to Integer coordinates. Use **TRACE** to check the area for a circle of radius 5. Then find the areas inside circles of radius 3, 4, and 7. Round your answers to two decimal places.

2. Use **TRACE** and whatever WINDOW settings you prefer to find the areas inside circles of radius 1.7, 3.2, and 24. Round your answers to two decimal places.

The next section explains another important, useful function that becomes much easier to use when it is expressed algebraically.

Problem Set: 6.4

1. In a *Rand McNally Road Atlas*, a map of Arizona is drawn to the scale of 38 miles per inch.

(a) On this map, the (straight line) distance between Yuma and Tucson measures $5\frac{1}{2}$ inches. How far is the real distance between these two cities? Round your answer to the nearest mile.

(b) Write a function that will compute the distance between any two points in Arizona from its measurement (in inches) on this map. Call this function d (for "distance").

(c) Copy the table of Display 6.31. (Yes, these are all real places in Arizona.) Then enter the function d into your graphing calculator and use it to fill in the distances in this table. Round your answers to the nearest mile.

(d) The longest north-south distance in Arizona is about 380 miles. How long is the state, top to bottom, on this map? Explain how you found your answer.

380

6.4 Describing Functions With Algebra

6.39

These exercises reinforce the message that machine assisted computation is so much easier than handwork that it's worth the effort to deal with the algebra.

1. $A(3) = 28.27$; $A(4) = 50.27$; $A(7) = 153.94$

2. $A(1.7) = 9.08$; $A(3.2) = 32.17$; $A(24) = 1809.56$

Problem Set: 6.4

1. This is a straightforward exercise in constructing, using, and graphing a simple linear function. The measurements are deliberately given in fraction form, just as they are read from a ruler, to give students practice in converting such information for use with their calculators.

   (a) 209 miles. By doing this computation, the students should see how to set up the function in part (b).
   (b) $d(x) = 38x$
   (c) The answers, from top to bottom, are 95 mi.; 238 mi.; 109 mi.; 176 mi.; 124 mi.; 240 mi.; 81 mi.; 297 mi.; 21 mi.; 418 mi.
   (d) An implicit exercise in inverses. Divide by 38, getting 10 in.

NOTES

Chapter 6

(e) Draw a graph of *d* on a piece of paper. (You may use your calculator to help you.) What maximum and minimum values should you choose for the *x*-axis? For the *y*-axis? Why? On your graph, mark the points that represent each distance of Display 6.31.

	Places	Distance	
		Map (in.)	Real (mi.)
(1)	Phoenix – Oracle	$2\frac{1}{2}$	
(2)	Bullhead City – Friendly Corners	$6\frac{1}{4}$	
(3)	Cottonwood – Snowflake	$2\frac{7}{8}$	
(4)	Flagstaff – Sentinel	$4\frac{5}{8}$	
(5)	Casa Grande – Sierra Vista	$3\frac{1}{4}$	
(6)	Skull Valley – Tombstone	$6\frac{5}{16}$	
(7)	Tuba City – Steamboat Canyon	$2\frac{1}{8}$	
(8)	Moccasin – Geronimo	$7\frac{13}{16}$	
(9)	Rough Rock – Round Rock	$\frac{9}{16}$	
(10)	Red Rock – San Luis	11	

Display 6.31

2. Find an atlas of the United States in your library. Look up the map of your state. (If you are in Arizona, choose some other state.) Then write a problem just like problem 1, choosing towns and cities in your state for the locations in your problem. (Even if the map you find may not say exactly what its scale is in miles per inch, it will have some scale notation on it. In this case, explain how you figure out what the scale is.) Test how good a question writer you are by having a classmate work out the answers to your questions.

3. Betsy and Oliver are sister and brother model railroaders. They have an HO scale railroad layout, called the "B & O Road," in their basement. The word *scale* here refers to a ratio of lengths; HO scale is $\frac{1}{8}$ inch to the foot. In order for their HO layout to look realistic, Betsy and Oliver must make sure that all the measurements of their models are in proportion with this ratio.

Published by IT'S ABOUT TIME, Inc. © 2000 MATHconx, LLC

381

(e) The minimum x and y values should be 0 because both axes are distance scales. Part (d) provides a rough idea of relevant size, but using its value as the maxima for x and y is too restrictive. There are diagonal distances in Arizona that are longer than the maximum north-south distance. One such distance is (11) in Display 6.31. To choose appropriate maxima, one really should know a little about the shape of Arizona. The maximum diagonal is northwest to southeast, a distance of about 475 miles; this makes a good maximum for the y-axis. Anything reasonably close to that, up to 500 miles or so, would do as well for graphing purposes. This means that a good maximum choice for x would be $12\frac{1}{2}$ in. to 13 in. or so. See Display 6.15T. Note that the city reference number is in ( ).

2. This problem combines the mathematics of problem 1 with a library activity, a little geography, some writing, and a little extra problem solving. It can be made into a small group activity, if you wish, with two different groups answering each other's questions.

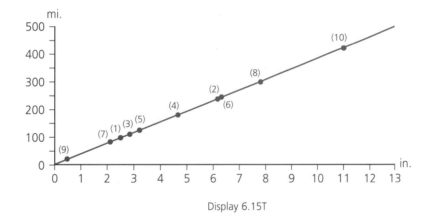

Display 6.15T

3. This problem and the next two explore some simple linear functions in a model railroad setting. Various parts exhibit the connections among formulas, tables, ordered pairs, and graphs. The problems also provide practice in estimation and help build general numeracy skills. They look at conversion from one measurement scale to another, including the relationship between the English system and the metric system.

(a) Betsy and Oliver want to make a model of their own house to put on the layout. After they measure the parts of their house, they need to convert the measurements to HO scale so that they can build the model accurately. Write a function h that will convert their measurements (in feet) to HO scale measurements (in inches).

(b) Copy the table in Display 6.32. Then enter the function h into your graphing calculator and use it to fill in the measurements in this table. Round your answers to the nearest $\frac{1}{16}$ inch.

	House Parts	Real (ft.)	Scale (in.)
(1)	outside length	30	
(2)	outside width	24	
(3)	height to eaves	18	
(4)	front door height	$6\frac{1}{2}$	
(5)	front door width	3	

Display 6.32

(c) Draw a graph of h on a piece of paper. (You may use your calculator to help you.) What maximum and minimum values will you choose for the x-axis? For the y-axis? Why? On your graph, mark the points that represent each measurement of Display 6.32.

(d) What railroad is the real B & O Road? Where is it? Why is it important in American history?

4. (This problem continues the story, begun in problem 3, of the B & O model railroad.) Betsy and Oliver have just found the plans for a small town station in a British railroad magazine. They want to build it in HO scale, but all the measurements are in meters!

(a) Write a function m that will convert their measurements (in meters) to HO scale measurements (in inches). (Remember: 1 inch = 2.54 cm.)

382

Published by IT'S ABOUT TIME, Inc. © 2000 MATHconx, LLC

(a) $h(x) = \frac{1}{8}x$, where x is in feet and $h(x)$ is in inches. (It can also be written as $h(x) = \frac{x}{8}$, but that may cause some confusion when graphing it.)

(b) Answers, top to bottom: $3\frac{3}{4}$ in., 3 in., $2\frac{1}{4}$ in., $\frac{13}{16}$ in., $\frac{3}{8}$ in.

(c) The minimum value for both x and y should be 0 because they are distance measurements. However, unlike the analogous question in problem 1, there is no natural choice for the maximum value of x. Its use for house measurements shows that it should at least allow x to be 30 feet. But it could also be used to convert dimensions of entire railroad yards. Any choice for maximum x that allows for a readable graph is OK. The choice for maximum y should have some reasonable relationship to the maximum value of x, but there's no definite rule here, either. The test is whether or not the relationship between x and y is understandable from the picture. See Display 6.16T. Note that the house part numbers are in ( ).

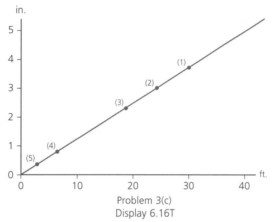

Problem 3(c)
Display 6.16T

(d) This is strictly an American history question, without mathematical relevance. The B & O Road is the Baltimore and Ohio Railroad, the first public railroad in the United States. Constructed in the 1830s to provide a way across the Allegheny Mountains, it reached Wheeling, WV, by 1852 and provided a connection to St. Louis, MO, by 1857. The B & O pioneered in the use of steam locomotives after the successful run of Peter Cooper's engine, *Tom Thumb*, in 1830. It is still a major east coast railroad, serving the Allegheny region.

4. This problem covers the same skills as problem 3 with the added wrinkle of metric conversion.

(a) Finding the conversion factor from the in./cm relationship requires a little careful reasoning about the arithmetic. You need meters in terms of feet; then you can apply the HO scale conversion from before. This is a foreshadowing of composite functions.

$$1 \text{ foot} = 12 \cdot 2.54 \text{ cm} = 30.48 \text{ cm} = 0.3048 \text{ m}$$

so

$$1 \text{ m} = \frac{1}{0.3048} \text{ ft.} = 3.28 \text{ ft. (approx.)}$$

Thus, the desired function is $m(x) = \frac{3.28}{8}x$ or $m(x) = 0.41x$, where x is measured in meters and $m(x)$ is in inches.

(b) Copy the table in Display 6.33. Then enter the function *m* into your graphing calculator and use it to fill in the measurements in this table. Round your answers to the nearest $\frac{1}{10}$ inch.

(c) The graph of the function *m* is a straight line. What is its slope? What is its *y*-intercept?

	Station Parts	Real (m.)	Scale (in.)
(1)	building length	10	
(2)	building width	7	
(3)	platform length	45	
(4)	platform width	4.3	
(5)	freight door height	2.6	
(6)	front door width	1.25	

Display 6.33

5. Estimate (in feet or meters) the real measurement of each of the following objects. Then use either the function *h* from problem 3 or the function *m* from problem 4 to help you find the corresponding measurement in HO scale. Round your answer to the nearest $\frac{1}{10}$ inch.

(a) the dimensions of your classroom (length, width, height)

(b) your own height

(c) 4 feet $8\frac{1}{2}$ inches, the distance between the rails of a standard gauge railroad track

(d) the length of a boxcar

(e) the length of a pickup truck

(f) the height of a cat

(g) the length of a football field

(h) the height of your school building

(i) the height of the World Trade Center

(j) the length of an ocean going supertanker

6. Converting temperatures from Fahrenheit to Celsius works like the Celsius to Fahrenheit function *F* that you studied in this section. This problem asks you to write a similar description of the Fahrenheit to Celsius function, which we'll call C.

Published by IT'S ABOUT TIME, Inc. © 2000 MATHconx, LLC

(b) Answers, top to bottom: 4.1 in., 2.9 in., 18.5 in., 1.8 in., 1.1 in., 0.5 in.

(c) The slope is $\frac{3.28}{8}$, which equals 0.41; the *y*-intercept is 0.

5. This problem provides a chance to combine using functions with size esti-mation. If it piques some students' curiosity, it could be used for some good discussion time.

(a) This depends on your room.

(b) Answers will vary a little. A person 5 feet tall would measure $\frac{5}{8}$ inch (about 0.6 in.) in HO scale.

(c) 0.6 in.

(d) Boxcars usually are 40 to 50 feet long; 5 to 6.3 in.

(e) About 16 feet; 2 in.

(f) About 16 in. (standing on all fours); less than 0.2 in.

(g) 120 yds. = 360 ft., including the end zones; 45 in. = 3 ft. 9 in.

(h) Answers will vary from school to school.

(i) 1350 feet; 168.8 in. An HO gauge model would be about 14 feet high.

(j) The supertanker *Globtik Tokyo*, the largest ship in the world when she was launched in 1972, measures 378.85 m (1242 ft., nearly $\frac{1}{4}$ mile) from stem to stern. An HO gauge model would be 155.25 in. (about 13 feet) long.

6. Most of this problem mimics the text, to reinforce the processes described there. The line relationship question is a bit more sophisticated and can be expanded into a preliminary, informal discussion of inverses, if you see fit. Such a discussion is not necessary at this point, however.

NOTES

_____

_____

_____

_____

_____

_____

_____

_____

Chapter 6

(a) Write C as an algebraic formula in the form

$$C(x) = \underline{\hspace{2cm}}$$

where x stands for a given Fahrenheit temperature. Explain how you got your algebraic expression.

(b) Your assignment as assistant weather forecaster has changed. Now you have to translate the Fahrenheit temperature of 24 major U.S. cities into Celsius for transmission to the station's Canadian affiliates. The list of cities and their latest Fahrenheit temperatures appears in Display 6.34. Enter these temperatures into one of your calculator's lists. Then use your function to have your calculator list the corresponding Celsius temperatures automatically.

City	°F	°C
Anchorage, AK	18	
Atlanta, GA	59	
Bismarck, ND	28	
Boston, MA	48	
Cincinnati, OH	51	
Dallas, TX	56	
Denver, CO	49	
Detroit, MI	44	
Hartford, CT	45	
Honolulu, HI	86	
Los Angeles, CA	76	
Memphis, TN	57	
Miami, FL	78	
Minneapolis, MN	30	
New Orleans, LA	60	
New York, NY	50	
Phoenix, AZ	82	
Pittsburgh, PA	47	
Portland, ME	42	
Reno, NV	58	
Richmond, VA	54	
St. Louis, MO	55	
Seattle, WA	49	
Washington, DC	53	

Display 6.34

Published by IT'S ABOUT TIME, Inc. © 2000 MATHconx, LLC

(a) $C(x) = \frac{5}{9}x - \frac{160}{9}$

(b) See Display 6.17T.

City	°F	°C
Anchorage, AK	18	–8
Atlanta, GA	59	15
Bismarck, ND	28	–2
Boston, MA	48	9
Cincinnati, OH	51	11
Dallas, TX	56	13
Denver, CO	49	9
Detroit, MI	44	7
Hartford, CT	45	7
Honolulu, HI	86	30
Los Angeles, CA	76	24
Memphis, TN	57	14
Miami, FL	78	26
Minneapolis, MN	30	–1
New Orleans, LA	60	16
New York, NY	50	10
Phoenix, AZ	82	28
Pittsburgh, PA	47	8
Portland, ME	42	6
Reno, NV	58	14
Richmond, VA	54	12
St. Louis, MO	55	13
Seattle, WA	49	9
Washington, DC	53	12

Display 6.17T

Chapter 6

(c) The function C can be represented as a straight line. What are its slope and its y-intercept?

(d) Copy the coordinate axes and the dotted line shown in Display 6.35.

    (i) Draw the graph of C on these axes. Think of the y-axis as the range of C.

    (ii) Draw the graph of F on the same coordinate axes. This time think of the y-axis as the range of F.

    (iii) What is the equation for the dotted line? Do you see any interesting relationships among these three lines? If so, describe what you see.

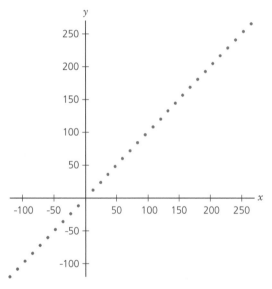

Display 6.35

7. Internet connection services allow you to connect with the World Wide Web by means of telephone hookups. One such service, InfoMatic, has a $10 monthly service fee plus a connect time charge of $15 per hour. The hourly charge is billed for actual connection time, which its computer tracks automatically and exactly.

(a) Write the formula for a function f that computes the total monthly bill for InfoMatic based on the time used. Then use f to compute the March bill for a subscriber

(c) The slope is $\frac{5}{9}$; the y-intercept is $-\frac{160}{9}$.

(d) See Display 6.18T. Part (iii) asks students to recognize that the lines for C and F are mirror images of each other; that is, they are reflections with respect to the line $y = x$. This displays, but does not explain, a basic property of inverse functions, which will be discussed formally later. These two functions are inverses of each other; each undoes what the other one does.

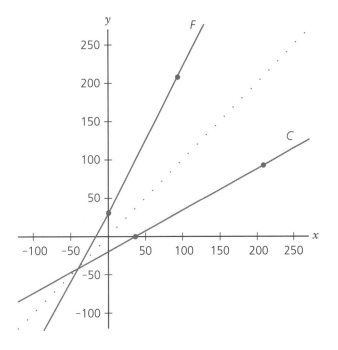

Display 6.18T

7. This problem relates to the material of Chapter 3. Parts (a) and (b) are straightforward. Parts (c)–(e) add a new wrinkle—a function that has to be defined in two pieces. Part (f) draws on some ideas from Chapter 5 to compare the values of linear functions.

(a) $f(x) = 15x + 10$, where x is measured in hours and $f(x)$ is measured in dollars. $f(2\frac{2}{3}) = \$50$; $f(4.1) = \$71.50$.

Chapter 6

who used 2 hours and 40 minutes of connect time that month, and also for a second subscriber who used 4 hours and 6 minutes of connect time.

(b) The function *f* can be represented as a straight line. What are its slope and its *y*-intercept? Copy the coordinate axes shown in Display 6.36 and draw the graph of *f* on these axes. Think of the *y*-axis as the range of *f*.

(c) Another online service, DataLine, has a monthly service fee of $25 which includes 2 free hours of connect time. Additional connect time is charged at $20 per hour. Describe a function, *g*, that computes the total monthly bill for DataLine based on the time used. Then use *g* to compute the March bill for a subscriber who used 1 hour and 37 minutes of connect time that month, and also for a second subscriber who used 4 hours and 15 minutes of connect time.

(d) Draw the graph of *g* on the same coordinate axes you used for part (b). Think of the *y*-axis as the range of *g*.

(e) The graph of *g* that you drew in part (d) should have two straight line pieces. Write an algebraic formula for each piece, and say for which domain values each formula applies.

(f) For which amounts of connect time is InfoMatic the better deal? For which amounts is DataLine the better deal? When are they exactly the same?

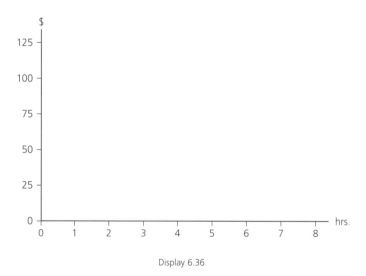

Display 6.36

Published by IT'S ABOUT TIME, Inc. © 2000 MATHconx, LLC

(b) The slope of *f* is 15; its *y*-intercept is 10. See Display 6.19T.

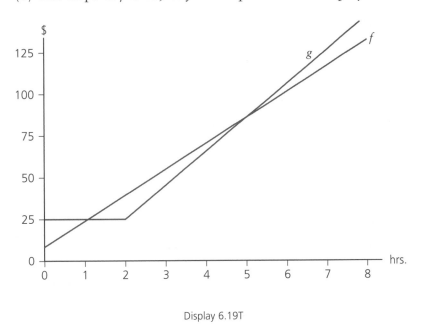

Display 6.19T

(c) The description of *g* in this part can be verbal, rather than by formulas. Part (e) asks for formulas. $g(1\frac{37}{60}) = \$25$; $g(4.25) = \$70$.

(d) See Display 6.19T.

(e) Between 0 and 2 hours, $g(x) = 25$. From 2 hours on, $g(x) = 20x - 15$. Finding the latter formula requires some of the ideas from Chapter 3. By the description of the function, the slope of this line (the rate) is 20. One point on the line is $(2, 25)$, so the *y*-intercept can be found by solving $25 = 20 \cdot 2 + b$ for *b*.

(f) The functions *f* and *g* agree at 1 hour (which is easy to see) and again at 5 hours, which looks about right from the graph, but needs to be verified. One way to find this second point is to set $f(x) = g(x)$ and solve for *x*.

$$15x + 10 = 20x - 15$$

implies equality at $x = 5$. Thus, between 1 and 5 hours of connect time, DataLine is the better deal. For less than 1 hour or more than 5 hours of connect time, InfoMatic is the better deal.

6.5 Growth Functions

A rich uncle has died and left you $100,000 on the condition that you put it in a bank account and leave it untouched for at least 5 years. You want to get the most for your money, so you talk with the managers of the three banks in your neighborhood. All three banks need more money to lend other customers, so each one offers you a special deal.

- "Put your money with us!" says Bank 1. "We'll give you 10% of your initial deposit each year it stays with us. You'll make another $50,000 in 5 years!"

- "Put your money with us!" says Bank 2. "We'll pay you 9% annual interest, and we'll compound it every year."

  "What does 'compound it every year' mean?" you ask.

  "At the end of each year, we'll add to your account the interest earned and we'll base the next year's interest on that new, larger amount. That way you'll earn interest on your interest!"

- "Put your money with us!" says Bank 3. "We'll pay you 8% annual interest, and we'll compound it every quarter."

  "What does 'compound it every quarter' mean?" you ask.

  "We won't wait until the end of a year to add on the interest you've earned; we'll do it every quarter-year— every 3 months. That way your interest goes to work for you faster!"

All three banks advertise that "interest is paid from day of deposit to day of withdrawal."

In your opinion, which of these three banks is offering you the best deal? Which offer is the worst? Explain your thinking.

6.40

Learning Outcomes

After studying this section, you will be able to:

Explain why an exponential function is appropriate for modeling growth;

Evaluate exponential functions and compare the effects of different growth rates;

Describe compounding situations using exponential functions;

Evaluate exponential functions and draw their graphs with a graphing calculator.

About Words

In everyday English and also in chemistry, a *compound* is something made by combining other things (ingredients).

Published by IT'S ABOUT TIME, Inc. © 2000 MATHconx, LLC

387

6.5 Growth Functions

The purpose of this section is to introduce and explain exponential functions as a useful way to model growth. It begins with a compound interest example that illustrates the distinction between linear growth and exponential growth. This example provides a concrete application of mathematics to students' everyday lives along with some practice in handling percents. The effect of increasing the frequency of compounding is explored. The question of what fractional exponents mean is raised, but not settled.

The section depends on and reinforces these concepts from Chapters 2 and 3,

- the definition of whole number exponent;
- the Associative and Distributive Laws;
- algebra as a way of identifying and clarifying patterns;
- the slope a straight line.

The first half of this section repeats the ideas about compound interest that were presented in Chapter 2, and then extends them to the idea of continuous compounding. The irrational number e is introduced as a "device that works" for handling continuous compounding with a calculator. The notions of a continuous process and a limiting value are handled informally and intuitively. A more extensive treatment of exponential functions and growth appears in Chapter 2 of Year 3.

Note that the adjectives "limiting" and "continuous" as used in this section are to be understood as ordinary English words. This informal usage is consistent with their formal mathematical usage, but an explanation of their formal meanings is neither essential nor desirable at this stage of the students' development.

6.40

Don't expect to settle this question now. It is the motivating theme for the first half of the section. With any luck, you'll get some division of opinion. Even the students who respond based on the classroom "gamesmanship" of assuming that the highest number is not the best deal simply because you asked the question probably will have some difficulty distinguishing between Banks 2 and 3. Once you get the students interested and engaged in the question, move on. The subsequent text gives them increasingly efficient ways to find the answer.

Assessments   Blackline Masters   Extensions   Supplements
For Additional Support Materials see page T-243

Thinking Tip

Make a table. Making a table of values sometimes can help you see patterns that show you how a process works.

How can you figure out which bank is offering you the most interest for your money? One way is to make a table showing the total amount of money you would have in each account at the end of each year. For Bank 1, that's easy. They will pay you 10% of your initial deposit each year. (Recall interest paid only on the original deposit is called simple interest.) That's an additional $10,000 a year. The amounts for Bank 2 are a little more difficult to compute, but they're not so bad if you take them one at a time. At the end of Year 1 you'll have 9% more than you started with. The amount at the end of Year 2 will be 9% more than the amount at the end of Year 1; and so on.

6.41

Copy the table in Display 6.37 and fill in the columns for Banks 1 and 2.

Year	Bank 1	Bank 2	Bank 3
0	$100,000.00	$100,000.00	$100,000.00
1	$110,000.00		
2			
3			
4			
5	$150,000.00		

Display 6.37

Did you fill in the Bank 2 column by hand, or did you use your calculator? (Either way is OK.) Do you see how to compute each entry by a single multiplication step? (You don't have to do it this way, but it's easier.) In case you missed it, here's how that works.

To fill in the amount for the end of Year 1, add 9% of $100,000 to the original $100,000. That's

$$\$100,000 + 0.09 \cdot \$100,000$$

By the Distributive Law, this is the same as
$$(1 + 0.09) \cdot \$100,000$$
which is
$$(1.09) \cdot \$100,000$$

That is, increasing a number by 9% is the same as multiplying it by 1.09. This means that you can find each entry of the Bank 2 column by multiplying the one above it by 1.09.

388

6.41

It is important to have the students fill in the Bank 2 column right now. If they just read about it, they are not as likely to appreciate the ensuing discussion of how to use the Distributive Law to compute each entry as a single multiple of the previous one.

All the values for the table in Display 6.37 are shown in Display 6.20T. Only the amounts for Banks 1 and 2 are asked for here; hold the other information until the students are allowed to wrestle with the tedious computations of more frequent compounding. Finding an easier way to do that is what motivates the exponential function. The pattern in the computations for Bank 2 provides the key.

Chapter 6

Additional Support Materials:

Assessments	Qty
Form (A)	1
Form (B)	1

Blackline Masters	Qty
Student pp.	
388	1
391-392	1

Extensions	Qty

Supplements	Qty
Growth Functions	1

Thinking Tip

Look for a pattern. Sometimes thinking about different ways to fill in a chart or table uncovers useful hidden patterns.

Besides being easy to find the amounts this way, there's a pattern here that will make it easier to fill in the next column. This process tells us that the yearly amounts for Bank 2 are found as in Display 6.38.

Year	Bank 2
0	$100,000
1	$1.09 \cdot \$100,000$
2	$1.09 \cdot (1.09 \cdot \$100,000)$
3	$109 \cdot (1.09 \cdot (1.09 \cdot \$100,000))$
4	
5	

Display 6.38

What are the missing entries for 4 years and 5 years in Display 6.38?

a

6.42

Because multiplication is associative, this clumsy pattern can be abbreviated by using exponents. Display 6.39 shows how.

Year	Bank 2
0	$100,000
1	$1.09 \cdot \$100,000$
2	$1.09^2 \cdot \$100,000$
3	$1.09^3 \cdot \$100,000$
4	
5	

Display 6.39

1. **What are the missing entries for year 4 and year 5 in Display 6.39?**

2. **Explain what associativity has to do with the change from Display 6.38 to Display 6.39.**

b

6.43

Now let's summarize this pattern. Notice that the only thing that changes as we move down the list in Display 6.39 is the number of years. The amount of money *is a function of* how many years it has been in the account. This function—we'll call it B_2, for Bank 2—depends on the number n of years according to the formula

$$B_2(n) = 1.09^n \cdot \$100,000$$

389

1b

6.42

4 years: $1.09 \cdot (1.09 \cdot (1.09 \cdot (1.09 \cdot \$100,000)))$
5 years: $1.09 \cdot (1.09 \cdot (1.09 \cdot (1.09 (1.09 \cdot \$100,000))))$

6.43

1. 4 years: $1.09^4 \cdot \$100,000$; 5 years: $1.09^5 \cdot \$100,000$

2. Associativity allows us to multiply all the 1.09 factors together first, before multiplying by $100,000. For instance, associativity allows the line for 2 years to be rewritten as follows.
   $$1.09 \cdot (1.09 \cdot \$100,000) = (1.09 \cdot 1.09) \cdot \$100,000 = 1.09^2 \cdot \$100,000$$

NOTES

Chapter 6

6.5 Growth Functions

This kind of function is called an **exponential function** because the independent variable (in this case, n) is used as an exponent.

Writing this process as an exponential function makes it much easier to find how much money would be in the account after any number of years. Instead of having to build up to the answer one year at a time, we can just put the number of years in for n and let the calculator compute it. For instance, the amount of money in the account after 10 years is

$$B_2(10) = 1.09^{10} \cdot \$100,000$$

(How much is that?)

This exponential pattern can be used to fill in the Bank 3 column, too, but we have to be a little careful. The following questions show you why.

6.44

1. If the bank's *annual* interest rate is 8%, what do you think their *quarterly* interest rate is?

2. If you deposit $100,000, how much money should you have at the end of the first quarter? At the end of 6 months? At the end of the first year?

3. The Bank 3 amount function can be written as

$$B_3(n) = 1.02^n \cdot \$100,000$$

Where does the number 1.02 come from? What does n represent in this case? Explain. (*Hint:* Look back at your answers to parts 1 and 2.)

4. Use this formula for $B_3(n)$ to fill in the Bank 3 column of Display 6.37.

5. Write a formula to describe the way Bank 1 computes the amount you would have at the end of each year. Call this function B_1. Explain how it works.

Now that you have formulas for the way your money would grow in each bank, you can use them to decide which bank gives you the best deal for *any* time period.

390

Published by IT'S ABOUT TIME, Inc. © 2000 MATHconx, LLC

6.44

1. Since a quarter is one-fourth of a year, the quarterly interest rate should be (and is) 2%, one-fourth of 8%.

2. If your students handle these questions correctly, they will have the key to the rest of this section. $102,000. $104,040. $108,243.22.

3. Since the quarterly rate is 2%, which is 0.02, at the end of each quarter there is $1 + 0.02 = 1.02$ times as much money as there was at the beginning. This is compounded each quarter, so n represents the number of *quarters* (3 month periods) that the money is in the bank.

4. See Display 6.20T.

Years	Bank 1	Bank 2	Bank 3
0	$100,000.00	$100,000.00	$100,000.00
1	$110,000.00	$109,000.00	$108,243.22
2	$120,000.00	$118,810.00	$117,165.94
3	$130,000.00	$129,502.90	$126,824.18
4	$140,000.00	$141,158.16	$137,278.57
5	$150,000.00	$153,862.40	$148,594.74

Display 6.20T

5. Since Bank 1 does *not* compound the interest (that is, they do not pay interest on the interest), this is a linear function. The bank pays $10,000 per year, simple interest.

$$B_1(n) = \$10,000 \cdot n + \$100,000$$

NOTES

1. Which bank gives you the most money for the 5 year period? Which gives you the least? Do these results agree with your answers at the beginning of this section?

6.45

2. If you only had to keep the money in the bank for three years, which bank would give you the most money? Which would give you the least? Justify your answer.

3. Suppose you decide to leave your money in the bank for an extra year. Which bank pays the most for the 6 year period? Which pays the least? Justify your answer.

Which (if any) of the functions B_1, B_2, and B_3 have graphs that are straight lines? Which do not? Defend your answers.

6.46

Earning interest is a way of making your money grow, and compounding is a way of making it grow faster. Compound interest functions are examples of **growth functions**, which express the amount of something at a particular time based on how much of it there was just before that time.[†] The compounding process is a good illustration of how the growth of an amount of anything (people, gerbils, rabbits, rats, bacteria, crocodiles) adds more fuel to the growth "engine" as it runs along. Before looking at some other examples of growth, let us take a careful look at the compound interest effect.

We have seen that, the more often interest is compounded, the faster the total amount grows. Is there any limit to how much faster you can make the money increase just by compounding the interest more frequently? Think about that question as we work through the following situation together.

(6.47)

You have $10,000 to invest for one year. Two investment companies are competing for your money. One offers you $12\frac{3}{4}\%$ simple interest. The other company offers you 12% interest, but says that you can decide how often you want it to be compounded. Which is the better deal?

[†] Growth functions are exponential functions. You will learn more about exponential functions and growth in Year 3.

391

6.45

These questions are straightforward applications of the three algebraic formulas for the bank functions.

1. $B_1(5) = \$10,000 \cdot 5 + \$100,000 = \$150,000$
    $B_2(5) = 1.09^5 \cdot \$100,000 = \$153,862.40$
    $B_3(20) = 1.02^{20} \cdot \$100,000 = \$148,594.74$

    Therefore, Bank 2 offers the most money after 5 years; Bank 3 offers the least. These amounts should be in the students' filled-in table for Display 6.37.

2. This answer also comes directly from the students' table for Display 6.37.
    $B_1(3) = \$10,000 \cdot 3 + \$100,000 = \$130,000$
    $B_2(3) = 1.09^3 \cdot \$100,000 = \$129,502.90$
    $B_3(12) = 1.02^{12} \cdot \$100,000 = \$126,824.18$

    Therefore, Bank 1 offers the most money after 3 years; Bank 3 again offers the least.

3. After 6 years, Bank 2 again offers the most money, but now Bank 1 offers the least.
    $B_1(6) = \$10,000 \cdot 6 + \$100,000 = \$160,000$
    $B_2(6) = 1.09^6 \cdot \$100,000 = \$167,710.01$
    $B_3(24) = 1.02^{24} \cdot \$100,000 = \$160,843.72$

6.46

One reason for discussing exponential functions here is to provide natural examples of functions that do not have straight line graphs. Only B_1 has a straight line graph. Its slope is 10,000 and its y-intercept is 100,000. To verify that the other two functions do not have straight line graphs, you can compute the rate of change (the slope) between different pairs of points. For instance, using the students' data for Display 6.37, the graph of B_2 must contain the points (0, 100,000), (1, 109,000), and (2, 118,810). The slope of the line between the first two of these points is

$$\frac{109,000 - 100,000}{1 - 0} = 9000$$

whereas the slope of the line between the second and third points is

$$\frac{118,810 - 109,000}{2 - 1} = 9810$$

Since the rate of change from point to point is not constant, the curve that goes through them cannot be a straight line. A similar computation takes care of B_3.

6.47

This is an important example that deserves some time and class discussion. It forms the intuitive basis for how e (the natural base of logarithms) works. In the rest of this section, e will be used pretty much as a magic number that underlies the e^x function of calculators, but students should have some feeling for what this function does and when it is appropriate to use it.

Some students might suggest a more efficient strategy for answering this better deal question than the one which is about to appear in the text. For instance, they might say, "Compute the $12\frac{3}{4}\%$ simple interest and the 12% interest compounded very often, and compare the answers." However, the slightly more leisurely strategy used here has the added benefit of illustrating how increasingly frequent compounding does not result in unlimited growth.

Published by IT'S ABOUT TIME, Inc. © 2000 MATHconx, LLC

One way to approach this investment problem is to try different compounding periods for the 12% rate and, in each case, compute the total amount of money you would have at the end of the year. Then you could compare these results with those of your investment at $12\frac{3}{4}$% simple interest, which is

$$1.1275 \cdot \$10,000 = \$11,275$$

Display 6.40 provides a way to keep track of what you find.

Total Amount After 1 Year at 12%			
compounded...	function	$n =$	amount
yearly	$A_y(n) = 1.12^n \cdot \$10,000$	1	
quarterly	$A_q(n) = 1.03^n \cdot \$10,000$	4	
monthly	$A_m(n) =$		
weekly	$A_w(n) = (1 + \underline{\quad})^n \cdot \$10,000$		
daily	$A_d(n) =$		

Display 6.40

6.48

Make a copy of Display 6.40 to fill in as you answer these questions. Parts of the first two lines are already done for you. (Use your calculator to do the computations.)

1. A_y is the function for 12% interest compounded yearly. Since the total time is only one year, $n = 1$ in this case. Compute and fill in the total amount you would have at the end of the year.

2. A_q is the function for 12% interest compounded quarterly. Explain why 1.03 instead of 1.12 appears in this formula, and why $n = 4$. Then compute and fill in the total amount you would have at the end of the year.

3. What does A_m stand for? Fill in its formula. What is n in this case? Compute and fill in the total amount you would have at the end of the year.

4. What does A_w stand for? Fill in the missing part of the formula, then complete this row of the table.

5. What does A_d stand for? Complete this row of the table.

Published by IT'S ABOUT TIME, Inc. © 2000 MATHconx, LLC

6.48

A completed copy of Display 6.40 appears in Display 6.21T. These questions are well suited to small group work. Students should look back at the early part of this section for examples of how similar computations were handled.

Total Amount After 1 Year at 12%			
compounded...	function	$n =$	amount
annually	$A_y(n) = 1.12^n \cdot \$10{,}000$	1	$11,200.00
quarterly	$A_q(n) = 1.03^n \cdot \$10{,}000$	4	$11,255.09
monthly	$A_m(n) = 1.01^n \cdot \$10{,}000$	12	$11,268.25
weekly	$A_w(n) = (1 + \frac{0.12}{52})^n \cdot \$10{,}000$	52	$11,273.41
daily	$A_d(n) = (1 + \frac{0.12}{365})^n \cdot \$10{,}000$	365	$11,274.75

Display 6.21T

1. $11,200.00 as shown in the completed table.

2. You must divide the *annual* interest rate of 0.12 by 4 to get the quarterly interest rate. The result, 0.03, is added to 1 to account for interest *and* principal. See the explanation right after Display 6.37 in the student text. $n = 4$ because there are 4 quarters in a year.

3. A_m is the function for 12% interest compounded monthly. The monthly interest rate is 0.01.

4. A_w is the function for 12% interest compounded weekly. The missing part of the formula is the weekly interest rate, which is $\frac{0.12}{52}$.

5. A_d is the function for 12% interest compounded daily.

NOTES

6. Explain how to find the total amount at the end of the year if the 12% interest were compounded every hour. Don't compute the exact amount, but estimate about how much it would be. Do you think finding the exact answer to this question would be worth the effort? Why or why not?

As you filled in Display 6.40, did you notice how the differences between the total amounts in the last column kept shrinking as the compounding periods got shorter? Look again at your figures for that column. Notice that, at the end of 1 year,

A_q is about \$55.00 larger than A_y ;
A_m is about \$13.00 larger than A_q ;
A_w is about \$5.00 larger than A_m ;
A_d is about \$1.35 larger than A_w .

Even if we compounded every hour or every minute, the total amount at the end of the year wouldn't get much bigger than the amount you found using A_d. In fact, this compounding process is limited by an exponential function that describes something called "continuous compounding." Continuous compounding is a lot like compounding every second of every minute of every day.

This limiting function depends on a very special number called *e*. Exponential functions involving *e* are so useful that many calculators have a special key for them, labeled e^x. The story of where this number *e* comes from and *why* it works the way it does will have to wait until you have learned some more mathematics. However, your graphing calculator makes it easy to see *how* it works for growth functions. Here's how to use this function key to settle the simple vs. compound interest question we've been working on.

For \$10,000 and an annual interest rate of 12%, the amount resulting from continuous compounding is given by

$$A(n) = e^{0.12n} \cdot \$10,000$$

where *n* is the number of years. To see what happens at the end of 1 year, just substitute 1 for *n*. Press the e^x key on your calculator and fill out the rest of the formula like this.

e^(0.12)∗10000

6. You would have to find the hourly interest rate, which is 0.12 divided by the number of hours in a year. Then 1 + this number would have to be raised to the power of the number of hours in the year. Since the difference in total amount between weekly and daily compounding is only $1.34 and the total differences seem to be shrinking each time, the total amount for hourly compounding should be less than $1 more than the amount for daily compounding. In terms of money, finding an exact answer probably is not worth the effort. However, since the daily rate is only 25 cents less than the $12\frac{3}{4}\%$ simple interest amount, it might be worth the effort to satisfy our curiosity about whether or not we actually have a larger amount. Students who like this sort of challenge might compute the actual amount on their calculators. The exact total is $11,274.96, only 21 cents more than the daily compounding amount.

Note that the month by month comparisons of the various possible interest rates make an ideal spreadsheet or calculator list exercise. Compounding can be done recursively with a simple interest formula for a single time period repeated down the column.

NOTES

Chapter 6

6.5 Growth Functions

This is the largest amount you can possibly get from a 12% rate in 1 year, no matter how often the interest is compounded. The $12\frac{3}{4}\%$ simple interest offer was better (by about 3 cents)!

6.49

1. What if you invest your $10,000 for two years? Which is better—$12\frac{3}{4}\%$ simple interest or 12% compounded continuously? How much better?

2. How can you get your calculator to approximate the value of e?

The example we just did illustrates the general form of continuous compounding functions. If you know the interest rate r and the principal P (the original deposit amount), then the amount of money you end up with depends on the number of years n you let it grow. The formula for such a function is

$$A(n) = e^{\,r \cdot n}\, P$$

Continuous compounding applies to many things besides money. It is the key to describing the growth of large groups of people, mice, bacteria, or any species that reproduces itself. As an example of this, let us look at world population.

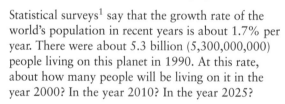

Statistical surveys[1] say that the growth rate of the world's population in recent years is about 1.7% per year. There were about 5.3 billion (5,300,000,000) people living on this planet in 1990. At this rate, about how many people will be living on it in the year 2000? In the year 2010? In the year 2025?

Unlike bank accounts, the compounding of population growth does not take place annually or quarterly on some special day. It's going on all the time. Every second of every hour, many people are being born and many others are dying. This means that the growth rate, the overall effect of these births and deaths, can be viewed as a continuous process. To answer these questions, then, we can use a continuous compounding function. In this case, r stands for the growth rate and P stands for the original population.

$$A(n) = e^{\,r \cdot n}\, P$$

$$A(n) = e^{.017n} \cdot 5,300,000,000$$

---

[1] The population growth rates in this section are taken from *Atlas of the Environment*, Prentice Hall Press, 1990.

394

Published by IT'S ABOUT TIME, Inc. © 2000 MATHconx, LLC

6.49

1. $12\frac{3}{4}\%$ simple interest for 2 years yields a total of \$12,550. The total for 12% compounded continuously is given by e^(0.12∗2)∗10000 = \$12,712.49, which is \$162.49 better.

2. This question is not essential to the flow of the section, but it is natural to ask and easy to answer. Moreover, it prompts students to recall that anything raised to the power 1 is itself. Entering e^(1) yields 2.718281828. This answer is only approximate; the actual number *e* is irrational, so its decimal expression is infinite and nonrepeating.

NOTES

Chapter 6

Now the questions are easy to answer. To find the approximate world population in the year 2000, which is 10 years after 1990, we just compute $A(10)$.

$$A(10) = e^{.017 \cdot 10} \cdot 5{,}300{,}000{,}000$$

1. **Do it.** Use your calculator to compute $A(10)$.

2. If you want to find the population in the year 2010, what n should you use? Write the formula for that case, then use it to compute the approximate world population in 2010. About how much of this increase over the year 2000 is the effect of compounding? Explain.

3. Compute the approximate world population in the year 2025.

4. Enter the function $A(n)$ into your graphing calculator. Then graph it for the years 1990 to 2050. As you do this, answer these questions.

   (a) What key must you use for n when you enter the formula?

   (b) Use 5.3 for P. What unit of measure will your answer be in?

   (c) Proper WINDOW settings are important for getting a useful picture. Why is setting X from 0 to 60 reasonable? What does it mean?

   (d) Why is 5 a reasonable minimum for Y? What does this 5 represent? What is a reasonable maximum for Y?

5. Now evaluate your function for the years 2000, 2010, 2030, and 2050. (The first two of these should agree with answers you got before.)

Not all countries have the same population growth rate. In recent years, the rate in the United States has been about 0.9% per year. The 1990 census said that the U.S. population at that time was about 249 million.

6.51

1. Write a formula for a function U that gives the U.S. population n years after 1990, assuming the same annual growth rate.

395

Published by IT'S ABOUT TIME, Inc. © 2000 MATHconx, LLC

6.50

These largely computational questions not only reinforce the ideas just presented, but also give students practice with the calculator and with such routine things as specifying the correct order of operations, rounding large numbers, using the decimal equivalents of percents, etc.

1. $A(10)$ is approximately 6.3 billion people. The calculator will give you the "exact" number 6,282,115,712, but the digits after the first two are meaningless because there were only two significant digits in the initial population number.

2. $A(20) = e^{0.017 \cdot 20} \cdot 5.3$ (billion) = approximately 7.4 billion people. The effect of the compounding is about 0.1 billion (that's 100 million) more people. In the decade between 1990 and 2000, the population grew by about 1 billion; in the decade between 2000 and 2010, it grew by about 1.1 billion.

3. $A(35) = e^{0.017 \cdot 35} \cdot 5.3 =$ approximately 9.6 billion people.

4. (a) You will have to use the variable key, which is X,T,θ on the TI-82 and X,T,θ,n on the TI-83.
   (b) The answer will be in billions of people.
   (c) That's the span of years from 1990 (the starting year) to 2050.
   (d) Ymin=5 represents 5 (billion) people, a reasonable minimum because there were actually 5.3 billion people in 1990, the starting year. A reasonable maximum can be any number close to where you think the population might be in 2050; Ymax=15 (billion people) will do, for instance.

5. Approximate values: $A(10) =$ 6.3 billion; $A(20) =$ 7.4 billion; $A(40) =$ 10.5 billion; $A(60) =$ 14.7 billion.

6.51

These questions are deliberately phrased a little more tersely than the previous ones because we expect students to discuss with each other how to go about answering them.

1. $A(n) = e^{0.009n} \cdot 249$, with the answer in millions of people.

2. Use the function U to compute the approximate U.S. population in the years 2000, 2025, and 2050.

3. At this rate of growth, how many years will it take the U.S. population to double? In what year will that occur? Explain how you found your answers.

Problem Set: 6.5

1. You just received a brand new Prestige Platinum credit card. You are allowed to charge up to $10,000, and you don't have to make any payments for an entire year. However, the annual interest rate on the unpaid amount is 24%, compounded monthly. You buy a new motorcycle for $8,000 and charge it to your Prestige Platinum card.

   (a) If you don't charge anything else and don't make any payments for a year, how much do you owe at the end of that time? Explain how you found your answer.

   (b) If you were charged simple interest at the rate of 24%, how much would you owe? Which amount is more, this one or your answer to part (a)? How much more? Explain why you think your answer is reasonable.

2. Make a table just like Display 6.40, except that the time period is 2 years. Use the same interest rate, 12%. What is the least simple interest rate (rounded up to the nearest quarter-percent) that would be a better deal than any of these compounding arrangements for the two year period? Justify your answer.

3. Make a table just like Display 6.40, except that the annual interest rate is 16%. Add on a row at the bottom, in which you put the continuous compounding function that limits all the compounding functions above it. Compute the total amount you get using this continuous compounding function.

4. A local bank recently advertised a CD (Certificate of Deposit) at an annual interest rate of 6%, compounded monthly. They claim that it has an effective annual yield of 6.17%.

   (a) A CD of this type was purchased for $1,000. Compute its value at the end of 1 year and at the end of 5 years.

   (b) What do you think effective annual yield means? Explain.

   (c) This same bank advertises that its Access Account has an interest rate of 3.20%, compounded daily. What is

2. $U(10) = 272$ million; $U(35) = 341$ million; $U(60) = 427$ million.

3. A little ingenuity is required to handle this question efficiently. Perhaps the easiest way is to enter the function U into the graphing calculator, and then TRACE its graph until the y-value is about 498 (million). This occurs about 77 years after 1990, in 2067.

Problem Set: 6.5

1. (a) The monthly interest rate is 2%, so the amount owed is $1.02^{12} \cdot \$8,000$, which equals $10,145.93.
    (b) The total amount owed at the 24% simple interest rate is $1.24 \cdot \$8,000$, which equals $9,920.00. The answer to part (a) is $225.93 more, as you would expect, because compounding keeps adding to the amount on which the interest is computed.

2. See Display 6.22T. If the $12\frac{3}{4}\%$ rate were just compounded annually, it would be better once again. However, when it is used as simple interest, the total amount would be only $12,550, which is far less. For simple interest, each additional quarter-percent adds $25 a year, so $13\frac{3}{4}\%$ is the least simple interest amount that is a better deal.

Total Amount After 2 Years at 12%			
compounded...	function	$n =$	amount
annually	$A_y(n) = 1.12^n \cdot \$10,000$	2	$12,544.00
quarterly	$A_q(n) = 1.03^n \cdot \$10,000$	8	$12,667.70
monthly	$A_m(n) = 1.01^n \cdot \$10,000$	24	$12,697.35
weekly	$A_w(n) = (1 + \frac{0.12}{52})^n \cdot \$10,000$	104	$12,708.98
daily	$A_d(n) = (1 + \frac{0.12}{365})^n \cdot \$10,000$	730	$12,711.99

Display 6.22T

3. See Display 6.23T.

Total Amount After 1 Year at 16%			
compounded...	function	$n =$	amount
annually	$A_y(n) = 1.16^n \cdot \$10,000$	1	$11,600.00
quarterly	$A_q(n) = 1.04^n \cdot \$10,000$	4	$11,698.59
monthly	$A_m(n) = (1 + \frac{0.16}{12})^n \cdot \$10,000$	12	$11,722.71
weekly	$A_w(n) = (1 + \frac{0.16}{52})^n \cdot \$10,000$	52	$11,732.23
daily	$A_d(n) = (1 + \frac{0.16}{365})^n \cdot \$10,000$	365	$11,734.70
continuously	$A_c(n) = e^{0.16n} \cdot \$10,000$	1 yr.	$11,735.11

Display 6.23T

the effective annual yield of this account? Explain how you found your answer.

(d) Find a bank in your neighborhood (or a bank ad in your local paper) that advertises the interest rate and the effective annual yield of an account. Write down the name of the bank and the description of the account. Then check the bank's claim by computing the effective annual yield of the account. Write a short explanation of your work.

5. In recent years, the annual population growth rate in China has been about 1.4%. *The World Almanac* says that there were about 1.151 billion people in China in 1991.

(a) Write a formula for a function C that gives the population of China n years after 1991, assuming the same growth rate. (Design your function to give the answer in millions of people.)

(b) Use the function C to compute the approximate population of China in the years 2000, 2025, and 2050.

(c) Put the formula for C into your graphing calculator. Then graph it, setting the window values like this: X from 0 to 60 with a scale of 10; Y from 800 to 2800 with a scale of 500.

(d) At this rate of growth, how many years will it take the population of China to double? In what year will that occur? Explain how you found your answers.

(Keep this function C in your calculator. You will need it for problem 7.)

6. In recent years, the annual population growth rate in India has been about 2.1%. *The World Almanac* says that there were about 866 million people in India in 1991.

(a) Write a formula for a function I that gives the population of India n years after 1991, assuming the same growth rate. (Design your function to give the answer in millions of people.)

(b) Use the function I to compute the approximate population of India in the years 2000, 2025, and 2050.

Published by IT'S ABOUT TIME, Inc. © 2000 MATHconx, LLC

4. (a) $1,061.68; $1,348.85.
    (b) The effective annual yield is the rate of interest you get in one year, expressed as if it were simple interest. For instance, in part (a), the interest on $1,000 is $61.68, which is 6.17% of $1000.
    (c) If we compute the interest for one year on a $100 deposit, we will get the effective annual yield right away

    $$(1 + \frac{0.032}{365})^{365} \cdot \$100 = \$103.25$$

    The interest is $3.25 on a $100 deposit, which is equivalent to a simple interest rate of 3.25%. This is the effective annual yield.

5. (a) $C(n) = e^{.014n} \cdot 1151$ millions of people.
    (b) $C(9) = 1306$ million; $C(34) = 1853$ million; $C(59) = 2629$ million.
    (d) TRACE can be used to find where the y-value of this function is approximately 2302 million. This occurs 49 years after 1991, in the year 2040.

6. (a) $I(n) = e^{.021n} \cdot 866$ millions of people.
    (b) $I(9) = 1046$ million; $I(34) = 1768$ million; $I(59) = 2990$ million.

NOTES

....

....

....

....

....

....

....

....

....

....

....

Chapter 6

(c) Put the formula for *I* into your graphing calculator. Then graph it, setting the WINDOW values like this: X from 0 to 60 with a scale of 10; Y from 800 to 2800 with a scale of 500.

(d) At this rate of growth, how many years will it take the population of India to double? In what year will that occur? Explain how you found your answers.

(Keep this function *I* in your calculator. You will need it for problem 7.)

7. If you did problems 5 and 6 above, display the graphs of both the functions *C* and *I* on the same set of axes. Where (approximately) do these two curves intersect? What do the coordinates of the intersection point tell us about the populations of these two countries?

8. In recent years, the annual population growth rate in Kenya has been about 4%. At that rate of growth, how many years will it take for the population of Kenya to double? Explain your answer.

Published by IT'S ABOUT TIME, Inc. © 2000 MATHconx, LLC

(d) TRACE can be used to find where the y-value of this function is approximately 1732 million. This occurs 33 years after 1991, in the year 2024.

7. The curves cross approximately at the point (40.6, 2033.2). This tells us that if these rates of growth do not change, about 40.6 years after 1991— sometime in the year 2031—the populations of India and China will be equal; each country will have about 2033.2 million people in it. Note that the point of intersection can be found on a TI-82 (TI-83) graphing calculator by using CALC menu and selecting intersect.

8. This might be a good problem for group discussion. Note that the current population of Kenya is *not* given; it is not needed. The students must come to see that the solution hinges on finding the n for which $e^{0.04n} = 2$. Once they see this, it is a relatively simple matter to put this function into the graphing calculator and trace it. Of course, appropriate WINDOW settings will have to be chosen; X from 0 to 30 or so, and Y from 1 to 2 would be good guesses at such settings. The population doubles in about 17.4 years.

NOTES

6.6 Links in a Chain: Composition of Functions

Two commonsense ideas make functions a powerful mathematical tool.

1. What "comes out" of a function is completely controlled by what "goes in."

2. Complicated processes often can be broken down into or built up from very simple functions.

The second of these ideas is the topic of this section. It is an example of *analysis*, the process of separating something into simpler parts so that it can be better understood. Chemical analysis, for example, examines a thing by trying to discover which (chemical) elements it is made of and how much of each element it contains. Chemicals that are not the basic elements are called *compounds* because they are put together from the elements. When you study chemistry, one of the first things you come across is the "periodic table." This is a way of organizing the chemical elements into groupings and patterns so that they might be better understood when they appear in compounds.

In many uses of mathematics we do a similar kind of analysis. If there is a process in which output depends on input, we try to describe it as a function. (This is the abstraction step.) Then we try to break this function into simpler functions so that, by applying each simpler function in turn, we end up with the same result as we get from the original function.

Here's an example of how a function can be broken into simpler functions. This one doesn't come from mathematics; it's from a newspaper cartoon of many years ago. Display 6.41 shows the input and output of cartoonist Rube Goldberg's bottle opener. It begins by feeding an elephant a bag of peanuts and ends by pulling the cork from the bottle. If we believe Rube Goldberg, this is a function. Pulling the cork from a bottle depends on feeding the elephant a bag of peanuts. Each time you put a bag of peanuts in, a cork comes out. But how does it work?

Learning Outcomes

After studying this section, you will be able to:

Describe function composition as a followed-by process;

Identify function composition in real world situations;

Construct the composite of two functions, and describe it in words and by an algebraic formula.

Thinking Tip

Break things into simpler parts. You get better understanding and control of a concept if you find how it can be built up from simpler ideas.

Published by IT'S ABOUT TIME, Inc. © 2000 MATHconx, LLC

6.6 Links in a Chain: Composition of Functions

399

6.6 Links in a Chain: Composition of Functions

The main idea of this section is function composition. Much of the power of the function concept stems from the ability to build complex processes out of simple ones by composition. Indeed, much of modern technology, from computer programming to spreadsheet structures to factory assembly lines, is founded on the ability to string together a series of predictable steps.

Chapter 6

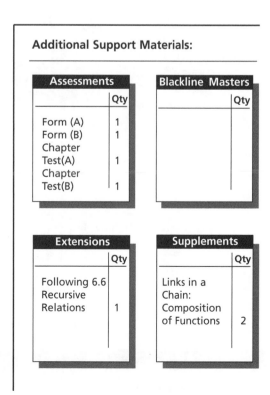

Additional Support Materials:

Assessments	Qty
Form (A)	1
Form (B)	1
Chapter Test(A)	1
Chapter Test(B)	1

Blackline Masters	Qty

Extensions	Qty
Following 6.6 Recursive Relations	1

Supplements	Qty
Links in a Chain: Composition of Functions	2

Display 6.41

The steps that go from the elephant to the bottle are shown in Display 6.42, along with the inventor's explanation of how they work. The output of the first step is the falling spike, which becomes the input of the second step. The output of the second step is the exploding balloon, which becomes the input of the third step.

Elephant (A) eats peanuts (B) — as bag gets lighter weight (C) drops and spike (D) punctures balloon (E) — explosion scares monkey (F) — his hat (G) flies off and releases hook (H), causing spring (I) to pull string (J) which tilts tennis racket (K) — racket hits ball (L), making it spin around on attached string, thereby screwing corkscrew into cork (M) — ball hits sleeping dog (N) who jumps and pulls cork out of bottle with string (O) — my how simple!

RUBE GOLDBERG™ and © property of Rube Goldberg Inc. Distributed by United Media. Used with permission.

Display 6.42

6.52

1. What is the output of the third step of the bottle opener?

2. What are the input and the output of the fourth step?

3. Describe the input and the output of each step from the fifth one to the end of the process (when the cork is pulled).

PuPublished by IT'S ABOUT TIME, Inc. © 2000 MATHconx, LLC

400

6.52

There can be some variation in these answers, depending on how students see the steps working. There is no need to be very fussy about precision here, nor to spend a lot of time on these questions. The main idea is for students to see a sequence of steps in which the output of each becomes the input of the next. They may get the idea just fine from questions 1 and 2, in which case you might want to skip question 3 entirely. Here are some reasonable, but not unique answers to these questions.

1. The monkey's hat flies off.

2. 4th step: input is flying hat; output is released hook.

3. 5th step: input is released hook; output is pulled string.
   6th step: input is pulled string; output is tilted tennis racquet.
   7th step: input is tilted tennis racquet; output is spinning ball and corkscrew device. This step is tricky; it requires a little compromise in the abstraction process. To preserve the function idea, you can only have one output. The description suggests two here, but they can be regarded as a single result if you focus on the spinning device, not on the ball and the corkscrew as separate items.
   8th step: input is spinning ball and corkscrew device; output is surprised dog.
   9th step: input is surprised dog; output is pulled cork.

NOTES

_____

_____

_____

_____

_____

_____

_____

_____

Chapter 6

The process of following one function by another, so that the images from the first function are in the domain of the second, is called **function composition**. The function that results from this putting together process is called the **composite** of the original functions.

About Words

In English, *to compose* something means to put it together or make it up (from pieces). A *composer* of a song or a symphony doesn't make up the sounds, but *puts them together* in a creative, artistic way. *Function composition* means putting together two or more functions to create a single function.

The composite of a function f followed by a function g is usually denoted by the symbol $g \circ f$. That seems backwards, doesn't it? It's not, if you remember how images of functions are symbolized. If we start with some x and apply f first, we get $f(x)$. Now, if we apply g to that, we get $g(f(x))$. That is,

$$(g \circ f)(x) = g(f(x))$$

Display 6.43 shows an example of this process. It starts with a function f from $\{a, b, c, d\}$ to $\{1, 2, 3, 4\}$ and continues with a function g from $\{1, 2, 3, 4\}$ to $\{*, \$, \#\}$. The composite function $g \circ f$ goes from $\{a, b, c, d\}$ to $\{*, \$, \#\}$.

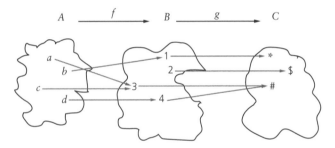

Display 6.43

The composite function $g \circ f$ of Display 6.43 goes from set A to set C. Copy and complete this listing of values for $g \circ f$. The first row is done for you.

6.53

$(g \circ f)(a) = g(f(a)) = g(3) = \#$

$(g \circ f)(b) = g(f(b)) = g(\_) = \_\_$

$(g \circ f)(c) = \_\_\_\_\_ = \_\_\_ = \_$

$(g \circ f)(d) = \_\_\_\_\_ = \_\_\_ = \_$

When functions are written as formulas, their composite doesn't have to be described one element at a time. You can use algebra to do it all at once. Here is an example. Suppose you want the composite of the "add 3" function, $f(x) = x + 3$, and the "squaring" function, $g(x) = x^2$. If you want to use f first, then g, you're saying "add 3 to the number, then square the

Published by IT'S ABOUT TIME, Inc. © 2000 MATHconx, LLC

401

6.53

$$(g \circ f)(a) = g(f(a)) = g(3) = \#$$
$$(g \circ f)(b) = g(f(b)) = g(1) = *$$
$$(g \circ f)(c) = g(f(c)) = g(3) = \#$$
$$(g \circ f)(d) = g(f(d)) = g(4) = \#$$

NOTES

Chapter 6

result." (Of course, "the number" can be any number in the domain of *f*.) We say all of this very easily with algebra.

$(g \circ f)(x) = g(f(x))$ Do *f* first, then do *g* to get the result.

$\qquad = g(x + 3)$ *f* adds 3 to any number.

$\qquad = (x + 3)^2$ *g* squares any number.

Thus, $(g \circ f)(x) = (x + 3)^2$. For instance,
$(g \circ f)(5) = g(5 + 3) = 8^2 = 64$.

6.54

Let *f* and *g* be the two functions just described.

1. Calculate $(g \circ f)(4)$ and $(g \circ f)(-4)$.

2. Write an algebraic formula for $(f \circ g)(x)$. Are the functions $g \circ f$ and $f \circ g$ equal? Why or why not?

Now think of two other functions, *h* and *j*, defined by the formulas

$$h(x) = 2x \quad \text{and} \quad j(x) = 5 - x$$

3. Describe in words what *h* and *j* do to a number.

4. Write formulas to describe the composite functions $h \circ j$ and $j \circ h$.

5. Calculate $(h \circ j)(7)$ and $(j \circ h)(7)$.

6. Are the two composite functions $h \circ j$ and $j \circ h$ equal? Why or why not?

Here is an example that shows how composition of functions often occurs in business. Imagine yourself in this situation.

(6.55) Your rock band has just recorded a *great* album! By careful planning and hard work, you were able to make a master tape for $20,000 (of your own money). A small record company has offered you a contract for producing and marketing your album as a CD. There's a lot of legal language, but the offer boils down to the following.

1. The company will market the CD at a list price of $15.

2. Your band will be paid 10% of the net amount that the company receives for the sale of your album, after retailer and distributor discounts. (Your 10% is called a *royalty*.)

402

Published by IT'S ABOUT TIME, Inc. © 2000 MATHconx, LLC

6.54

These questions reinforce the notation and terminology of function composition in an algebraic setting. They also illustrate the noncommutativity of the composition process.

1. $(g \circ f)(4) = 49$; $(g \circ f)(-4) = 1$

2. $(f \circ g)(x) = f(g(x)) = f(x^2) = x^2 + 3$. No, they are not equal. To justify this (from the definition of equal functions), students need to come up with a number that has different images under $f \circ g$ and $g \circ f$. Almost any number works.

3. h doubles the number; j subtracts the number from 5.

4. $(h \circ j)(x) = h(j(x)) = h(5 - x) = 2(5 - x)$;
   $(j \circ h)(x) = j(h(x)) = j(2x) = 5 - 2x$

5. $(h \circ j)(7) = -4$; $(j \circ h)(7) = -9$

6. No, they are not equal. The previous part is an example of a number (a domain element) that has different images under the two composite functions.

6.55

This is a somewhat simplified, but essentially typical description of a retail marketing arrangement for recordings, books, and the like. It begins a long, detailed example in which function composition is discussed relatively late. However, time spent on the details of this example provides several additional payoffs.

- This realistic business setting is quite similar to what will face any students who try to market anything on their own.

- It gives students practice with some basic arithmetic skills—percents, estimation, roundoff, etc.

- It reminds them of how to use spreadsheets or calculator lists to handle repetitive and/or comparative calculations.

- It exhibits the use of some linear functions, expressed both algebraically and graphically, in a real world situation.

It would be reasonable to spend a full class on this example before continuing with the development of function composition.

Chapter 6

3. Each month you will receive a statement showing the number of CDs sold and your total royalty amount for that month.

It sure is exciting to be offered a contract! You don't exactly understand all the technical words in this offer, but the company assures you that it is "a standard recording contract." You sign it right away and wait for the money to start rolling in.

While you're waiting, you dream about the "big bucks" your band will get in royalties. Let's see...

> 1000 CDs at $15 each is $15,000
> 2000 CDs at $15 each is $30,000

How about making a table with your calculator to get a better idea of the money involved?

Clear the lists on your graphing calculator. We're going to use several lists in this example, in order. We'll call the first one L1, the second one L2, and so on, which is probably what your calculator calls them, too. We'll use *n* to represent the number of CD's sold.

6.56

1. In L1, list some possible values for *n*, from 500 to 10,000 in steps of 500: that is, list 500, 1000, 1500,... , 10,000. (Do you know how to do this automatically, without putting in each amount by hand? If not, find out.)

2. In L2, list the amount of money (in dollars) collected by the stores for these sales (without sales tax). This amount is usually called "gross sales." What formula will make L2 list the gross sales amount for each number of CDs in L3? Enter it. At this point, your calculator lists should look something like Display 6.44.

3. Can you compute how much you should be paid in royalties from these various sales figures? If you can, do it in L3, then explain your thinking. If you can't compute the royalty amount, explain what extra information you need.

403

6.56

The main purpose of this example extends beyond calculators or spreadsheets to functions and their composition. Therefore, it is highly directed. It is important for the later development that students set up their lists in the form described.

1. You might have to help the students here. Most graphing calculators have an automatic sequence generator. For instance, from the LIST menu of the TI-82 (TI-83) calculators, choose seq(. This requires five pieces of information to generate a sequence: formula, variable, first variable value, last variable value, increment. In this case, you could enter

    seq(500X,X,1,20,1)→L1

    to generate the sequence and store it in the first list. The X here is the variable key. Another way to enter and store this same sequence of values is

    seq(X,X,500,10000,500)→L1

2. The formula is $15n$ because the retail price of a CD is $15. For TI-82 (TI-83) calculators, at the top of L2 enter 15∗L1.

3. This is a trap to keep students from just going through the arithmetic motions without connecting what they're doing to the real world. It is tempting to compute royalties at 10% of gross sales (or estimate that it would be a little less); however, this overlooks the effects of the retailer and distributor discounts, which are the two other pieces of information needed.

    Students who compute the royalty amount should somehow explain how they are handling the discounts. It may be that a student whose family is involved in retailing will have a feeling for this, but, even so, getting close to the correct amount will be mostly a matter of luck because the exact discount percentages (which will be specified shortly) could vary quite a bit and still be realistic. A good first guess would be less than half of the 10% figure. The nonmathematical lesson being set up here is "understand a contract before you sign it."

Chapter 6

L₁	L₂	L₃
500	7500	
1000	15,000	
1500	22,500	
⋮	⋮	
9500	142,500	
10,000	150,000	

Display 6.44

Display 6.44 represents a function. The amount of gross sales depends entirely on the number of CDs sold. In the language of this chapter, "gross sales" is the dependent variable and "number of CDs sold" is the independent variable. This technical language can be shortened by saying that the gross sales amount *is a function* of the number of CDs sold. We'll call this function g.

The formula for L2 suggests an easy way to write this function algebraically. If n is a particular number of CDs sold, then $g(n)$ is the gross sales amount for that number of CDs, and

$$g(n) = 15n$$

6.57

1. **Compute $g(800)$.**

2. **Compute $g(5114)$.**

3. **Suppose you knew that gross sales amounted to $127,365. How would you find the number of CDs sold? What is that number?**

Six months later, the album is on the market and your band gets its first royalty check. In the first month, 5114 CDs have been sold, but the check amount is only $3,451.95. There must be some mistake! You call the record company.

"There's no mistake," they say. "Your royalty is 10% of *net* sales, not of gross sales. It's all explained in the contract you signed."

• Back to the fine print in the contract.

• The retail stores get a 40% discount off the list price. That is, the wholesale price of the CD is 60% of its list price.

404

Published by IT'S ABOUT TIME, Inc. © 2000 MATHconx, LLC

6.57

This is a quick, routine exercise in using function notation. The computations may be done by hand or with a calculator. The last question suggests an inverse process.

1   $12,000.00

2. $76,710.00

3. Divide by 15, getting 8491 CDs.

NOTES

_____

Chapter 6

- The distributor gets a 25% discount off the wholesale price. The remaining 75% of the wholesale price is the net sales price.

- Your band's royalty is 10% of the net sales price.

Remembering what you learned in math class, you see that each of these three steps is a function.

- The wholesale amount is 60% of the gross sales amount. That is, if the gross sales amount is x, then the wholesale amount, $w(x)$, is found by

$$w(x) = 0.6x$$

The function w turns gross sales amounts into wholesale amounts.

- The net sales amount is 75% of the wholesale amount. That is, if the wholesale amount is x, then the net sales amount, $s(x)$, is found by

$$s(x) = 0.75x$$

The function s turns wholesale amounts into net sales amounts.

- The royalty is 10% of the net sales amount. That is, if the net sales amount is x, then the royalty, $r(x)$, is found by

$$r(x) = 0.1x$$

The function r turns net sales amounts into royalty amounts.

Each royalty amount, then, is an image of an image of an image of an image of n. Each amount depends on the amount from the step before. The lists of your calculator can illustrate this chain of functions. To see how, work through the following questions.

Published by IT'S ABOUT TIME, Inc. © 2000 MATHconx, LLC

NOTES

6.58

Recall that L1 in your calculator contains some sample numbers of CDs sold and L2 contains the corresponding gross sales amounts.

1. In L3, enter a formula to compute the wholesale amounts that correspond to the gross sales amounts in L2. What function does this formula represent?

2. The correspondence between L1 and L2 represents the gross sales function, *g*. What function does the correspondence between L1 and L3 represent? Write it as a formula, if you can.

3. In L4, enter a formula to compute the net sales amounts that correspond to the wholesale amounts in L3. What function does this formula represent?

4. What function does the correspondence between L1 and L4 represent? Write it as a formula, as simply as you can.

5. In L5, enter a formula to compute the royalty amounts that correspond to the net sales amounts in L4. What function does this formula represent?

6. What function does the correspondence between L1 and L5 represent? Write it as a formula, as simply as you can.

7. If 3500 CDs are sold, how much royalty money does your band get? What if 9000 CDs are sold? Explain how to read the answers from the calculator lists.

8. If 37,458 CDs are sold, how much royalty money does your band get? Explain how to get the answer *without* entering new data into your lists. (*Hint:* Look at your answer to part 6.)

Question 8 above shows that you don't really need the calculator lists to compute your band's royalty on the sale of a particular number of CDs. You only need the effect of the chain of functions represented by the lists. The four simpler functions—*g*, *w*, *s*, and *r*—are put together, one after another, to form the composite "royalty function"

$$r \circ (s \circ (w \circ g))$$

This way of using function composition is what makes electronic spreadsheets such powerful tools for handling numbers. Entire bookkeeping systems can be built up step by step from simple functions in this way.

406

Published by IT'S ABOUT TIME, Inc. © 2000 MATHconx, LLC

6.58

These questions illustrate function composition. They are good for small group work in class. The later questions in this set mimic the patterns of the earlier ones, gradually building up the composition process in stages. Thus, students who need help with the answers to 1 and 2 should see, by analogy, how to handle 3 and 4, and so on.

1. $0.6*L2$, which represents the function w.

2. This represents the composite function $w \circ g$, which can be written
$$(w \circ g)(n) = w(g(n)) = 0.6 \cdot (15n) = 9n$$

3. $0.75*L3$, which represents the function s.

4. This represents the composite function $s \circ (w \circ g)$, which can be written as follows.
$$(s \circ (w \circ g))(n) = s((w \circ g)(n)) = 0.75 \cdot 9n = 6.75n$$

5. $0.1*L4$, which represents the function r.

6. This represents the composite function $r \circ (s \circ (w \circ g))$, which can be written
$$r \circ ((s \circ (w \circ g)))(n) = r((s \circ (w \circ g))(n)) = 0.1 \cdot 6.75n = 0.675n$$

7. $2,362.50; $6,075.00. Find 3500 or 9000 in L1 and follow its images across the other lists until you get to L5.

8. The composite function formula of part 6 shows how to calculate the royalty amount from n, the number of CDs sold. In this instance, the royalty is $0.675 \cdot 37,458 = \$25,284.15$.

NOTES

Making spreadsheets is only one of many applications of function composition. Following one function by another to form a new function is one of the most useful, basic ideas in all of mathematics. It is useful in two ways.

- It lets us break down a complicated process into simpler steps. Since each step is easier to understand, the entire process becomes easier to use.

- It lets us combine a series of steps into a single function that can be used more efficiently than going through each step separately.

The royalty function described above is an example of combining steps into a single, more efficient function. The following questions ask you to break down a familiar process into simpler pieces.

The Celsius to Fahrenheit function F described in Section 6.4 was defined by the formula

$$F(x) = \frac{9}{5}x + 32$$

6.59

1. Write F as the composite of two simpler functions. Try out your answer by converting 20°C to Fahrenheit using your two step process. Compare your answer with what you get by using the original function F. (You should get the same thing.)

2. Does it matter which of your two functions is used first in forming the composite? Why or why not?

REFLECT

Function is one of the most basic, most important ideas in all of mathematics. This simple idea of an unambiguous way to get from one set to another is at the heart of many, many complex theories and powerful applications. In this chapter you have seen many different kinds of functions—sequences, step functions, linear functions, growth functions, and others. Some were defined by algebraic formulas, some came from diagrams, some were just described in words. In all these instances, the basic idea is the same: Given any "input" (domain) element, a function *always* relates it to *exactly one* "output" (range) element. Such relationships occur surprisingly often—in science, in business, in everyday life, almost anywhere you look. Recognizing them as functions is often the way to link the power of mathematics to the real world.

Published by IT'S ABOUT TIME, Inc. © 2000 MATHconx, LLC

6.59

1. This function can be broken down in a natural way into two separate steps, each of which is a function.

   (a) Multiply by $\frac{9}{5}$: $m(x) = \frac{9}{5}x$
   (b) Add 32: $a(x) = x + 32$

   Thus, $F = a \circ m$, as can be seen from this.

   $F(x) = (a \circ m)(x) = a(m(x)) = a(\frac{9}{5}x) = \frac{9}{5}x + 32$

   $F(20) = (a \circ m)(20) = a(m(20)) = a(\frac{9}{5} \cdot 20) = a(36) = 36 + 32 = 68° \text{ F}$

2. Yes, it matters. The composite function $m \circ a$ calls for addition of 32 first, then multiplication by $\frac{9}{5}$, which gives a different result. For example,

   $(m \circ a)(20) = m(a(20)) = m(20 + 32) = m(52) = \frac{9}{5} \cdot 52 = 93.6$

NOTES

Published by IT'S ABOUT TIME, Inc. © 2000 MATHconx, LLC

Chapter 6

Problem Set: 6.6

1. Determining the correct postage for a piece of mail is actually a composite of two functions:

    (i) finding the weight of the letter or package by using a scale, and

    (ii) matching the weight with a postage amount by using a chart or table of postage rates.

    Describe two other processes from everyday life that can be thought of as composite functions.

2. In each of these parts there are formulas for two functions, f and g, on the set of rational numbers. In each case,
    (i) find formulas for the functions $g \circ f$ and $f \circ g$, and
    (ii) use your formulas to compute $(g \circ f)(10)$ and $(f \circ g)(10)$.

    (a) $f(x) = 4x$ and $g(x) = x + 6$

    (b) $f(x) = x - 2$ and $g(x) = \frac{x}{4}$

    (c) $f(x) = {}^-3x$ and $g(x) = x + 5$

    (d) $f(x) = x^2$ and $g(x) = x - 1$

    (e) $f(x) = 0.5x$ and $g(x) = 2x$

    (f) $f(x) = x^2$ and $g(x) = x^3$

3. (a) A function f on the rational numbers is defined by the formula

    $$f(x) = 7x - 3$$

    Define two functions, g and h, such that $f = h \circ g$.

    (b) A function p on the rational numbers is defined by the formula

    $$p(x) = 5x^2 + 8$$

    Define three functions, q, r, and s, such that $p = s \circ (r \circ q)$.

4. A function p matches each integer with its opposite (the integer with the same absolute value, but the opposite sign). A function d matches each integer with its double.

    (a) Write formulas for the functions p and d.

    (b) Write a formula for the composite function $d \circ p$; then compute $(d \circ p)(15)$ and $(d \circ p)({}^-12)$.

    (c) Write a formula for the composite function $p \circ d$; then compute $(p \circ d)(15)$ and $(p \circ d)({}^-12)$.

    (d) Are these two composite functions equal? Why or why not?

Published by IT'S ABOUT TIME, Inc. © 2000 MATHconx, LLC

408

Problem Set: 6.6

Some of these exercises provide reinforcing echoes of topics seen in earlier chapters and earlier sections of this chapter. By viewing them from the perspective of composite functions, students may gain new insights into these "old" ideas.

2. (a) $(g \circ f)(x) = 4x + 6$; $(g \circ f)(10) = 46$
   $(f \circ g)(x) = 4(x + 6) = 4x + 24$; $(f \circ g)(10) = 64$

   (b) $(g \circ f)(x) = \dfrac{x - 2}{4}$; $(g \circ f)(10) = 2$
   $(f \circ g)(x) = \dfrac{x}{4} - 2$; $(f \circ g)(10) = 0.5$

   (c) $(g \circ f)(x) = -3x + 5$; $(g \circ f)(10) = -25$
   $(f \circ g)(x) = -3(x + 5) = -3x - 15$; $(f \circ g)(10) = -45$

   (d) $(g \circ f)(x) = x^2 - 1$; $(g \circ f)(10) = 99$
   $(f \circ g)(x) = (x - 1)^2$; $(f \circ g)(10) = 81$

   (e) $(g \circ f)(x) = 2(0.5x) = x$; $(g \circ f)(10) = 10$
   $(f \circ g)(x) = 0.5(2x) = x$; $(f \circ g)(10) = 10$

   (f) $(g \circ f)(x) = (x^2)^3 = x^6$; $(g \circ f)(10) = 1,000,000$
   $(f \circ g)(x) = (x^3)^2 = x^6$; $(g \circ f)(10) = 1,000,000$

3. An important thing to watch for here is that students compose their functions in the proper order. These can be done in more than one way; the solutions given here are in some sense the most obvious ones, but other correct solutions are just as good.
   (a) $g(x) = 7x$; $h(x) = x - 3$
   (b) $q(x) = x^2$; $r(x) = 5x$; $s(x) = x + 8$

4. Besides reinforcing the concept of function composition, this problem and the next give students some practice with handling signed numbers.
   (a) $p(x) = -x$; $d(x) = 2x$
   (b) $(d \circ p)(x) = 2(-x) = -2x$; $(d \circ p)(15) = -30$; $(d \circ p)(-12) = 24$
   (c) $(p \circ d)(x) = -2x$; $(p \circ d)(15) = -30$; $(p \circ d)(-12) = 24$
   (d) Yes; the formula, which is the same in parts (b) and (c), shows that any domain number is taken to the same image by both functions.

Chapter 6

5. A function p matches each integer with its opposite (the integer with the same absolute value, but the opposite sign). A function t matches each integer with the integer that is two greater than the integer.

    (a) Write formulas for the functions p and t.

    (b) Write a formula for the composite function $t \circ p$, then compute $(t \circ p)(15)$ and $(t \circ p)(-12)$.

    (c) Write a formula for the composite function $p \circ t$, then compute $(p \circ t)(15)$ and $(p \circ t)(-12)$.

    (d) Are these two composite functions equal? Why or why not?

6. Earlier in **MATH** *Connections*, you saw that equations for straight lines can be written in the form $y = mx + b$, where m is the slope and b is the y-intercept. These equations are actually functions of x. That is,

    $$f(x) = mx + b$$

    The letters m and b are constants here. That is, they stand for particular numbers.

    (a) Describe f as the composite of two functions—a slope function and an intercept function.

    (b) These two functions tell you two different things about the picture of the function. What does the slope function tell you about the picture? What does the intercept function tell you?

    (c) Does the order in which you compose these two functions matter? Why or why not?

5. (a) $p(x) = -x$; $t(x) = x + 2$
   (b) $(t \circ p)(x) = -x + 2$; $(t \circ p)(15) = -13$; $(t \circ p)(-12) = 14$
   (c) $(p \circ t)(x) = -(x + 2) = -x - 2$; $(p \circ t)(15) = -17$; $(p \circ t)(-10) = 10$
   (d) No; a domain number is taken to two different images by these two composite functions, as parts (b) and (c) illustrate.

6. (a) The slope function (call it s) is defined by $s(x) = mx$, where m is the slope; the intercept function (call it i) is defined by $i(x) = x + b$, where b is the y-intercept. $f = i \circ s$.
   (b) The slope function tells you the angle of inclination that the line makes with the x-axis. Slope is the ratio of rise-over-run.
       The intercept function tells you the point where the line intersects the y-axis.
   (c) Yes, the order matters; the function f does *not* equal $s \circ i$.

NOTES

Chapter 6

7. Display 6.8 describes a 6% sales tax function. This is actually a composite $r \circ p$ of two functions, a percentage function p and a rounding function r.

   (a) Explain in your own words how p and r work on the sales amounts from $0.01 to $1.00.

   (b) Using the upper part of Display 6.8 as a model, define a 7% sales tax function for all sales amounts from $0.01 to $1.00. Describe this tax function first as a composite of a percentage function and a rounding function; then make a table for it.

6% Sales Tax Schedule

Sale		Tax
From	To	
$0.01	$0.09	$0.00
0.10	0.16	0.01
0.17	0.33	0.02
0.34	0.50	0.03
0.51	0.66	0.04
0.67	0.83	0.05
0.84	1.00	0.06

The tax to be collected is the amount indicated for each dollar of the sale price plus the amount indicated above for any fraction of a dollar.

Top Part of Display 6.8

8. (a) Is function composition commutative? How would you convince someone that your answer is correct?

   (b) Is function composition associative? How would you convince someone that your answer is correct?

Published by IT'S ABOUT TIME, Inc. © 2000 MATHconx, LLC

7. (a) The function p just takes 6% of the sales amount. The function r rounds this percentage *up* to the next whole cent, except for the sales amounts from $0.01 through $0.09, where its value is 0.

   (b) A similar tax function for 7% would start with a function that takes 7% of the sale amount. This would be followed by a rounding function which, as in Display 6.8, would round each percentage up to the next whole cent. The only uncertain part is deciding which values to leave at 0 tax. Display 6.8 appears to use the $0.01 through $0.09 interval somewhat arbitrarily. If this interval or any smaller interval from $0.01 up were used, it would be consistent with the pattern suggested here. We choose in this answer to leave $0.01 through $0.07 untaxed, and round the noninteger tax amounts to the next higher cent. See Display 6.24T.

Sale		Tax
From	To	
$0.01	$0.07	0¢
0.08	0.14	1¢
0.15	0.28	2¢
0.29	0.42	3¢
0.43	0.57	4¢
0.58	0.71	5¢
0.72	0.85	6¢
0.86	1.00	7¢

Display 6.24T

8. (a) No. Several examples in this section illustrate that the order in which the functions are composed sometimes (in fact, usually) makes a difference.

   Note that it is important to beware of a common misunderstanding here. Commutativity is a property of the operation, not of a particular instance of its use. That is, it doesn't make sense to say that an operation is commutative "sometimes"; either it is or it isn't. In order for an operation to be commutative, the order of the two elements being combined must *never* affect the outcome. One case in which the order affects the outcome is enough to render the operation noncommutative.

   (b) Yes. It is fairly easy to see this intuitively, and a formal proof is not expected at this level. A reasonable justification might be an example or two, along with a few words indicating why the examples appear to be typical in some sense. With some students, you might goad them a bit by reminding them of the example in the section where commutativity appeared to work and asking them why they think their examples can be trusted. However, this might not be a profitable use of time for others.

Published by IT'S ABOUT TIME, Inc. © 2000 MATHconx, LLC

Chapter 6

NOTES

Chapter 6

Chapter 7

Chapter 7 Planning Guide

Chapter 7 Counting Beyond 1, 2, 3

Chapter 7 focuses on counting. It summarizes basic ideas, language, and notation for sets, introduces Venn diagrams and tree diagrams, and establishes the Fundamental Counting Principle, all in concrete, commonsense contexts. This lays the groundwork for the topics of discrete mathematics that appear in later chapters.

Assessments Form A (A)	Assessments Form B (B)	Blackline Masters
Quiz 7.1-7.2(A) Quiz 7.3(A) Quiz 7.4-7.5(A) Chapter Test(A)	Quiz 7.1-7.2(B) Quiz 7.3(B) Quiz 7.4-7.5(B) Chapter Test(B)	No Blackline Masters for this chapter

Extensions	Supplements for Chapter Sections	Test Banks
7.5 The Genetic Code Following 7.5 Counting Jeans	7.2 Sets: What to Count — 1 Supplement 7.3 Venn Diagrams: Counting With Pictures — 1 Supplement 7.5 The Fundamental Counting Principle — 1 Supplement	To be released

Pacing Range 3 weeks including Assessments

Teachers will need to adjust this guide to suit the needs of their own students. Not all classes will complete each chapter at the same pace. Flexibility — which accommodates different teaching styles, school schedules and school standards — is built into the curriculum.

Teacher Commentary is indexed to the student text by the numbers in the margins (under the icons or in circles). The first digit indicates the chapter — the numbers after the decimal indicate the sequential numbering of the comments within that unit. Example:

7.9

(7.37)

7.9

(7.37)

Student Pages in Teacher Edition   **Teacher Commentary Page**

Observations

Rosalie Griffin, Teacher
Crosby High School, CT

"In Chapter 7 students are presented with problems using many familiar contexts which helps to set the stage for group discussions. These then can lead to very good cooperative learning situations in which the students compare their answers and discuss the counting methods that they have discovered. I have also found that students of all levels enjoy the section on Venn Diagrams which is presented very well here. In fact, the counting problems covered in this section are frequently seen on the SATs and *Connections* students handle them with ease. In many traditional courses, there is very little coverage of Venn Diagrams."

Chapter 7

Michael Garcia
Sharing NASA's Explorations

Exploration of our solar system has reached a whole new level of activity. NASA has launched several new spacecraft to explore planets. Every day, discoveries and data flow back to Earth.

Michael Garcia is an educator who specializes in math, physics and chemistry. He works for the Jet Propulsion Laboratory in Pasadena, California. His job is to translate the new images and data returning to Earth into programs for schools. One program Michael's team has built is a simulation using actual images from the Mars Pathfinder. Students can "launch" their own robotic spacecraft to Mars and virtually explore it for themselves.

Michael explains how coding systems, data sets, and their corresponding visualizations and diagrams are basic to the creation of interactive products. "All computers use a binary coding system, 'machine language', to operate or compute," he explains. "To complete a task, a computer must run an algorithm. This is a sequence of steps where it translates data, or a series of data sets, into logical notation.

"Likewise, all data returned by spacecraft is binary, meaning ones and zeros," continues Michael. "Computers use binary words to make pictures. Viewing a picture, we often need to adjust the contrast or 'stretch' the image to see hidden details. Here's where we need to apply mathematical equations.

"Also, in our simulations, we often need to create images of the data and data sets. So we might use Venn diagrams. This is an easy way to see how two or more really complex data sets merge together or relate to each other. We might, for example, want to see what's happening between a planet's magnetic field and the Sun's solar wind."

Michael truly enjoys his work. "Every day I get to explore data that is being seen for the first time. Then I put it into a format that can be understood and used by many other people, everywhere."

412

Published by IT'S ABOUT TIME, Inc. © 2000 MATHconx, LLC

Chapter 7   Counting Beyond 1 - 2 - 3

The major purpose of this chapter is to get students thinking about counting problems and techniques for their solution. We have tried to accomplish this by using familiar contexts where counting plays a role. For example, the number of possible lottery tickets in certain states, the number of possible ZIP codes, and the number of possible license plates are contexts with which many students are familiar. The counting techniques of this section will be used in the following chapter on probability and in later work on statistics and more advanced probability.

Chapter 7

Counting Beyond 1, 2, 3

CHAPTER 7

7.1 A Need to Count

A type of puzzle that appears in many newspapers and magazines involves taking several letters and rearranging them to form meaningful words. Usually three, four or five letters are given. For example, one day the letters *mslie* appeared. By rearranging the letters one can form the words *miles*, *limes* and *slime*.

Carmen, a student at Newton School enjoys working with such puzzles. One day Carmen looks at the letters *iter* and writes the words

> *rite* (What does this word mean?)

and

> *tier* (What does this word mean?)

1. Can you find any words that Carmen missed? If you can, write them.

7.1

2. The next day, in the newspaper puzzle, Carmen finds the letters *opst* and forms two meaningful words. Do you think that Carmen missed any words? If yes, how many meaningful words can you form from the letters *opst*? Write them.

413

Published by IT'S ABOUT TIME, Inc. © 2000 MATHconx, LLC

7.1 A Need to Count

A purpose of this section is get students to see a need for counting techniques. In particular, even with the use of calculators and computers, one needs to have some idea of the number of operations involved—a counting process. Moreover, we live in a world of codes, such as bar codes at a supermarket, which involve a need to count. No counting techniques are given in this section, but the ideas will be revisited in later sections.

7.1

1. Students should find that Carmen missed the word **tire.**

2. Students should find the words **stop, pots, post, tops,** and **spot.**

Additional Support Materials:

Assessments	Qty
Form (A)	1
Form (B)	1

Blackline Masters	Qty

Extensions	Qty

Supplements	Qty

Chapter 7

7.1 A Need to Count

Carmen decides that from now on she will write out *all* arrangements of the given letters, whether they make sense or not. Then she will look at the list and decide which ones are meaningful. The following day, in the newspaper puzzle, she finds the letters *pto* and writes the list

pto opt top pot otp tpo

7.2

1. Which arrangements in the above list are meaningful words to you?

2. The following day Carmen finds four different letters given. She writes out a list of 20 arrangements and claims that she has now listed *all* arrangements of the four letters. Do you agree with Carmen? That is, are there exactly 20 different arrangements of four different letters? If you agree, justify your answer. If you do not agree, how many arrangements do you think you can find? Explain how you arrived at your answer.

3. How many possible arrangements of five different letters can be made? (*Hint:* How many arrangements can be formed from two different letters? From three different letters? From four different letters?)

Thinking Tip

Look for a pattern.

How many? This question is behind the need for counting. The space age and the information age have brought with them a need for more people to know more about counting. An example of such a need occurred in the early 1960's when a group of scientists put a program on a computer to solve a problem. The computer was able to perform 100,000 operations (additions, subtractions, multiplications, and divisions) per second. These people believed that a computer could quickly solve any problem that involved arithmetic. The scientists waited two weeks but no solution appeared. The scientists then analyzed the problem and found the number of operations needed to solve the problem was greater than 10^{18}. Then they found the time the computer would need to solve the problem. They were surprised! See if you are.

414

Published by IT'S ABOUT TIME, Inc. © 2000 MATHconx, LLC

7.2

1. The words **opt, top,** and **pot** should be meaningful words to students.

2. See what students have to say about the 20 different arrangements. There are 24 different arrangements of four different letters and students may work out an example to get this number.

3. In order to see a pattern, students should see that there are 2 arrangements of 2 different letters, 6 arrangements of 3 different letters and 24 arrangements of 4 different letters. See if students observe the pattern $6 = 3 \cdot 2$, $24 = 4 \cdot 6 = 4 \cdot 3 \cdot 2$ and conjecture that there are $5 \cdot 4 \cdot 3 \cdot 2 = 120$ arrangements of five different letters. Students should not get frustrated if they do not observe this pattern. Indeed, learning to see such patterns is the object of this chapter.

NOTES

Chapter 7

A computer performs 100,000 operations per second.

a
7.3

1. **How many operations can this computer perform in an hour?**

2. **How many operations can this computer perform in a day?**

3. **How many operations can this computer perform in a year?**

4. **Approximately how long will it take this computer to perform 10^{18} operations?**

Counting also plays an important role in making codes such as bar codes on items at a supermarket or ZIP codes on mail.

1. **What is a code?**

b
7.4

2. **What other codes are you aware of that people often use?**

The postal ZIP codes were originally designed as a five-digit national coding system which identifies each postal delivery area. It was designed to simplify the delivery of mail. The first digit of the five-digit code identifies one of 10 regions of the nation. The first three digits identify a major city or major distribution center. The full five digits identify an individual post office or an area within a city. (Note: Four more digits were later added that identify a post office box number or street.)

What is your postal ZIP code?

c
7.5

The idea of *coding,* as in postal ZIP codes, is an important one. For example, a certain school has 720 students. Each student is to receive a *computer access password (or code word)* consisting of one or more letters chosen from the 26 letters of the alphabet. In order to use a computer in the school, students must first press the letter or letters of their code word. Four students have the codes given below.

Name	Code
Richard	A
Mary	V
Sook	D
William	F

415

Have students solve this problem using a calculator. Be prepared to give help where necessary. For example, you might ask them "How many seconds in a minute?" or "How many minutes in an hour?"

1. The answer is $60 \times 60 \times 10^5$ or its equivalent.
$$60 \times 60 \times 10^5 = 360,000,000$$
"three hundred sixty million"

2. The answer is $24 \times 360,000,000$
or
$$8,640,000,000 = 864 \times 10^7$$

3. The answer is $365 \times 864 \times 10^7$
$$31,536 \times 10^8 = 3.1536 \times 10^{12}$$
or its equivalent.

4. The answer is obtained by dividing 10^{18} by 3.1536×10^{12}
or
$$\frac{10^{18}}{3.1536 \times 10^{12}} = \frac{10^6}{3.1536} = \frac{1,000,000}{3.1536} \approx 317,098 \; years$$

That is, it will take this computer more than *three hundred thousand years* to solve this problem.

1. Get ideas from students on what the word **code** means to them. According to *Webster's Dictionary*, a code is a system of symbols (as letters, numbers, or words) used to represent assigned and often secret meanings.

2. Students should come up with ideas such as license plates for cars, telephone numbers, social security numbers, MAC numbers, combinations for locks, etc.

Check your local ZIP code.

Chapter 7

Code words with one letter can only be applied to 26 students. Therefore, some students have code words that contain more than one letter. Four students have the code words given below.

Name	Code
Alice	CA
Martin	BD
Mineo	WW
Kim	DB

7.6

Do you think it is necessary that some students have more than two letters in their code word? Explain your answer. This is an example of a counting problem.

In 1877, Edison's phonograph played the nursery rhyme *"Mary Had A Little Lamb,"* after he had recorded it on cylinders made of tinfoil—the first reproduction of a human voice. The tinfoil cylinder was followed by the wax cylinder, the hard rubber disc, and the shellac disc. The first commercial phonograph was introduced about 1925. Commercial long play records (LP) arrived in 1948. However, it is necessary to handle these records very carefully if you do not want to lose the musical quality. In addition, the tracking of a needle in the grooves of these records causes wear. This wear, together with dirt, can produce noises not originally recorded resulting in unpleasants sounds. Many of these problems have disappeared with the modern compact disc (CD). Compact discs arrived in the early 1980's. A compact disc is read by a laser beam, so playing a compact disk does not produce any damage. Moreover, many errors which result from dirt, scratches, and mishandling can be corrected.

On a compact disc, music is stored using the digits 0 and 1, which are called **binary digits** or **bits** (each one is called a **bit**). Information about the music is contained in microscopic pits and flat areas on the surface of the disc. A 1 is represented as the beginning or end of a pit and a flat area represents a 0. A series of pits and flat areas is read by a laser beam from the center to the outside edge in a spiral fashion. As the laser beam focuses on the pits and flat areas, the changes in the reflected beam are sensed by electronic circuits which interpret the 1's and 0's and prepare the signal for human ears. In order to protect the pits against wear, a covering of transparent plastic is used.

7.6

Using one letter, 26 students can be covered. With exactly two letters $26 \cdot 26 = 676$ students can be covered. Thus, $676 + 26 = 702$ students can be covered with one or two letters. It follows that it will be necessary for some students to have more than two letters in their codes. It is suggested that you do not give the students these answers, but rather let them experiment and listen to their ideas. If some students do get the correct answer, have them explain how they got the correct answer. Have the class ask questions of these students regarding their techniques. If no students come up with the correct answer, tell them that a purpose of this chapter is to provide them with tools for solving such problems.

NOTES

Chapter 7

Although many musical qualities are important, let us consider only volume. Music on a CD is sometimes soft and sometimes loud, in varying degrees. How loud or how soft must be given by the use of 0's and 1's. Let's see how this might be done. If we have only two levels, say *loud* and *soft,* we could code the sound as follows.

Level	Code
soft	0
loud	1

If the laser beam reads the message

0010111

the sound coming out of a speaker would be

soft - soft - loud - soft - loud - loud - loud

If the music coming out of a speaker is

soft - loud - loud - soft - loud - soft - soft

7.7

what binary message did the laser beam read?

Such music would probably provide very dull listening. Let's try a more sensitive code with four levels—*very soft, soft, loud,* and *very loud.* We might code the sound as follows.

Level	Code
very soft	00
soft	01
loud	10
very loud	11

If the laser beam reads the message

0111000001

the music coming out of a speaker would be

soft - very loud - very soft - very soft - soft

Published by IT'S ABOUT TIME, Inc. © 2000 MATHconx, LLC

417

7.7 The answer is 0110100.

NOTES

_____

a
7.8

1. If the music coming out of a speaker is

    loud - very loud - soft - soft - very soft - loud

    what binary message did the laser beam read?

2. We are presently using two bits in each code. What problems arise if we use a mixture of one bit and two bit codes?

(*Hint:* Consider:)

Level	Code
very soft	0
soft	1
loud	10
very loud	11

The previous question demonstrates problems that can arise if codes do not contain the same number of bits. In our efforts to find codes for the various sound levels, we shall restrict ourselves to lists in which all the codes contain the same number of bits—no mixtures.

b
7.9

1. If each code contains three bits (for example 101), how many different sound levels could be detected?

2. If we wanted to detect 1000 sound levels, can you guess how many bits would have to appear in each code? Explain your answer. (*Hint:* Try an organized list. Look for patterns.) This is an example of a *counting* problem.

In this section we have illustrated the use of counting in several different contexts. Many jobs such as managing a fast food restaurant, a supermarket, a gas station, or a department store, or working for a company that needs to take inventory, or working as a scientist or engineer, require that one be able to solve counting problems. Computer scientists and technicians and people working in the medical fields need to be able to solve counting problems. In the remainder of this chapter we shall try to assist you in developing that ability.

418

Published by IT'S ABOUT TIME, Inc. © 2000 MATHconx, LLC

7.8

1. The answer to the first question is 101101010010.

2. Let students offer answers to the second question. The point to be emphasized is that such codes can be ambiguous. In the example, given in the hint, is 1011 to be interpreted as

    loud - very loud

    or as

    soft - very soft - soft - soft

7.9

1. Let students experiment with this question. Some students might, in some fashion, come up with the correct result $2 \cdot 2 \cdot 2 = 8$. Let them explain how they arrived at their answer. Other students might list all possibilities

    000   001   010   011   100   101   110   111

2. Let students experiment again with this second question. Suggest that students look for a *pattern*.

Number of Bits in a Code Word	Number of Sound Levels
1	2
2	4
3	8
4	16
.	.
.	.
.	.

Thus, one wants to raise 2 to a power so that the result is not less than 1000. Using a calculator one finds that $2^9 = 512$ and $2^{10} = 1024$, so that 10 or more bits would have to appear in each code. Tell students that they will know how to solve problems like this by the time they finish the chapter.

NOTES
_____

....

....

....

....

....

Chapter 7

Problem Set: 7.1

1. (a) If we want to sort the patients in a large hospital into age groups: 0–9, 10–19, 20–29, 30–39, ... (years), by coding with bits, how many bits are needed in each code?

    (b) If we wanted a "finer" sorting in (a): 0–4, 5–9, 10–14, 15–19, ... (years), how many bits are needed in each code?

2. In 1977 two Voyager spacecraft were launched from Earth bound for the giant planets in the solar system—Jupiter, Saturn, Uranus, and Neptune, the last of which was visited in August, 1989. The Voyagers had five cameras for taking pictures and six instruments for making scientific measurements. All of the pictures and the scientific information were sent back to Earth using codes formed by bits (0's and 1's). More than four trillion bits have been sent back to earth by the Voyagers since they were launched. (Four trillion bits is enough to represent 5000 copies of the *Encyclopaedia Britannica*.) Information was sent to Earth at the rate of 21,000 bits per second.

    (a) How many hours of time were used by the Voyagers in sending four trillion bits to Earth?

    (b) Why might engineers be interested in an answer to the question in part (a)?

Problem Set: 7.1

1. (a) To a certain extent this is an open-ended question. The difficulty is how high one wants to take the age brackets. See if students come up with something like the following: After the interval 90–99, simply have one more category—100 or greater. This sorting would require 11 code words. If each code word had the same number of bits, as is implied in the problem, then 4 bits would be required.

   (b) Using the same idea as in part (a), 21 code words would be necessary which requires 5 bits.

2. (a) 21,000 bits/sec. corresponds to 7.56×10^7 bits/hour. Hence, about 52,910 hours were required to send four trillion bits to earth (1 trillion = 10^{12}).

   (b) Engineers might be interested for a number of reasons. For example, batteries or whatever type of energy is used to transmit information must last for this amount of time.

NOTES

7.2 Sets: What to Count

Learning Outcomes

After studying this section, you will be able to:

Use set notation;

Write set notation in several different ways;

Write the number of elements of a set as a function.

In a population census, a government is trying to determine the size of a population. Not all counting problems are as long and as tedious as a census. For example, one might be interested in counting the number of cars in a parking lot (Why?) or the number of students in this class (Why?) or the number of chairs in this classroom (Why?). In each of these examples one is counting the number of objects (cars, people, chairs) in a collection. Mathematicians refer to a collection of objects as a **set**. An object in a set is called an **element** of the set.

The word set, as used in mathematics, is not new to you. In Chapter 2 we used the idea of a *solution set* for an equation. For example, recall problems like the following.

a
7.10

See if 1, 2, 3, 4, or 5 are solutions to the equation

$$(x - 2) \cdot (x - 4) = 0$$

Write the solution set for this equation.

Then, in Chapter 3 you read about sets of points and used the *set-builder* notation. Recall problems like the following:

b
7.11

Translate the following description into set-builder notation. Then say what you think the picture looks like.

"The set of all ordered pairs (x,y) such that $x = 2$ and y is between 3 and 7, inclusive."

In this chapter we shall use the word set in a very broad way. For example, one could consider the set of shopping carts in a supermarket, the set of teachers in this school, or the set of people in the State of Wyoming. Capital letters, such as A, B, and C are often used in assigning names to sets. For example, one might say, "Let A be the set of students in this class." In this case A is a name for the set and "students in this class" is a description of the elements of the set. Using set-builder notation, one could write

$$A = \{x \mid x \text{ is a student in this class}\}$$

Published by IT'S ABOUT TIME, Inc. © 2000 MATHconx, LLC

7.2   Sets: What to Count

In this section students should be immersed in the notion of a set and the idea that counting techniques will involve counting the number of elements in a set. Set notation should become part of a student's mathematical language. We have chosen to use #( ) to indicate the number of elements in a set. Students should see the relation between this notation and function notation that they have previously used.

7.10

Answer is {2, 4}.

7.11

Answer is $\{(x, y) \mid x = 2, 3 \leq y \leq 7\}$

Additional Support Materials:

Assessments	Qty
Form (A)	1
Form (B)	1

Blackline Masters	Qty

Extensions	Qty

Supplements	Qty
Sets: What to Count	1

Chapter 7

Another method of writing a set is to actually list the elements. For example, if B is a name for the set of all natural numbers less than 8, then one could write

$$B = \{1, 2, 3, 4, 5, 6, 7\}$$

How could one write the set B using set-builder notation? Note that 5 is an element of B but 17 is not an element of B, and 17.4 is not an element of B.

Here are some practice questions about sets and set notation.

7.12

1. Consider the set of even integers between 2 and 12 inclusive. Give this set a name.

   (a) Write this set using set-builder notation.
   (b) Write this set by listing the elements.

2. Write each of the following sets by listing the elements:

   (a) The set A of all natural numbers greater than 5, but less than 10.
   (b) The set B of all odd natural numbers less than 12.
   (c) The set C of all natural numbers less than 20 which are multiples of 3.
   (d) The set D of all natural numbers less than 23 which are multiples of 4 or multiples of 5.
   (e) The set E of all natural numbers less than 27 which are multiples of 3 and also multiples of 4.
   (f) The set F of all students in the class whose first name begins with "P".
   (g) The set G of all states in the U.S. bordered by the Pacific Ocean.

3. If you toss a coin and A is a name for the set of all possible outcomes, how would you write the set A by listing the elements?

4. If you toss a standard six sided die and B is a name for the set of possible outcomes, how would you write the set B by listing the elements?

5. If you toss a pair of standard six sided dice and C is the set of possible sums that can be obtained, how would you write the set C by listing the elements?

6. If you are going to toss two coins and D is the set of possible outcomes, how would you write the set D by listing the elements?

Published by IT'S ABOUT TIME, Inc. © 2000 MATHconx, LLC

421

7.12

1. Let students give whatever name they want, say *A*. Then

    (a) *A* = {*x* | *x* is an even integer, 2 ≤ *x* ≤ 12}
    (b) *A* = {2, 4, 6, 8, 10, 12}

2. (a) *A* = {6, 7, 8, 9}
   (b) *B* = {1, 3, 5, 7, 9, 11}
   (c) *C* = {3, 6, 9, 12, 15, 18}
   (d) *D* = {4, 5, 8, 10, 12, 15, 16, 20}. *WARNING!* Make sure that students understand the use of the word "or". That is, a number which is a multiple of 4 or a multiple of 5 could be a multiple of both.
   (e) *E* = {12, 24} *WARNING!* Make sure that students understand the use of the word "and". That is, a number which is a multiple of 3 and a multiple of 4 must be a multiple of both.
   (f) Answers will vary by class.
   (g) {California, Oregon, Washington, Alaska, Hawaii}

3. See what students come up with. They might write things such as *A* = {head, tail} or *A* = {*h, t*}.

4. Students are expected to write something such as *B* = {1, 2, 3, 4, 5, 6}, but they might also write *B* = {one, two, three, four, five, six}.

5. *C* = {2, 3, 4, 5, 6, 7, 8, 9, 10, 11, 12}

6. One possible way is *D* = {*HH, HT, TH, TT*}. Another possibility is *D* = {2 heads, 2 tails, 1 head and 1 tail}. Note that the first set has one more element because it takes into account the order of occurrences of heads and tails.

NOTES

Chapter 7

Some sets have the property that you can count the number of elements. For example, if

$$A = \{5, 17, 23\}$$

then there are three elements in A. We write $\#(A) = 3$ to indicate that the number of elements in the set A is three. If

$$B = \{\text{Joan, Kim, Mary, Elena}\}$$

then $\#(B) = 4$. Notice the similarity between the $\#(\ )$ notation and the $f(\ )$ notation used in Chapter 6. Indeed, you can think of $\#$ as a function which assigns a whole number to certain sets.

a
7.13

1. If C is the set of students in your class, what is $\#(C)$?

2. **An eighth grade mathematics teacher asked students to do problems 7 through 12 for homework. If H is the set of problems assigned, what is $\#(H)$?**

It is possible that a set has no elements. Indeed, in Chapter 2 you were asked to try to solve equations like

$$0 \cdot k = 37$$

No matter what number you replaced k with, you got $0 \cdot k = 0$, not 37, so there was no solution to this equation. The solution set was written as $\{\ \}$ to represent the **empty set,** the set with no elements. Another notation used for the empty set is $\varnothing$. Since the empty set has no elements, we write

$$\#(\varnothing) = 0$$

b
7.14

1. **Let T (for tall) denote the set of all students in your class who are over 9 feet tall. What is $\#(T)$?**

2. **Describe three sets, each of which is the empty set. Be able to explain why your sets are empty.**

A purpose of this chapter is to find ways of counting the number of elements in a set.

422

Published by IT'S ABOUT TIME, Inc. © 2000 MATHconx, LLC

7.2 Sets: What to Count

7.13

1. Answer will vary with each class.

2. Answer #(H) = 6

7.14

1. $T = \varnothing$, so #(T) = 0

2. Students might write something like the following. Let B be the set of all students in the class who weigh more than 700 pounds.

NOTES

Problem Set: 7.2

1. Use set-builder notation to write the set *G* of all positive integers which are less than 98.

2. Use set-builder notation to write the set *H* of all positive integers which are greater than or equal to 38.

3. By listing the elements, write the set of all U.S. states that border Canada. Give this set a name.

4. By listing the elements, write the set of all U.S. states that border Mexico. Give this set a name.

5. Let *T* be the set of all U.S. states which are in the Southern Hemisphere. What is #(*T*)?

6. If *A* is the set of counting numbers less than 25 which are multiples of 3, what is #(*A*)?

7. If *D* is the set of counting numbers less than 27 which are multiples of 4 or multiples of 5, what is #(*D*)?

8. If you toss a standard six sided die and *B* is the set of possible outcomes, what is #(*B*)?

9. If you toss a pair of standard six sided dice and *C* is the set of possible sums that can be obtained, what is #(*C*)?

10. If *C* is the set of cards in a standard deck of cards, what is #(*C*)?

Published by IT'S ABOUT TIME, Inc. © 2000 MATHconx, LLC

423

Problem Set: 7.2

1. $G = \{x \mid x \text{ is a positive integer, } x < 98\}$

2. $H = \{x \mid x \text{ is a positive integer, } x \geq 38\}$

3. $A = \{$Washington, Idaho, Montana, Wisconsin, North Dakota, Michigan, Minnesota, New York, Vermont, New Hampshire, Maine$\}$

4. $A = \{$California, Arizona, New Mexico, Texas$\}$

5. $T = \varnothing$, so $\#(T) = 0$

6. $\#(A) = 8$

7. $\#(D) = 10$

8. $\#(B) = 6$

9. $\#(C) = 11$; $\{2, 3, 4, \cdots, 11, 12\}$

10. $\#(C) = 52$ for a standard deck.

NOTES

Chapter 7

7.3 Venn Diagrams: Counting With Pictures

Learning Outcomes

After studying this section, you will be able to:

Use the basic set operations with the help of Venn diagrams;

Solve counting problems using Venn diagrams;

Use Venn diagrams in developing reasoning abilities related to counting problems;

Divide a set into subsets in order to answer questions about counting.

In a class of 30 students, 17 watch MTV and 12 play video games. Five students watch MTV and play video games. See if you can answer the following questions.

7.15

1. How many students watch MTV but do not play video games?

2. How many students play video games but do not watch MTV?

3. How many students watch MTV or play video games (possibly both)?

4. How many students neither watch MTV nor play video games?

If you answered all four questions correctly, you should give yourself a pat on the back.

We now look at a method for getting answers to such questions. Let U be the set of all students in the class, M the set of students who watch MTV and G the set of students who play video games. We know that $\#(U) = 30$, $\#(M) = 17$, and $\#(G) = 12$. Our method involves using a picture known as a **Venn diagram** as illustrated in Display 7.1.

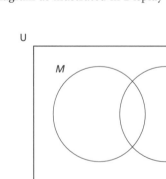

Display 7.1

424

7.3 Venn Diagrams: Counting With Pictures

Venn diagrams are extremely useful tools in the teaching of basic counting techniques. Their actual use in the real world, however, is limited. In addition, in this section students will become familiar with set operations such as union and intersection through the use of these diagrams.

7.15

The object here is to get students to come up with numbers and to orally give an account of how they arrived at their numbers. Even if a student gets the wrong answer to these questions, let them give their explanation. The correct answers are

1. 12

2. 7

3. 24

4. 6

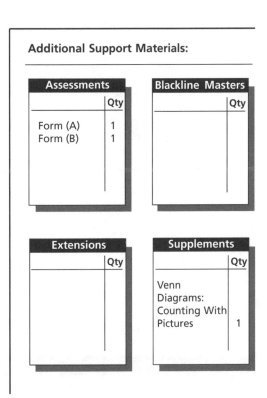

Additional Support Materials:

Assessments	Qty
Form (A)	1
Form (B)	1

Blackline Masters	Qty

Extensions	Qty

Supplements	Qty
Venn Diagrams: Counting With Pictures	1

Chapter 7

Think of all the students in the class being represented by points inside the rectangle *U*. Inside the circle *M* are the 17 students who watch MTV. Inside the circle *G* are the 12 students who play video games. The 5 students who watch MTV and play video games are in the region inside both circles which is colored green in Display 7.2.

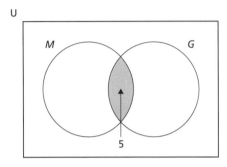

Display 7.2

The set of students in this common region is denoted *M*∩*G*, read (M intersect G, or the intersection of M and G.) That is, *M*∩*G* is the set of elements that are in *M and* in *G*. Moreover, #(*M*∩*G*) = 5.

Inside the circle *M* in Display 7.3, there are 17 students, 5 of whom are in the intersection. Hence 12 students must be located in the region colored blue of circle *M*.

About Words

The word *intersection* is used to indicate an overlapping of two figures or things. For example, one is familiar with the intersection of two streets. In the text, we have the overlapping of two sets; the intersection of two sets.

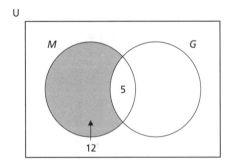

Display 7.3

425

NOTES

7.16

1. How many students are in the region which is colored yellow of circle *G* in Display 7.4?

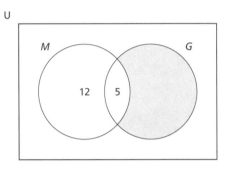

Display 7.4

2. How many students are in the region which is colored pink of Display 7.5?

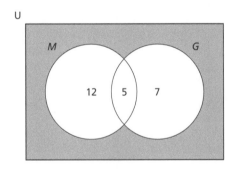

Display 7.5

Now let us return to the questions you discussed at the beginning of this section.

How many students watch MTV but do not play video games? These students are in the region which is colored blue in Display 7.6, so the answer is 12. The region colored blue in this display represents the set *M – G*, read "the difference of M and G." That is, *M – G* is the set of elements that are in *M* but not in *G*. Moreover, #(*M – G*) = 12.

Published by IT'S ABOUT TIME, Inc. © 2000 MATHconx, LLC

7.16

1. Seven

2. Six. You may want to bypass this question and let students deal with it after further preparation, when it reappears in 7.18, 2.

NOTES

_____

Chapter 7

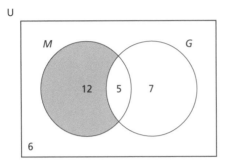

Display 7.6

How many students play video games but do not watch MTV?

7.17

1. Draw a copy of Display 7.7 and shade the region corresponding to this question.

2. How many students are in the region shaded in (1)?

3. How would you write the shaded region of activity 1 as the difference of two sets?

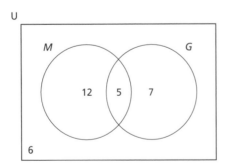

Display 7.7

How many students watch MTV or play video games (possibly both)?

427

7.17

1. Students should shade the region marked with a 7.

2. There are seven students in this set.

3. G–M

NOTES

Chapter 7

These students are in the regions which are shown in color of Display 7.8.

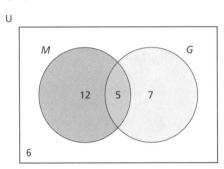

Display 7.8

About Words

The word *union* is used to indicate the joining or combining of several things into one. For example, a labor union combines many people for a common cause. In the text we have the joining of two sets, their union.

The answer is 24. The set of students in the shaded regions of this display is denoted $M \cup G$, read "M union G." That is, $M \cup G$ is the set of elements that are in M or in G (possibly both). Moreover $\#(M \cup G) = 24$.

7.18

How many students neither watch MTV nor play video games?

1. **Draw a copy of Display 7.9 and shade the region corresponding to this question.**

2. **How many students are in the region shaded in (1)?**

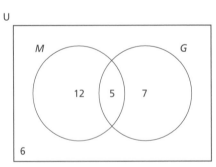

Display 7.9

Venn diagrams are sometimes used by business people to help organize their thoughts about sets and the number of elements in certain sets. The following problems are designed to give you practice in answering questions about the number of elements in certain sets. Many students enjoy such problems because they regard them as *puzzles*.

Published by IT'S ABOUT TIME, Inc. © 2000 MATHconx, LLC

7.18

1. Students should shade the region inside the rectangle but outside of both circles.

2. There are six students in this set.

NOTES

_____

_____

_____

_____

_____

_____

_____

_____

_____

_____

_____

_____

_____

_____

Chapter 7

1. Of 1000 people interviewed, an advertising agency found 786 people who read *Newsweek* magazine, 664 who read *Time* magazine, and 461 who read both magazines.

    (a) Of the 1000 people interviewed, how many people read at least one of the two magazines, *Newsweek* or *Time*? Justify your answer.

    (b) Of the 1000 people interviewed, how many people read one of the two magazines but not both? Justify your answer.

7.19

2. A survey is taken at an ice cream parlor. People are asked to list their two favorite flavors. 74 list vanilla as one of their favorite flavors while 37 list chocolate. If 19 list both flavors and 12 list neither of these two flavors, how many people participated in the survey?

3. In a survey of 100 students, 50 indicated that they liked rock music, 60 liked country and western music, and 45 of those who liked country and western music also liked rock. How many students in the survey liked country and western music but not rock?

4. Make up a problem like questions 1, 2, and 3 above, which will give your classmates practice in using a Venn diagram, and to answer questions about the number of elements in certain sets.

5. As a check to see if you have carefully read the text, draw four Venn diagrams like the one below (Display 7.10).

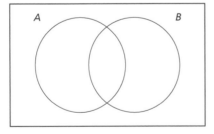

Display 7.10

Now, using your diagrams, indicate by shading, each of the following sets.

(a) $A \cap B$ (b) $A - B$ (c) $B - A$ (d) $A \cup B$

429

Published by IT'S ABOUT TIME, Inc. © 2000 MATHconx, LLC

7.19

1. From Display 7.1T

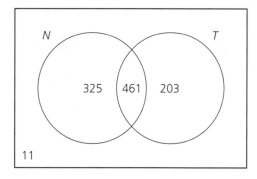

Display 7.1T

where
N = set of people interviewed who read *Newsweek*
T = set of people interviewed who read *Time*
The answers are
(a) 325 + 461 + 203 = 989; and (b) 325 + 203 = 528.

2. Ask for student solutions. The Venn diagram in Display 7.2T

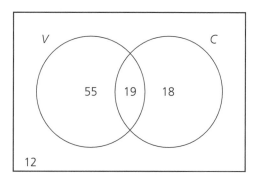

Display 7.2T

where
V = set of people in survey who list vanilla
C = set of people in survey who list chocolate
indicates that the answer is 55 + 19 + 18 + 12 = 104.

3. A Venn diagram gives the answer 15.

4. Have students react to other students' problems.

Chapter 7

5. Answers are below in Displays 7.3T–7.6T.

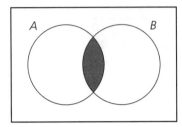

$A \cap B$

Display 7.3T

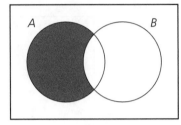

$A – B$

Display 7.4T

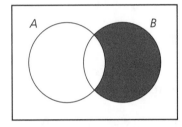

$B – A$

Display 7.5T

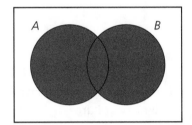

$A \cup B$

Display 7.6T

NOTES

NOTES

6. Jason says "If A and B are sets, then

$$\#(A \cup B) = \#(A) + \#(B)."$$

Is Jason correct? Explain.

7. How many natural numbers less than or equal to 100 are multiples of 2 or 5? How is this question related to question 6?

8. In this section, the ideas of intersection, union, and difference of two sets have been introduced using examples. Use set-builder notation to give general definitions of

   (a) $A \cap B$ (b) $A \cup B$ (c) $A - B$

A class of 30 students contains some men and some women. Let A be the set of women in the class and let B be the set of blue-eyed women in the class. Note that every element of B is an element of A. In such a case we say that B is a **subset** of A and write $B \subseteq A$.

As another example, If $A = \{3, 5, 7, 9, 15\}$ and $B = \{3, 9, 15\}$, then $B \subseteq A$ since every element of B is an element of A.

7.20

1. Let A be the set of students in your class. Describe at least three different subsets of A.

2. Do you think the following statements are true or false? Explain.

   (a) For any set A, $A \subseteq A$.
   (b) For any set A, $\varnothing \subseteq A$.
   (c) For any set A, $A \subseteq \varnothing$.

3. Suppose set B is a subset of A. Assuming $\#(A)$ and $\#(B)$ can be found, what relationship would you believe exists between $\#(A)$ and $\#(B)$? Explain.

4. What might a Venn diagram look like if it is known that $B \subseteq A$?

Venn diagrams were introduced by the British mathematician John Venn in 1881. As you have seen in this section, he used such pictures to show relationships between sets.

430

6. If $A \cap B = \emptyset$, Jason is correct. Otherwise Jason is wrong.

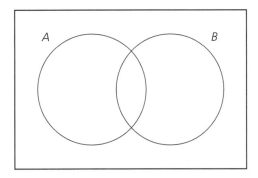

Display 7.7T

In the Venn diagram (Display 7.7T) if one counts the number of elements in A, which is #(A), and then adds the number of elements in B, which is #(B), the elements of $A \cap B$, which is number #($A \cap B$), have been counted twice. This number must be subtracted from #(A) + #(B). The correct formula, which always works, is

$$\#(A \cup B) = \#(A) + \#(B) - \#(A \cap B).$$

If $A \cap B = \emptyset$, so that #($A \cap B$) = 0, then

$$\#(A \cup B) = \#(A) + \#(B).$$

7. Let

A = set of counting numbers involved that are multiples of 2; and,
B = set of counting numbers involved that are multiples of 5.

Then, A = {2, 4, 6, 8,...,100} so that #(A) = 50. Now,
B = {5, 10, 15, 20,...,100} so that #(B) = 20. The set of counting numbers involved that are multiples of 2 or 5 is the set $A \cup B$. From the previous problem

$$\#(A \cup B) = \#(A) + \#(B) - \#(A \cap B)$$
$$\text{or, in this case,}$$
$$\#(A \cup B) = 50 + 20 - \#(A \cap B).$$

Thus, we need #($A \cap B$). Now, $A \cap B$ is the set of counting numbers involved that are multiples of 2 and 5, or

$$A \cap B = \{10, 20, 30,...,100\}$$

so that #($A \cap B$) = 10. It follows that

$$\#(A \cup B) = 50 + 20 - 10 = 60.$$

One might use the Venn diagram (Display 7.8T) to again see that #($A \cup B$) = 60.

Chapter 7

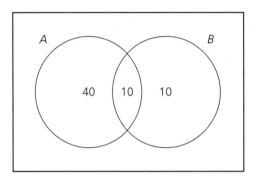

Display 7.8T

8. (a) $A \cap B = \{x \mid x$ is an element of A and of $B\}$
   (b) $A \cup B = \{x \mid x$ is an element of A or of B (possibly both)$\}$
   (c) $A - B = \{x \mid x$ is an element of A but not of $B\}$

7.20

1. Get a number of different answers from students.

2. In (a), ask the students if every element of A is an element of A. The statement is true. Part (b) may take some explaining. If one can find an element of $\varnothing$, then it is an element of A. The statement is true. In (c), the statement is false. In particular, take A to be any nonempty set.

3. $\#(B) \leq \#(A)$. Ask students why they cannot, in general, write $\#(B) < \#(A)$.

4. If $B \subseteq A$, then a Venn diagram might look like the following Display 7.9T.

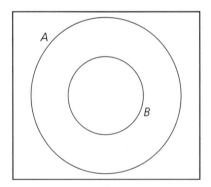

Display 7.9T

NOTES

Chapter 7

Do you think that figures other than circles could be used to show relationships between sets? If you believe that other figures could be used, do you think that a circle is the best figure to use or do you have another figure you like better? Explain.

a
7.21

1. Riverdale Mathematics Company in Delaware produces two products—books on mathematics and video games involving mathematics. They presently have 1520 books and 3417 video games in stock. What is the total number of items this company has in stock?

a
7.22

2. The audio department at a local L-Mart sells units that play cassette tapes or compact disks. The store presently stocks 54 units that play cassette tapes and 74 units that play compact disks. Of these units, 17 play both tapes and compact disks. What is the total number of units the audio department has in stock?

Which of the above two problems did you find easier to solve? Why?

b
7.23

Make up two counting problems like the problems above, one of which you think is easy to solve and one which you think is more difficult. Write a paragraph on how to write such pairs of problems.

7.24

Two sets A and B are said to be **disjoint** if $A \cap B = \varnothing$. That is, A and B are disjoint if they have no elements in common. For example, let B be a set of bicycles and let R be a set of rollerblades. Then $B \cap R = \varnothing$, so B and R are disjoint.

1. Give three different examples of pairs of disjoint sets.

2. What might a Venn diagram look like if it is known that A and B are disjoint sets?

b
7.25

3. What role does the idea of disjoint sets play in your solution of the problems above?

Published by IT'S ABOUT TIME, Inc. © 2000 MATHconx, LLC

431

7.21

There is no reason one could not use rectangles instead of circles. Indeed, some people do. Get students' opinions on this.

7.22

Answer to the first problem is 4937, while the answer to the second problem is 111.

7.23

Students should have no difficulty in determining that the first problem is the easier of the two. The reason is that in the first problem, the set of all items is separated into two sets which have an empty intersection. The second problem does not involve this property.

7.24

Have students compare problems.

7.25

1. Answers will vary.

2. If *A* and *B* are disjoint sets, a Venn diagram might look like the following Display 7.10T.

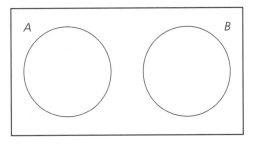

Display 7.10T

3. Again, the idea in the first problem is that the two sets described are disjoint and together form the entire set.

Chapter 7

We have been dividing a set into two parts which form disjoint sets. Why should we limit ourselves to two subsets? Let's look at the following example: A local compact disc store separates their discs into exactly one of the four musical categories—classical, jazz, popular, and rock. They presently have in stock 380 classical, 450 jazz, 250 popular, and 870 rock discs. Let S be the set of all discs they have in stock. Let

C be the set of classical discs
P be the set of popular discs
J be the set of jazz discs
R be the set of rock discs

so that

$$\#(C) = 380, \#(J) = 450, \#(P) = 250, \#(R) = 870$$

Then $S = C \cup J \cup P \cup R$ and moreover, *any two of the sets C, J, P, and R are disjoint.* A Venn diagram for this situation might be the following:

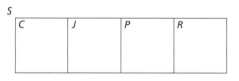

Display 7.11

To find $\#(S)$ one needs to count the number of discs in S. This number, however, can be obtained by counting the number of classical discs $\#(C)$, then adding the number of jazz discs $\#(J)$, then adding the number of popular discs $\#(P)$, and finally adding the number of rock discs $\#(R)$. That is,

$$\#(S) = \#(C) + \#(J) + \#(P) + \#(R)$$

$$\#(S) = 380 + 450 + 250 + 870$$

$$\#(S) = 1950$$

When a set can be divided into subsets, any two of which are disjoint, the counting becomes quite easy. This idea, as simple as it seems, is quite important for an understanding of more complicated counting methods.

How might all the students in your class be divided into four subsets, any two of which are disjoint?

7.26

432

One possibility is to divide students by grades, say *A*, *B*, *C*, and lower than *C*.

7.26

NOTES
_____

A set S can be divided into 5 subsets A, B, C, D and E in such a way that any two of these 5 sets are disjoint. If each of the 5 sets has exactly 8 elements, what is #(S)?

7.27

Problem Set: 7.3

1. Let A be the set {Hartford, Denver, Miami}. Write all subsets of A.

2. (a) Draw four copies of Display 7.12. In one shade $A \cap (B \cap C)$. In another diagram shade $(A \cap B) \cap C$. What did you find?

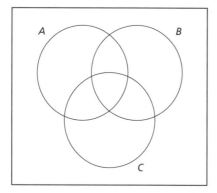

Display 7.12

What algebraic law(s) has the same structure? Why does it now make sense to talk about $A \cap B \cap C$? How would you describe an element of $A \cap B \cap C$?

(b) Use your two other diagrams to determine whether or not one can say that

$$A - (B - C) = (A - B) - C$$

7.27

$\#(S) = 5 \cdot 8 = 40$

Problem Set: 7.3

1. {Hartford}, {Denver}, {Miami}, {Hartford, Denver}, {Denver, Miami}, {Hartford, Miami}, {Hartford, Denver, Miami}, $\varnothing$.

2. (a) Students should see that $A \cap (B \cap C) = (A \cap B) \cap C$ (Display 7.11T). That is, there is an Associative Law for the "intersection" operation. This is a good place to talk about the meaning of the parentheses. It now makes sense to talk about $A \cap B \cap C$ since one can only take the intersection of two sets at a time, but it does not matter which two are selected first in finding this set. An element of $A \cap B \cap C$ is in all three sets.

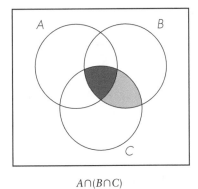
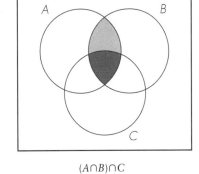

$A \cap (B \cap C)$ $(A \cap B) \cap C$

Display 7.11T

(b) In this case, students should find that $A - (B - C)$ is not the same set as $(A - B) - C$ (Display 7.12T).

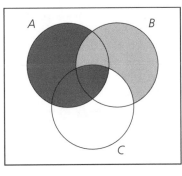

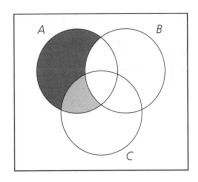

$A - (B - C)$ $(A - B) - C$

Display 7.12T

Chapter 7

3. Draw two copies of the diagram below (Display 7.13). In one shade $A \cup (B \cup C)$. In the other diagram, shade $(A \cup B) \cup C$.

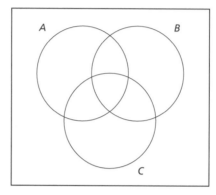

Display 7.13

(a) What did you find?

(b) Explain why it now makes sense to talk about $A \cup B \cup C$.

(c) How would you describe an element of $A \cup B \cup C$?

4. In many factories, items that have been made are checked for defects. Inspectors sometimes look not only for the kind of defects that an item might have, but also the number of defects.

The Turniton Co. makes TV sets. Each TV set they make is given a final test for defects in (i) the picture tube, (ii) the sound system, and (iii) the remote control system. Yesterday they made 1000 sets. They found that 54 units had a defective picture tube, 67 had a defective sound system, and 80 had a defective remote control system. Of these, 26 units had both a defective picture tube and a defective sound system, 20 had both a defective picture tube and a defective remote control system, 31 had both a defective sound system and a defective remote control system, and 14 had all three defects.

Published by IT'S ABOUT TIME, Inc. © 2000 MATHconx, LLC

3. (a) Students should see that $A \cup (B \cup C) = (A \cup B) \cup C$ (Display 7.13T). That is, there is an Associative Law for the union operation.
    (b) It now makes sense to talk about $A \cup B \cup C$ since one can only take the union of two sets at a time, but it does not matter which two are selected first in finding this set.
    (c) The element may be in any of the three sets and may be in more than one set.

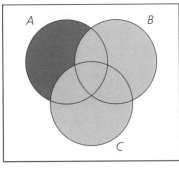

$A \cup (B \cup C)$

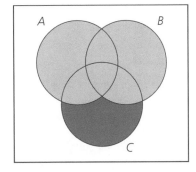

$(A \cup B) \cup C$

Display 7.13T

4. Let

    P = set of TV's with a defective picture tube
    S = set of TV's with a defective sound system
    R = set of TV's with a defective remote control

    The given information yields

    $\#(P) = 54$, $\#(S) = 67$, $\#(R) = 80$, $\#(P \cap S) = 26$, $\#(P \cap R) = 20$, $\#(S \cap R) = 31$, and $\#(P \cap S \cap R) = 14$

    In completing a Venn diagram for this problem (Display 7.14T), work backwards starting with $\#(P \cap S \cap R) = 14$.

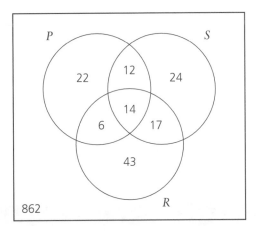

Display 7.14T

Chapter 7

If a set has no defects, it is considered to be "perfect." If a set has only one defect, it can be repaired and made perfect so it is called "repairable." Sets with two or more defects are considered "scrap" although some of the parts are reusable. Of the 1000 TV sets made yesterday,

(a) How many sets were repairable?

(b) How many sets were scrap?

(c) How many sets were perfect?

(d) Why might the manager of Turniton be interested in these numbers?

5. A local sports outlet sells many types of sports equipment, but they specialize in soccer equipment. In January, the manager decided to get into national advertising. A full page ad in sports magazines for a month was considered and three magazines seemed suitable — *Sports Illustrious*, *Popular Sports*, and *Soccer Monthly*. Advertising experts gave the following estimates on the number of readers:

Sports Illustrious	215,000
Popular Sports	320,000
Soccer Monthly	107,000
Sports Illustrious and *Popular Sports*	198,000
Popular Sports and *Soccer Monthly*	54,000
Sports Illustrious and *Soccer Monthly*	38,000
All Three Magazines	24,000

The manager finds that the company can only afford to advertise in two of the three magazines. The manager wants to advertise in the two magazines that will have the largest number of people seeing the ad. Which two magazines would the manager choose? Do you think that the manager should look at other factors rather than just the total number of readers? If so, what factors?

Published by IT'S ABOUT TIME, Inc. © 2000 MATHconx, LLC

From the Venn diagram one sees that the answer to (a) is 89, while the answer to (b) is 49. The answer to (c) is 862. (d) Student answers should vary. For example, the manager could be interested in repair costs.

5. Let I = set of people who read *Sports Illustrious*
   P = set of people who read *Popular Sports*
   S = set of people who read *Soccer Monthly*

In the Venn diagram Display 7.15T, the numbers are given in thousandths.

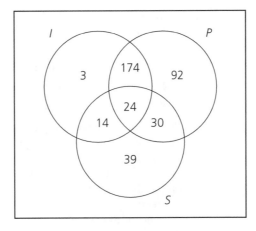

Display 7.15T

One finds #$(I \cup P)$ = 337, #$(I \cup S)$ = 284, and #$(P \cup S)$ = 373. In order to have the largest number of people seeing the ad, the manager should choose *Popular Sports* and *Soccer Monthly*. The manager might want to consider which magazines are read by soccer fans or what returns can be expected from people who see an ad in more than one magazine.

NOTES

6. Yesterday, 48 patients were admitted to the emergency room of a hospital in Washington, D.C. Some of these patients had basic medical insurance and some had catastrophic medical insurance.

    What is catastrophic medical insurance?

    A look at the records of these 48 patients indicated that 37 had basic medical insurance, 12 had catastrophic medical insurance, and 5 had both types of insurance.

    (a) How many patients had neither of these types of insurance?

    (b) How many of these patients had basic medical insurance but not catastrophic medical insurance?

    (c) Why might a hospital director be interested in these numbers?

7. (This problem is based on questions asked at a recent staff meeting in a bank.) The Rocky Mountain National Bank has 54,000 customers in Colorado and 29,000 customers in other states. The bank has 45,000 customers with an income of more than $25,000 a year, and 32,000 customers who owe the bank more than $5,000. Of the customers in Colorado, 15,000 owe the bank more than $5,000. Of all the customers with an income of more than $25,000 per year, 10,000 owe the bank more than $5,000. Of the customers in Colorado with an income of more than $25,000 per year, 8000 owe the bank more than $5,000. Let

    A = set of customers in Colorado

    B = set of customers with an annual income of more than $25,000 per year

    C = set of customers who owe the bank more than $5,000

    This bank considers customers in the set $C - (A \cup B)$ as "high risk" customers.

    (a) Describe, in words, a customer in the set $C - (A \cup B)$. Why might such a customer be considered a high risk customer?

    (b) Copy the Venn diagram (Display 7.14) and shade the region $C - (A \cup B)$.

    (c) Find $\#(C - (A \cup B))$.

Published by IT'S ABOUT TIME, Inc. © 2000 MATHconx, LLC

6. Catastrophic medical insurance is designed to cover costly medical expenses resulting from a prolonged illness or injury.

The Venn diagram in Display 7.16T can be used to answer the two questions which follow. We have used

B = set of patients with basic medical insurance.
C = set of patients with catastrophic medical insurance.

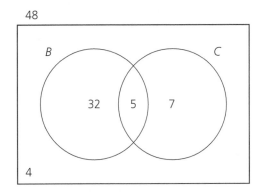

Display 7.16T

(a) Four patients had neither type of insurance.
(b) Thirty-two patients had basic medical insurance but not catastrophic medical insurance.

(c) A hospital director might be interested in these numbers to determine what costs would be paid by insurance companies and what costs would be expected to be paid by the individuals who may not be able to afford the medical expenses.

7. (a) A customer in $C - (A \cup B)$ is a person who owes the bank more than $5,000 but neither lives in Colorado nor has an income of more than $25,000 a year.
   (b) An answer is given in Display 7.17T.

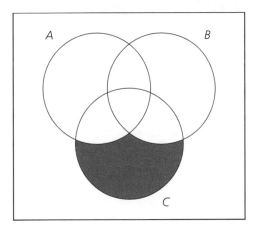

Display 7.17T

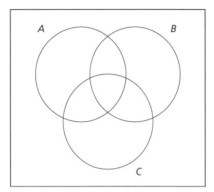

Display 7.14

8. *A set S can be divided into 26 subsets A, B, C,..., X, Y, Z in such a way that any two of these 26 sets are disjoint. If each of the 26 sets has exactly 15 elements, what is #(S)?*

Published by IT'S ABOUT TIME, Inc. © 2000 MATHconx, LLC

437

7.3 Venn Diagrams: Counting With Pictures

(c) The partially complete Venn diagram in Display 7.18T indicates the necessary information where numbers are given in thousandths. From the diagram $\#(C - (A \cup B)) = 15{,}000$.

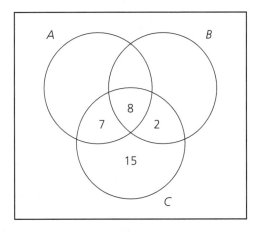

Display 7.18T

8. $15 \cdot 26 = 390$

NOTES

7.4 Using Tree Diagrams to Count

Learning Outcomes

After studying this section you will be able to:

Draw a tree diagram;

Translate situations into tree diagrams in order to solve counting problems;

Determine a set of outcomes using a tree diagram;

Describe patterns that come from partial trees.

At Krishna's Deli, customers have a choice of one of four types of meat—ham, chicken, beef, or turkey. Customers also have a choice of putting the meat on white, rye, or whole wheat bread.

Krishna claims that since there are four types of meat and three selections for bread, customers have a choice of seven different sandwiches. Is Krishna correct? Why?

7.28

Krishna's Deli  *Dan's Deli*

Down the street from Krishna's Deli is Dan's Deli. At Dan's Deli, customers have a choice of one of three types of meat—ham, chicken, or beef. Customers also have a choice of one of two types of bread—white or rye. Our problem is to find how many possible choices customers have at Dan's Deli.

One strategy for solving certain counting problems is to use a **tree diagram.** We shall discuss what is meant by a tree diagram using the example from Dan's Deli. Suppose a customer first selects the type of meat—ham (*H*), Chicken (*C*), or Beef (*B*). This first decision is illustrated in Display 7.15.

First Decision

H

C

B

Display 7.15

Published by IT'S ABOUT TIME, Inc. © 2000 MATHconx, LLC

7.4 Using Tree Diagrams to Count

Students should see that tree diagrams provide a useful counting technique. For some problems a tree diagram offers the most efficient method of solution. Our major object here, however, is to have students become familiar with tree diagrams so that they can be used in the next section as a foundation for the Fundamental Counting Principle.

7.28

No. Krishna is not correct. Students might remember the multiplication rule from previous years. Otherwise, students should be able to write a list to see that customers have a choice of twelve different sandwiches.

Ham on White	Beef on White
Ham on Rye	Beef on Rye
Ham on Whole Wheat	Beef on Whole Wheat
Chicken on White	Turkey on White
Chicken on Rye	Turkey on Rye
Chicken on Whole Wheat	Turkey on Whole Wheat

Additional Support Materials:

Assessments

	Qty
Form (A)	1
Form (B)	1

Blackline Masters

	Qty

Extensions

	Qty

Supplements

	Qty

Chapter 7

Each of the arrows represents one possible choice. Note that we have drawn our arrows from left to right. Sometimes you will see arrows drawn in other directions. For example, we might have illustrated these choices by drawing arrows from top to bottom as in Display 7.16.

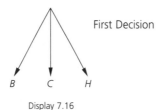

First Decision

Display 7.16

We shall continue to use the diagram in Display 7.15. The next step in constructing a tree diagram for this example is to indicate, by arrows, the second possible decision. In this case, for each choice of meat, a person has two choices of bread—white (W) or rye (R). These possibilities are illustrated in Display 7.17.

First
Decision

Second
Decision

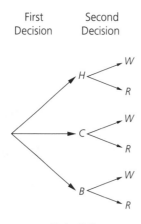

Display 7.17

Graphs, such as that in Display 7.17 are called *tree diagrams* because if you turn it so that the arrows face up, the result sort of looks like a tree with branches. Each arrow represents a **branch.** A complete choice at Dan's Deli is indicated by starting at the point on the left side of the tree diagram and following a path of arrows to a point on the right side. For example, the choice chicken on white bread is indicated by the blue arrows in Display 7.18.

Published by IT'S ABOUT TIME, Inc. © 2000 MATHconx, LLC

NOTES

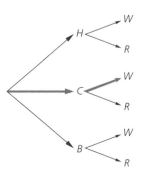

Display 7.18

The end points on the right side of the tree diagram correspond to different choices for sandwiches. Since there are six such end points, there are six different sandwiches available at Dan's Deli. That is, if S is the set of sandwiches available at Dan's Deli, then $\#(S) = 6$. An important way to view this result is the following: For each of the 3 initial branches in the tree diagram there are 2 subsequent branches for a total of $3 \cdot 2 = 6$ possible choices.

Tree diagrams, such as that in Display 7.18, frequently make it easy to list the elements of a set. For example, if S denotes the set of sandwiches available at Dan's Deli, one can simply read down the list of choices from the diagram. In this case one might write

$$S = \{HW, HR, CW, CR, BW, BR\}$$

where HW stands for "ham on white," HR stands for "ham on rye," etc.

7.29

1. (a) Draw a tree diagram for choices at Dan's Deli in which the first decision represents the type of bread to be used and the second decision is the type of meat.
   (b) In terms of the number of different sandwiches available, does it matter whether one specifies bread or meat first? Explain.
2. (a) Using a tree diagram, find the number of different sandwiches which are available at Krishna's Deli.
   (b) Let V be the set of sandwiches available at Krishna's Deli. Write this set V by listing the elements.

Published by IT'S ABOUT TIME, Inc. © 2000 MATHconx, LLC

440

7.29

1. (a) Display 7.19T gives a possible tree diagram.

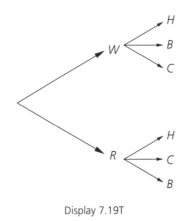

Display 7.19T

(b) It does not matter. The result is the same—six different selections.

2. (a) See Display 7.20T.

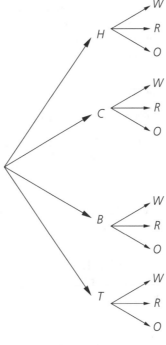

Display 7.20T

The letters represent: *H*-ham, *C*-chicken, *B*-beef, *T*-turkey, *W*-white, *R*-rye, and *O*-whole wheat.

(b) One way is to write
$V = \{HW, HR, HO, CW, CR, CO, BW, BR, BO, TW, TR, TO\}$.

Chapter 7

As another example, a coin is to be tossed twice. The result of each toss will be a head, denoted *H*, or a tail, denoted *T*. A tree diagram for this activity might look like the following (Display 7.19):

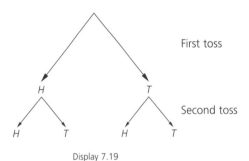

First toss

H   *T*

Second toss

H   *T*   *H*   *T*

Display 7.19

By starting at the top point and following a path of arrows (branches) one is able to visualize all the possible outcomes. For each of the 2 possible outcomes of the first toss there are 2 possible outcomes for the second toss. Thus there are $2 \cdot 2 = 4$ paths that one can follow. If *S* is the set of all possible outcomes, then $\#(S) = 4$. This set of all possible outcomes might be written as

$$S = \{HH, HT, TH, TT\}$$

Sometimes people will use ordered pair notation and write

$$S = \{(H,H), (H,T), (T,H), (T,T)\}$$

where, for example, (H,T) indicates a head on the first toss and a tail on the second toss.

1. Explain how the tree in Display 7.19 divides the set *S* into a pair of disjoint subsets, each of which has two elements.

7.30

2. A coin is to be tossed 3 times. Two possible outcomes are (H, T, H) and (T, H, H). Let *S* denote the set of all possible outcomes.

   (a) Use a tree diagram to find $\#(S)$.
   (b) Write the set *S* by listing all the elements.
   (c) Did you find your tree useful in writing the list in part (b)? Why?

441

Published by IT'S ABOUT TIME, Inc. © 2000 MATHconx, LLC

7.30

1. Looking at the tree, one should observe that the tree divides the set S into two disjoint sets—the first being the set of outcomes where H is the result of the first toss and the second set is the set of outcomes where T is the result of the first toss. i.e.,

$$S = \{HH, HT\} \cup \{TH, TT\}$$

or

$$S = \{(H, H), (H, T)\} \cup \{(T, H), (T, T)\}$$

2. (a) See Display 7.21T. It follows that $\#(s) = 8$.

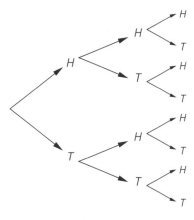

Display 7.21T

(b) $S = \{HHH, HHT, HTH, HTT, THH, THT, TTH, TTT\}$

(c) Students should find that the tree diagram in Display 7.21T is useful in making the list. A list can be found by starting at the left and working to the right (e.g., HHH, HHT, etc.).

NOTES

Chapter 7

Trees form a useful visual tool for getting the grasp on certain counting problems. In particular, trees are a valuable aid in gaining an understanding of the Fundamental Counting Principle which appears in the next section.

Thinking Tip

Look for a pattern.

Problem Set: 7.4

1. A company has main centers in New York and San Francisco. A fiber optic line is to be constructed from New York to one of the cities Chicago or Omaha, then from that city to one of the cities Denver, Phoenix, or Albuquerque, and finally on to San Francisco. Use a tree to determine the number of ways in which this line may be routed.

2. Mary and Felicia agree to play tennis until one of them wins three games. Use a tree diagram to determine the number of different ways this can happen.

3. A coin is tossed 5 times. Two possible outcomes are (H, H, T, H, T) and (T, H, T, T, T). Let S denote the set of all possible outcomes. By drawing part, but not all, of a tree diagram, see if you can determine $\#(S)$.

4. The World Series of Baseball involves one team from the National League (N) and one team from the American League (A). They play until one of the teams has won four games. Jason says that there are 24 different ways the series can be played and lists two examples—*NANNAN* and *AANANNA*. Jason uses *NANNAN* to mean the National League team won the first, third, fourth, and sixth games, while the American League team won the second and fifth games.

   (a) Is Jason correct when he says there are 24 different ways the series can be played?

   (b) Is it necessary to draw a complete tree in order to answer part (a)?

   (c) Who might be interested in knowing an answer to the question in part (a)?

Published by IT'S ABOUT TIME, Inc. © 2000 MATHconx, LLC

MATH *Connections*: A Secondary Mathematics Core Curriculum

Problem Set: 7.4

1. Using

    N-New York   *D*-Denver
    C-Chicago   *P*-Phoenix
    O-Omaha   *A*-Albuquerque
                      S-San Francisco

    one obtains a tree diagram such as that in Display 7.22T.

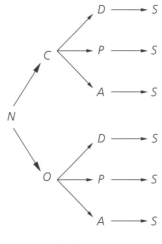

Display 7.22T

There are six ways in which the line may be routed.

NOTES

2.   Let *M*-Mary wins and *F*-Felicia wins. One could use a tree diagram such as that in Display 7.23T. Note that when a letter is underlined, the games stop.

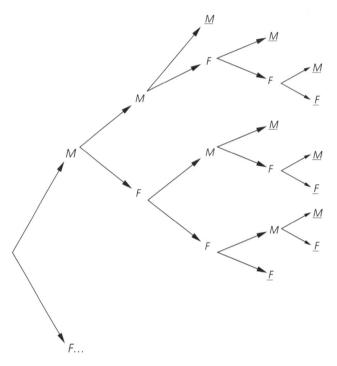

Display 7.23T

Students should recognize the symmetry of such a graph and realize that the number of possible paths beginning with *M* is the same as the number of paths beginning with *F*. Thus the answer is 2 · 10 = 20.

3.   The object here is to see how little of a tree diagram a student has to draw in order to see a pattern and use the symmetry involved to get the correct answer which is 32.

4.   (a) Jason is way off. There are 70 different ways this series can be played.
     (b) From the symmetry, students should be aware that they need only consider one initial branch where, say *N* is the winner. At the end, simply double this result. A partial tree is given in Display 7.24T. When a letter is underlined, the series stops. For clarity of the tree diagram, the arrows have been omitted.
     (c) Student answers will vary. Makers and vendors of souvenirs might be interested in covering all bases for production and inventory purposes. To make sure all bases are covered involves knowing how many bases are possible.

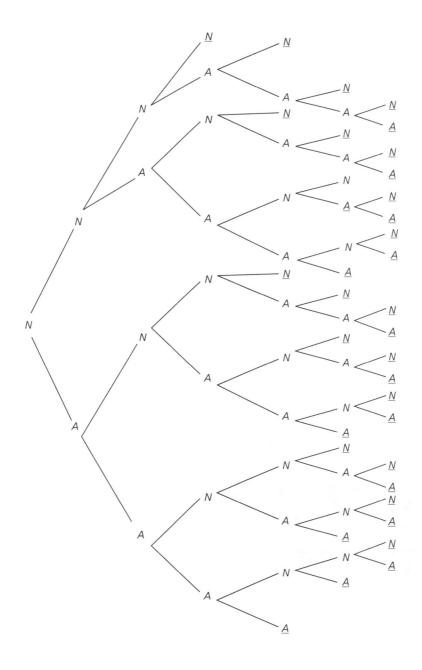

Display 7.24T

Chapter 7

5. Display 7.20 represents nine city blocks; the lines indicate streets. A person at the point *A* in the lower left hand corner wishes to travel to the point *B* in the upper right hand corner along the streets. At any corner, the person must go North or East. How many different paths could this person take from *A* to *B*? (Problems like this one play a role in routing ambulances, fire trucks, etc.)

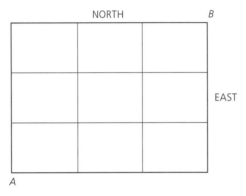

Display 7.20

6. Are there four children in your family or do you know someone from a family with four children? If the first child born in a certain family is a girl (*G*), the second a boy (*B*), the third a girl (*G*) and the fourth a boy (*B*), we could write *GBGB* to indicate the order in which the children were born. Use a tree diagram to determine how many different orders are possible for a family with four children.

443

Published by IT'S ABOUT TIME, Inc. © 2000 MATHconx, LLC

5. Use *N* for a North block and *E* for an East block. The first move from *A* can be either *N* or *E*. Note that each path from *A* to *B* must contain exactly three *E*'s and three *N*'s. By symmetry, one need only follow one initial branch (Display 7.25T) which gives 10 paths. Doubling this number gives a total of 20 paths.

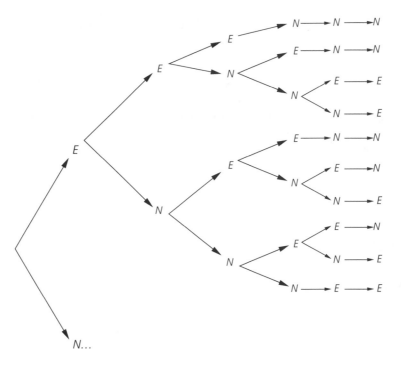

Display 7.25T

6. One could use a partial tree diagram as shown in Display 7.26T. There are 16 possible outcomes ($2 \cdot 2 \cdot 2 \cdot 2$).

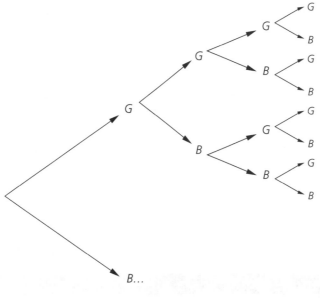

Display 7.26T

7.5 The Fundamental Counting Principle

Learning Outcomes

After studying this section, you will be able to:

Solve a variety of problems using the Fundamental Counting Principle;

Model various situations which lead to the use of the Fundamental Counting Principle;

Use the Fundamental Counting Principle to explain why a counting process works in certain models.

In the last section we looked at a tree diagram for customer choices at Dan's Deli. Customers had a choice of three meats—ham (H), chicken (C), or beef (B), plus a choice of white (W) or rye (R) bread. The tree diagram appears again in Display 7.21

First Decision   Second Decision

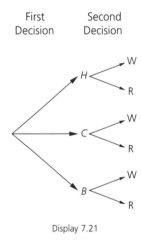

Display 7.21

A **complete branch** in a tree diagram is a path from the starting point to an end point following the arrows (branches) in the diagram. For example, the path marked in blue in Display 7.22 is a complete branch.

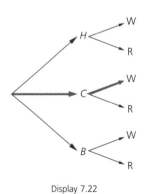

Display 7.22

Published by IT'S ABOUT TIME, Inc. © 2000 MATHconx, LLC

444

7.5 The Fundamental Counting Principle

It is extremely important for students to understand the ideas of this section. The Fundamental Counting Principle will be used in the following chapter on probability and in later material on statistics. The notion of a "permutation" is within easy grasp, but this word is not used in the text of this section. In addition, the idea of "factorial", along with its properties, is one which many teachers emphasize in this section.

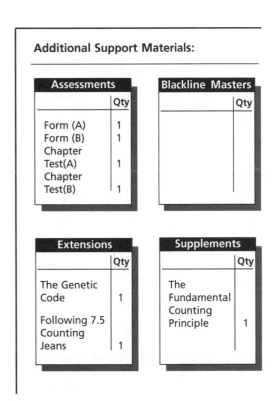

Additional Support Materials:

Assessments	Qty
Form (A)	1
Form (B)	1
Chapter Test(A)	1
Chapter Test(B)	1

Blackline Masters	Qty

Extensions	Qty
The Genetic Code	1
Following 7.5 Counting Jeans	1

Supplements	Qty
The Fundamental Counting Principle	1

Chapter 7

1. How many complete branches are there in the tree diagram of Display 7.21?

2. In a tree diagram for Krishna's Deli of the previous section, how many complete branches are there?

a
7.31

The tree diagram (which we will just call a *tree*) in Display 7.21 is called a **two-level tree.** The first level indicates the first decision, which in this case is meat, and the second level indicates the second decision, which is bread. There are three branches to get to the first level and each entry at the first level has two branches to get to the second level. We ask that you think carefully about this statement—*Each entry at the first level has two branches to get to the second level. No matter what first-level entry you pick, you have the same number of branches to the second level.* The number of first-level entries is 3. For each of these entries there are 2 branches to the next level. There are $3 \cdot 2 = 6$ complete branches.

This idea is important enough to state as a *principle.* A **principle** is a basic rule which we accept and use to solve problems. If applied properly, such a rule will lead us to the correct results. We ask you to help by filling in the blank with the question mark.

Principle: If the first level of a tree has *m* entries and, if every first-level entry has exactly *n* branches to the second level, the two-level tree has exactly **?** complete branches.

b
7.32

For lunch you decide to have a sandwich and a dessert. You have a choice of a ham sandwich or a chicken sandwich. For dessert you have a choice of ice cream, pie, yogurt, cake, or pudding. By thinking of a tree, but without drawing one, determine the number of different lunches you could have. What are your first-level entries? What are your second-level entries?

The above principle can be extended to trees with more than two levels.

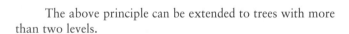

Published by IT'S ABOUT TIME, Inc. © 2000 MATHconx, LLC

7.31

1. There are six complete branches.

2. In the tree diagram for Krishna's Deli of the previous section, Display 7.20T of the Teacher Commentary, there are twelve complete branches.

7.32

In the *Principle*, the __?__ should be replaced by *mn*. In the example which follows, there are $2 \cdot 5 = 10$ different lunches.

NOTES

Chapter 7

a

7.33

1. A three-level tree has two first-level entries. For each first-level entry there are four second-level entries. For each second-level entry there are two third-level entries. Draw a picture of such a tree. What is the total number of complete branches?

2. In a three-level tree there are *n* first-level entries. For each first-level entry there are *m* second-level entries. For each second-level entry there are *r* third-level entries. Complete the following sentence.

There are _____ complete branches.

These problems and examples, based on ideas from trees, illustrate the Fundamental Counting Principle.

FUNDAMENTAL COUNTING PRINCIPLE

Two Actions: If one action can be taken in *m* ways, and for each of those *m* ways a second action can be taken in *n* ways, then the two actions can be taken in $m \cdot n$ ways.

Three Actions: If one action can be taken in *r* ways, and for each of those *r* ways a second action can be taken in *s* ways, and for each of those *s* ways a third action can be taken in *t* ways, then the three actions can be taken in $r \cdot s \cdot t$ ways.

K Actions: If one action can be taken in n_1 ways, and for each of those n_1 ways a second action can be taken in n_2 ways, and for each of those n_2 ways a third action can be taken in n_3 ways and so on up to a *k*th action that can be taken in n_k ways, then the sequence of *k* actions can be taken in

$$n_1 \cdot n_2 \cdot n_3 \cdot \ldots \cdot n_k$$

ways.

We shall sometimes write FCP for the Fundamental Counting Principle.

b

7.34

Explain how the two-action and three-action parts of the FCP are special cases of the *K*-action part. What are $n_1, n_2, n_3, \ldots, n_k$ in each case? Do you think it is necessary to memorize the FCP? Why?

446

7.33

1. Students might draw a tree similar to the following Display 7.27T.

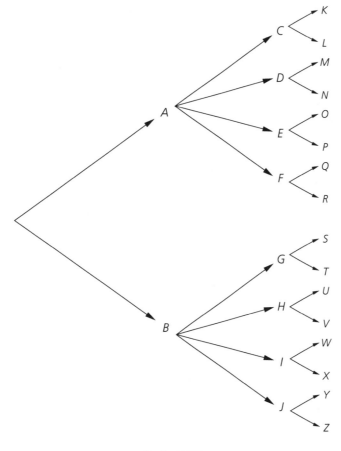

Display 7.27T

There are $2 \cdot 4 \cdot 2 = 16$ complete branches.

2. There are $n \cdot m \cdot r$ complete branches.

7.34

Student answers will vary. The idea is that in the two action part, $k = 2$, $n_1 = m$, and $n_2 = n$. In the three action part, $k = 3$, $n_1 = r$, $n_2 = s$, and $n_3 = t$. With the tree image in mind, students should have little difficulty remembering the Fundamental Counting Principle.

Here is a question that is easily answered by the FCP. In a certain class, the students Sal, Kim, Mac, Anna, and Jane are responsible for checking student homework. One of these five students is to be selected as chairperson and another as vice chairperson. In how many ways can this be done?

Suppose our first action is to select a chairperson—this can be done in 5 ways. After that, our second action is to select a vice chairperson. Since a chairperson has already been selected, we have only 4 ways of taking this second action. By the FCP, a chairperson and a vice chairperson can be selected in $5 \cdot 4 = 20$ different ways.

1. If we first select a vice chairperson and then a chairperson, do we get the same answer?

2. Suppose that in addition to a chairperson and a vice chairperson we also had to select some other person in the group as a secretary. In how many ways can the three people be chosen?

a

7.35

The FCP offers a way of solving many counting problems for which a tree diagram is impractical. For example, in the state of Euphoria, license plates for automobiles consist of 2 letters followed by 3 digits. Letters and digits may be repeated. Thus WR135, WW211, and ST308 are possible license plates. Our problem is to determine how many license plates are possible. One might consider the following sequence of actions.

Action 1: Choose the first letter—26 possible ways
Action 2: Choose the second letter—26 possible ways
Action 3: Choose the first digit—10 possible ways
Action 4: Choose the second digit—10 possible ways
Action 5: Choose the third digit—10 possible ways

By the FCP there are $26 \cdot 26 \cdot 10 \cdot 10 \cdot 10 = 26^2 \cdot 10^3 = 676,000$ possible license plates. Try to imagine what a tree diagram would look like for this problem.

1. How many license plates are possible in the state of Euphoria if letters and digits may not be repeated?

2. How many license plates are possible in the state of Euphoria if letters and digits may be repeated, but the last digit cannot be 0?

b

7.36

Published by IT'S ABOUT TIME, Inc. © 2000 MATHconx, LLC

447

1b

7.35

1. Yes. Again there are 5 choices for the vice chairperson and then 4 choices for the chairperson. The actions are commutative.

2. $5 \cdot 4 \cdot 3 = 60$ different ways

7.36

1. $26 \cdot 25 \cdot 10 \cdot 9 \cdot 8 = 468,000$ different plates

2. $26 \cdot 26 \cdot 10 \cdot 10 \cdot 9 = 608,400$ different plates

NOTES

Chapter 7

REFLECT

We hope that the material in this chapter has helped you develop an ability to count. The extensions and applications of those tools will assume even greater importance as you progress further into the ideas of probability and statistics. Good Luck!

Problem Set: 7.5

1. The word "digit" refers to one of the numbers 0, 1, 2, 3, 4, 5, 6, 7, 8, or 9. In a certain state lottery one picks 4 digits. For example, one might pick 2337, 1279, or 9993. How many different selections are possible?

2. A license plate in a certain state consists of two letters followed by three digits. How many possible license plates are there if the letters and digits may be repeated?

3. If license plates are to have three letters followed by three digits, how many different license plates can be made if all the digits must be different and the letters may be repeated on any one plate?

4. Five vice presidents of a certain company are to be placed in five offices. In how many different ways can such placements be made?

5. A company has 783 employees. Carefully explain why there must be at least two employees with the same pair of initials.

6. How many digits are in a Social Security number? How many Social Security numbers are possible?

7. Radio and TV station names, like WPVI and KYW begin with a W or K followed by either two or three letters.

    (a) How many names of stations are possible?

    (b) The FCC is a government agency. What does FCC stand for?

    (c) Why might a person who works for the FCC be interested in how many names of stations are possible?

8. A mathematics class has 17 students. A photographer arrives to take a class picture. Since some students are tall and some are short, the photographer asks the students to arrange themselves in different orders along a line so she can select the arrangement that looks best. If the students

Published by IT'S ABOUT TIME, Inc. © 2000 MATHconx, LLC

Problem Set: 7.5

1. One has to fill four slots (i.e., take four actions) __ __ __ __ .

   The first slot can be filled in any one of 10 ways. The second slot can then be filled in 10 ways, the third in 10 ways, and the fourth in 10 ways. By the FCP there are
   $$10 \cdot 10 \cdot 10 \cdot 10 = 10^4 = 10,000 \text{ different selections.}$$

2. There are $26^2 10^3 = 676,000$ possible license plates.

3. Answer is given by $26^3 \cdot 10 \cdot 9 \cdot 8 = 12,654,720$

4. One vice president can be assigned an office in 5 ways. A second vice president can then be assigned an office in 4 ways, etc. The answer is given by
   $$5 \cdot 4 \cdot 3 \cdot 2 \cdot 1 = 120$$

   Note that at some point in this section the teacher should introduce the factorial notation. This could be such a point. Tell students that
   $$5! = 5 \cdot 4 \cdot 3 \cdot 2 \cdot 1 = 120$$

   and give several other examples such as
   $$7! = 7 \cdot 6 \cdot 5 \cdot 4 \cdot 3 \cdot 2 \cdot 1 = 5040$$

   Get students to see, for example, that
   $$8! = 8 \cdot 7! = 8\,(5040) = 40,320$$

   If students have a calculator with ! operation, make sure they know how to use it. On the TI-82 (TI-83), for example, to compute 7! one keys

   7 MATH PRB 4 ENTER

5. There are $26^2 = 676$ different pairs of initials. Since there are 783 employees, at least two must have the same pair of initials.

6. A Social Security number consists of

   $$\underline{3 \text{ digits}} - \underline{2 \text{ digits}} - \underline{4 \text{ digits}}$$

   The answer is given by
   $$10^3 \cdot 10^2 \cdot 10^4 = 10^9 = 1,000,000,000$$

7. (a) There are 18,252 possible names that begin with K and the same number that begin with W. Hence the answer is 36,504.
   (b) FCC stands for Federal Communications Commission.
   (c) A person who works for the FCC would be interested in the number of possible names since that number limits the number of possible stations using these requirements for station names.

8. There are $17! = 3.556874281 \cdot 10^{14}$

   different arrangements. Hence the time required is 17! seconds. Assuming each year has 365 days, this result corresponds to
   $$\frac{17!}{31,536,000} = 11,278,774.36 \text{ years}$$

   There are 31,536,000 seconds in a year, assuming that a year contains 365 days.

Chapter 7

are able to form one new arrangement every second, how long will it take for them to arrange themselves in every possible order? (*Hint:* Use a calculator.)

9. In a coastal state there are 19,953,134 registered automobiles.

   (a) If one is restricted to use only digits and a license plate must contain at least one but no more than n digits (a digit may be used more than once on a plate), what is the smallest value of n so that a sufficient number of plates can be made?

   (b) How does the result of part (a) change if one is allowed to use either digits or letters, with the letters I, L, O, and S being prohibited because of possible confusion with certain digits?

10. In a certain computer programming language, an "identifier" is a list (sequence) of a certain number of symbols where the first symbol is a letter of the English alphabet and each of the remaining symbols may be either a letter or a digit. For example, F43Y2 is an identifier of length 5 (it contains five symbols).

    (a) What is the total number of identifiers of length five possible for use in this computer language?

    (b) How many possible identifiers are there of length 1 or more, up to and including 5?

11. A midwestern state presently licenses 1,570,000 cars and trucks and the number is increasing at the rate of about 10,000 a year. The state requires a license to consist of three letters of the alphabet followed by three digits, and no letter or digit can be repeated in a license plate. A state senator is concerned that the state will soon run out of license plates. If the above rate of increase remains in effect, in how many years will the state run out of license plates?

12. In computer science a **binary string** is a list (sequence) of 0's and 1's. For example, 0010110 is a binary string of length 7; 1001 is a binary string of length 4, and 01101 is a binary string of length 5.

    (a) How many binary strings are there of length 7?

    (b) How many binary strings are there of length 7 which begin and end with 0?

9. (a) You might suggest that students put the results in a table similar to the following Display 7.28T.

No. of Digits	No. of Plates	Cumulative Total
1	10	10
2	100	110
3	1000	1110
4	10,000	11,110
5	100,000	111,110
6	1,000,000	1,111,110
7	10,000,000	11,111,110
8	100,000,000	111,111,110

Display 7.28T

Stop. One needs at least 8 digits.

(b) This question may be challenging to some students because intermixing of letters and numbers is permitted. The number of possibilities thus created may at first confuse students. A breakdown into components of the first three entries in Display 7.29T follows. For this question, a table might look similar to Display 7.29T.

1. $22 + 10 = 32$

2. $22 \cdot 22 = 484$
$22 \cdot 10 = 220$
$10 \cdot 22 = 220$
$10 \cdot 10 = \underline{100}$
1024

3. $22 \cdot 22 \cdot 22 = 10,648$
$22 \cdot 10 \cdot 22 = 4840$
$22 \cdot 22 \cdot 10 = 4840$
$10 \cdot 22 \cdot 22 = 4840$
$10 \cdot 10 \cdot 22 = 2200$
$10 \cdot 22 \cdot 10 = 2200$
$22 \cdot 10 \cdot 10 = 2200$
$10 \cdot 10 \cdot 10 = \underline{1000}$
$32,768$

No. of Digits or Letters	No. of Plates	Cumulative Total
1	32	32
2	1024	1056
3	32,768	33,824
4	1,048,576	1,082,400
5	33,554,432	34,636,832

Display 7.29T

Stop. The answer is now 5.

Chapter 7

10. (a) There are $26 \cdot 36^4 = 43,670,016$ identifiers of length 5.
    (b) For the second question one might use the table in Display 7.30T.

Length	No. of Identifiers
1	26
2	936
3	33,696
4	1,213,056
5	43,670,016
TOTAL	44,917,730

Display 7.30T

11. The state senator should not be concerned. There are 11,232,000 possible license plates. The population would have to increase by 9,662,000 in order to reach this number. At the present rate this would take about 966.2 years.

12. Answers are given by
    (a) $2^7 = 128$
    (b) Since the first and the last digits must be 0, the only actions to be taken are in the choice of the 5 digits between the two 0's, which yields $2^5 = 32$ different strings.

NOTES

NOTES

(c) How many binary strings are there of length 7 which begin or end with 0?

(d) How many binary strings are there of length 7 which have 0 as the second digit?

(e) How many binary strings of length 7 contain exactly one 0?

(f) How many binary strings of length 7 begin with 01 and have a 0 as the fourth digit?

13. Let us return to the example of Section 7.1 concerning the storage of information on a compact disc (CD). Information about the music on a CD is stored using the binary digits 0 and 1. We are only interested in the loudness level or volume of the sound. As previously stated, we might code these levels as

Volume	Code
soft	0
loud	1

or

Level	Code
very soft	00
soft	01
loud	10
very loud	11

(a) How many volume levels can be coded if each code contains

   (i) three bits

   (ii) four bits

(b) If one wishes to code 1000 different sound levels, how many bits must appear in each code word, assuming all code words contain exactly the same number of bits?

Published by IT'S ABOUT TIME, Inc. © 2000 MATHconx, LLC

(c) There are $2^6 = 64$ strings which begin with 0 and $2^6 = 64$ which end with 0. There are $2^5 = 32$ strings which begin and end with 0. The answer is given by $64 + 64 - 32 = 96$.

For students who need a more formal treatment, let

A = set of strings of length 7 which begin with 0.

B = set of strings of length 7 which end with 0.

Then, $\#(A \cup B) = \#(A) + \#(B) - \#(A \cap B) = 64 + 64 - 32 = 96$.

(d) Since the string must look like $\_0\_\_\_\_\_$ we have only 6 slots to fill. This can be done in $2^6 = 64$ ways.

(e) The one 0 can appear in any of the 7 positions.

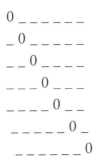

```
0 _ _ _ _ _ _
_ 0 _ _ _ _ _
_ _ 0 _ _ _ _
_ _ _ 0 _ _ _
_ _ _ _ 0 _ _
_ _ _ _ _ 0 _
_ _ _ _ _ _ 0
```

Since each of the other positions must contain a 1, there only are 7 different strings.

(f) The string must look like $0\ 1\ \_\ 0\ \_\ \_\ \_$ so that only 4 slots have to be filled. This can be done in $2^4 = 16$ different ways.

13. (a) Using the FCP, it is seen that (i) 8 sound levels can be coded if each code contains three bits and (ii) 16 sound levels can be coded if each code contains four bits.

(b) In order to code 1000 different sound levels, it is necessary to use 10 bits in each code.

NOTES

NOTES

Chapter 8 Planning Guide

Chapter 8 Introduction to Probability: What Are the Chances?

Chapter 8 makes immediate use of Chapter 7. Combining counting with chance, it presents the probability function for events of equally likely outcomes. Later sections describe how to simulate uncertain situations by using random number tables or by calculator programs.

Assessments Form A (A)	Assessments Form B (B)	Blackline Masters
Quiz 8.1-8.2(A) Quiz 8.3(A) Project 8.4-8.5(A) Chapter Test(A)	Quiz 8.1-8.2(B) Quiz 8.3(B) Chapter Test(B)	Student pp. 455-456,477, 489-490

Extensions	Supplements for Chapter Sections	Test Banks
8.3 What Are the Odds?	8.1 Basic Ideas of Probability — 1 Supplement 8.2 Intuition and Probability — 1 Supplement	To be released

Pacing Range 2-3 weeks including Assessments

Teachers will need to adjust this guide to suit the needs of their own students. Not all classes will complete each chapter at the same pace. Flexibility — which accommodates different teaching styles, school schedules and school standards — is built into the curriculum.

Teacher Commentary is indexed to the student text by the numbers in the margins (under the icons or in circles). The first digit indicates the chapter — the numbers after the decimal indicate the sequential numbering of the comments within that unit. Example:

8.9   8.37

Student Pages in Teacher Edition

8.9   8.37

Teacher Commentary Page

Observations

Bryan Morgan, Teacher
Oxford Hills Comprehensive High School, ME

"Chapter 8 covers the role of chance in the real world and the role of mathematics in determining the Probability of outcomes. I have found that Probability is best learned through doing, so make sure to do a great deal of these problems with your students, then let them do the rest on their own. The more problems they do the better, so give them lots of problems and then let them take the problems apart. They'll need to discuss them and clear up all the misconceptions they have since with Probability there are no cut and dried formulas. The students will need to discover how one problem is different from another, which is why there are so many problems to solve. This chapter lays a solid foundation for Probability which will be built on later in the program. I really like the way this program builds difficulty gradually. It comes back to subjects in more formal and traditional settings when the students are more algebraically and academically mature. I point this out to teachers all the time – when they look at Year 1 they shouldn't judge the difficulty of the program and similarly when they look at Year 3 they shouldn't judge that it will be impossible for their students to do. It builds the difficulty so gradually that the kids don't even notice it."

Chapter 8

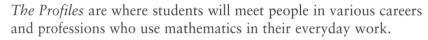
Stafford Thompson
Predicting the Unknown

Stafford Thompson is a senior actuarial analyst at CIGNA Health Care. "I really enjoy being a mathematician," he explains. "I like being able to identify problems, put them into a mathematical context, and then solve them!"

Stafford had always liked math. The summer after 11th grade found him at a camp for actuarial science. "I had no idea what an actuary was, but I knew they offered calculus and linear algebra, so I wanted to go." He went on to Florida Agricultural and Mechanical University in Tallahassee. He earned a B.S. in Mathematics with a concentration in Actuarial Science.

It's commonly believed that actuaries just help insurance companies predict when policyholders will get sick or die. In fact, actuaries perform many interesting types of statistical analysis. They can figure the probability of a baseball player hitting a fan on the head with a foul ball. They can predict the chance that space shuttle debris will land on your house. They can also calculate the probability of serious injury to Michael Jackson, whose voice is insured for millions.

Stafford uses his actuarial skills to predict how profitable an investment will be. "We use the law of large numbers. We can't really predict what a person will do. But with many millions of individuals, we can do a very reliable job." Using probability, averages and measures of variance, Stafford forecasts the values of various investments. "We look at current and past rates over a 10 to 15 year history," he explains. "We try to predict the rate of inflation. There's a lot of educated guesswork."

Stafford's long-term goal is to teach Actuarial Science at a university. "I want to prepare other students for an actuarial career."

"I like my job," he concludes. "I like the opportunity to use my skills. I enjoy making money, and actuarial science provides a foundation for any entrepreneurial dreams you may have. Using financial analysis, I've learned how to build a business from the ground up."

452

Chapter 8   Introduction to Probability: What Are The Chances?

This chapter on probability builds on students' previous middle school education in this area, although the only formal prerequisites are the counting techniques of the previous chapter. The role of "chance" in the lives of all of us is an important one and it is hoped that students will sense the precision of mathematics in formalizing our ideas about events where the outcomes are uncertain. Sections 1–3 of this chapter are essential for later material in **MATH** *Connections*. Sections 4 and 5 are quite challenging and highly recommended for those students with interest in preparing for the sciences.

Chapter 8

Introduction to Probability: What Are the Chances?

CHAPTER 8

8.1 Basic Ideas of Probability

Last night on the Late News, a weather forecaster stated, "There is a 40 percent chance of rain tomorrow."

Write a paragraph on what this statement from the forecaster means to you.

8.1

8.2

1. If a weather forecaster stated that there is a 90 percent chance of rain tomorrow, would this affect any plans you have? What other people might have plans that would be affected by this forecast?

2. Is there a chance that you will pass this mathematics course? Are you sure that you will pass this course? Are you certain that you will not pass this course? Explain!

Almost every day we hear someone use the word *chance*. When the word chance is used, it is frequently applied to some future activity (rain tomorrow) or an event (passing a course at the end of a term) for which we are *not certain* of the outcome. The two questions above refer to events which, in general, are not certain, the occurrence of rain and the passing of this course.

Published by IT'S ABOUT TIME, Inc. © 2000 MATHconx, LLC

453

8.1 Basic Ideas of Probability

A purpose of this first section is to have students connect the ideas of probability with daily events in their lives. It is important that students begin to relate the common word "chance" to "probability." It is also important for students to realize that a probability must be a number between 0 and 1 inclusive.

8.1

This should be a short (5 minute) writing project to be completed in class. See what students write and have a discussion among students. In particular, a weather forecaster studies maps, which give pictures of the weather systems. The forecaster knows how these systems—highs, lows, air masses, and fronts—normally develop and move. If past maps show that the present weather system is not moving normally, the forecaster must determine the chances that it will continue to move in the same way, or will begin to move in a more nearly normal way. If the normal way would result in rain, then the forecaster is determining the chances of rain.

8.2

These questions are for class discussion.

1. If you plan to come to school tomorrow, you might bring an umbrella but otherwise not change any plans you have. However, if you have tickets for a World Series Game, your plans might change significantly.

2. Another set of discussion questions. Get students to give their ideas about the meaning of *sure* and *certain*.

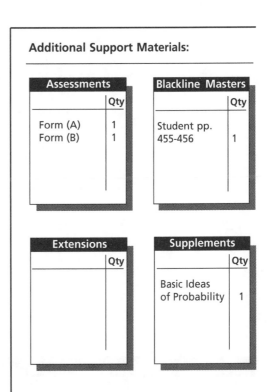

Additional Support Materials:

Assessments	Qty
Form (A)	1
Form (B)	1

Blackline Masters	Qty
Student pp. 455-456	1

Extensions	Qty

Supplements	Qty
Basic Ideas of Probability	1

Chapter 8

8.3

1. List three other events that are not certain.

2. Some events are *certain*. For example, it is certain that a human being cannot live for a year without food or water. List three other events that are certain.

3. Some events are *impossible*. For example, it is impossible for you to run 500 miles per hour. List three other events that are impossible.

In the language of mathematics, the word *probability* is used instead of *chance*. The phrase "there is a 40 percent chance of rain" becomes "the probability of rain is 0.40."

The following diagrams may help you understand what is happening. A weather forecaster states that there is a 40% chance of rain tomorrow. Let E stand for the event "it rains tomorrow." On a number line, we look at the interval [0,1].

The forecaster is telling us that the probability of rain tomorrow is the number indicated by x on this number line.

In mathematical notation we write $P(E) = 0.40$

which is read "The probability of E is 0.40".

If an event E is certain, we take $P(E) = 1$.

If an event E is impossible, we take $P(E) = 0$.

Published by IT'S ABOUT TIME, Inc. © 2000 MATHconx, LLC

8.3

1. See what ideas students have. For example, are they certain that they will not get a cold next week?

2. Students are likely to come up with ideas like "tomorrow, 2 + 2 will equal 4" or "the sun will come up tomorrow."

3. See what ideas students have. For example, they might come up with something like "it is impossible for me to buy a new car."

NOTES

Chapter 8

The following problems will help you learn more about describing events and assigning numbers or probabilities to them.

1. For each of the following events, select a number on the line below the statement which indicates the probability you would assign to the given event E. Also write your answers in the form "$P(E) = number$". Be prepared to explain your choices. The word "I" refers to you, the reader.

(a) I will watch TV sometime tomorrow.

$P(E) = $ _____

(b) I will listen to a CD (compact disc) sometime tomorrow.

$P(E) = $ _____

(c) I will drink a soda tomorrow.

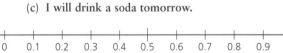

$P(E) = $ _____

(d) It will rain tomorrow.

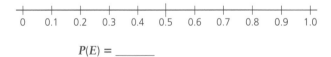

$P(E) = $ _____

Published by IT'S ABOUT TIME, Inc. © 2000 MATHconx, LLC

455

8.4

It is suggested that a set of these questions be copied and handed out to each student. Blackline Masters are provided. Have them fill in the x's and then have a class discussion as to why they filled in the probabilities the way they did.

NOTES

_____

Chapter 8

(e) It will snow tomorrow.

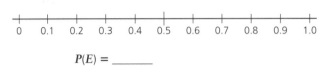

$P(E) =$ _____

(f) I will run 500 miles next weekend.

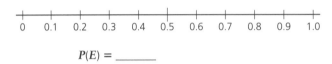

$P(E) =$ _____

Now we can make our ideas a little more formal. The basic concept is the following: For any event, call it E, we assign a number between 0 and 1 inclusive, denoted $P(E)$. We call $P(E)$ **the probability of E** and frequently say $P(E)$ is the **probability that E will happen.**

8.5

1. Describe an event E for which you believe $P(E) = \frac{1}{2}$. That is, the probability for the event E would be the number indicated below.

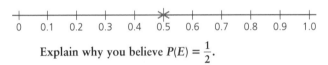

   Explain why you believe $P(E) = \frac{1}{2}$.

2. Describe an event E for which you believe $P(E) = \frac{1}{4}$. Explain why you believe $P(E) = \frac{1}{4}$.

3. On a recent TV show a medical doctor said to a group of people, "The patient has a better than even chance of surviving." What does this doctor's statement mean to you? On what basis does a doctor make such a statement?

We frequently use past experience to arrive at a probability for an event. For example, consider a baseball player who made 51 hits in the last 300 times at bat. If someone asked "What is the probability that this player will

456

Published by IT'S ABOUT TIME, Inc. © 2000 MATHconx, LLC

8.5

1. Getting a head on a toss of a coin, or getting a tail on a toss of a coin, are likely candidates from students.

2. This one should get some interesting solutions from students. If they do not come up with something interesting, you might suggest something geometric like the following. Take a rectangle and divide it into 4 equal parts. Think of it as a dart board. If you are blindfolded, throw a dart and hit the board. What is the probability that your dart is in the upper left hand section?

probability $= \frac{1}{4}$	

3. An "even" chance of surviving would mean that in the past with similar patients, half survived and half did not survive. A "better than even" chance would mean that in the past, with similar patients, more than half survived and less than half did not survive. See what students write.

NOTES

....

....

....

....

....

....

....

Chapter 8

make a hit the next time at bat?" the answer would likely be "The probability is $\frac{51}{300} = 0.17$." In this case, past experience was used to determine a probability.

8.6

1. In the last 8 games, a baseball player walked 13 times, made a hit 11 times, and struck out 26 times. The player is now coming up to bat. What probability would you assign to the event that this player strikes out?

2. Bates Insurance Company sells auto insurance. During the past year, 783 of their customers were not involved in an accident, 132 were involved in minor accidents, and 18 were involved in major accidents. What probability would you assign to the event that a new customer is involved in a minor accident during the next year? (Round your answer to two decimal places.)

In probability, our goal is to assign numbers between 0 and 1 inclusive to events that interest us. In particular, the events usually involve situations or activities for which we do not know the outcome. We have seen that people sometimes assign such numbers or probabilities on the basis of past experience. In order to have "past experience" available, it is frequently useful, or necessary, to perform experiments.

Consider the activity of tossing two coins. Before the coins are tossed we do not know what the outcome will be. We could get two tails, two heads, or one head and one tail. Let us ask, "What is the probability of getting two tails?" Our event E is given by

E: two tails

and we want a number $P(E)$ which is between 0 and 1 inclusive. One method to determine $P(E)$ is the following.

I tossed two coins 50 times and counted the number of times two tails appeared. I found that 11 times out of 50 tosses there were two tails. The results of this experiment were, for

Published by IT'S ABOUT TIME, Inc. © 2000 MATHconx, LLC

457

8.6

1. $\frac{26}{50}$ or 0.52

2. $\frac{132}{933} = 0.14$ to two decimal places. This assumes that the two accident customer sets are disjoint.

NOTES

Chapter 8

8.1 Basic Ideas of Probability

me, a past experience. On this basis, one could say that $P(E) = \frac{11}{50} = 0.22$. However, a friend of mine tossed two coins 50 times and got two tails 14 times. For my friend, on the basis of past experience, one could say that $P(E) = \frac{14}{50} = 0.28$. Which answer is correct, 0.22 or 0.28? Neither should be taken as the correct answer. Both are estimates of the probability $P(E)$. These estimates came from two experiments. The first experiment was my tossing two coins 50 times and the second experiment was my friend tossing two coins 50 times. *Estimates of probabilities will usually change from one experiment to another.*

8.7

1. Take two coins and toss them 25 times. Count the number of times two tails appeared. What is your estimate of $P(E)$? Write your answer in decimal form. How does your estimate compare with that of other students in the class?

2. For all of the experiments described above there is a formula which we have been using to compute $P(E)$. Write this formula in the form

$$P(E) = \underline{\hspace{3cm}}$$

Be as precise as you can.

In summary, *probability* is primarily concerned with situations in which we are not certain of the outcome. A probability is a number between 0 and 1 inclusive which measures, to some extent, our confidence that a particular outcome will occur. These numbers may result from nothing more than a "gut" feeling, from past experience, from experiments, or from a combination of these. They may also be the result of *intuition*, which is the subject of the next section.

Problem Set: 8.1

1. In the last 24 attempts, a basketball player made 5 field goals.

   (a) What probability would you assign to the event that this player makes a field goal on the next attempt?

   (b) What probability would you assign to the event that this player misses on the next attempt?

458

Published by IT'S ABOUT TIME, Inc. © 2000 MATHconx, LLC

8.7

1. Have students compare their estimates of $P(E)$. See if students will come up with the idea of pooling their results. What estimate of $P(E)$ comes from such a pooling? Do they think that this is a better estimate of $P(E)$ than any individual estimate?

2. One would hope that students would come up with something similar to the following.

$$P(E) = \frac{\text{number of times two tails appeared}}{\text{number of times coins were tossed}}$$

Problem Set: 8.1

1. (a) $\frac{5}{24}$ (b) $\frac{19}{24}$

NOTES

Chapter 8

2. In the last 3 games, a baseball player walked 4 times, made a hit 3 times, and struck out 10 times. The player is now coming to bat. What probability would you assign to the event that this player does *not* strike out?

3. Insurance companies sometimes make use of probabilities based on past experience in determining insurance rates. Life insurance costs, automobile insurance costs, etc. can depend on such probabilities. Consider the following scenario: In a certain state, past experience indicates that nine out of every one hundred cars are involved in accidents during a year. Thus the probability of a particular car being involved in an accident next year is taken to be $\frac{9}{100} = 0.09$. Some accidents (fender benders) are minor ones, but others involve major repairs. The Wingate Insurance Company insures 200,000 cars in this state.

   (a) How many of these cars can the company expect to be involved in accidents during the next year? Explain!

   (b) The average (mean) cost to the insurance company is $1,500 per accident. How much money can the Wingate Co. expect to pay next year for auto repairs? Explain!

   (c) In order to survive, the company needs $50,000,000 left after paying for auto repairs. If each car owner is going to pay the same amount, how much must the company charge each insured owner? Explain!

Published by IT'S ABOUT TIME, Inc. © 2000 MATHconx, LLC

459

2. $\frac{7}{17}$

3. (a) $(0.09)(200,000) = 18,000$
   (b) $(18,000)(1500) = \$27,000,000$
   (c) $385

NOTES

Chapter 8

4. Consider the following situation. You have a cup filled with five marbles. Four of the marbles are white and one is green. Without looking into the cup you reach in and pull out a marble. If it is green you stop. If it is white, you put the marble aside and select another marble, and so forth until you pull out the green marble. Obviously you cannot determine beforehand which draw is going to get you the green marble. It could be the first draw, the second draw, the third, draw, the fourth draw, or the fifth draw. Without performing any experiment, which draw do you think is the one most likely (has the highest probability) to give you the green marble? Now design an experiment to see if your guess is correct. Write a short report on the results of this experiment.

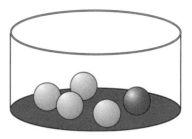

Published by IT'S ABOUT TIME, Inc. © 2000 MATHconx, LLC

4. This problem is a good one for class discussion and group activity. First have the students discuss the problem and then make guesses as to which draw is most likely to yield the green ball. Experience indicates that some students will say 2 or 3. Now have students work in small groups to design an experiment to obtain an answer. See if students realize that the first draw, second draw, etc., are equally likely—that is, have the same probability. A summary of the experiment might take this form.

Draw	1st	2nd	3rd	4th	5th
Probability	$\frac{1}{5}$	$\frac{4}{5}\cdot\frac{1}{4}=\frac{1}{5}$	$\frac{3}{5}\cdot\frac{1}{3}=\frac{1}{5}$	$\frac{2}{5}\cdot\frac{1}{2}=\frac{1}{5}$	$\frac{1}{5}\cdot\frac{1}{1}=\frac{1}{5}$

NOTES

Chapter 8

8.2 Intuition and Probability

We have seen how you could assign probabilities based on your personal belief that something will or will not happen. We have also seen how you could assign probabilities based on past experience or on the results of experiments. The *theory* of probability to a large extent was developed on *intuition*. If I am going to toss a coin, is there any reason to believe that a tail is more likely to appear than a head? Most people would answer "no." Their answer is not based on experiments they performed, but rather on their intuition and the symmetry of a coin. In this section we shall see how probabilities based on intuition can be assigned.

A Word to Know: Intuition refers to an ability to look at a situation and have quick and ready ideas, based largely on feelings or beliefs.

....

A Word to Know: Theory refers to a careful study of a topic based on accepted ideas or formulas and how they relate to each other. For example, music theory studies how accepted arrangements of tones relate to each other to produce music.

....

Historically, the study of probability began with games involving dice.

What games do you know about that use dice?

8.8

Since the first questions about "chance" or "probability" had to do with games played with dice, let's begin with such an activity.

A **die** is one of a pair of dice. Each die is a cube with faces marked with 1, 2, 3, 4, 5, or 6 spots (or dots). If a die is tossed or rolled, symmetry suggests that landing with one face up is just as likely as any other face.

Consider the question "If a die is tossed, what is the probability that 4 spots show?" This means "What is the probability that the face with 4 spots is facing up?" We could

Learning Outcomes

After studying this section you will be able to:

Make probability assignments using the ratio of the number of favorable outcomes to the total number of outcomes;

Explain what it means for events to be equally likely;

Compute probabilites in a variety of contexts.

Published by IT'S ABOUT TIME, Inc. © 2000 MATHconx, LLC

8.2 Intuition and Probability

In this section, students are expected to recognize the symmetry of objects like a coin or a die. It is important that they be able to use these ideas of symmetry, along with the given definition of probability and their knowledge of counting techniques, in actually assigning numbers as probabilities.

8.8

Students should come up with answers like Monopoly, Parcheesi, Craps, Sorry, Risk, Pictionary, Payday, and Trivial Pursuit.

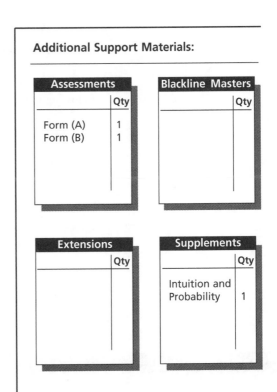

Additional Support Materials:

Assessments	Qty
Form (A)	1
Form (B)	1

Blackline Masters	Qty

Extensions	Qty

Supplements	Qty
Intuition and Probability	1

Chapter 8

perform an experiment to estimate this probability, but instead will use our *intuition* to find the probability. There are six possible results and there is no reason to suppose that one result is more likely to occur than any other. When this happens we say that the results are *equally likely*. Thus the probability of rolling one particular number, in this case 4, is taken to be $\frac{1}{6}$. We frequently write this as

$$P(4) = \frac{1}{6}$$

Similarly, $P(5) = \frac{1}{6}$ and $P(2) = \frac{1}{6}$ etc.

Consider the following more complicated question: "If a die is tossed, what is the probability that the result is an even number?" In this case the result could be a 2, 4, or 6. Thus there are three acceptable numbers out of a total of 6 possible numbers. This probability is $\frac{3}{6}$. We sometimes write this as

$$P(\text{even number}) = \frac{3}{6}$$

A die is tossed. Assign probabilities to each of the following.

8.9

1. *P*(odd number)

2. *P*(number larger than 2)

3. *P*(number smaller than 3)

4. *P*(number is a multiple of 3)

5. *P*(number is divisible by 4)

6. *P*(10), the probability of obtaining 10 spots

The previous examples and problems suggest the following **intuitive definition of probability:**

$$Probability = \frac{number\ of\ acceptable\ outcomes}{total\ number\ of\ possible\ outcomes}$$

or, as one sometimes will see

$$Probability = \frac{number\ of\ favorable\ outcomes}{total\ number\ of\ possible\ outcomes}$$

Remember: *These definitions only apply to situations where the "possible ways" are equally likely to occur.*

462

8.9

It may be necessary to explain to students what a die is. Usually, students know about a pair of dice but sometimes are not familiar with the fact that a die is one of a pair of dice. They should have, and be able to explain, the following results.

1. $\dfrac{3}{6} = \dfrac{1}{2}$

2. $\dfrac{4}{6} = \dfrac{2}{3}$

3. $\dfrac{2}{6} = \dfrac{1}{3}$

4. $\dfrac{2}{6} = \dfrac{1}{3}$

5. $\dfrac{1}{6}$

6. 0

NOTES

Chapter 8

When we say that people or objects are chosen at **random,** we mean that each person or object is equally likely to be chosen. When one talks about tossing a *fair* coin, one means that the possible results of "head" or "tail" are equally likely. Similarly, when one talks about tossing or rolling a *fair* die, one means that any one of the numbers 1, 2, 3, 4, 5, or 6 is equally likely to appear.

If we say that the probability of getting a 4 is $\frac{1}{6}$ when a die is rolled, what idea comes to mind? The idea is the following. If the die were rolled many, many times, then $\frac{1}{6}$th of the time a 4 would show.

If a die is rolled 100 times, is it possible that a 4 would never show?

8.10

However, it is our "belief" that if a fair die is rolled millions of times, then a 4 would show about $\frac{1}{6}$th of the time. Thus probability is related to our beliefs that certain things will happen "in the long run."

Problem Set: 8.2

1. The numbers 1 to 100 are written on slips of paper and placed in a box. After the slips are mixed, you select one of the slips without looking into the box.

   (a) What is the probability that the number on the slip is greater than 84?
   (b) What is the probability that the number on the slip is less than 10?
   (c) What is the probability that the number on the slip is divisible by 7?
   (d) What is the probability that the number on the slip is a multiple of 5 and a multiple of 7?
   (e) What is the probability that the number on the slip is a multiple of 5 or a multiple of 7?

2. A science quiz consists of ten true-false questions. One student has not spent any time studying for the quiz and simply guesses the answer to each question. What is the probability that this student will get the correct answer to all of the questions?

8.10

This should be fairly easy for students, but a class discussion should help everyone accept the fact that 100 tosses of a die can occur without yielding a 4.

Problem Set: 8.2

1. (a) $\frac{16}{100} = 0.16$ (b) $\frac{9}{100} = 0.09$ (c) $\frac{14}{100} = 0.14$

   (d) $\frac{2}{100} = 0.02$ (e) $\frac{32}{100} = 0.32$

2. From the Fundamental Counting Principle there are 2^{10} possible ways to answer the questions. Only one way has all answers correct, so the probability is $\frac{1}{2^{10}}$.

NOTES

Chapter 8

3. From a standard deck of 52 cards that has been well shuffled, a card is drawn face down.

   (a) What is the probability that the card drawn is a 7 of spades?
   (b) What is the probability that the card drawn is a 7?
   (c) What is the probability that the card drawn is a king?
   (d) What is the probability that the card drawn is a spade?

4. A person in your area code region dialed a seven-digit number at random. What does it mean to you to say "a person dialed a seven-digit number at random?" What is the probability that this person dialed your telephone number?

5. Cards bearing the letters A, B, E, and T are placed in front of a monkey. The monkey successively picks one of the cards at random and does not replace the card. What does it mean to you that the monkey picked a card at random? What is the probability that the monkey picked B E A T (in that order)?

6. A fair coin is tossed seven times and the results are listed in order. (H for head; T for tail)

   (a) What is the probability that the outcome is TTHHHHH?
   (b) What is the probability of all tails?
   (c) What is the probability of getting exactly one head?
   (d) What is the probability that the first toss was a head and the third toss was a tail?
   (e) What is the probability that the first toss was a tail and the last toss was a head?

7. The eleven letters in the word "CONNECTICUT" are written on slips of paper and put into a bowl. The slips of paper are thoroughly mixed and one of them is picked at random.

   (a) What is the probability that the letter N is picked?
   (b) What is the probability that the picked letter is a vowel?
   (c) What is the probability that the picked letter is in the word "PENNSYLVANIA" ?
   (d) What is the probability that the picked letter is in the word "MAMMAL"?
   (e) What is the probability that the picked letter is in the alphabet?

3. (a) $\dfrac{1}{52}$

    (b) Since there are 4 sevens, the answer is $\dfrac{4}{52} = \dfrac{1}{13}$.

    (c) Since there are 4 Kings, the answer is $\dfrac{4}{52} = \dfrac{1}{13}$.

    (d) Since there are 13 spades, the answer is $\dfrac{13}{52} = \dfrac{1}{4}$.

4. Get students to discuss how a person might dial a seven-digit number at random. Usually a person knows about where each number is located so that simply selecting a slot or a key is really not random. By the Fundamental Counting Principle there are 10^7 possible ways of dialing. Since only one is the correct number, the answer is $\dfrac{1}{10^7}$.

5. Get students to discuss what it means for the monkey to pick a card at random. By the Fundamental Counting Principle there are 24 different ways for the monkey to pick the cards, assuming that the monkey cannot pick the same card twice. Thus, the answer is $\dfrac{1}{24}$.

6. There are 2^7 possible outcomes.

    (a) $\dfrac{1}{2^7}$ (b) $\dfrac{1}{2^7}$

    (c) The one head can occur in any one of the seven slots so that the answer is $\dfrac{7}{2^7}$.

    (d) Show students that by writing H_T_ _ _ _ there are 2^5 ways of filling in the five empty slots. Hence, the answer is $\dfrac{2^5}{2^7} = \dfrac{1}{4}$.

    (e) Same answer as the previous part.

7. (a) $\dfrac{2}{11}$ (b) $\dfrac{4}{11}$ (c) $\dfrac{4}{11}$ (d) 0   (e) 1

NOTES

Chapter 8

Published by IT'S ABOUT TIME, Inc. © 2000 MATHconx, LLC

8. In this problem you are asked to make reasonable guesses. Make sure you are able to explain how you arrived at your answers.

   A fair die is rolled 120 times. How many times would you expect

   (a) the number 5?

   (b) an even number?

   (c) an odd number?

   (d) a number greater than 2?

   (e) a number which is a multiple of 3?

   (f) a number greater than 7?

   (g) a number less than 1?

   (h) a number less than 7?

9. A fair die is tossed.

   (a) What is $P(5)$, the probability of obtaining 5 spots?

   (b) What is $P(5)$ if you are told that the result was a number greater than 2?

   (c) What is $P(5)$ if you are told that the result was a number less than 6?

   (d) What is $P(5)$ if you are told that the result was an odd number?

   (e) What is $P(5)$ if you are told that the result was an even number?

10. The numbers 1 to 100 are written on slips of paper and placed in a box. After the slips are mixed, one of the slips is selected at random.

    (a) What is the probability that the number on the slip is greater than 89?

    (b) What is the probability that the number on the slip is greater than 89 if you are told that the number is greater than 75?

    (c) What is the probability that the number on the slip is greater than 89 if you are told that the number is odd?

    (d) What is the probability that the number on the slip is greater than 89 if you are told that the number is a multiple of 3?

Published by IT'S ABOUT TIME, Inc. © 2000 MATHconx, LLC

8. (a) A 5 should be *expected* one-sixth of the time or on 20 rolls.
   (b) 60 times   (c) 60 times   (d) 80 times   (e) 40 times
   (f) 0 times   (g) 0 times   (h) 120 times

9. (a) $\frac{1}{6}$ (b) $\frac{1}{4}$ (c) $\frac{1}{5}$ (d) $\frac{1}{3}$ (e) 0

10. (a) $\frac{11}{100} = 0.11$ (b) $\frac{11}{25}$ (c) $\frac{5}{50} = \frac{1}{10} = 0.1$ (d) $\frac{4}{33}$

Get students to see that additional information reduces the number of possible outcomes.

NOTES

Chapter 8

11. The **Slot Machine,** invented by Charles Fey of San Francisco in 1895, is a gambling device frequently called a "one-armed bandit." (A number of states have outlawed these devices.) To play, you drop a coin into a slot and pull a lever on the side of the machine which causes a set of reels to spin. The number of reels varies from 3 to 5 but a "standard" slot machine has 3 reels, each having 20 picture symbols such as those given in the following table.

Picture	Reel 1	Reel 2	Reel 3
Bar	1	3	1
Bell	1	3	3
Plum	5	1	5
Orange	3	6	7
Cherry	7	7	0
Lemon	3	0	4
	20	20	20

Each reel randomly stops at one of its 20 pictures. The prizes also can vary but are generally listed on the machine.

(a) If the Jackpot, the biggest prize, is won by a person who gets 3 bars, what is the probability of winning the Jackpot?

(b) If a prize, smaller than the Jackpot, is won by a person who gets all three pictures alike, other than the bars, what is the probability of winning a smaller prize?

12. When a deer crosses a road there are two things that can happen–either the deer is hit by a car or the deer is not hit by a car. Therefore, the probability of a deer safely crossing a road is $\frac{1}{2}$. Do you agree or disagree? Write a paragraph explaining your answer.

Published by IT'S ABOUT TIME, Inc. © 2000 MATHconx, LLC

466

11. (a) Out of $20^3 = 8000$ outcomes, there are 3 ways to win the Jackpot, so the answer is $\frac{3}{8000}$.

    (b) Out of 8000 outcomes, there are 160 ways to win a smaller prize, so the answer is $\frac{160}{8000} = \frac{1}{50}$.

12. See what students write. Have a class discussion. The important point is that the probability of $\frac{1}{2}$ assumes that "the deer is hit by a car" and "the deer is not hit by a car" are equally likely events which, indeed, is not what one would intuitively accept.

NOTES

Chapter 8

8.3 Sample Spaces and Equally Likely Events

Learning Outcomes

After studying this section you will be able to:

Write or describe a sample space for an experiment;

Construct sample spaces in which the elements are equally likely;

Use the complement of an event in calculating probabilities;

Find the probability of the union and intersection of events;

Explain some of the history of probability.

The tossing or rolling of a fair die is an experiment. You do not know what will happen before you do the actual experiment. The set of possible outcomes is given by

$$S = \{1, 2, 3, 4, 5, 6\}$$

The set S is called a *sample space* for this experiment. As in the previous section we assign a probability to each element of this sample space as follows:

$$P(1) = \frac{1}{6}, \ P(2) = \frac{1}{6}, \ P(3) = \frac{1}{6}, \ P(4) = \frac{1}{6}, \ P(5) = \frac{1}{6}, \ P(6) = \frac{1}{6}$$

Each element of S is assigned the same probability since we assume that any outcome is just as likely as any other outcome. That is, the outcomes are **equally likely.**

A Phrase to Know: A sample space is the set of all possible outcomes of an experiment.

The tossing of a fair coin is also an experiment. You do not know the outcome before you do the actual experiment. Use H to denote a head and T to denote a tail.

8.11

(a) Write the sample space S for this experiment by listing the elements.

(b) What probability should be assigned to each element of the sample space?

(c) Are the elements of the sample space equally likely?

467

Published by IT'S ABOUT TIME, Inc. © 2000 MATHconx, LLC

8.3   Sample Spaces and Equally Likely Events

The notion of a sample space is fundamental in the study of probability. Knowing the elements of a sample space and whether or not the elements are equally likely forms the basis for the development of higher order thinking and problem solving in probability. This section concentrates on these basic ideas.

8.11

1. (a) Students should be expected to write something like
$$S = \{H,T\}$$
or
$$S = \{Head, Tail\}$$
    (b) $P(H) = \dfrac{1}{2}$ and $P(T) = \dfrac{1}{2}$
    (c) The elements are equally likely.

Additional Support Materials:

Assessments	Qty
Form (A)	1
Form (B)	1

Blackline Masters	Qty

Extensions	Qty
What Are The Odds?	1

Supplements	Qty

Chapter 8

8.3 Sample Spaces and Equally Likely Events

Return to our experiment of tossing a die. What if one is interested in the probability that the result is a number greater than 4? We make use of our intuitive definition of probability as follows.

If $A = \{5, 6\}$, then A is a subset of S, and we are interested in whether or not the result is an element of A. It is customary to write

$$P(\text{number greater than } 4) = P(A)$$

or

$$P(A) = \frac{2}{6}$$

Another way to look at this result is the following.

$$P(A) = \frac{\#(A)}{\#(S)}$$

(Recall that $\#A$ indicates the number of elements in set A.) As another example, consider the probability that the result is an even number. From our intuitive definition of probability

$$P(\text{even number}) = \frac{3}{6}$$

If we let $B = \{2, 4, 6\}$, then B is a subset of S, and we are interested in whether or not the result is an element of B. It is customary to write

$$P(\text{even number}) = P(B)$$

or

$$P(B) = \frac{3}{6}$$

Note that

$$P(B) = \frac{\#(B)}{\#(S)}$$

8.12

1. One is interested in the probability that the result in S is a number less than 3.

   (a) By listing the elements, write a set C, which corresponds to this event.
   (b) What is $P(C)$?

2. One is interested in the probability that the result in S is a multiple of 3.

   (a) By listing the elements, write a set D, which corresponds to this event.
   (b) What is $P(D)$?

468

8.12

1. (a) $C = \{1, 2\}$ (b) $P(C) = \dfrac{2}{6}$

2. (a) $D = \{3, 6\}$ (b) $P(D) = \dfrac{2}{6}$

NOTES

Chapter 8

We can formalize the ideas of these examples as follows: Let S be the set of all possible outcomes of an experiment–that is, S is a **sample space** of the experiment. We shall assume that the sample space is of such a nature that the elements of S are *equally likely*. If A is a subset of S, then A is called an **event** in S and we define the probability of A, denoted $P(A)$, by

$$P(A) = \frac{\#(A)}{\#(S)}$$

1. What is $P(S)$?

2. What is $P(\varnothing)$?

a
8.13

3. A pair of fair dice is rolled and one looks at the sum of the numbers on the two dice. Write a sample space S for this experiment. Do you think that the elements of S are equally likely? Explain!

Remember that there are several ways to specify sets. One way is to list the elements. Another way is to write a description of the elements in a set. In some cases, one simply describes the elements of a sample space.

Consider the experiment of picking a card at random from a standard deck of 52 cards. We are interested in the probability that the card picked is a King. There are four Kings in a deck of cards. Our sample space S consists of the set of 52 cards in the deck. Each element of S is equally likely. The event of interest is the event that the card picked is a King. Let A be the set of Kings. Then,

$$P(A) = \frac{\#(A)}{\#(S)} = \frac{4}{52} = 0.076923 \text{ (to six decimal places)}$$

The following problems will help you to simplify some complicated probability problems.

b
8.14

1. In a certain class of 30 students there are 7 with blue eyes. A student is to be selected at random.

   (a) What is a reasonable sample space S for this experiment? What is $\#(S)$?

   (b) If B denotes the set of blue eyed students in the class, what is $P(B)$?

   (c) The set B' (read "B prime") is the set of elements in S which are *not* in B. This set B' is called the *complement* of B. For this example, where B denotes the set of blue eyed students in the class, describe the students who are in B'.

Published by IT'S ABOUT TIME, Inc. © 2000 MATHconx, LLC

469

1. $P(S) = 1$ 2. $P(\varnothing) = 0$

8.13

3. $S = \{2, 3, 4, 5, 6, 7, 8, 9, 10, 11, 12\}$. The elements of S are not equally likely, since only the sum $1 + 1 = 2$, while, for example, $1 + 6 = 2 + 5 = 3 + 4 = 7$.

1. (a) A reasonable sample space S is the set of students in the class. Thus, $\#(S) = 30$.

8.14

   (b) $P(B) = \#(B)/\#(S) = \dfrac{7}{30}$

   (c) The set B' consists of those students in the class who do not have blue eyes.

NOTES

Chapter 8

(d) In the Venn diagram of Display 8.2, shade the region which represents B'.

S

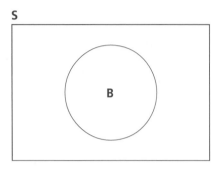

Display 8.2

(e) What do you observe about $P(B) + P(B')$?

This problem illustrates the following important properties of probabilities: *If S is a sample space for an experiment and A is an event in S, then*

$$P(A) + P(A') = \underline{?}$$

or

$$P(A) = \underline{?} - P(A')$$

2. A fair coin is tossed 5 times. What is the probability that at least one head appears? (*Hint:* Calculate the probability that no heads appear and use your knowledge of complement.)

3. In a class of 30 students, 17 play video games and 12 watch MTV. It turns out that 5 students play video games and watch MTV. A student in this class is to be selected at random.

(a) What is a reasonable sample space S for this experiment? What is $\#(S)$?

(b) Let A be the set of students who play video games. What is $P(A)$?

(c) Let B be the set of students who watch MTV. What is $P(B)$?

(d) Describe, in words, the students in the set $A \cap B$. What is $P(A \cap B)$?

(e) Describe, in words, the students in the set $A \cup B$. What is $P(A \cup B)$?

470

(d) The region in S, but outside of B, should be shaded.

(e) Students should observe that
$$P(B) + P(B') = 1$$

In completing the statements, students should have

$$P(A) + P(A') = 1$$
$$\text{or}$$
$$P(A) = 1 - P(A')$$

2. Let A be the event "no head appears." Then A' represents the event "at least one head appears," so
$$P(A') = 1 - P(A) = 1 - \left(\frac{1}{32}\right) = \frac{31}{32}$$

3. (a) A reasonable sample space is the set S of students in this class. Thus, $\#(S) = 30$.

   (b) $P(A) = \frac{17}{30}$ (c) $P(B) = \frac{12}{30}$

   (d) Students in $A \cap B$ play video games *and* watch MTV.
   $$P(A \cap B) = \frac{5}{30}$$

   (e) Students in $A \cup B$ play video games *or* watch MTV (possibly both).
   $$P(A \cup B) = \frac{24}{30}$$

NOTES

Chapter 8

(f) If S is a sample space, and A and B are events in S, then there is an equation that relates $P(A \cup B)$, $P(A)$, $P(B)$, and $P(A \cap B)$. From the work that you have done thus far on this problem, can you conjecture what that equation is? Write your equation in the form

$$P(A \cup B) = \underline{\hspace{2cm}}$$

What happens to the equation if A and B are disjoint?

(g) Describe, in words, the students in the set A'. What is $P(A')$?

(h) What is the probability that the selected student plays video games but does not watch MTV?

The French mathematicians Blaise Pascal (1623–1662) and Pierre Fermat (1601–1665) are generally given credit for the development of the area of mathematics we now call "Probability." However, more than 100 years before Pascal and Fermat, an Italian physician and mathematician named Girolamo Cardano (1501–1576) had computed many numbers relating to games involving dice and wrote the first book on the subject titled *The Book on Games of Chance*. More than fifty years before Pascal and Fermat, an Italian scientist Galileo Galilei (1564–1642) also computed a list of numbers related to dice games.

Galileo Galilei

Galileo made numerous contributions to science. Write a list of as many as you can. Check resource books in the library, a CD-ROM, or the Internet for information.

8.15

Historically, there is a record of Chevalier deMere approaching Pascal in 1654 with several questions about gambling which may have been based on deMere's own gambling activities. Historians are quick to point out that the questions were old and well known. In particular, one of deMere's questions was the following: If you throw two dice, how many throws must one be allowed in order to have a better than even chance of getting two sixes at least once?

See if you can make a reasonable guess at an answer to the question posed by deMere.

8.16

Published by IT'S ABOUT TIME, Inc. © 2000 MATHconx, LLC

(f) $P(A \cup B) = P(A) + P(B) - P(A \cap B)$. If A and B are disjoint, then $P(A \cap B)$ is 0, and $P(A \cup B) = P(A) + P(B)$.

(g) A' is the set of students who do not play video games. $P(A') = \dfrac{13}{30}$

(h) The probability is $\dfrac{12}{30}$

8.15

Students should be familiar with some of Galileo's contributions to science from their science courses. The following is a partial list of his contributions.

1. He made the first practical use of the telescope to discover many new facts about astronomy. He made larger and more powerful telescopes than had been made before.

2. He discovered the law of the pendulum. At the age of 20, as a university student, he observed a great lamp swinging from the ceiling of a cathedral in Pisa. He used his pulse beat to time the motions of the lamp and observed that each swing took the same amount of time. Later, he introduced a simple pendulum to time the pulse rate of medical patients.

3. Galileo is credited with the Law of Falling Bodies. He reasoned that all bodies are pulled to earth with the same acceleration, regardless of their weight. This was a new theory, at the time, and the followers of Aristotle, who said heavy bodies fell faster than lighter ones, bitterly opposed Galileo's ideas.

4. Galileo invented the sector, a drafting tool which is still used today.

5. He observed that the Milky Way was a mass of stars.

6. He discovered the four bright satellites of Jupiter.

7. He discovered that the Moon was not smooth and was not shining by its own light.

8.16

This is not a trivial problem. The fact that this problem was brought to the attention of a mathematician is evidence of the subtle nature of the problem. It is doubtful whether any students will come up with the correct answer, but good reasoning should be applauded.

The usual solution is obtained as follows. It is convenient to determine first the probability of not obtaining any sixes. If one throws once there are thirty-six possible results with two dice and thirty-five of these do not give two sixes. Thus, the chance of not getting two sixes in one roll is

$$Q_1 = \frac{35}{36}$$

If one throws twice, there are 36×36 possible results and 35×35 of them do not give two sixes either time. Thus,

$$Q_2 = \left(\frac{35}{36}\right)^2$$

Chapter 8

For many years the mathematics of chance, now called probability, was used primarily to solve problems dealing with gambling. Today, the mathematics of chance is used in almost every area of human interest. For example, in the 18th century, records of births in city hospitals were examined to look for patterns in the sex of a child (male or female). It was discovered that the patterns were similar to the patterns of heads and tails that resulted from repeatedly tossing a coin. Scientists then developed methods to study patterns in the sex of a child as if it resulted from a game of chance played by nature.

Life insurance policies take into account the chance that a person with a certain medical history will die within a certain period; opinion polls indicate the chance that a person will be elected President of the United States; and hereditary traits are viewed by biologists as being assigned by chance. We'll stop here, for the moment, but the list of uses of the mathematics of chance is very long indeed.

We have already mentioned that games involving dice were instrumental in the development of probability. Consider the toss of a pair of fair dice. We look at the sum of the numbers obtained. A possible sample space for this experiment would be the set

$$\{2, 3, 4, 5, 6, 7, 8, 9, 10, 11, 12\}$$

However, the elements of this set are not equally likely.

8.17

1. **Explain why a sum of 5 is more likely than a sum of 2.**

2. **Explain why a sum of 12 is less likely than a sum of 9.**

It follows that for our definition of probability, this is not a suitable sample space. A reasonable sample space can be obtained as follows: Suppose the dice are colored so that one die is red and the other is green. Display 8.3 gives the possible "sum" outcomes from tossing the pair of dice.

472

In a similar way, one finds that in n throws the chance of not getting any "two sixes" is

$$Q_n = \left(\frac{35}{36}\right)^n$$

Hence the opposite or complementary event, that of getting "two sixes" at least once, has the chance (probability)

$$P_n = 1 - Q_n = 1 - \left(\frac{35}{36}\right)^n$$

In order to have a better than even chance one must have $P_n > \frac{1}{2}$ and one finds

$$P_{24} = 0.4914 \text{ and } P_{25} = 0.5055$$

Thus, the answer to the question is 25.

With some classes, one might want students to work in groups. Even if they just come up with the idea of working with the opposite event, this would represent a real problem solving ability.

8.17

1. Students should see that there is only one way to get a sum of 2 but several ways of getting a sum of 5. Thus, a sum of 5 is more likely than a sum of 2.

2. Again, students should see that there is only one way to get a sum of 12, but several ways of getting a sum of 9. Thus, a sum of 9 is more likely than a sum of 12.

NOTES

Chapter 8

Green die

	1	2	3	4	5	6
1	2	3	4	5	6	7
2	3	4	5	6	7	8
3	4	5	6	7	8	9
4	5	6	7	8	9	10
5	6	7	8	9	10	11
6	7	8	9	10	11	12

Red die

Display 8.3

The 36 sum entries form a sample space. These sum entries are equally likely and form a suitable sample space for this experiment. There is a total of 36 entries. This number could also be calculated from the FCP (remember the Fundamental Counting Principle) since there are 6 possible results for the red die and 6 possible results for the green die. The number of possible results for the pair of dice is thus $6 \cdot 6 = 36$.

8.18

1. What is the probability of obtaining a sum of 7?

2. What is the probability that the sum is an odd number?

3. What is the probability that the sum is greater than 9?

4. What is the probability that the sum is less than 5?

5. What is the probability that the sum is a multiple of 3?

6. What is the probability that the sum is even, if it is known that the sum is greater than 3?

7. What is the probability that the sum is 8, if it is known that one of the dice showed a 3? (Be careful!)

8. Which is more probable—the sum is even or the sum is odd?

9. What is the probability that the sum is greater than 9, if it is known that one of the dice showed a 4?

10. What is the probability that the sum is an even number or is a multiple of 3?

Published by IT'S ABOUT TIME, Inc. © 2000 MATHconx, LLC

473

8.18

1. $\frac{1}{6}$
2. $\frac{18}{36} = \frac{1}{2}$
3. $\frac{6}{36} = \frac{1}{6}$
4. $\frac{6}{36} = \frac{1}{6}$
5. $\frac{12}{36} = \frac{1}{3}$
6. $\frac{17}{33}$
7. $\frac{2}{11}$
8. The two events have the same probability.
9. $\frac{2}{11}$
10. $\frac{24}{36} = \frac{2}{3}$

NOTES

Chapter 8

In this section you have been introduced to the concept of probability and a number of the basic laws of probability. In later material you will see many applications of these ideas.

Problem Set: 8.3

1. A card is selected at random from a standard deck of 52 cards. What is the probability of each of the following?

    (a) The card selected is a 5?
    (b) The card selected is a Queen of Diamonds?
    (c) The card selected is a King or Queen?
    (d) The card selected is a Diamond?

2. An eight sided die (octahedron) has eight faces with the numerals 1, 2, 3, 4, 5, 6, 7, or 8 appearing on each face and each number of dots appears exactly once. If this die is tossed, what is the probability that

    (a) The result is an even number?
    (b) The resulting number is less than 5?
    (c) The resulting number is a multiple of 4?

3. In a class of 35 students, 8 play in the band and 9 are members of the art club. It turns out that 3 students are in the band and in the art club. Let A denote the set of students in the class who are in the art club and B the set of students in the class who play in the band.

    (a) What is $P(A \cup B)$?
    (b) What is $P(A')$?
    (c) What is the probability that a student in the class, selected at random, plays in the band but is not a member of the art club?
    (d) What is the probability that a student in the class, selected at random, is neither in the band nor in the art club?

4. In a group of 1000 people, an advertising agency found 786 people that read *Newsweek* magazine, 664 that read *Time* magazine, and 461 people that read both magazines. One of the people in the group is selected at random.

Problem Set: 8.3

1. (a) $\frac{4}{52}$ (b) $\frac{1}{52}$ (c) $\frac{8}{52}$ (d) $\frac{13}{52}$

2. (a) $\frac{4}{8}$ (b) $\frac{4}{8}$ (c) $\frac{2}{8}$

3. A Venn diagram can help.
   (a) $\frac{14}{35}$ (b) $\frac{26}{35}$ (c) $\frac{5}{35}$ (d) $\frac{21}{35}$

4. A Venn diagram might help. A reasonable sample space is the set of 1000 people interviewed. Let
   W — set of people who read *Newsweek*
   T — set of people who read *Time*

NOTES

Chapter 8

(a) What is the probability that this person reads at least one of the two magazines, *Newsweek* or *Time*?

(b) What is the probability that this person reads at least one of the two magazines but not both?

(c) What is the probability that this person reads *Time* magazine if you are told that this person does not read *Newsweek*?

5. Assuming that boys and girls are equally likely to be born, what is the probability that in a family with three children, all three are girls?

6. A standard slot machine has 3 reels, each having 20 picture symbols as given in the following table.

Picture	Reel 1	Reel 2	Reel 3
Bar	1	3	1
Bell	1	3	3
Plum	5	1	5
Orange	3	6	7
Cherry	7	7	0
Lemon	3	0	4
	20	20	20

Each reel randomly stops at one of its 20 pictures. The Jackpot prize is won by a person who gets 3 bars. A smaller prize is won by getting all three pictures, other than the bars, alike. What is the probability of not winning *any* of the above mentioned prizes?

7. Roulette is the oldest casino game still in existence. Dictionaries frequently define roulette as a gambling game in which players bet on which compartment of a revolving wheel a small ball will come to rest. The compartments are numbered and colored. A dealer oversees the betting, makes the payoffs, rotates the wheel and spins an ivory ball. If the ball rests in the compartment housing one of the numbers or colors that you've bet, you win. Very simply—the wheel rotates, the ball spins, and you win or lose.

Two similar wheel games were very popular in Europe in the early 1700's; one was known as "Hoca" and the other as "E-O." These games, however, had properties which led to illegal gambling procedures. It was Gabriel deSantine, a police official in Paris, who around 1765 supported the

475

Published by IT'S ABOUT TIME, Inc. © 2000 MATHconx, LLC

(a) In this part we want $P(W \cup T)$. Now,
$$\#(W \cup T) = \#(W) + \#(T) - \#(W \cap T) = 989$$
Thus, $P(W \cup T) = \dfrac{989}{1000}$

(b) From a Venn diagram one sees that the probability is
$$\dfrac{(325 + 203)}{1000} = \dfrac{528}{1000}.$$

(c) If you are told that this person does not read *Newsweek*, then our sample space becomes the 214 people who do not read this magazine. Of this number, 203 read *Time*. Thus, the probability is $\dfrac{203}{214}$.

5. The children could be specified by writing, for example, *BGG* to indicate a boy first, a girl second, and a girl third. By the Fundamental Counting Principle there are 8 such lists. Only 1 of these involves all three being girls. The probability is $\dfrac{1}{8}$.

6. There are 3 ways to win the Jackpot and 160 ways to win a smaller prize. Thus the probability of winning some prize is $\dfrac{163}{8000}$. The probability of the complement of this event—not winning any prize is $1 - \dfrac{163}{8000} = \dfrac{7837}{8000}$. So about 98% of the trials win nothing for the player.

7. (a) The probability of winning on 17 is $\dfrac{1}{38}$. The probability of losing is $1 - \dfrac{1}{38} = \dfrac{37}{38}$.

   (b) The probability of winning on red is $\dfrac{18}{38}$. The probability of losing is $1 - \dfrac{18}{38} = \dfrac{20}{38}$.

NOTES

Chapter 8

development of the fairer game of roulette. This new game eventually became more popular than the other wheel games.

The roulette wheels in Europe are slightly different than those in the United States. In the United States, a roulette wheel has 38 compartments around its rim. One is numbered 0 and another is numbered 00, both in green compartments. The others are numbered from 1 to 36, of which half are colored red and the other half are colored black. There are many different bets that can be made. For example, you can bet on a number such as 17 or you can bet on the color of a compartment, such as "red".

(a) If you bet on the number 17, what is the probability that you win? What is the probability that you lose?

(b) If you bet on the color "red", what is the probability that you win? What is the probability that you lose?

EXPLORATION

We have mentioned that the Italian scientist Galileo Galilei (1564–1642) computed a list of numbers relating to dice games. In particular, Galileo was asked about probabilities in games played with 3 dice. He figured out the probabilities by using a table as we have done for games with 2 dice.

(a) What sums can be obtained with 3 dice? Construct your own table which indicates the number of ways each possible sum may be obtained.

(b) What sum(s) is/are most likely when 3 dice are rolled?

(c) Which is more probable with 3 dice—a sum of 10 or sum of 15?

(d) Which is more probable with 3 dice—a sum which is an odd number or a sum which is an even number?

(e) What is the probability, with 3 dice, that the sum is greater than 10?

(f) What is the probability that all 3 dice showed a 5?

(g) What is the probability that all 3 dice showed the same number of dots?

(h) What is the probability, with 3 dice, that the sum is an even number or a multiple of 3?

Published by IT'S ABOUT TIME, Inc. © 2000 MATHconx, LLC

EXPLORATION

This should be an in depth problem. Give students time (a week?) to work on this problem. Students should come up with reasonable tables. One standard table makes use of the previous table for two dice in the following way. The sum of three dice can be any one of 3, 4, 5, 6, 7, 8, 9, 10, 11, 12, 13, 14, 15, 16, 17, or 18. Suppose one gets a 4 on the third die and looks at a sum such as 10. This means that the sum on the first and second die must have been 6. From the previous table this can occur in 5 ways. Suppose the third die shows a 6 and you consider a sum of 17. This means that a sum of 11 was obtained on the first two dice. From the previous table this can occur in 2 ways. Continuing in this fashion, one completes the following table in Display 8.1T.

Sum of Three Dice

	3	4	5	6	7	8	9	10	11	12	13	14	15	16	17	18	
1	1	2	3	4	5	6	5	4	3	2	1						
2		1	2	3	4	5	6	5	4	3	2	1					
3			1	2	3	4	5	6	5	4	3	2	1				
4				1	2	3	4	5	6	5	4	3	2	1			
5					1	2	3	4	5	6	5	4	3	2	1		
6						1	2	3	4	5	6	5	4	3	2	1	
	1	3	6	10	15	21	25	27	27	25	21	15	10	6	3	1	Frequency

TOTALS

Display 8.1T

The numbers 1–6 on the left side column give the number of dots on the third die. The sum of the totals in the last row is equal to 216. This should have been anticipated from the Fundamental Counting Principle since there are $6 \cdot 6 \cdot 6 = 216$ possible outcomes which are equally likely. The probability of getting a sum of 11 is thus $\frac{27}{216}$, etc.

(a) Should be answered by something like the above.

(b) The sums of 10 and 11 are the most likely sums, each having a probability of $\frac{27}{216}$.

(c) A sum of 10 (probability of $\frac{27}{216}$) is more likely than a sum of 15 (probability of $\frac{10}{216}$).

(d) The probability of an even number is $\frac{108}{216}$ while the probability of an odd number is also $\frac{108}{216}$. Thus, even and odd are equally likely.

(e) From the table one sees that this probability is $\frac{1}{2}$.

Chapter 8

(f) There is only one way this can happen so the answer is $\frac{1}{216}$.

(g) There are 6 ways in which this can happen so the answer is $\frac{6}{216}$.

(h) There are 108 ways to get an even number and 72 ways to get a multiple of 3. However, 36 of these numbers are even and multiples of 3. The answer is $\frac{(108 + 72 - 36)}{216} = \frac{144}{216} = \frac{2}{3}$.

NOTE

1. There are many patterns that are mathematically interesting in the table presented in this solution. For example, the numbers in Pascal's Triangle are there if one looks for them. You may wish to exploit such properties at this time.

2. Another idea which some teachers have used in working with groups on material such as this is to have one group make up additional problems (questions) for the other groups.

NOTES

NOTES

8.4 Simulation With Random Number Tables

Suppose that students in your class were asked to pick a digit between 0 and 9 inclusive and write it on a slip of paper. The slips are put into a box and mixed. Then someone draws the slips, one at a time, out of the box and writes a list of the numbers on the slips. The result could be

4, 7, 8, 3, 4, 0, 1, 2, 1, 9, 5, 6, 7, 9, 8, 4, 3, 2, 5, 7, 0, 1, 4, 6, 7, 7, 8, 9, 2, 3

This is one way a person might try to construct a list of random numbers, or in this case, random digits. If one performed this activity many, many times, the long list that results should contain each digit about the same number of times. That is, each digit is equally likely.

Our experience has been, however, that when students are asked to list a digit between 0 and 9 inclusive, they tend to shy away from 0 and 9, and select a number in between. The resulting list would not be a true random number list because it is *biased* by students shying away from 0 and 9.

A Word to Know: An experiment is **biased** if one or several outcomes are more likely than others.

Another way of obtaining a list of random digits would be to take a large piece of cardboard and section it off into rectangles with equal areas with numbers as follows.

0	1	2	3	4	5	6	7	8	9
1	2	3	4	5	6	7	8	9	0
2	3	4	5	6	7	8	9	0	1
3	4	5	6	7	8	9	0	1	2
4	5	6	7	8	9	0	1	2	3
5	6	7	8	9	0	1	2	3	4
6	7	8	9	0	1	2	3	4	5
7	8	9	0	1	2	3	4	5	6
8	9	0	1	2	3	4	5	6	7
9	0	1	2	3	4	5	6	7	8

Learning Outcomes

After studying this section, you will be able to:

Describe ways of forming lists of random digits;

Change random digits into outcomes of an experiment;

Simulate the queuing process at a bank using random number tables.

8.4 Simulation With Random Number Tables

The use of random numbers in simulating activities represents a widely used application of probability. From studying this section, students should realize that generating lists of random numbers is not a trivial exercise and is frequently biased. They should also sense the power that is inherent in simulating day to day activities.

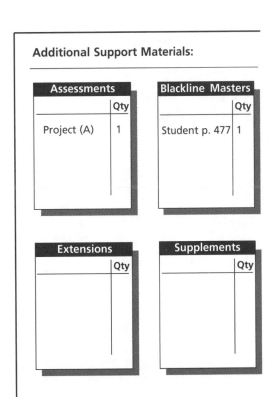

Additional Support Materials:

Assessments	Qty
Project (A)	1

Blackline Masters	Qty
Student p. 477	1

Extensions	Qty

Supplements	Qty

Chapter 8

8.4 Simulation With Random Number Tables

Now we could pin the piece of cardboard to the wall and throw darts at it, writing down the results in the order that they landed. The result could be something like

2,7,4,9,2,1,0,7,4,8,6,5,2,6,8,9,0,3,2,2,5,8,9,7,9,7,9,3,2,1,5,5,7,9

Do you think that this method leads to a list which is biased?

a
8.19

In order to construct a list of random digits, what we are seeking is an experiment with sample space

S = {0, 1, 2, 3, 4, 5, 6, 7, 8, 9}

where the elements are equally likely. That is, each element has a probability of $\frac{1}{10}$.

Can you think of experiments that have this sample space S where the elements are equally likely?

b
8.20

Mathematicians have found various ways to construct lists of random digits. The following table in Display 8.4 is a list of random digits made from a rather complex computer program.

TABLE OF RANDOM DIGITS

8 5 0 5 2 9 4 9 9 2 3 9 6 5 5 0 3 8 7 0 4 1 6 1 2 0 9 8 6 9 9 6 **8** 6 6 2 7
1 9 8 5 4 1 5 6 7 5 5 5 9 9 4 3 6 0 0 9 6 0 2 3 4 4 9 1 5 1 5 6 1 9 3 9 1 8

Display 8.4

A Word to Know: To simulate an activity means to copy that activity as close as you can without actually performing the activity.

Now we shall explain how such a table is used to simulate the toss of a coin. Why do we want to simulate an activity? If one wished to toss a coin many, many times, the activity would take a long time and be very tiring. However, if we could let a computer do the job for us, the activity could be done in a very short time and we would have lots of energy left to do more pleasant things. For the moment we shall think of ourselves as a computer with the list of random digits given in Display 8.4.

If we would actually toss a fair coin, the probability of a Head is $\frac{1}{2}$ and the probability of a Tail is $\frac{1}{2}$. If we select a

Published by IT'S ABOUT TIME, Inc. © 2000 MATHconx, LLC

478

One might tend to throw a dart at the middle of the board in which case the result is biased.

8.19

See what students come up with. They might suggest, for example, having students in the class looking randomly at the license plates on cars and writing down the digits they see.

8.20

NOTES

_____

Chapter 8

random digit, the probability is $\frac{5}{10} = \frac{1}{2}$ that the number is between 0 and 4 inclusive and the probability is $\frac{5}{10} = \frac{1}{2}$ that the number is between 5 and 9 inclusive. Thus we have the following scheme (Display 8.5).

Simulation Scheme	
Random Digit	Result of Coin Toss
0–4	H–Head
5–9	T–Tail

Display 8.5

If we apply this scheme to our table of random digits, the first row

8 5 0 5 2 9 4 9 9 2 3 9 6 5 5 0 3 8 7 0 4 1 6 1 2 0 9 8 6 9 9 6 9 8 6 6 2 7

becomes

T T H T H T H T T H H T T T T H H T T H H H H T H H H T T T T T T T T T T H T

There are 38 entries in the above list and we might interpret these entries as the results of tossing a fair coin 38 times. Note that there are 14 Heads and 24 Tails. Is this what you expected? Are the results close to what you expected?

1. Using the simulation scheme, change the second row of our table random digit (Display 8.4) into H's and T's. How many Heads occur? How many Tails occur? Is this what you expected?

8.21

2. Let's think of the first two rows of our table random digit as 76 throws of a fair coin. Using the above scheme, how many Heads occur? How many Tails occur? Is this what you would expect?

3. Find several schemes, different from that of Display 8.5, which could be used to simulate the toss of a coin.

In the previous discussion, we started looking at Heads and Tails by beginning at the 8 in the first row of our random digit table, and reading from left to right. Picking a starting point is also part of the art of simulation. We should somehow randomly select a starting point. One rather crude way we might do this is the following. Put our random digit table under your pencil. Close your eyes and let your pencil come down on the table. Whatever digit is closest is your starting point. This

8.21

1. The second row
1 9 8 5 4 1 5 6 7 5 5 5 9 9 4 3 6 0 0 9 6 0 2 3 4 4 9 1 5 1 5 6 1 9 3 9 1 8
becomes
H T T T H H T T T T T T T T H H T H H T T H H H H H H T H T H T T H T H T H T
There are 17 Heads and 21 Tails. This is probably not exactly what students expected but the results should be close to what they expected.

2. There are 31 Heads and 45 Tails. Students probably expected 38 Heads and 38 Tails. It is a subjective opinion as to whether the results from the two rows of the random digit table are close to their expectations.

3. Get students to come up with some ideas. One idea might be the following.

Random Digit	Result of Coin Toss
0, 2, 4, 6, 8	Head
1, 3, 5, 7, 9	Tail

NOTES

Chapter 8

starting point is called the **seed** of your simulation. The writer did this and came up with the seed 8 which appears underlined in bold type in Display 8.6.

8 5 0 5 2 9 4 9 9 2 3 9 6 5 5 0 3 8 7 0 4 1 6 1 2 0 9 8 6 9 9 6 **8** 6 6 2 7
1 9 8 5 4 1 5 6 7 5 5 5 9 9 4 3 6 0 0 9 6 0 2 3 4 4 9 1 5 1 5 6 1 9 3 9 1 8

Display 8.6

Thus, if I were going to simulate ten tosses of a coin, I would use the random digits

8 6 6 2 7 1 9 8 5 4

so the results would be

T T T H T H T T T H

8.22

1. Can you think of other ways of selecting a seed?

2. How might you use our table of random digits to simulate ten tosses of a fair die? Explain.

There is no reason we should restrict ourselves to random digits—that is, integers between 0 and 9 inclusive. Why not look for random numbers, again integers, between 0 and 99 inclusive? Such a list might look like that in Display 8.7.

37 10 87 39 25 74 91 05 21 59 28 84 72 63 51 22 31 90
24 54 00 39 76 57 48 91 38 46 47 93 04 17 83 12 73 29 etc.

Display 8.7

Note that 00 will be considered 0; 01 as 1; 02 as 2, etc. In this case, each number should have a probability of $\frac{1}{100}$.

We can use the random digits in Display 8.8 to form a new list by pairing digits. Recall our original table of random digits.

TABLE OF RANDOM DIGITS

8 5 0 5 2 9 4 9 9 2 3 9 6 5 5 0 3 8 7 0 4 1 6 1 2 0 9 8 6 9 9 6 9 8 6 6 2 7
1 9 8 5 4 1 5 6 7 5 5 5 9 9 4 3 6 0 0 9 6 0 2 3 4 4 9 1 5 1 5 6 1 9 3 9 1 8

Display 8.8

By pairing digits we obtain a list of numbers between 0 and 99 inclusive. Again note that 00 will be considered 0, 01 as 1, 02 as 2, etc. Using the idea of pairing we obtain the following table of random numbers (Display 8.9).

TABLE OF RANDOM NUMBERS

85 05 29 49 92 39 65 50 38 70 41 61 20 98 69 96 98 66 27 19 85 41 56 75 55 99
43 60 09 60 23 44 91 51 56 19 39 18 etc.

Display 8.9

8.22

1. Again, solicit student ideas. One might be the following. Take the last digit of your telephone number and look for the first occurrence of that digit in the table. Use that as a seed.

2. This is a good problem for students working in groups. One way might be the following. Take our table of random digits and write the same list, but omit any number which is not in the set from 1 to 6 inclusive. The result would be the following for ten tosses.

5 5 2 4 2 3 6 5 5 3

NOTES

Chapter 8

1. Can you think of other ways of constructing such a table of random numbers?

8.23

2. How might one use the table of random numbers in Display 8.9 to simulate ten tosses of a fair coin?

3. How might one use the table of random numbers to simulate ten tosses of a fair die?

Simulation is used in situations other than coin tossing or die rolling. Indeed, it is a serious business. Government agencies such as those involved with transportation and the distribution of energy, make extensive use of simulation. Simulations are frequently used to model the traffic at toll booths on a highway. The DuPont Company recently completed a simulation of the entire operation of a large hospital. In all of these applications, a basic tool was a random number table (in most cases generated on a computer).

As an example, we shall simulate the arrival times of customers arriving at a bank in a midsize town. Getting this type of information can be tricky and frequently requires several people working together. In this case we consider a group of people who observed customers arriving at the bank. Beginning at 1 p.m. a record was kept of the number of customers who arrived during each minute, for a total of 100 minutes. During some one minute periods, 3 customers would arrive. During other one minute periods, 5 customers would arrive, etc. We put this information into the following table (Display 8.10).

Number of Customers Arriving During a One Minute Period	Number of One Minute Periods During Which This Number Arrived
0	7
1	15
2	18
3	30
4	9
5	8
6	6
7	-?-

Display 8.10

During no one minute period did more than 7 customers arrive.

What number must appear in the -?- position of the last row in Display 8.10?

8.24

481

8.23

1. At this point, students might suggest something like the following. Write the numbers from 0 to 99 on slips of paper, put the slips into a box and thoroughly mix. Pick a number from the box, record it, put it back, mix again, and pick another slip. Continue this process to obtain as many such random numbers as you wish.

2. One way is to pick a seed and use the following scheme.

Random Number	Result of Coin Toss
00–49	Head
50–99	Tail

3. One way is to ignore any number which is 96 or greater and use the following scheme.

Random Number	Result of Toss of Die
00–15	1
16–31	2
32–47	3
48–63	4
64–79	5
80–95	6

8.24

Since there was a total of 100 one minute periods observed, the numbers in the right hand column must sum to 100. Thus, the number 7 must appear in the -?- position.

NOTES

Chapter 8

A Phrase to Know: If something could occur b ways but actually occurs only a ways, we say that the **fraction of occurrences** of that something is $\frac{a}{b}$. The number $\frac{a}{b}$ is often written in decimal form.

If we change the numbers in the right hand column to "fraction of occurrences", one has the following table (Display 8.11).

Number of Customers Arriving During a One Minute Period	Fraction of Occurrences
0	0.07
1	0.15
2	0.18
3	0.30
4	0.09
5	0.08
6	0.06
7	-?-
	1.00

Display 8.11

8.25   **What number, in decimal form, must go in the -?- position of the last row in Display 8.11?**

The table of fractions of occurrence in Display 8.11 is read in the following way: For 7% of the one minute intervals observed, no customers arrived. For 15% of the one minute intervals observed, exactly one customer arrived, etc.

We want to use a random number table to simulate the arrival of customers, but first we must set up a scheme. The scheme should follow the same pattern as in Display 8.11. A rather natural scheme would be the following (Display 8.12).

Published by IT'S ABOUT TIME, Inc. © 2000 MATHconx, LLC

8.25 Since the answer to the previous question was 7, the answer to this question is $\frac{7}{100} = 0.07$.

NOTES

ARRIVAL SCHEME	
Number of Customers Arriving During a One Minute Period	Random Number
0	00–06
1	07–21
2	22–39
3	40–69
4	70–78
5	??–??
6	??–??
7	93–99

Display 8.12

What would be the appropriate integers for the ??–?? positions in Display 8.12?

8.26

In order to apply the scheme, we will use the random number table of Display 8.13 which was generated by a complex computer program.

RANDOM NUMBER TABLE

98 09 87 43 12 01 97 65 23 47 34 04 18 97 34 59 42 23 32 46 99 14 19 92
85 49 73 75 24 77 52 51 68 34 49 74 15 21 81 31 45 87 91 49 10 21 76 39
42 58 90 21 73 58 37 05 23 40 25 07 28 64 56 43 97 98 41 32 39 83 67 34

Display 8.13

Our next step is to find a seed in this random number table. We selected the underlined "73" in Display 8.14.

RANDOM NUMBER TABLE

98 09 87 43 12 01 97 65 23 47 34 04 18 97 34 59 42 23 32 46 99 14 19 92
85 49 **73** 75 24 77 52 51 68 34 49 74 15 21 81 31 45 87 91 49 10 21 76 39
42 58 90 21 73 58 37 05 23 40 25 07 28 64 56 43 97 98 41 32 39 83 67 34

Display 8.14

It follows that we shall make use of the random numbers

73 75 24 77 52 51 68 34 49 74 15 21 81 etc.

8.26

The completed lines would appear as

5	79–86
6	87–92

NOTES

Let's simulate the arrival of customers for 15 minutes. Making use of our scheme, we form the following table (Display 8.15).

Minute	Random Number	Number of Customers Arriving
1	73	4
2	75	4
3	24	2
4	77	4
5	52	3
6	51	3
7	68	3
8	34	2
9	49	3
10	74	4
11		
12		
13		
14		
15		

Display 8.15

8.27 **What entries in the Display 8.15 would be appropriate for the last five minutes of simulation?**

Notice that this table is set up to follow the same pattern that we actually observed when watching customers arrive.

Simulations, such as those developed in this section, form an important tool in the study of complex systems.

Problem Set: 8.4

1. For fifty consecutive one minute time periods, the number of customers arriving at a bank are recorded. The results are given in Display 8.16.

484

Published by IT'S ABOUT TIME, Inc. © 2000 MATHconx, LLC

8.4 Simulation With Random Number Tables

8.27

The last five minutes of simulation would be the following.

Minute	Random Number	Number of Customers Arriving
11	15	1
12	21	1
13	81	5
14	31	2
15	45	3

Problem Set: 8.4

1. An appropriate scheme would be the following Display 8.2T.

Number of Customers Arriving During a One Minute Period	Random Number
1	00–21
2	22–49
3	50–63
4	64–83
5	84–91
6	92–93
7	94–97
8	98–99

Display 8.2T

Student answers on a final table will vary and depend on the seed selected.

Number of Customers Arriving During a One Minute Period	Number of One Minute Periods During Which This Number Arrived
1	11
2	8
3	7
4	10
5	4
6	1
7	8
8	1

Display 8.16

Set up an arrival scheme based on random numbers. Select a seed in the random number table of Display 8.13. Construct a table, similar to that in Display 8.15, which simulates the number of customers arriving during 10 one minute periods.

2. In a grocery store, the service times needed by customers at checkout counters were recorded. The service times were rounded to the nearest half minute. The fraction of occurrences are given in Display 8.17.

Service Times (in Minutes)	Fraction of Occurrences
0	0
$\frac{1}{2}$	0.04
1	0.09
$\frac{3}{2}$	0.24
2	0.31
$\frac{5}{2}$	0.15
3	0.08
$\frac{7}{2}$	0.04
4	0.03
$\frac{9}{2}$	0.01
5	0.01

Display 8.17

Set up a service time scheme based on random numbers. Select a seed in the random number table of Display 8.13. Construct a table that simulates the service time for twelve consecutive customers.

485

2. An appropriate scheme would be the following Display 8.3T.

Service Times (in Minutes)	Random Number
0	None
$\frac{1}{2}$	00–03
1	04–12
$\frac{3}{2}$	13–36
2	37–67
$\frac{5}{2}$	68–82
3	83–90
$\frac{7}{2}$	91–94
4	95–97
$\frac{9}{2}$	98
5	99

Display 8.3T

Student answers on a final table will vary and depend on the seed selected.

NOTES

Chapter 8

8.5 Simulation Using Calculators

Learning Outcomes

After studying this section, you will be able to:

Find lists of random numbers on a TI-82 (TI-83);

Change random numbers from a TI-82 (TI-83) into outcomes of an experiment;

Write programs on a TI-82 (TI-83) for simulating various activities.

In the last section we saw how to simulate a number of activities by using random number tables. Computers and calculators are capable of making lists of random numbers. Usually, however, they do not produce lists of integers but rather decimal numbers between 0 and 1. With a TI-82 (TI-83) such a list can be made by using the following steps:

1. Turn on the calculator by pressing the ON key.

2. Press MATH ◁ 1 . When ◁ is pressed the PRB (probability menu) and 1: are highlighted. Pressing the 1 key selects the rand (random) operation.

3. Your calculator should display rand with a blinking cursor. Now press ENTER. On the author's calculator the number

.4972695102

appeared. Pressing ENTER again gave the two numbers

.4972695102

.9999157586

Pressing ENTER again gave the three numbers

.4972695102

.9999157586

.1794355993

Continuing in this fashion, the following list was obtained.

.4972695102

.9999157586

.1794355993

.417296993

.289041425

.7068343753

.3053351791

etc.

Published by IT'S ABOUT TIME, Inc. © 2000 MATHconx, LLC

486

8.5 Simulation Using Calculators

Based on ideas from the previous section, this section combines the power of a calculator and the power of simulation. This is an excellent section for having students extend their knowledge of programming on a calculator. Note that programming a TI-82 is similar to programming a TI-83.

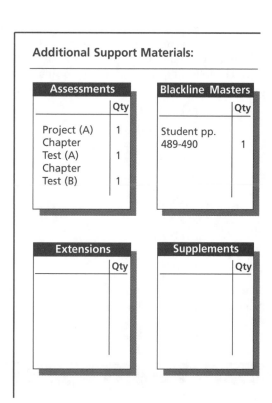

Additional Support Materials:

Assessments	Qty
Project (A)	1
Chapter Test (A)	1
Chapter Test (B)	1

Blackline Masters	Qty
Student pp. 489-490	1

Extensions	Qty

Supplements	Qty

Chapter 8

At this point, you should use your TI-82 (TI-83) and generate a list of random numbers.

8.28

1. Why do you think that the 4th and 5th numbers in the above list have fewer digits than the other numbers in the list?

2. How might one use such a list of random numbers to generate a list of random whole numbers between 0 and 99 inclusive? Can you think of more than one way?

3. How might one use such a list of random numbers to simulate ten tosses of a fair coin? Is there more than one way to do this?

We now know how to obtain a list of random numbers between 0 and 1 on a graphing calculator. A big question remains: Can we get that calculator to toss a coin for us many times and tell us how many heads appeared (and thus also the number of tails that appeared)? In order to do this we need to write a program for the calculator. The calculator does not know how to toss a coin or even how to simulate the toss of a coin unless we give the calculator instructions on how to do it. The set of instructions is called a **program.** If you do not know how to write a program, review the Appendix C—Programming the TI-82 (TI-83).

We need to give our program, or set of instructions, a name. The name may have no more than 8 symbols. I decided to call my program COIN but you can call yours whatever you like. The following program is used to simulate the tossing of a coin N times, where N is a counting number of your choice.

```
Prgm1:COIN
:Disp "WHAT IS N
?"
:Input N
:0→H
:For(T,1,N)
:rand→R
:If R<0.5
:H+1→H
:End
:Disp H
```

Before we see how this program works, let's play with it for a while. Your teacher will help you put this program into your

487

8.28

1. The last digit was a 0 which the calculator did not include.

2. One way would be to round these decimal numbers to two decimal places and multiply the result by 100.

3. One could use a scheme such as the following.

Random Number	Result of Coin Toss
≤0.5	Head
>0.5	Tail

NOTES

Chapter 8

calculator. How do we run the program? Press PRGM, select your "coin" program, press ENTER. The question "*What is N?*" appears on the screen. How many times do you want a coin to be tossed? I chose 50, but you can choose any number you wish (don't make it too big; it still takes some time). Press 5 0 and ENTER. After a second or so, my calculator showed 29. That is, in the 50 tosses of a coin, a head appeared 29 times. Your number, of course, could be quite different. Why?

8.29 **Run the program again simply by pressing** ENTER. **Did you get the same number of heads? Explain!**

Now let's see if we can get some idea of how and why this program works. The program appears below with the lines numbered.

```
1.      Prgm1:COIN
2.      :Disp "WHAT IS N
3.      ?"
4.      :Input N
5.      :0→H
6.      :For(T,1,N)
7.      :rand→R
8.      :If R<0.5
9.      :H+1→H
10.     :End
11.     :Disp H
```

Line 1   simply gives a name to your program. Note that when you are asked for a program name, the ALPHA mode is already in use.

Line 2   asks you for the number of times, N, that you wish a coin to be tossed.

Line 3   is the end of Line 2.

Line 4   tells the calculator what value for N you have selected.

Line 5   introduces a counter H which will count the number of times a head has appeared.

Line 6   introduces a counter T which will count the number of times the calculator has simulated the toss of a coin. The 1 and the N give the beginning and ending values of T.

Line 7   selects a random number and gives it the name R.

488

Published by IT'S ABOUT TIME, Inc. © 2000 MATHconx, LLC

8.29

Students should realize that the calculator is beginning with a new seed and hence will probably have a different number of heads.

NOTES

Line 8   tests to see if R is less than 0.5. If so, we want to call the result a head. Otherwise, the result is a tail.

Line 9   adds 1 to the counter H if the result in line 8 is a head. In this way H keeps track of the total number of heads obtained.

Line 10   tells the calculator that the process of tossing a coin one time is now complete. If your number, N, of tosses has been reached, the calculator will stop. If not, the calculator returns to line 7 and goes through the process again.

Line 11   asks the calculator to display the number of heads that were obtained in the N tosses of a coin.

REFLECT

In this chapter you have been exposed to many ideas about probabilities and events that happen by chance. Uncertainty surrounds all of us all of the time. It is probability that enables us to measure, in some sense, that uncertainty. Later, in **MATH** *Connections*, you will return to the study of probability at a higher level and see connections between probability and statistics.

Problem Set: 8.5

A purpose of the following two problems is to put together ideas that you have learned in **MATH** *Connections*. Some of the ideas you have studied in earlier chapters.

1. Run your coin flipping program from this section 30 times, using an N value of 50 each time. This would be just like flipping a real coin 50 times, and then repeating the whole process 29 more times. Record the results of each run of the program. Thus you should end up with a list of 30 numbers, each number being a number between 0 and 50. Each number represents the number of heads that you got with 50 flips.

   (a) Organize your results into a frequency table, so that you count the number of times you got 20 heads, the number of times you got 21 heads, and so on.

   (b) Form a histogram from the results in part (a).

   Note: On the TI-83 you could do parts (a) and (b) by entering the raw data into the statistics part of the calculator. Tracing the histogram gives you the number of 24s, 25s, 26s and so on.

Published by IT'S ABOUT TIME, Inc. © 2000 MATHconx, LLC

489

Problem Set: 8.5

1. Students typically do not have good intuition about actual phenomena which have a random component. The idea behind this problem is to sharpen the students' ideas about how random events actually occur.

The fundamental connection to make between the theory of probability and actual random events is that if an event has probability say $\frac{1}{3}$, and if the experiment is performed many times, the event should occur about $\frac{1}{3}$ of the time. But what does that "about" really mean? In practice, if a fair coin is flipped 50 times, how many heads might actually come up?

This question can be answered using the binomial distribution, which is a bit too advanced to introduce at this level, but we can come up with an experimental answer using the coin flipping program. This also makes an important connection between probability and the statistics that was studied at the beginning of the year. The basic relationship we will use is

$$\text{experimental probability of event} = \frac{\text{number of occurrences of event}}{\text{number of repetitions of experiment}}$$

The theoretical probabilities for the coin flipping experiment are shown in the table of Display 8.4T, both in table form and as a histogram. The formula for calculating the probability of x heads in n flips of a coin is the binomial distribution formula

$$\frac{n!}{x!(n-x)!}p^x(1-p)^{n-x}$$

where for our problem n is 50, and p (the probability of heads) is 0.5. For example, when we flip a coin 50 times, the probability of getting exactly 25 heads is about 0.112 or 11.2%. Perhaps most important, we see that we will virtually always get between 15 and 35 heads.

Chapter 8

(c) Combine your data with your classmates data to form one big frequency table. If you combine the results from 10 groups, then you would have data corresponding to 300 trials of this experiment instead of just 30 trials. Now form a histogram for the data from the entire class.

(d) Based on the data you collected, write a paragraph or two addressing the following questions. How likely is it that if you flip a coin 50 times you will get exactly 25 heads? How likely is it that you will get fewer than 15 heads? How likely is it that you will get between 20 and 30 heads?

(e) Bart makes the following proposition to his little sister. He says, "I am going to flip a coin 50 times. If I get 23, 24, 25, 26, 27 or 28 heads, you have to do my chores this week. If the number of heads is anything else, I will do your chores this week. Out of 51 possible outcomes, I only get 6 outcomes and you get the other 45 outcomes. How about it?" Should Bart's sister take his offer or not?

2. Many games that use dice involve rolling a pair of dice, and adding together the total number of spots on the two dice. The possible results from rolling two dice would be the numbers 2 through 12. (Why?) When one die is rolled, the numbers one through six should come up with approximately equal probability. Will the numbers 2 through 12 come up with equal probability when two dice are rolled? If not, what would the probabilities be?

In order to determine the probability of an event, one method is to use your intuition. Often in real life, exact calculation of probabilities is extremely difficult or impossible. Another approach is to repeat an experiment many times and record the results to estimate the probability of an event. A third approach is to program a computer or calculator to repeat the experiment many times and have it store the results, from which you can estimate the probability of the event.

(a) Determine the intuitive probabilities of the numbers 1 through 6 coming up when one die is rolled, *based on the assumption that all numbers are equally likely.*

(b) Determine the probabilities of the numbers 1 through 6 coming up by actually rolling a die. To do this, roll a die 100 times and record the results. Organize your results into a frequency table, and then make a histogram. Now combine your results with your

Published by IT'S ABOUT TIME, Inc. © 2000 MATHconx, LLC

# of Heads	Probability	# of Heads	Probability
10	0.000	26	0.108
11	0.000	27	0.096
12	0.000	28	0.079
13	0.000	29	0.060
14	0.001	30	0.042
15	0.002	31	0.027
16	0.004	32	0.016
17	0.009	33	0.009
18	0.016	34	0.004
19	0.027	35	0.002
20	0.042	36	0.001
21	0.060	37	0.000
22	0.079	38	0.000
23	0.096	39	0.000
24	0.108	40	0.000
25	0.112		

Display 8.4T

A typical histogram for part (b) would look like Display 8.5T. The histograms that your students will come up with are empirical histograms. Since you are repeating the experiment 30 times, you might expect to get 25 heads about 3 or 4 times (11% of 30 is 3.3). You use your empirical histogram to calculate experimental probabilities by dividing the number in each category by 30. For example, if you got 25 heads 4 times in 30 trials, the estimated probability of getting 25 heads would be $\frac{4}{30} \approx 0.133$ or about 13.3%.

A typical histogram for part (c) would look like Display 8.6T (assuming 10 groups of three students and hence 300 repetitions of the experiment). This part makes use of the data from the entire class. This time, the estimated probabilities should be closer to the theoretical ones shown in the table. This time you divide the number in each category by the total number of trials for the class (300 or so). The idea here is that the more you repeat an experiment, the closer the probability estimates should be to the theoretical probabilities. Still, even with data from the whole class, it is likely that not all of the probability estimates will be close to the theoretical ones. Many trials are often needed to get good estimates for all probabilities.

Chapter 8

classmates' results to form a frequency table and histogram which summarizes the results of all the experiments of yours and your classmates. For example, if there were 5 groups doing this experiment, you would have the results from 500 rolls of a die.

(c) Determine the probabilities of the numbers 1 through 6 coming up using computer simulation. The program below can be used to simulate the rolling of a die 99 times. The results are stored in the statistics part of the calculator in list L1. You can then make a histogram of the results. Use a WINDOW setting of Xmin=0.5, Xmax=6.5, Xscl=1, Ymin=0, Ymax=30, Yscl=10, then use **TRACE** to find the number in each category.

```
PROGRAM: DIE
:For(I,1,99)
:int(rand*6)+1→L1(I)
:End
```

Read the following two paragraphs to learn how this program works.

Since **rand** is a random number between 0 and 1, rand*6 is a random number between 0 and 6. Then int(rand*6) finds the integer part of rand*6, meaning it rounds rand*6 down to an integer from 0 to 5. So int(rand*6)+1 is an integer from 1 to 6, which is what we want when we simulate a die. This result is then stored in list L1 so that all the results can be plotted as a histogram.

The **For** and **End** statements form what is called a "For loop." The statement between the **For** and **End** statements is executed 99 times. This means that 99 simulated rolls of a single die will be stored in list L1. The letter **I** is called an index. **I** starts out equal to 1, then each time through the loop its value increases by 1, up to 99. This way the first simulated die is stored in L1(1), the second simulated die stored in L1(2), and so on.

(d) Use the results of parts (a) through (c) to determine or estimate the probabilities of getting each of the numbers 2 through 12 when you roll two dice and add the results. Use whatever method or methods you can, including intuitive calculation (the Fundamental Counting Principle might help), repeated trials with real dice, or calculator simulation.

Published by IT'S ABOUT TIME, Inc. © 2000 MATHconx, LLC

491

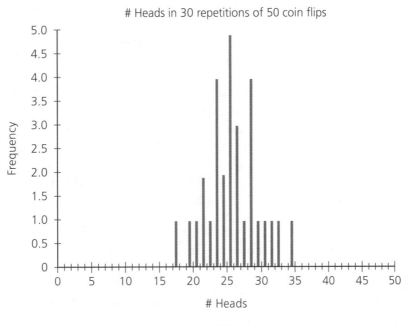

Display 8.5T

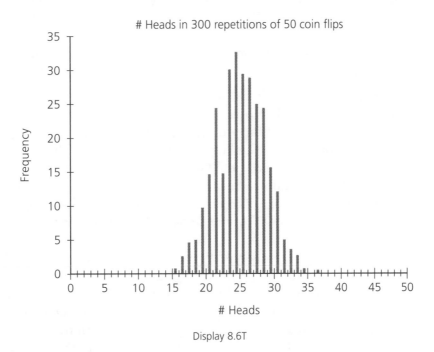

Display 8.6T

For part (d), we have seen that the probability of 25 heads should come out to be about 11% or so. It is quite unlikely (nearly 0 probability) that one would get fewer than 15 heads. The probability of getting between 20 and 30 heads is estimated by adding the probabilities of getting 20 heads through 30 heads together. This should come out to about 88%. Thus, generally one would expect to get between 20 and 30 heads, but a number out of this range is not highly unusual.

Chapter 8

For part (e), we add the probabilities for 23 through 28 heads together. These account for about 60% of the total probability, even though they represent only 6 of the 51 outcomes. Thus, Bart is getting the best of it; Bart's sister should not take the offer.

Remember that all of the probabilities we are quoting here are the theoretical probabilities; the probabilities that your students will be using will be estimated from the calculator experiment. Probabilities estimated from just 30 trials will not be very accurate. Ideally, through group discussion, the students will decide to use the data from the entire class instead of the data from only their own group. We don't recommend that you show them the theoretical probabilities or the binomial formula at this point.

2. The goals of problem 2 are similar to those of problem 1, so read through the Teacher Commentary for that problem first.
    This time we are rolling dice. When one die is rolled, the outcomes (the numbers 1 through 6) are equally likely. When two dice are rolled, and the results added together, the outcomes (2 through 12) are not equally likely. The goal of the project is to get students to estimate the probabilities for these outcomes, and use this knowledge to solve a problem involving dice.

    (a) With equally likely outcomes, each of the numbers would have probability $\frac{1}{6}$.

    (b) To estimate the probability of getting a six, for example, take the number of sixes in 100 rolls and divide by 100 (as explained in the Teacher Commentary for problem 1). The histogram for 100 rolls will probably not come out looking "the way it should." The combined data for the whole class should come out closer to the equally likely ideal (a flat histogram). Remember to divide the frequencies in the histogram by the number of trials to get probabilities (divide by 100 for one student group; 500 for the combined results of 5 student groups, and so on).

    (c) Since the TI-83 can only hold 99 values in a list, we use 99 trials instead of 100. Thus, to estimate probabilities, divide the number of occurrences of an outcome by 99. Otherwise, the results using the program should be similar to the results using a real die. Of course, it is much faster to roll a die 99 times by calculator than to roll a real die 99 or 100 times. Thus, students could repeat this process many times and combine the results to get more accurate results. You probably would want to put them in groups and see if they could figure this out themselves.

(d) Some students may be able to figure out the theoretical probabilities using the Fundamental Counting Principle. For example, there are 36 outcomes for rolling 2 dice (6 times 6). The list of outcomes is

$$(1, 1), (1, 2), ..., (1, 6)$$
$$(2, 1), (2, 2), ..., (2, 6)$$
$$\vdots$$
$$(6, 1), (6, 2), ..., (6, 6)$$

Since there are three ways to get a sum of 4 ((1,3), (2,2), (3,1)) the probability of getting a total of 4 is $\frac{3}{36}$. It may be better to leave these fractions unreduced for comparison.

We expect that most students would use the calculator simulation approach (certainly it is faster than using actual dice). The program for rolling two dice would be

```
: For(I,1,99)
: int(rand * 6) → A
: int(rand * 6) + 1 → B
: A + B → L1(I)
: End
```

Set the WINDOW for Xmin = 0; Xmax = 13; Xscl = 1; and Ymin = 0; Ymax = 30; Yscl = 1.

By running this program just as you did for a single die, you should get probabilities similar to the theoretical ones calculated, as explained above. The shape of the experimental histogram should be approximately tent shaped, with the largest probability at 7, and the smallest at 2 and 12. By combining different runs, you can get more accuracy (see if some of the student groups come up with this idea themselves). Remember, the probability of a 4, for example, would be the number of 4's divided by the number of trials.

Chapter 8

Note: The program in part (c) can be modified to simulate the roll of two dice. Just roll one die and store the result in memory *A*, roll a second die and store the result in memory *B*, and then add *A* and *B* and store the result in list L1.

(e) Sandy and Rodrigo are playing a board game called Monopoly. Two dice are rolled each time. It's Sandy's turn. If Sandy rolls a 4, 6, 7 or 8 she loses. Do you think she will lose the game on her next roll or not? Justify your answer using your results from part (d).

(f) Write an essay on the three methods of calculating probabilities you have used in this problem (intuitive calculation, actual repeated trials, and calculator simulation). Which method is most reliable? Why? Which is the easiest? Why? Which do you prefer? Why? Relate your discussion to your answers to parts (d) and (e).

(g) If three dice are rolled and the resulting numbers are added together, what are the possible results and their probabilities?

Published by IT'S ABOUT TIME, Inc. © 2000 MATHconx, LLC

(e) The theoretical probability of getting a 4, 6, 7 or 8 would be

$$\frac{3}{36} + \frac{5}{36} + \frac{6}{36} + \frac{5}{36} = \frac{19}{36}$$

which is a little more than $\frac{1}{2}$. Thus, it is more likely that she will lose than not. Of course, the experimental probabilities that your students calculate won't be exact, so it is possible they will come to the opposite conclusion. The process and the explanation are more important than their conclusion.

(f) Obviously, calculator simulation is faster than actual repeated trials and should be just about as accurate. Calculation based on the Fundamental Counting Principle is the most reliable, since the accuracy of a simulation depends on the number of trials. The students should see this clearly in parts 2 and 3.

(g) The possible sums for the three dice are {3, 4, 5, 6,..., 17, 18}.
$P(3) = P(18) = \frac{1}{216}$; $P(4) = P(17) = \frac{3}{216}$; $P(5) = P(16) = \frac{6}{216}$;
$P(6) = P(15) = \frac{10}{216}$; $P(7) = P(14) = \frac{15}{216}$; $P(8) = P(13) = \frac{21}{216}$;
$P(9) = P(12) = \frac{25}{216}$; $P(10) = P(11) = \frac{27}{216}$. See Display 8.1T.

NOTES

Chapter 8

Appendix A: Using a TI-82 (TI-83) Graphing Calculator

A graphing calculator is a useful tool for doing many different mathematical things. Once you begin to use it, you'll find that it is powerful, fast, and friendly. In fact, your biggest difficulty may be just getting started for the first time! Because this machine can do a lot, it has lots of complicated looking buttons. But you don't have to know about *all* of them before you start to use *any* of them! The sooner you make friends with your electronic assistant, the more it will be able to help you. Let us introduce you to each other by trying a few simple things.

The Cover

The face of the calculator is protected from dirt and scratches by a cover that slides on and off from the top. When you're using the calculator, this cover slips on the back so that you won't lose it. Always put the cover back over the face of the calculator when you finish using it.

On, Off, 2nd , and Clear

To get the calculator's attention, just press ON (at the lower left corner of the calculator). What happens? Do you see a dark block blinking in the upper left corner of the screen? That's the **cursor**, which tells you where you are on the screen. The cursor is always at the spot that will be affected by the next button you push.

Notice that the word OFF is printed in color above the ON button, a little to the left of its center. Notice also that there is one key of the same color. It is the key marked 2nd at the left end of the second row.

When you push 2nd , it makes the next key that you push behave like what is marked above it on the left.

Try it: Push 2nd . What has happened to the cursor? Do you see an up arrow inside it as it blinks? That's to remind you that 2nd key has been pushed and will affect the next key

Using a TI-82 (TI-83) Graphing Calculator

This appendix is *not* intended to replace the manual for the TI-82 (TI-83) graphing calculators. Rather, it has two purposes.

- It serves as a gentle introduction to the machine by way of some simple calculations, and

- It provides a convenient reference for some of the more commonly used elementary procedures.

Before using the graphing calculators with your class for the first time, **please check each one to see that it is reset to its factory settings and that it actually turns on and off.** It will be easier to answer your students' questions if all the calculators have working batteries and behave the same when they are first turned on.

NOTES

you choose. Now push [ON]. What happens? Did the cursor disappear? You should have a blank screen; the calculator should be off.

It's always a good idea to turn your calculator off when you finish using it. If you forget, the calculator will turn itself off after a few minutes to save its batteries. Sometimes when you are using it, you may put it aside and do something else for a little while. If it is off when you pick it up again, don't worry; just press [ON]. The screen will show what was there before it shut down.

Pressing [CLEAR] gives you a blank screen that is ready for new work. But the last thing you did is still stored. Press [2nd] then [ENTER] to bring it back.

Basic Arithmetic

Doing arithmetic on a graphing calculator is no harder than on a simpler calculator. In fact, it's easier. This calculator has a screen that lets you keep track of the problem as you enter it. Let's try a few simple exercises. Turn your calculator on.

- Pick two 3-digit numbers and add them. To do this, just key in the first number, press [+] and then key in the second number. Your addition problem will appear on the screen. Press [ENTER] to get the answer.

If you make a mistake when entering a number, you can go back and fix it. The [◁] key lets you move back (left) one space at a time. When you get to your mistake, just key in the correct number over the wrong one. Then move forward (right) to the end of the line by using the [▷] key.

For instance, to add 123 and 456, press 1 2 3 [+] 4 5 6 [ENTER]. The screen will show your question on the first line and the answer at the right side of the second line, as in Display A.1.

```
123+456
            579
```

Display A.1

Published by IT'S ABOUT TIME, Inc. © 2000 MATHconx, LLC

A-2

A.1

Basic Arithmetic

These questions are largely for routine practice. The use of seven-digit numbers helps to encourage the students to use the shortcuts, rather than just rekeying the entries. In parts 3 and 4, it serves the additional purpose of requiring them to deal with an answer displayed in scientific notation.

NOTES

- Now let's try the other three basic arithmetic operations. To clear the screen, press CLEAR. Then try subtracting, multiplying, and dividing your two 3-digit numbers. For instance, if your numbers are 123 and 456, press

$$1\ 2\ 3\ \boxed{-}\ 4\ 5\ 6\ \boxed{\text{ENTER}}$$

$$1\ 2\ 3\ \boxed{\times}\ 4\ 5\ 6\ \boxed{\text{ENTER}}$$

$$1\ 2\ 3\ \boxed{\div}\ 4\ 5\ 6\ \boxed{\text{ENTER}}$$

Your screen should look like Display A.2.

Notice that the display uses $*$ for multiplication (so that it is not confused with the letter x) and / for division.

```
123-456
              -333
123*456
            56088
123/456
       .2697368421
```

Display A.2

- Here are two, button pushing shortcuts.

If you don't want to redo a problem with just a small change in it, you don't have to reenter the whole thing. 2nd ENTER will bring back the last problem you entered. Just move to the place you want to change, key in the change, and press ENTER. For instance, add 54321 and 12345, as in Display A.3.

```
54321+12345
            66666
```

Display A.3

NOTES

Now, to subtract 12345 from 54321, press [2nd] [ENTER]; the next line will show 54321 + 12345. Move your cursor back to the + sign (using [◁]) and press [−]; then press [ENTER]. Did you try it? Your screen should look like Display A.4.

```
54321+12345
                66666
54321−12345
                41976
```

Display A.4

Let's check to see that 41976 is the correct answer by adding 12345 to it and seeing if we get the first number back again. Since you want to do something to the last answer, *you don't have to reenter it*. Press [+]. Does your calculator show Ans+ and the cursor? It should. If you press an operation key right after doing a calculation, the machine assumes that you want to perform this operation on the last answer. It shows that last answer as Ans. Now key in 12345 and press [ENTER]. You should get back the first number, 54321.

A.1

1. Pick two seven-digit numbers and add them. What do you get?

2. Now subtract the second number from the first. Can you do it without rekeying the numbers? What do you get?

3. Now multiply your two seven-digit numbers. What do you get? What does the E mean?

4. Check the last answer by dividing the second of your seven-digit numbers into it. (Do it without rekeying the last answer.) Do you get your first number back again?

Published by IT'S ABOUT TIME, Inc. © 2000 MATHconx, LLC

1. This is straightforward.

2. To do this without rekeying, use the entry key [2nd] [ENTER] to get back the addition line, move back to the + sign using the [◁] key, press [−], then press [ENTER].

3. The fact that the numbers chosen have seven digits guarantees that their product appears in scientific E notation. For example, the product of 1234567 and 2345678 appears as 2.895896651E12. This means that the product is actually

$$2.895896651 \times 10^{12} \text{ or } 2,895,896,651,000$$

4. To check without rekeying the answer, just press [÷], then key in the second seven-digit number. For our example, the display will show Ans/2345678. When you press [ENTER] the first seven-digit number will appear.

NOTES

Multiply 98765432 by 123456. Now check the product in two ways.

a

A.2

- Divide by pressing ⟨ ÷ ⟩ then entering 123456. Does it check?

- First reenter the product; then divide it by 123456. (The product is in scientific notation. To enter it as a regular number, remember that the positive number after the E tells you to move the decimal that many places to the right.) Does it check?

1. Divide 97533 by 525 and by 625. One of the answers you get will be exactly right, and the other one will be a very close approximation.

b

A.3

   - Which is which?

   - How can you tell?

   - If you hadn't been told that one of the answers is an approximation, how could you know?

2. When an answer is too long to be displayed with ten digits, the calculator shows a ten-digit approximation. Does it do this by just chopping off (truncating) the rest of the digits, or by rounding off? What test would you give your calculator to tell which way it does this?

1. Pick any three-digit number and note it down.

c

A.4

2. Repeat its digits in the same order to form a six-digit number (like 123123, for example). Key this number into your calculator.

3. Divide your number by 7.

4. Divide your answer by 11. (How do you do this without reentering the answer?)

5. Divide the last number by 13. What do you notice about the result? Do you think that it is just a coincidence?

6. Pick another three digit number and repeat steps 2–5.

7. Try to beat the system; see if you can pick a three-digit number that doesn't work this way. What might you try? Why?

8. Can you actually prove that the pattern you see *works every time*? How might you try to do this?

Published by IT'S ABOUT TIME, Inc. © 2000 MATHconx, LLC

A-5

This exercise illustrates the fact that some answers, particularly those expressed in scientific notation, are approximations. It also gives students a chance to deal with two other matters;

- rewriting a number from scientific notation to standard form, and
- experiencing the wraparound feature of the calculator's screen display.

To do the second check, students must convert the product $1.219318517\text{E}13$ to the form 12,193,185,170,000 and key in

$$12193185170000 \boxed{\div} 123456 \boxed{\text{ENTER}}$$

This is too long to fit on a single line of the calculator display, so it is *automatically* wrapped around to the second line. There is no need to press any sort of "carriage return" key. In fact, trying to do so probably will result in an error. The screen should look like Display A.1T.

> 12193185170000/1
> 23456
>   98765431.98

Display A.1T

These questions relate to the fact that answers are displayed with a maximum of 10 digits.

1. The easiest way to identify the exact answer is by observing that one of these answers has fewer than 10 digits; that one is exact. The next question actually tells the student this fact. The other is not, but you can't be *sure* just because it has 10 digits. The decimal form of the answer does not terminate because the divisor has prime factors other than 2 or 5.

    Multiplying back to check your answer by using Ans $\boxed{\times}$ will give exactly the original dividend *both* times; the calculator holds a more exact approximation than it shows. However, if you rekey each answer and multiply it by its divisor, you will get an inexact original dividend in one of these cases.

2. An easy test is to divide 2 by 3. The display .6666666667 clearly shows that the calculator rounds, rather than truncates.

This question illustrates how the efficiency of a calculator permits students to focus on emerging patterns without getting tangled in computation. Steps 2 – 5 result in the original three-digit number, regardless of what was chosen to begin with. Step 7 is intended to encourage students to think about finding exceptional cases. For instance, most students will choose three different digits for their first three-digit number, and very few will use 0. They might reasonably guess that a number with repeated digits or with

The Two Minus Signs

The calculator has two minus signs. The one on the blue key looks like $\boxed{-}$ and the one on the gray key looks like $\boxed{(-)}$. The blue one, on the right, is for subtraction. It is grouped with the keys for the other arithmetic operations. To subtract 3764 from 8902, for example, you would key in

$$8 \ 9 \ 0 \ 2 \ \boxed{-} \ 3 \ 7 \ 6 \ 4 \ \boxed{\text{ENTER}}$$

(Go ahead; do it. Do you get 5138?)

The gray minus key, next to the $\boxed{\text{ENTER}}$ key at the bottom, is for making a number negative. It is grouped with the digit keys and the decimal point. To add the numbers -273, 5280, and -2116, for example, you would key in

$$\boxed{(-)} \ 2 \ 7 \ 3 \ \boxed{+} \ 5 \ 2 \ 8 \ 0 \ \boxed{+} \ \boxed{(-)} \ 2 \ 1 \ 1 \ 6 \ \boxed{\text{ENTER}}$$

(Try it.) Notice that the display shows these negative signs without the parentheses, but they are smaller and raised a little. To see the difference between this negative sign and the subtraction sign, try subtracting the negative number -567 from 1234. Here are the keystrokes.

$$1234 \ \boxed{-} \ \boxed{(-)} \ 567$$

The display should look like this:

$$1234 - {}^{-}567$$

Raising to a Power

To raise a number to a power, press $\boxed{\wedge}$ just before entering the exponent. Thus, to compute 738^5, press

$$7 \ 3 \ 8 \ \boxed{\wedge} \ 5 \ \boxed{\text{ENTER}}$$

The screen should look like Display A.5.

```
738^5
          2.1891817E14
```

Display A.5

Published by IT'S ABOUT TIME, Inc. © 2000 MATHconx, LLC

MATH *Connections*: A Secondary Mathematics Core Curriculum

zeroes in it would not work in the same way. Even though that turns out not to be the case, such conjectures are evidence that students are developing good thinking and exploration skills.

Proving that this "trick" works all the time is well within the reach of many students at this level. It rests on the fact that multiplication undoes what division does (and vice versa). Multiplying the three divisors, $7 \times 11 \times 13$, produces the number 1001, and multiplying a three-digit number by 1001 has the effect of repeating its digits. Thus, step 2 multiplied the original number by 1001, and steps 3, 4, and 5 divided by 1001 in three stages.

NOTES

The Menu Keys

Many keys bring a menu to the screen. A menu is a list of functions—things that the calculator is ready to do for you. For instance, press each of the keys across the row that starts with MATH . Don't worry about what all those lists say; just pick one out and look at it as you read the rest of this paragraph. Notice that it is actually a double menu. There are two cursors on it, shown as dark blocks. The one in the top left corner can be moved along the top line by using the ◁ and ▷ keys. Each time you move it to a new place on the top line, the menu below changes. The items in each lower menu are reached by using the other cursor, which can be moved up and down along the left side of the screen by using the △ and ▽ keys.

Once you have put the cursor on the choice you want, you actually make the choice by pressing ENTER . This makes the calculator go back to its "home" screen and display your choice. To make the calculator do what you have chosen, press ENTER again.

1. **How many separate calculator functions can be reached through the menus of the** MATH **key?**

2. **How many separate calculator functions can be reached through the menus of the** MATRX **key?**

A.5

Entering Data in a List

The data handling tools are found through the statistics menu.
*   Turn your calculator on and press STAT . You'll see a menu that looks like Display A.6.

EDIT CALC
1:Edit…
2:SortA(
3:SortD(
4:ClrList

TI-82

EDIT CALC TESTS
1:Edit…
2:SortA(
3:SortD(
4:ClrList
5:SetUpEditor

TI-83

Display A.6

A-7

The Menu Keys

These questions serve the purpose of getting the students to focus on the dual nature of the menus. They also emphasize the wide ranging power of these machines. Finally, they provide a simple exercise in counting possibilities in a somewhat novel setting.

1. On the TI-82. 10 + 6 + 6 + 4 = 26; on the TI-83. 10 + 9 + 7 + 7 = 33.

2. On the TI-82.   5 + 11 + 5 = 21; on the TI-83. 10 + 16 + 10 = 36.

Entering Data in a List

This part is self explanatory. There are no differences between the TI-82 (TI-83) for this process.

NOTES

- To enter data, make sure that the top cursor is on EDIT and the left cursor is on 1: . Then press ENTER . Your screen display should look like Display A.7, with the cursor right under L1.

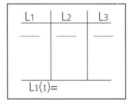

Display A.7

Note: If the display shows numbers in the L1 column, you'll have to clear the data memory. There are two ways to do this.

Get out of this display (by pressing 2nd QUIT) and go back to the STAT menu. Press 4 . When ClrList appears, press 2nd 1 then ENTER ; Done will appear. Now go back to the STAT screen and choose 1:Edit .

or

Without leaving this display, use the △ and ◁ keys to move your cursor to the top of the column and highlight L1. Press CLEAR and then the ▽ key. List L1 should be cleared.

- Now it's time to enter the data. The calculator stores in its memory each data number you enter, along with an L1 label for that entry. The first number is called L1(1), and the second is called L1(2), and so on. (We'll ignore the L2 and L3 labels for now.) Key in the first data number, then press ENTER . Notice that L1(2) now appears at the bottom of the screen. Key in the second data number and press ENTER ; and so on, until you have put in all the data. If you make a mistake, just use the arrow keys to move the cursor to your error, type over it correctly, then move back to where you were.

At this point, the calculator has all your data stored in a way that is easy to use, and the data will stay stored even after the calculator is turned off.

NOTES

Summaries of 1-Variable Data

It is easy to get summary information about data that is stored in a single list.

- Bring up the STAT menu.

- Move the top cursor to CALC. The side cursor should be on 1:1-Var Stats. Press [ENTER].

- 1:1-Var Stats will appear on your screen. Enter the list you want the calculator to summarize. For instance, if you want a summary of the data in list L1, press [2nd] [1] ; then press [ENTER].

That's all there is to it! A screenful of information will appear. Sections 1.3–1.7 in Chapter 1 of Book 1 explain how to interpret that information.

Putting Data in Size Order

The TI-82 (TI-83) have built-in programs that will put your data in size order automatically. Do you have any data stored in L1? If not, enter ten or a dozen numbers at random, so that you can see how the following steps work.

1. Turn the calculator on and go to the STAT menu.

2. To see what is stored in L1, [ENTER] 1:Edit . Then move the cursor left to L1, if it's not there already. Make sure you have some data in this list.

3. Go back to the STAT menu and choose 2:Sort A(then press [ENTER]. Tell the calculator to sort the L1 list by pressing [2nd] [1], then [ENTER]. Your calculator screen should now say Done. To see what it has done, reopen List 1 (using [STAT] 1:Edit) . Your data should now be listed in ascending order — that is, from smallest to largest as you read down the list. The A in SortA(stands for ascending order.

Now go back to the STAT menu and choose 2:SortD(then press [ENTER]. Tell the calculator to sort the L1 list again. (Press [2nd] [1] [ENTER].)

1. When the screen says Done, what has your calculator done? (Look at L1 again to help you answer this question.)

A.6

2. What does the "D" in SortD(stand for?

Published by IT'S ABOUT TIME, Inc. © 2000 MATHconx, LLC

A-9

Summaries of 1-Variable Data

This is another self explanatory part with no differences between the TI-82 (TI-83) calculators. You may need to remind students that the downward pointing arrow at the beginning of the last line of the display indicates that there are more lines of information below, which can be read by pressing ▽ .

Putting Data in Size Order

A.6

This should be a very quick exercise.

1. It sorts the numbers from largest to smallest as you read down the list.
2. The D stands for descending order .

If you haven't covered median yet, you can ignore the rest of this part until you get to Section 1.4 of Year 1.

NOTES

_____

_____

_____

_____

_____

_____

_____

_____

_____

_____

_____

Once the data are in size order, it is easy to find the median. For example, if you have 21 data items in all, the median is just the 11th one in the sorted list. Scroll through the data (using the ⟨ △ ⟩ key) until you find L1(11). Its value is the median. If you have 20 data items, the median is halfway between the 10th and 11th items in the sorted list. Scroll through the data until you find L1(10) and L1(11). Then calculate the number halfway between them.

Finding the mode is just as easy. Count repeated items in this list. The one that is repeated the most times is the mode.

The Graph Window

This kind of calculator is called a graphing calculator because it can *draw graphs*. The screen on a graphing calculator can show line drawings of mathematical relationships. It does this with two kinds of coordinate systems—*rectangular coordinates* or *polar coordinates*. In this part we shall use only rectangular coordinates; polar coordinates will appear much later. (If you are not familiar with the idea of a rectangular coordinate system, you should review the first section of Chapter 3 in Book 1 now.)

Your calculator leaves the factory with standard coordinate axes built in. To see what they look like, turn on your calculator and press ⟨GRAPH⟩ (in the upper right corner). You should see a horizontal and a vertical axis crossing the middle of the screen. The horizontal axis is called the *x*-**axis**, and the vertical axis is called the *y*-**axis**. (If your screen doesn't show this, press ⟨ZOOM⟩ and choose 6:ZStandard .) Examine this display carefully; then answer the following questions.

A.7

1. Assuming that the dots along each axis mark the integer points, what is the largest possible value on the *x*-axis? On the *y*-axis?

2. What is the smallest possible value on the *x*-axis? On the *y*-axis?

3. Does it look as if the same unit of measure is being used on both axes?

4. Why do you suppose the spacing between the units is not exactly the same everywhere on an axis? Do you think that this might cause a problem?

Published by IT'S ABOUT TIME, Inc. © 2000 MATHconx, LLC

The Graph Window

A.7

These questions are intended to get students to understand the purpose for some of the display adjustments that are available from various menus. These adjustment options will be described shortly.

1. 10 for both;
2. -10 for both;
3. No;
4. Because the numbers of dots across and down are not multiples of 10. Both this and the apparent difference in unit length on the axes could be misleading later if not understood properly. The students probably can only guess at this now.

NOTES

The standard coordinate axis setting can be changed in several ways. This is done using the menu that appears when you press WINDOW . Try that now. You should get Display A.8.

```
WINDOW FORMAT
  Xmin = -10
  Xmax = 10
  Xscl = 1
  Ymin = -10
  Ymax = 10
  Yscl = 1


      TI-82
```

```
WINDOW
  Xmin = -10
  Xmax = 10
  Xscl = 1
  Ymin = -10
  Ymax = 10
  Yscl = 1
  Xres = 1

      TI-83
```

Display A.8

Xmin and Xmax are the smallest and largest values on the *x*-axis (the horizontal axis); Ymin and Ymax are the smallest and largest values on the *y*-axis (the vertical axis).

Xscl and Yscl are the scales for marking off points on the axes. The setting 1 means that each single integer value on the axis is marked. To see how the scale value works, change Xscl to 2. (Move the cursor down, using ▽ , then just key in 2 in place of 1.) Now press GRAPH . What change do you notice? Now go back to the WINDOW menu (press WINDOW) and change Yscl to 5. Return to the graph (press GRAPH). What has changed?

You can ignore the Xres = 1 line on the TI-83 for now. (If you're really curious, see p. 3–11 of the TI-83 Guidebook.)

Change the WINDOW settings so that they look like Display A.9. Then look at the graph and answer these questions.

A.8

1. Where on the screen is the origin of the coordinate system?

2. Does it look as if the same unit of measure is being used on both axes?

3. Does it look as if the spacing between the units is the same everywhere on an axis?

4. What happens when you press △ then ▽ ?

A.8

1. These settings provide a coordinate system with the origin in the lower left corner of the screen.
2. The integer points are marked on the axes, using the same distance as the unit of measure on both.
3. The units are uniformly spaced on each axis because the array of dots in the screen display is 95 by 63. The scale in this case is actually 10 dots to the unit in each coordinate direction.
4. When the two arrow keys are pressed, a cursor in the form of a cross appears exactly in the center of the screen, and the coordinates of its location are shown at the bottom: $x = 4.7$ and $y = 3.1$. This is discussed further in the next couple of paragraphs.

NOTES

```
WINDOW FORMAT
  Xmin=0
  Xmax=9.4
  Xscl=1
  Ymin=0
  Ymax=6.2
  Yscl=1

        TI-82
```

```
WINDOW
  Xmin=0
  Xmax=9.4
  Xscl=1
  Ymin=0
  Ymax=6.2
  Yscl=1
  Xres=1

        TI-83
```

Display A.9

If you have worked through the previous questions, you found that pressing ⬚ △ , ⬚ ▽ puts a cross exactly in the middle of your screen and two numbers at the bottom. The cross is the cursor for the graphing screen, and the numbers are the coordinates of the point at its center. In this case, the cursor is at (4.7, 3.1). It can be moved to any point on the graph by using the four arrow keys ⬚ △ , ⬚ ▽ , ⬚ ◁ , ⬚ ▷ at the upper right of the keypad.

A.9 Move the cursor to the point (4, 3). How far does the cursor move each time you press ⬚ ◁ or ⬚ ▷ ? How far does it move each time you press ⬚ △ or ⬚ ▽ ? Now move the cursor directly down to the bottom of the screen. What are the coordinates of the lowest point you can reach?

These new WINDOW settings are better than the standard one in some ways, and worse in others. Let's look again at the Standard coordinate system and compare it with the one we just saw. To get back to the standard settings, press ⬚ ZOOM , then press ⬚ 6 to choose ZStandard. The Standard coordinate axes should appear immediately.

A.10 These questions refer to the Standard coordinate axes.

1. Where is the cursor to begin with? How do you find it if you can't remember?

2. Try to move the cursor to the point (4,3). How close can you get to it?

3. How far does the cursor move each time you press ⬚ ◁ or ⬚ ▷ ?

4. How far does it move each time you press ⬚ △ or ⬚ ▽ ?

This is a simple exercise in understanding cursor movement. It also prepares the student for an investigation of scale changes. In this case, the cursor moves 0.1 unit each time you press any arrow key. This can be seen from the change in coordinates at the bottom of the screen. The lowest point directly beneath (4, 3) on this screen is (4, 0).

A.10

This is an important exploration for understanding how the calculator deals with coordinate systems.

1. The cursor is at (0, 0) to begin with; it can be found by pressing [△] [▽] or [◁] [▷] .

2. (4.0425532, 2.9032258)

3. 0.212766 of a unit, with some minor variations.

4. 0.3225807 of a unit, with some minor variations.

NOTES

5. Move the cursor directly down to the bottom of the screen. What are the coordinates of the lowest point you can reach?

6. In what ways is this coordinate system better than the one we set up for the previous set of questions? In what ways is it worse?

7. How might we fix the bad features of this system without losing the good ones?

Another useful WINDOW setting is 8:ZInteger in the ZOOM menu. When you press [8], coordinate axes appear, but they are still the standard ones. Press [ENTER] to get the Integer settings.

These questions refer to the Integer coordinate axes.

1. Try to move the cursor to the point (4, 3). How close can you get to it?

A.11

2. How far does the cursor move each time you press [◁] or [▷]?

3. How far does it move each time you press [△] or [▽]?

4. Why is this setting named Integer?

5. In what ways is this coordinate system better than the one we set up for the previous set of questions? In what ways is it worse?

6. How might we fix the bad features of this system without losing the good ones?

To plot a point (mark its location) on the graphing screen, go to the point-drawing part of the DRAW menu, like this.

Press [2nd] [PRGM] and move the top cursor to POINTS .

Choose 1 to make the [ENTER] key mark cursor locations. If you want to mark some points and erase others, choose 3. This lets the [ENTER] key change the state of any point the cursor is on; it will mark one that isn't already marked, and will unmark one that is. (*Hint:* If you have plotted too many points and you want to start over, you can go to ZOOM menu and press [6]. This will wipe out everything you have plotted and return to the Standard coordinate settings. If you were using different coordinate settings, you will have to redo them in the WINDOW menu.) If you want to erase some points, see Drawing Points on a graph section in the TI Guidebook.

A-13

Published by IT'S ABOUT TIME, Inc. © 2000 MATHconx, LLC

5. (4.0425532, -10)

6. There are many ways of answering these questions. A major advantage of the standard system is that it allows for negative coordinate values. It also has the same maximum and minimum values on each axis. The fact that the cursor does not move in "nice" increments is a nuisance, as is the fact that the horizontal single step amounts differ from the vertical ones. Students might also find it annoying that points with integer coordinates can't always be reached exactly.

7. This might be asking a lot of students who are unfamiliar with the calculator, but class discussion could be productive. To fix the drawbacks listed above while retaining the advantages, change the WINDOW settings so that the x-axis goes from -4.7 to 4.7 and the y-axis goes from -3.1 to 3.1. Remember to use $\boxed{(-)}$, instead of $\boxed{-}$, when entering the negative values. This will give you a coordinate system with $(0, 0)$ in the middle of the screen, so that it will handle both positive and negative values. The cursor will move in increments of 0.1 in either direction, and hence all the points with integer coordinates can be reached exactly. The disadvantage to this system is its limited range. The exercises give students a chance to explore other options.

A.11

1. This Exploration should be easier than the previous one. The cursor can be moved exactly to $(4, 3)$.

2. & 3. It moves exactly 1 unit each time any arrow key is pressed.

4. That is, all the points that can be plotted exactly must have integer coordinates; hence, it is called the Integer setting.

5. & 6. The last two parts are open ended, as in the previous Exploration.

NOTES

Problem Set: Appendix A

1. What WINDOW settings do you need in order to put the origin at the upper right corner of your screen? What can you say about the coordinates of the points that can be plotted on this screen?

2. What WINDOW settings do you need in order to put the origin at the upper left corner of your screen? What can you say about the coordinates of the points that can be plotted on this screen?

3. Choose the Integer setting for the coordinate axes and plot the points (30, 14), (-5, 20), (-26, -11), and (6, -30). Then write the coordinates of two points that lie within the area of the graph window but cannot be plotted exactly with this setting.

4. Find WINDOW settings to form a coordinate system such that the points (120, 80) and (-60, -40) are within the window frame.

   (a) How far does the cursor move each time you press ◁ or ▷?

   (b) How far does it move each time you press △ or ▽?

   (c) Can you put the cursor exactly on (120, 80)? If not, how close can you come? Plot this point as closely as you can.

   (d) Can you put the cursor exactly on (-60, -40)? If not, how close can you come? Plot this point as closely as you can.

   (e) Can you put the cursor exactly on (0, 0)? If not, how close can you come?

5. Find WINDOW settings to form a coordinate system such that the cursor can be put exactly on the points (20, 24.5) and (-17.3, -14).

   (a) What is the initial position of the cursor?

   (b) How far does it move each time you press ◁ or ▷ ?

   (c) How far does it move each time you press △ or ▽ ?

   (d) Can you put the cursor exactly on (0, 0)? If not, how close can you come?

Published by IT'S ABOUT TIME, Inc. © 2000 MATHconx, LLC

Problem Set: Appendix A

1. Set Xmax and Ymax to 0. All points that can be plotted must have both coordinates negative (or zero).

2. Set Xmin and Ymax to 0. All points that can be plotted must have a nonnegative x-coordinate and a nonpositive y-coordinate.

3. Any point within the axes ranges that does not have integers for both coordinates cannot be plotted exactly.

4. This can be done in many different ways. Answers to the specific questions depend on the choice of coordinate extremes.

5. Perhaps the easiest (but not the only) way to do this is to set

   Xmin = -17.3, Xmax = 20, Ymin = -14, and Ymax = 20

   If these settings are used, then the rest of the answers are
   (a) (.95319149, 5.25)
   (b) approx. .3968 (with slight variations)
   (c) .6209677 (with minor variations in the last digit)
   (d) (.15957447, .28225806)

NOTES

Drawing Histograms

Drawing a histogram is very easy. All you have to do is choose a few numbers to tell the calculator how wide and how tall to make the bars, as follows. Turn your calculator on and press [WINDOW]. The screen should look like Display A.10, maybe with different numbers.

```
WINDOW FORMAT
  Xmin = -10
  Xmax = 10
  Xscl = 1
  Ymin = -10
  Ymax = 10
  Yscl = 1

      TI-82
```

```
WINDOW
  Xmin = -10
  Xmax = 10
  Xscl = 1
  Ymin = -10
  Ymax = 10
  Yscl = 1
  Xres = 1

      TI-83
```

Display A.10

The numbers in this WINDOW list tell the calculator how to set the horizontal (X) and vertical (Y) scales.

- Xmin, an abbreviation of *X minimum*, is the smallest data value the picture will show. You should set it at some convenient value less than or equal to the smallest value in your data set.

- Xmax, an abbreviation of *X maximum*, is the largest data value the picture will show. Set it at some convenient value greater than or equal to the largest value in your data set.

- Xscl, an abbreviation of *X scale*, says how to group the data. It is the size of the base interval at the bottom of each bar of the histogram. For instance, Xscl = 10 will group the data by 10s, starting from the value of Xmin that you chose.

- Ymin is the smallest frequency of any data group. It is never less than 0, which usually is a good choice for it.

- Ymax represents the length of the longest bar. Choose a convenient number that is not less than the largest frequency of any data group, but not much larger.

- Yscl determines the size of the steps to be marked on the vertical (frequency) scale. For small data sets, set it to 1. If your setting for Ymax is much larger than 10, you might want to set Yscl larger than 1. A little experimenting will show you how to choose a helpful setting.

Published by IT'S ABOUT TIME, Inc. © 2000 MATHconx, LLC

A-15

Drawing Histograms

This is a self explanatory section. No exercises are included because there is ample opportunity to practice this process while working on problems in the text, particularly in Section 1.3 of Year 1.

NOTES

- If you have a TI-83, the last line at the bottom of this display is Xres = 1. It's a pixel resolution setting for graphing functions; ignore it for now.

Now your calculator is ready to draw a histogram.

- Press [STAT PLOT] (actually, [2nd] [Y=]), choose 1: and press [ENTER] .

- Choose these settings from each row by moving the cursor to them with the arrow keys and pressing [ENTER] each time.

  – Highlight On.

  – Highlight the histogram picture.

  – Set Xlist to the list containing your data (L1, L2, etc.).

  – Set Freq:1 .

Now press [GRAPH] — and there it is!

Drawing Boxplots

The TI-82 (TI-83) calculators can draw boxplots. All they need are the data and a few sizing instructions. Here's how to do it.

- Turn the calculator on, press [STAT] and choose 1:Edit... from the EDIT menu. Check which list contains the data you want to use. Let's assume it's in L1.

- Press [WINDOW] and set the horizontal (X) and vertical (Y) scales. (If you have forgotten how to set your WINDOW, refer to "The Graph Window" section.) Choose convenient numbers for the X range—Xmin less than your smallest data value and Xmax greater than your largest data value, but not too small or too large. (You don't want the picture to get squeezed into something you can't see well!) Also set Xscl to some convenient size.

- The Y settings don't matter as much. However, for the TI-82, if you set Ymin to –1 (Be sure to use the [(–)] key!) and Ymax to 4, the X scale will appear nicely in a readable

Published by IT'S ABOUT TIME, Inc. © 2000 MATHconx, LLC

Drawing Boxplots

This is another self explanatory section. No exercises are included because there is ample opportunity to practice this process while working on problems in the text, particularly in Section 1.5 of Year 1.

NOTES

location under the boxplot. For the TI-83, Ymin = -2 and Ymax = 2 work a little better.

- Press ⎡STAT PLOT⎤ (actually, ⎡2nd⎤ ⎡Y=⎤), choose 1: and press ⎡ENTER⎤ . Select these settings from each row by moving the cursor to them with the arrow keys and pressing ⎡ENTER⎤ each time.

    On; the boxplot picture; L1 from the Xlist; 1 from Freq

- Now press ⎡GRAPH⎤ —and there it is!
- To read the five-number summary, press ⎡TRACE⎤ and use the ⎡◁⎤ and ⎡▷⎤ to display the five numbers one at a time.

Graphing and Tracing Lines

If you want the calculator to graph a line or a curve, you must first be able to describe the line or curve by an algebraic equation. Once you have the equation for what you want to draw, you must put it in the form

$$y = [\text{something}]$$

For a straight line, that's not a problem; we often put the equation in this form, anyway. For some other kinds of curves, putting them in this form can be a little messy. In this section we shall deal only with straight lines.

All graphing begins with the ⎡Y=⎤ key. When you press this key for the first time, you get the screen in Display A.11.

Y₁ =
Y₂ =
Y₃ =
Y₄ =
Y₅ =
Y₆ =
Y₇ =

Y1 = Y2 = Y3 = Y4 = Y5 = Y6 = Y7 =

Plot1   Plot2   Plot3
\Y1 =
\Y2 =
\Y3 =
\Y4 =
\Y5 =
\Y6 =
\Y7 =

TI-82   TI-83

Display A.11

Published by IT'S ABOUT TIME, Inc. © 2000 MATHconx, LLC

Graphing and Tracing Lines

This section should be helpful for students when they get to Chapter 3 of Year 1.

NOTES

These lines allow you to put in as many as ten different algebraic equations for things you want drawn. (The subscript number gives you a way to keep track of which equation goes with which picture on the graph.) To see how the process works, we'll make the first example simple—two straight lines through the origin.

Key in -.5X on the $Y_1=$ line, *using the* $\boxed{X,T,\theta}$ *key to make the* X; then press $\boxed{\text{ENTER}}$.

(It is important to use $\boxed{X,T,\theta}$ for X because that's how the calculator knows that you are referring to the horizontal axis.)

Key in -.25X on the $Y2=$ line and $\boxed{\text{ENTER}}$ it.

Be sure to use the $\boxed{(-)}$ key for the negative sign. If you don't, you'll get an error message when you ask for the graph. If you want to wipe out one of these equations and redo it, just move the cursor back to the equation and press $\boxed{\text{CLEAR}}$.

Now your work is done. Press $\boxed{\text{GRAPH}}$ and just watch as the calculator draws the lines. If you forget which line goes with which equation, or if you want to see the coordinates of the points along your lines, press $\boxed{\text{TRACE}}$ and then move the cursor with the $\boxed{\triangleleft}$ and $\boxed{\triangleright}$ keys. When you do this, the coordinates of the cursor's position appear at the bottom of the screen. For the TI-82, a number appears in the upper right corner to tell you which equation you're tracing. For the TI-83, the equation appears in the upper left hand corner. In this example, when you press $\boxed{\text{TRACE}}$ you will be on $Y_1=$ -.5X, the first of the two lines we entered. Try it. Now move back and forth along this line.

To switch from one line to another, use the $\boxed{\triangle}$ and $\boxed{\triangledown}$ keys. Notice that, in this case, either of these keys gets you to the other line. That's because we are only graphing two equations. If we were graphing more than two, these keys would move up and down the *list of equations*, regardless of where the graphs appeared on the screen.

There is a way to remove the graph of an equation from the screen without erasing the equation from your list. For example, let us remove the line $Y1=$ -.5X from the picture. Go back to the $\boxed{Y=}$ list. Notice that the = sign of each equation appears in a dark block. This shows that the graph of

A-18

Published by IT'S ABOUT TIME, Inc. © 2000 MATHconx, LLC

NOTES

this equation is turned on. To turn it off, move the cursor to the = sign and press [ENTER] . The dark block will disappear. To turn it back on, put the cursor back on = and press [ENTER] again.

Approximating Data by a Line

This section refers to a situation that commonly arises in the analysis of two variable data. Such data can be represented as points on a coordinate plane, and it is often useful to know if the pattern of points can be approximated by a straight line. A common way of doing this is called *least-squares approximation*. An explanation of this process and its use appears in Chapter 4 of Year 1. This calculator section provides a simple example of how to get the TI-82 (TI-83) to give you a least-squares approximation of a set of data.

Let's look at a very small, simple data set. (The process is exactly the same for bigger, more complicated data sets.) Here are four points of two variable data.

$$(1, 2) \quad (2, 3) \quad (3, 5) \quad (4, 6)$$

If you plot these points on a coordinate plane, you will see that they don't all lie on the same line. (Don't just take our word for it; make a sketch!) The calculator uses the least-squares method to find automatically the line of "best fit." Section 4.3 (in Chapter 4) describes how this method works and what best fit means. These are the instructions for getting the calculator to do all the tedious work for you.

First of all, you need to have the data entered in two *separate data storage lists. You get to* these lists by pressing [STAT] and choosing 1:EDIT... from the EDIT menu. When you press [ENTER], you should get Display A.12.

Display A.12

Published by IT'S ABOUT TIME, Inc. © 2000 MATHconx, LLC

Approximating Data by a Line

This simple example relies on some of the calculator's default choices. For instance, the data are entered in lists L1 and L2, which are the default comparison lists for LinReg. To compare other data lists with this function, you must specify your list choices. See the calculator's instruction manual for details.

Note that when you go through the linear regression process described here, the correlation coefficient r shows up automatically on the TI-82, but not on the TI-83. To get it on the TI-83, go to the CATALOG menu, choose DiagnosticOn, and [ENTER] it. Then you will get both r^2 and r in the linear regression display.

NOTES

If the columns already contain data that you don't want, you can clear them out in either of two ways.

- Press [STAT] and choose 4:ClrList from the menu that appears. When the message ClrList appears, enter the name of the list you want to clear. (Press [2nd] [1] for L1, [2nd] [2] for L2, etc.) Then press [ENTER] ; the screen will say Done. Now press [STAT] to return to the process of entering data.

- Go to the MEM screen (press [2nd] [+]) and choose 2:Delete... (press [2]). Choose 3:List... from the menu that appears. The screen will show the name of each data storage list that contains data. Use the arrow keys to pick the ones that you want to clear out; press [ENTER] for each one. Now press [STAT] to return to the process of entering data.

Enter the first coordinate of each data point into list L1; put its second coordinate in list L2. The four data points of our example should appear as shown in Display A.13.

L1	L2	L3
1	2	-------
2	3	
3	5	
4	6	
-------	-------	
L2(5) =		

Display A.13

Now we are almost done. Press [STAT] and go to the CALC menu. Choose LinReg(ax + b) . When you press [ENTER] , the screen will display an algebraic description of the line of best fit. For our example, it looks like Display A.14.

- The second line, $y = ax + b$, just tells you that the information is for slope-intercept form. (Notice that the TI-82 (TI-83) use a, not m, for the slope here.)

- The third line says that the slope is 1.4.

- The fourth line says that the y-intercept is .5.

Note: On the TI-82, the last line shows the **correlation coefficient,** a measure of how good the fit is. The correlation coefficient is not discussed in your textbook. A detailed explanation of how it works will have to wait until you study

NOTES

statistics in more depth. But, in case you are curious about it, here is a little more information. The correlation coefficient is always a number between -1 and 1, inclusive. 1 and -1 stand for a perfect fit, with all points exactly on the line. (1 is for lines with positive slope; -1 is for lines with negative slope.) The closer r is to 0, the worse the fit.

```
LinReg
y = ax + b
a = 1.4
b = .5
r = .9899494937
```
TI-82

```
LinReg
y = ax + b
a = 1.4
b = .5
```
TI-83

Display A.14

Putting together this information about our example, we see that the least-squares line is described by the equation

$$y = 1.4x + .5$$

Graph the line $y = 1.4x + .5$. Are any of the four data points on it? How can you be sure?

A.12

Using Formulas to Make Lists

Sometimes it is useful to make a new list of data from an old one by doing the same thing to each data value. For instance, you might want to add a fixed number to each value, square each value, or find the distance of each value from some particular number. Instead of computing the new list one entry at a time, you can do it all at once if you can express your process as a formula.

Here's how the process works.

- Go to the STAT menu. Enter a list of data in L1, and then clear L2 and L3.

- To add 5 to each entry in L1, move the cursor over to the second column, then up to the heading, L2. The bottom line of your display should read L2= (without any number in parentheses).

A-21

A.12

There are two ways to check whether or not the points are exactly on the line. One is to substitute each one into the equation and see if the result is true. The other is to have the calculator plot the line with the Integer setting and move the [TRACE] cursor to the x-values 1, 2, 3, and 4. Either way, the students can see that none of the points are exactly on the line. By using the calculator, they will see the actual y-value of each point on the line with the same x-value as the data point they are checking, thus seeing how close the line comes to each data point.

Using Formulas to Make Lists

This section probably will be more useful to students after they have covered functions expressed as formulas. It is not essential to their basic understanding of the calculators. The process explained here is very much like that used in working with electronic spreadsheets. However, there is one crucial difference: The data must be in the "domain" list *before* the formula is entered at the top of the output column. Unlike spreadsheets, the TI-82 (TI-83) calculators do not store the formula. They simply use the formula to calculate the column entries, and then store only the entries. If you change a domain entry later, the corresponding entry in the output column will *not* change.

NOTES

- The trick here is to let the symbol L_1 stand for each element of the list L_1. That is, we make L_1 *a variable*. Key in $L_1 + 5$; the bottom of your screen should read $L_2 = L_1 + 5$.

- Now press [ENTER] and watch the entire column for L_2 fill out automatically!

- To list in L_2, the square of each entry in L_1, put the cursor on L_2 (at the top of the column). Then enter $L_1 \hat{} 2$ (or $L_1 * L_1$).

- Now let us list in L_3 the midpoint between the L_1 entry and the L_2 entry. Put the cursor back on L_3 at the top of the column and press [CLEAR]. This removes the old formula. Now key in $(L_1 + L_2)/2$ and press [ENTER].

1. List at least ten data values in L_1.

A.13

2. Write a formula to list in L_2 the distance between 17 and each entry in L_1. Remember: Distances are never negative numbers. Then use it.

3. Write a formula to list in L_3 the square of the difference (which may be negative) between each entry in L_1 and 17. Then use it.

4. Write a formula to list in L_4 the square root of each entry in L_3. Then use it.

5. How are columns L_2 and L_4 related? Explain.

Drawing Circles

To draw circles directly on a graph, use 9:Circle(in the DRAW menu. (The DRAW menu appears when you press [2nd] [DRAW].) 2:Line(can be used to draw segments, which lets you add radii, diameters, and other segments to your drawings of circles.

Before beginning, make sure that all the functions on your Y= screen are turned off. If they are not, their graphs will appear when you draw circles and segments. Also make sure that all STAT PLOTS are turned off.

Follow these instructions to draw a circle directly on a graph.

1. From the ZOOM menu, choose ZStandard (to clear any unusual WINDOW settings). Then choose ZSquare or ZInteger, which displays the graph window.

1. This is mostly routine practice, but it also illustrates how to get absolute value without using the abs function.

2. L2 = abs (17 − L1) or L2 = abs (L1− 17)

3. L3 = (L1 − 17)^2 or L3 = (L1 − 17) ∗ (L1 − 17)

4. L4 = $\sqrt{L3}$

5. They are the same. Squaring makes a number positive and the calculator's value for square root is the positive root. The net effect of these two steps is to make positive whatever number you start with; that is, to give you its absolute value.

Drawing Circles

This material probably will be most useful for Year 2, particularly in Chapter 4.

These questions are for practicing the calculator skill just described. (a) and (b) are straightforward. For (c), students can choose any radii for the four circles; they have to enter the center point in each case.

This is another skill reinforcement exercise.

1. Circles will look oval in Standard WINDOW setting and in any setting where the x and y axes are of equal length in calculator units. To get a circle that looks round, choose the ZSquare WINDOW setting in the ZOOM menu.

2. This is straightforward. Answers as to which method is easier are likely to vary, depending on the learning style preferences of the individual students.

NOTES

2. From the DRAW menu, choose 9:Circle(.

3. Choose a point for the center by moving the cursor to this point and pressing [ENTER] .

4. Choose the radius for your circle by moving the cursor this many units away from the center and pressing [ENTER] .

You can continue to draw circles by repeating the last two steps. To clear the screen before drawing a new circle, use :ClrDraw in the DRAW menu. If you want to stop drawing circles, press [CLEAR] .

> **Follow the steps above to draw each of these items.**
>
> 1. a circle with center (0, 10) and radius 5
>
> 2. a circle with center (12, −7) and radius 15
>
> 3. four circles with center (0, 0)

a

A.14

You can also draw a circle from the Home Screen (the calculator's primary display WINDOW) by following these instructions. (You can use this same method to draw circles from a program.)

1. From the Home Screen, choose Circle(from the DRAW menu.

2. Input the coordinates of the center, followed by the radius; then press [ENTER] . For example, if you enter (0, 10, 5), the calculator will draw a circle with center at (0, 10) and radius 5, using whatever ZOOM WINDOW setting is current.

3. To return to the Home Screen, press [CLEAR] .

> **1. Draw a circle with center (3, 2) and radius 7 directly from the Home Screen. (If your graph does not look like a circle, how can you adjust the graph WINDOW so that it does?)**
>
> **2. Draw four concentric circles around (0, 0) directly from the Home Screen. Earlier you were asked to draw this figure directly on a graph. Which method is easier for you? Why?**

b

A.15

Published by IT'S ABOUT TIME, Inc. © 2000 MATHconx, LLC

NOTES

Using a Spreadsheet

Computers give us many different tools for doing and using mathematics. One of these tools is called a **spreadsheet**. These days, a spreadsheet is an easy-to-use and very powerful computer program, but the idea of a spreadsheet is really much simpler and older than computers. Originally, a spreadsheet was just an oversized piece of paper, with lines and columns that made it easier for accountants and bookkeepers to keep their work in order.

You can make a spreadsheet on a lined piece of paper.

- Make a narrow border across the top and down the left side of the sheet.

- Divide the rest of the paper into columns from top to bottom. Six columns of about equal width will do for now.

- In the left margin, number the lines, beginning with 1, to the bottom of the page.

- Across the top margin, name each column with a letter from A to F in alphabetical order.

Your paper should look something like Display B.1.

	A	B	C	D	E	F
1						
2						
3						
4						
5						
6						
⋮						

Display B.1

B-1

Using a Spreadsheet

This appendix is *not* intended to replace a manual for your electronic spreadsheet program. Rather, it has two purposes.

- It serves as a gentle introduction to electronic spreadsheets by way of some simple exercises.

- It provides a convenient reference for some of the more commonly used elementary procedures.

The instructions provided here are fairly generic. They have been crafted to apply equally well to Microsoft Excel and to Lotus 1-2-3, with appropriate comments about specific differences. You should be able to use this Appendix with virtually any electronic spreadsheet program. However, if you are using an older and/or less common spreadsheet, it probably would be a good idea to work through these instructions with it in some detail. In any event, your spreadsheet manual should be regarded as the definitive reference source.

NOTES

The Cell Names

Each box in this grid has its own address — the letter of its column followed by the number of its row. For instance, C4 refers to the box, third column (column C), on the fourth line (row). The electronic spreadsheets that computers handle look just like this, and each position in them is addressed in just the same way. Electronic spreadsheet manuals often call the boxes **cells**. We'll do the same thing, so that you become used to the term.

B.1

Here are a couple of questions to get you comfortable with the way cells are addressed.

• Make a copy of Display B.1 and shade in these cells: A2, B3, C4, D5, E6, A6, B5, D3, E2. What shape do you get?

• If you wanted Display B.1 to be shaded in a checkerboard pattern, with alternating cells filled in, which cells would you shade? Write out all their addresses. (There's more than one way to do this.)

The advantage of electronic spreadsheets over handmade ones is that the electronic ones do the computations for you, *IF* you ask them properly. If you know how to speak the language of your spreadsheet program, you can get it to do all the hard work very quickly. The main idea to remember is

A spreadsheet is powerful because it can find and work with numbers that appear anywhere on it by using the cell names.

Therefore,

When working with a spreadsheet, always try to build what you want, step by step, from the first data you enter. The fewer numbers you have to enter, the easier it is for the spreadsheet to do your work.

Published by IT'S ABOUT TIME, Inc. © 2000 MATHconx, LLC

The Cell Names

B.1

The first question makes an X centered at C4. The second question can be done in two ways, depending on whether or not Cell A1 is to be shaded. If it is, then the cells to be shaded are

A1, C1, E1, B2, D2, F2, A3, C3, E3, B4, D4, F4, A5, C5, E5, B6, D6, F6

Otherwise, the shaded cells are

B1, D1, F2, A2, C2, E2, B3, D3, F3, A4, C4, E4, B5, D5, F5, A6, C6, E6

NOTES

___

Appendix B: Using a Spreadsheet

The rest of this appendix shows you how to get an electronic spreadsheet to work for you. For practice, each new process will be introduced by using it to deal with this problem.

> You are sent to the local supermarket to buy at least 2 pounds of potato chips for a club picnic. The club treasurer tells you to spend as little money as possible.

Now, there are many different brands of potato chips, and each brand comes in several different size bags. How can you compare prices in a useful way? Well, the bag sizes are measured in ounces. If you divide the price of the bag by the number of ounces, you'll get the price per ounce (this approach is called *unit* pricing). We'll set up a spreadsheet to tell you the price per ounce of every kind of potato chip bag your market sells.

> *Don't just read the rest of this appendix*: **DO IT! Work along with the instructions using your own spreadsheet.**

B.2

B.3

Entering Numbers and Text

There are three different kinds of things you can put in a cell — numbers, text, and formulas. Most spreadsheets distinguish between numbers and text automatically.

1. If you enter numerical symbols only, the entry is treated as a number.

2. If you begin an entry with letters or other symbols not related to numbers (even if numbers are entered along with them), the entry is treated as text.

[Note: If you want a number (such as a date or a year) or a number related symbol (such as $) to be treated as a text entry, you have to tell the machine somehow. Check your user's manual for the way your spreadsheet program does it.]

Display B.2 lists the prices of different brands and sizes of potato chips, including the special sale prices for the day. These are actual data from a supermarket. To enter these data in

Published by IT'S ABOUT TIME, Inc. © 2000 MATHconx, LLC

B.2 It is important to have the students actually work through this example, step-by-step, on a computer, if possible. If you have enough access to computers to allow for small group work, that probably would be best. If you only have access to one computer for demonstration purposes, have students take turns working through the steps. Either way, check their understanding at each stage and discuss difficulties as they arise.

Entering Numbers and Text

B.3 It is tempting not to repeat the brand names for different sizes of the same brand. However, Is will cause serious problems when the rows are sorted because the brand name will not be carried along with the rest of the information for some rows. Discourage this particular economy of effort, or be prepared to have some students starting over again when they hit the sort step.

NOTES

their most useful form, you should use *three* columns—one for the brand, one for the weights (in ounces), and one for the prices. Put the information of Display B.2 into columns A, B, and C now.

Brand of Chip	No. of Ounces	$Cost of Bag
Cape Cod	11 oz.	2.49
Eagle Thins	9.5 oz.	1.99
Humpty Dumpty	6 oz.	1.19
Humpty Dumpty	10 oz.	1.68
Lay's	6 oz.	0.95
Lay's	14 oz.	2.79
O'Boisies	14.5 oz.	2.79
Ruffles	6 oz.	1.39
Ruffles	14 oz.	2.79
Tom's	6 oz.	1.39
Tom's	11 oz.	1.69
Wise	6 oz.	1.39
Wise	10 oz.	1.48

Display B.2

The standard column width of your spreadsheet probably is not big enough to handle some of the brand names. Find the Column Width command and adjust the width of column A to 15 spaces. While you're at it, you might as well adjust the width of column B (the ounces) and column C (the price) each seven spaces wide. This will make the display look a little neater.

Published by IT'S ABOUT TIME, Inc. © 2000 MATHconx, LLC

NOTES

Appendix B: Using a Spreadsheet

Entering Formulas

If you want the spreadsheet to calculate an entry from other data, you have to give it a formula to use. You also have to begin with a special symbol to let it know that a formula is about to be entered. The special symbol depends on the type of spreadsheet you have. Excel uses the symbol = ; Lotus 1-2-3 uses the symbol + ; your software might use something else.

Calculate the price per ounce of Cape Cod chips by entering the formula C1/B1 into cell D1. As soon as you enter it, the number 0.226363 should appear. This is correct, but more accurate than we need. Three decimal places should be enough. Find the spreadsheet command that fixes the number of decimal places and use it to set the column D display to 3 places.

Copying Formulas

To get the price per ounce of Eagle Thins, all you have to do is copy the formula from cell D1 to cell D2. Do that. (Check the spreadsheet manual to see how to copy from one cell to another.) As soon as you do it, the number 0.209 will appear. Now look at the formula itself. Notice that it says C2/B2; that is, when you copied the formula one cell below where it started, the spreadsheet automatically changed the cell addresses inside it by that amount. This automatic adjustment process is one of the most powerful features of the spreadsheet. Next we'll use it to get the price per ounce of *all* the other kinds of chips at once!

Repeated Copying

You can copy a cell entry over and over again, all at once, along as much of a row or column as you mark out. If the entry is a formula, the spreadsheet will automatically adjust the cell addresses in it at each step. In some spreadsheet programs (such as Excel), this is done by the Fill command. In others (such as Lotus 1-2-3), it is done as part of the Copy command, by highlighting the entire region of cells into which you want the formula copied.

Published by IT'S ABOUT TIME, Inc. © 2000 MATHconx, LLC

Repeated Copying

B.4

C3 /B3   C7 / D7   C13 /D13

NOTES
_____

Find out how this works for your spreadsheet. Then copy what's in D2 into cells D3 through D13 and watch all the per ounce prices appear immediately. At this point, your spreadsheet should look something like Display B.3.

	A	B	C	D
1	Cape Cod	11	2.49	0.226
2	Eagle Thins	9.5	1.99	0.209
3	Humpty Dumpty	6	1.19	0.198
4	Humpty Dumpty	10	1.68	0.168
5	Lay's	6	0.95	0.158
6	Lay's	14	2.79	0.199
7	O'Boisies	14.5	2.79	0.192
8	Ruffles	6	1.39	0.232
9	Ruffles	14	2.79	0.199
10	Tom's	6	1.39	0.232
11	Tom's	11	1.69	0.154
12	Wise	6	1.39	0.232
13	Wise	10	1.48	0.148

Display B.3

 What *formula* is being used in cell D3? In D7? In D13?

B.4

Inserting Rows and Columns

Now let's put in column headings so that the spreadsheet is easier to understand. Move the cursor to the beginning of row 1 and use the Insert Row command of your spreadsheet to put in two rows at the very top. (Cape Cod should now be in cell A3.) We'll use the first row for headings and leave the second row blank. Enter Brand in A1, ounce in B1, price in C1 and enter $/oz. in D1. Change the width of column D to 7 spaces.

Because we've moved everything down, the row numbers no longer correspond to the number of brands listed. Make space to renumber the rows that list the brands, like this: Move the cursor to the top of the first column and use the Insert Column command to put two new columns at the far left. (Cape Cod should now be in cell C3.)

Published by IT'S ABOUT TIME, Inc. © 2000 MATHconx, LLC

B-6

NOTES

Numbering Rows

Now let's try a little experiment. We'll number the brands in two different ways. Make the two new columns, A and B, only 4 spaces wide. Now put the numbers 1 through 13 down these two columns, starting at the third row, in these two ways.

B.5

- In column A, enter each number by hand—the number 1 in A3, the number 2 in A4, and so on, down to the number 13 in A15.

- In column B, enter the formula B2+1 in cell B3. The number 1 will appear because the spreadsheet treats the empty cell B2 as if it had 0 in it. Now copy this formula into all the cells from B3 through B15.

Do columns A and B match? (They should. If they don't, ask your teacher to help you find what went wrong.) At this point, your display should look like Display B.4.

	A	B	C	D	E	F
1			Brand	oz.	$/bag	$/oz.
2						
3	1	1	Cape Cod	11	2.49	0.226
4	2	2	Eagle Thins	9.5	1.99	0.209
5	3	3	Humpty Dumpty	6	1.19	0.198
6	4	4	Humpty Dumpty	10	1.68	0.168
7	5	5	Lay's	6	0.95	0.158
8	6	6	Lay's	14	2.79	0.199
9	7	7	O'Boisies	14.5	2.79	0.192
10	8	8	Ruffles	6	1.39	0.232
11	9	9	Ruffles	14	2.79	0.199
12	10	10	Tom's	6	1.39	0.232
13	11	11	Tom's	11	1.69	0.154
14	12	12	Wise	6	1.39	0.232
15	13	13	Wise	10	1.48	0.148

Display B.4

Published by IT'S ABOUT TIME, Inc. © 2000 MATHconx, LLC

Numbering Rows

B.5

The experiment actually takes place in the next step, when the rows are placed in order with respect to the per ounce price of the various bags of chips. The numbers entered by hand will go along with their original rows; however, the numbers entered by formula will remain as they are, numbering the rows from best deal to worst.

NOTES

Ordering Data

Another handy feature of an electronic spreadsheet is that it can put in order data that is listed in a column. It can put numbers in size order, either increasing or decreasing. Most spreadsheets can also put text entries in alphabetical order. To do this, you need to find the Sort command and tell it what list of data you want to rearrange. (In Excel, Sort is in the Data menu; in Lotus 1–2–3, it's in the Select menu.) The computer prompts you for a little more information, such as whether you want ascending or descending order, then does the sorting.

(Note: Some spreadsheets move entire rows when they sort; others can be told just to rearrange the data in a single column. Check your user's manual to see how your spreadsheet works. In this example, we assume that the spreadsheet moves entire rows when it sorts.)

Let's rearrange the potato chip list according to the price per ounce, from most expensive to least expensive. Follow your spreadsheet's instructions to sort the per ounce prices in column F in ascending order. Which kind of potato chip is the best buy? Which is the worst buy?

Look at columns A and B.

B.6

1. **Do they still match? What has happened? Explain.**

2. **What would have happened if you had entered the number 1 in B3, then entered the formula =B3+1 in B4? Explain.**

Now that we have all this information, how do we find out how much it will cost the club for the 2 pounds of potato chips? Here's one plan.

- Compute the number of ounces in 2 pounds.

- Multiply the cost of 1 ounce by the total number of ounces needed.

(*Warning*: There's something wrong with this approach; what is it?)

B.7

We'll do this on the spreadsheet because it provides an example of a different way to use cell addresses. To find the total number of ounces, we just multiply the number of pounds (2) by 16. Make these entries on the spreadsheet.

B-8

Ordering Data

1. See B.5.

2. Because the B3 entry is not a variable, the 1 would stay with the Cape Cod row, causing the numbering in column B to start over at that point.

The problem with this approach is that the chip prices are not bulk prices. You can't buy the chips by the ounce; they're sold in bags of certain fixed sizes. We deal with this after discussing the use of constant cell addresses. Cell D18 will have the value 32.

NOTES

- In C17, enter number of lbs.; in D17, enter 2.

- In C18, enter number of oz.; in D18, put the formula that multiplies the entry in D17 by 16. (What is that value?)

Constant Cell Addresses

To find out how much 2 pounds of each kind of potato chip will cost, first set column G to display in currency format. Then move the cursor to cell G3. (This should be the first blank cell at the end of row 3.) We want this cell to show the number of ounces to be bought (in D18) multiplied by the price per ounce (in F3). Let's try it.

- Enter the formula D18*F3 in G3. The result should be $4.74.
  (Is your first kind the Wise 10 oz. bag?)

- So far, so good. Now copy this formula to the next line, in G4. What do you get? $0.00? How come?

- Look at the formula as it appears in G4. Does it say D19*F4? What happened?

Remember that when you shift a formula from one location to another, the spreadsheet automatically shifts every cell address in exactly the same way. We copied this formula to a location one row down from where it was, so the spreadsheet added the number 1 to the row number of each cell address in the formula. Now, we want that to happen to one of these addresses, but not to the other. That is, the cost of the kind of potato chip in row 4 should use the price per ounce in F4, but it should still use the total number of ounces from D18.

To prevent the spreadsheet from automatically adjusting a cell address when a formula is moved, enter the cell address with a $ in front of its column letter and a $ in front of its row number.

B.8

This means that you should go back to cell G3 and enter the multiplication formula $D$18*F3. Now copy this to G4. Do you get $4.92? Good. (If not, what went wrong? Ask your teacher if you need help figuring it out.) Now copy this formula into cells G5 through G15. Column G now should show the cost for 2 pounds of each kind of potato chip in your list.

Published by IT'S ABOUT TIME, Inc. © 2000 MATHconx, LLC

Constant Cell Addresses

B.8

This is a fairly standard way of keeping a cell address fixed. However, some spreadsheets, particularly some older ones, use a different convention to distinguish between variable and constant cell addresses. Consult the user's manual; then advise your students accordingly.

NOTES

Go to G1, make this column 7 spaces wide and enter the word cost as the column heading.

B.9

1. According to column G, which kind of potato chip is the best buy?

2. Why is that *not* necessarily the best buy for your club?

3. What's wrong with letting this answer tell you what kind to buy? (*Hint*: How many *bags* would you have to buy?)

The INT Function

As the hint in the box above suggests, using the information in column G to guide your choice may not be a good idea because the supermarket sells potato chips by the bag. In order to know how much it will cost to get at least 2 pounds of chips, you first must know how many bags you'll need.

How do you do that? Easy, right? Just divide 32 oz. (2 lbs.) by the number of ounces in a single bag. If you get a mixed number, add 1 to the whole-number part.

For example, if you want at least 32 oz. in 10 oz. bags, divide 32 by 10. You get 3.2 as an answer, but, since you can't buy 0.2 of a bag of chips, you need 4 bags.

There's a spreadsheet function—called INT—that makes this very easy to compute automatically. The INT function gives you the greatest integer less than or equal to the number you put into it. For instance,

$$\text{INT}\left(3\tfrac{1}{3}\right) = 3$$

$$\text{INT}(2.98) = 2$$

$$\text{INT}(5) =$$

Let's use this function to carry out the computation we just did, finding how many 10 oz. bags of Wise potato chips we need in order to have at least 2 pounds. But instead of entering the numbers in separately, we'll get them from other cells on the spreadsheet. Move to cell H3 and enter the formula

$$\text{INT}(\$D\$18/D3) + 1$$

Published by IT'S ABOUT TIME, Inc. © 2000 MATHconx, LLC

B.9

1. Wise
2. and 3. See B.7 for explanations.

The INT Function

B.10

1. 32 (the number of ounces in 2 pounds).
2. The $ symbols keep this cell address from changing when the formula is copied elsewhere.
3. 10 (the number of ounces in a single bag)
4. 3.2
5. 3
6. 4
7. INT($D$18/D4)+1.

NOTES

Just to make sure you understand what we're doing, answer these questions before moving on.

1. What does $D$18 stand for?

2. Why are the $ symbols there?

3. What does D3 stand for?

4. What number is $D$18/D3?

5. What number is INT($D$18/D3)?

6. What number is INT($D$18/D3)+1?

7. If you copy this formula to cell H4, how will it read?

a

B.10

Now use the Fill command to copy this formula into cells H4 through H15. For each kind, the number you get says how many bags you need in order to have at least two pounds of chips. Put the heading bags at the top of this column H, and make the column 5 spaces wide.

Now we can finish the problem. To find the cost of at least 2 lbs. of each kind of chip, multiply the number of bags you need by the cost of a single bag. Enter a formula in I3 that does this; then copy it into I3 through I15. Finish your spreadsheet display by renaming column G cost 1 and naming column I cost 2 and changing the width of column I to 6 spaces.

1. If you *must* get at least 2 lbs. of chips and you want to spend as little as possible, which kind do you buy?

2. How many bags do you buy?

3. What does it cost you?

b

B.11

The next questions show the power of spreadsheets for testing out different variations of a situation. Each part is exactly the same as above, except that the total number of pounds of chips is different. Answer each one by changing as little as possible on your spreadsheet.

1. If you *must* get at least 3 lbs. of chips and you want to spend as little as possible, which kind do you buy? How many bags do you buy? What does it cost you?

2. If you *must* get at least 4 lbs. of chips and you want to spend as little as possible, which kind do you buy? How many bags do you buy? What does it cost you?

c

B.12

B.11

1. Tom's 11 oz. size
2. 3
3. $5.07. The finished spreadsheet should look like Display B.1T.

	A	B	C	D	E	F	G	H	I
1			Brand	oz.	$/bag	$/oz.	cost 1	bags	cost 2
2									
3	13	1	Wise	10	1.48	0.148	4.74	4	5.92
4	11	2	Tom's	11	1.69	0.154	4.92	3	5.07
5	5	3	Lay's	6	.95	0.158	5.07	6	5.70
6	4	4	Humpty Dumpty	10	1.68	0.168	5.38	4	6.72
7	7	5	O'Boisies	14.5	2.79	0.192	6.16	3	8.37
8	3	6	Humpty Dumpty	6	1.19	0.198	6.35	6	7.14
9	6	7	Lay's	14	2.79	0.199	6.38	3	8.37
10	9	8	Ruffles	14	2.79	0.199	6.38	3	8.37
11	2	9	Eagle Thins	9.5	1.99	0.209	6.70	4	7.96
12	1	10	Cape Cod	11	2.49	0.226	7.24	3	7.47
13	8	11	Ruffles	6	1.39	0.232	7.41	6	8.34
14	10	12	Tom's	6	1.39	0.232	7.41	6	8.34
15	12	13	Wise	6	1.39	0.232	7.41	6	8.34
16									
17			number of lbs.:	2					
18			number of oz.:	32					

Display B.1T

B.12

If the spreadsheet has been set up as described, each group of questions can be answered by changing only one entry on the spreadsheet, the total number of pounds shown in D17. Here are the answers.

1. 3 lbs.: 5 bags of Wise 10 oz. size, at a total cost of $7.40
2. 4 lbs.: 6 bags of Tom's 11 oz. size, at the total cost of $10.14

3. If you *must* get at least 5 lbs. of chips and you want to spend as little as possible, which kind do you buy? How many bags do you buy? What does it cost you?

Problem Set: Appendix B

1. These two questions refer to the potato chip spreadsheet that you just made.

   (a) Add a column J that shows the total number of ounces of potato chips of each kind that you get when you buy enough bags to get at least two pounds of them. What formula will compute these numbers?

   (b) Add a column K that shows the number of *extra* ounces (more than 2 pounds) that you get when you buy enough bags to get at least two pounds of potato chips. What formula will compute these numbers?

2. Make a spreadsheet like the one for the potato chips to deal with this problem.

   (a) Your favorite aunt runs a shelter for homeless cats. As a present for her birthday, you decide to give her 5 pounds of canned cat food. You want to spend as little money as possible. The brands, sizes, and prices for the canned cat food at the supermarket are shown in Display B.5. What brand and size is the best buy, and how many cans of it should you get? What will it cost?

   (b) Your best friend thinks you have a great idea. She decides to buy your aunt 5 pounds of canned cat food, too. If you both chip in and buy a combined present of 10 pounds of canned cat food, what is the best buy of canned cat food for your combined present? Explain your answer?

Published by IT'S ABOUT TIME, Inc. © 2000 MATHconx, LLC

3. 5 lbs.: 14 bags of Lay's 6 oz. size, at the total cost of $13.30

Problem Set: Appendix B

1.   (a) Formula for column J (as it appears for J3): H3*D3
   (b) Formula for column K (as it appears for K3): J3—$D$18
       Note that the formula J3—32 also works for the original 2 lb. problem, but it doesn't adjust automatically for the 3, 4, and 5 lb. problems.

2. A spreadsheet solution for this problem is shown in Display B.2T. Much of it can be constructed by mimicking the potato chip spreadsheet setup. The only new wrinkle is the "n for x" pricing. This invites the insertion of two new columns, F for the number of cans that are bought for the price shown in column E; column G is for the price per can. The row order shown in Display B.2T results from sorting with respect to price per oz. (column H), from least to most.

Here is how each column is constructed. Except for "number of oz.," each formula is shown as it would be in row 3; the data in its column is obtained by using Fill to copy the formula to the other cells in the column.

A   Number entered consecutively from 1 to 12.

B   Formula: B2+1

C   Brand entered individually, in alphabetical order (smaller size first within brands).

D   Ounces per can entered individually. Number of lbs. entered by hand in D16. Formula for number of oz.: D16*16

E   Prices entered individually; total price for group of cans, where appllicable.

F   Number of cans bought for price in column E; entered individually.

G   Display set to 3 decimal places. Formula: E3/F3

H   Display set to 3 decimal places. Formula: G3/D3

I   Cost (if sold in bulk) for D16 pounds. Formula: $D$17*H3

J   Number of cans required for at least D16 pounds. Formula: INT($D$17/D3) +1

K   Cost for number of cans in column J. Formula: J3*G3
    (a) The best deal for 5 lbs. is the 14 oz. size of Puss'n Boots; 6 cans are required
    (b) However, the best deal for 10 lbs. is the 13 oz. size of 9 Lives; 13 cans are required, for a total cost of $6.37

Brand of Cat Food	No. of Ounces	Cost
Alpo	6 oz.	3 for $1.00
Alpo	13.75 oz.	$ .65
Figaro	5.5 oz.	$ .37
Figaro	12 oz.	$ .66
Friskies	6 oz.	$ .35
Friskies	13 oz.	$ .58
Kal Kan	5.5 oz.	4 for $1.00
Puss 'n Boots	14 oz.	$ .55
9 Lives	5.5 oz.	3 for $ .88
9 Lives	13 oz.	$ .48
Whiskas	5.5 oz.	3 for $1.00
Whiskas	12.3 oz.	$ .55

Display B.5

3. Here's a bonus question.

(a) Invent a problem about breakfast foods that is like the potato chip and cat food problems.

(b) Go to your local supermarket and gather the brand, size, and price information that you will need to solve your problem.

(c) Using the data you gather for part (b), set up a spreadsheet that solves the problem you invented in part (a).

Published by IT'S ABOUT TIME, Inc. © 2000 MATHconx, LLC

	A	B	C	D	E	F	G	H	I	J	K
1			Brand	oz.	price	#	$/can	$/oz.	cost 1	bags	cost 2
2											
3	10	1	9 Lives	13	0.49	1	0.490	0.038	3.02	7	3.43
4	8	2	Puss' n Boots	14	0.55	1	0.550	0.039	3.14	6	3.30
5	6	3	Friskies	13	0.58	1	0.580	0.045	3.57	7	4.06
6	12	4	Whiskas	12.30	0.55	1	0.550	0.045	3.58	7	3.85
7	7	5	Kal Kan	5.50	1.00	4	0.250	0.045	3.64	15	3.75
8	2	6	Alpo	13.75	0.65	1	0.650	0.047	3.78	6	3.90
9	9	7	9 Lives	5.50	0.88	3	0.293	0.053	4.27	15	4.40
10	4	8	Figaro	12	0.66	1	0.660	0.055	4.40	7	4.62
11	1	9	Alpo	6	1.00	3	0.333	0.056	4.44	14	4.67
12	5	10	Friskies	6	0.35	1	0.350	0.058	4.67	14	4.90
13	11	11	Whiskas	5.50	1.00	3	0.333	0.061	4.85	15	5.00
14	3	12	Figaro	5.50	0.37	1	0.370	0.067	5.38	15	5.55
15											
16			number of lbs.:	5							
17			number of oz.:	80							

Display B.2T

Note that there is an interesting detail here, if you want to take the time to pursue it. Notice that the 5th, 6th and 7th kinds of cat food show the same price per oz. in column H. But the bulk costs of D17 ounces in column I is different! How can that be? A brief discussion can lead to the fact that the computer stores the answers to its computations in a much more exact form than it usually shows.

3. Students' answers to the bonus question will vary.

NOTES

Appendix C: Programming the TI-82 (TI-83)

After you have been using the TI-82 (TI-83) for a while, you may notice that you are repeating certain tasks on your calculator over and over. Often you are repeating the same sequence of keystrokes, which can become very tiresome. Programs give you a way to carry out long sequences of keystrokes all at once, saving you a great deal of time and energy.

In this appendix we will show you some simple TI-82 (TI-83) programs and how to enter and use them. In the textbook, there are some other programs which you will find useful in solving problems.

Correcting Mistakes

When you enter a program you will almost surely make some keying mistakes. You can use the arrow keys to back up and key over any mistakes. To insert something new, rather than keying over what is already there, give the insert command (INS above the ⌐DEL⌐ key) by keying

$$\boxed{\text{2nd}} \quad \boxed{\text{DEL}}$$

Use the ⌐DEL⌐ key to delete the current character.

Entering Programs

To enter a program, give the ⌐NEW⌐ command under the ⌐PRGM⌐ menu by keying

$$\boxed{\text{PRGM}} \quad \boxed{\triangleleft} \quad \boxed{\text{ENTER}}$$

Your calculator should look like Display C.1. You are now in program writing mode. Whatever you key in will be stored in the program you are creating, rather than being executed directly. To get out of program writing mode, give the QUIT command.

Published by IT'S ABOUT TIME, Inc. © 2000 MATHconx, LLC

APPENDIX C

Display C.1

Next you need to name your program so that you can use it. We will start with a very short and not very useful program just to test your ability to enter a program and run it. Give your program the name ADD. Normally, to enter the capital letters that are above and to the right of some of the keys you must press the [ALPHA] key first. When naming a program, however, the calculator goes into ALPHA mode automatically. This means you *don't* have to press the [ALPHA] key when entering the letters in the program name. Key in

Your calculator screen should now look like Display C.2

Display C.2

We now need to enter the actual program commands. Our test program will ask for two numbers and then add them. Each line of the program begins with a colon. At the end of each line of the program press [ENTER] . The first line of our program asks for the first of the two numbers it will add. The two numbers that we tell the calculator to add are called the *input* for the program. The Input command is the first item under the I/O section of the PRGM menu. We will store the input in memory A. Key in

Published by IT'S ABOUT TIME, Inc. © 2000 MATHconx, LLC

The TI screen should now look like Display C.3.

```
PROGRAM: ADD
: Input A
: ■
```

Display C.3

The next line in the program asks for another number and stores it in memory location B. Enter the second line now, based on the way you entered the first line. Your screen should now look like Display C.4.

```
PROGRAM: ADD
: Input A
: Input B
```

Display C.4

The third line adds the numbers stored in memories A and B and stores the result in memory C. Key in

[ALPHA] [A] [+] [ALPHA] [B] [STO ▷] [ALPHA] [C] [ENTER]

The new screen is in Display C.5.

```
PROGRAM: ADD
: Input A
: Input B
: A + B→C
: ■
```

Display C.5

We finish our program with a statement which displays the result of adding the two numbers (now stored in memory C). The display command Disp is the third item under the I/O section of the PRGM menu.

C-3

APPENDIX C

Key in

PRGM ▷ 3 ALPHA C

The resulting screen is in Display C.6

```
PROGRAM: ADD
: Input A
: Input B
:A + B→C
:Disp C
:■
```

Display C.6

We are done writing the program! To quit programming mode use the QUIT key (above the MODE key). The program is automatically saved. Key in

2nd QUIT

You are now back to the Home Screen, where you started.

Running Programs
To run the program we just keyed in, we go to the EXEC section of the PRGM menu, key in the number of the program we want to run, and then press ENTER . We will assume that the program named ADD that we just entered is program number 1. Key in

PRGM 1 ENTER

If you entered the program correctly, a question mark appears asking for input. (If there is an error, look at the next section on editing programs.) This question mark is produced by the first line of your program. You are being requested to type in the first of two numbers, which will then be added by the program. Let's suppose that we want to add the numbers 4 and 5. Press 4 then press ENTER . A second question mark appears asking for the second number. Press 5 and press ENTER again. The result, 9, should appear. The screen now looks like Display C.7.

Published by IT'S ABOUT TIME, Inc. © 2000 MATHconx, LLC

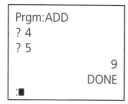

Display C.7

To run the program again, just press the [ENTER] key. You don't have to go through the **PRGM** menu to run the program the second time, as long as no other calculations have been performed in between. Try adding two other numbers to see how this works.

Quitting Programs

If you are in the middle of running a program and you want to stop the program, press [ON] key. To try this out, run the ADD program again, but this time when the first question mark appears, press [ON] . The screen should look like Display C.8.

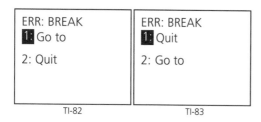

Display C.8

Press [2] to quit the program and return to the Home Screen. Pressing [1] puts you back in program writing mode at the point in the program where you stopped the program.

Editing Programs

If your program doesn't work, or if you just want to make changes to a program, you use the EDIT section of the **PRGM** menu. Key in

Published by IT'S ABOUT TIME, Inc. © 2000 MATHconx, LLC

APPENDIX C

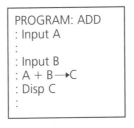

This should put you back in the ADD program (assuming it is program 1). Your screen should look just as it did when you left the program writing mode (see Display C.6). Use the arrow keys and the insert [INS] and delete [DEL] keys as explained in the Correcting Mistakes section.

To open space for a new line, put the cursor at the beginning of a line, give the insert command [INS] and then press [ENTER]. To try this on your ADD program, use the arrow keys to put the cursor at the beginning of the second line of the program and key in

[2nd] [DEL] [ENTER]

Your screen should look like Display C.9.

```
PROGRAM: ADD
: Input A
:
: Input B
: A + B→C
: Disp C
:
```

Display C.9

The blank line we just created will not affect the program, so we can just give the QUIT command to leave the program writing mode.

A Useful Program

Now that you have some practice with writing, editing and running programs, let's take a look at a program that you might really find useful.

Graphing With Parameters

Suppose that we want to graph the equation of a straight line, say $y = ax + 5$, for several values of a. The constant a is called a *parameter*. First we can enter the expression AX + 5 as expression Y1 under the Y= menu. We can then store numbers in memory A and press [GRAPH]. The problem is that we only see the graph for one value of A at a time. The following program allows you to easily produce graphs for many values of A and keep all of the graphs on the screen together.

Published by IT'S ABOUT TIME, Inc. © 2000 MATHconx, LLC

Enter the program shown in Display C.10, using what you learned from the **Entering Programs** section. Name the program PARAMS. Note: DrawF is item 6 under the DRAW menu (above the [PRGM] key) for the TI-82. Y1 is item number 1 of the Function sub menu under the **Y-vars** menu (above the [DRAW] [VARS] key). For the TI-83, Y1 is found by keys [VARS] [▷] [1] [1] [ENTER]

```
PROGRAM: PARAMS
: Input  A
: DrawF  Y1
: ■
```

Display C.10

The program is simple, but saves quite a few keystrokes. You put in a value for A, and then the function is graphed using the DrawF command.

To use this program you must store your function in function memory Y1 and then *turn off* Y1 (put the cursor on the = and press ENTER). Your Y= WINDOW should look like Display C.11. Notice that the = is *not* highlighted, indicating the function is off.

```
Y1 = AX + 5
Y2 =
Y3 =
Y4 =
Y5 =
Y6 =
Y7 =
Y8 =
```

Display C.11

To set the graph WINDOW to the Standard setting, press the 6 under the ZOOM menu. Your WINDOW settings should appear as in Display C.12.

Published by IT'S ABOUT TIME, Inc. © 2000 MATHconx, LLC

APPENDIX C

WINDOW FORMAT	WINDOW FORMAT
Xmin=−10	Xmin=−10
Xmax=10	Xmax=10
Xscl=1	Xscl=1
Ymin=−10	Ymin=−10
Ymax=10	Ymax=10
Yscl=1	Yscl=1
	Xres=1
TI-82	TI-83

Display C.12

Now run the program. Try starting with an A value of 1. Press [1] then [ENTER] in response to the question mark. You should see a graph of the function $y = 1x + 5$. To run the program again, first press the [CLEAR] key (to get back to the Home Screen) then [ENTER]. Try an A with a value of −2 this time. Now both the graphs of $Y = AX + B$ for $A = 1$ and for $A = -2$ should be on the screen, as shown in Display C.13.

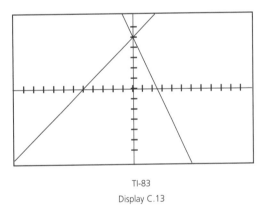

TI-83

Display C.13

If you want to clear the graph screen, use ClrDraw, which is item 1 under the DRAW menu.

You only need to change the function stored in Y_1 to graph any other function with one parameter. For instance, try graphing the function $y = a^x$ for various a values.

Appendix C: Programming the TI-82 (TI-83)

GLOSSARY   I.a. and I.b.

absolute temperature scale (Kelvin scale) A scale calibrated where water boils at 373° and freezes at 273°. The scale starts at absolute zero and has the same-size degrees as the Celsius scale.

absolute value The (nonnegative) distance of a number from 0.

acronym A type of abbreviation for a string of words.

algorithm A systematic procedure (steps or rules) performing a sequence of operations or computations.

analysis The process of separating something into simpler parts so that it can be better understood.

Associative Laws $(a + b) + c = a + (b + c)$ *(addition)*
$a(b \cdot c) = (a \cdot b)c$ *(multiplication)*

axis One of the reference lines in a coordinate system.

biased (experiment) An experiment or event in which one or several outcomes are more likely to occur than others.

bimodal (data set) A set made up of two distinct data groupings that are relatively far from each other.

binary digits The digits 0 and 1.

boxplot A five-number summary in picture form.

break-even point In business, the value of which the revenue and expenses are equal, i.e., the profit and/or loss are zero.

category data Data that can be classified into groups and titled—labels, names, etc.

Celsius temperature scale A scale calibrated where water boils at 100° and freezes at 0°.

chance A situation favoring some purpose. A word used interchangeably with *probability* and *likelihood*.

coefficient A number or variable that precedes a variable.

commutative A term that means a different order of variables or constants in an expression or an equation.

Published by IT'S ABOUT TIME, Inc. © 2000 MATHconx, LLC

Commutative Laws $a + b = b + a$ *(addition)*
$a \cdot b = b \cdot a$ *(multiplication)*

compound interest Interest paid on the principal and accrued interest.

constant A number, letter or symbol that represents one value only.

convention An agreement to do something in a particular way.

coordinate Each of the numbers or letters used to identify the position of a point in a coordinate system.

coordinate system A graphical method that uses two or more numbers or letters to locate a position in space.

data Factual information.

defined on A function is *defined on* a particular set if that set is in the domain of the function.

dependent variable The variable that represents the range of a function or the variable, the values of which are determined by the values of another variable to which it is related.

deviation The difference between a data value and some measure of center, such as the mean.

disjoint (sets) Two or more sets that have no elements in common.

Distributive Law $a(b + c) = ab + ac$
$(a + b)c = ac + bc$
$a(b - c) = ab - ac$
$a(b + c - d) = ab + ac - ad$

domain (of a function) The set of all possible "input" elements for the function. The elements of the independent variable.

dotplot A data display in which each data item is shown as a dot above its value on a number line.

ellipsis The symbol ... used to indicate something is missing or omitted.

empty set The set with no elements.

equally likely (events) Events that have the same probability of occurring.

equation A symbolic statement that two quantities are equal.

Published by IT'S ABOUT TIME, Inc. © 2000 MATHconx, LLC

event A subset of a sample space.

exponential decay The description of a function in the form $y = a^x$, where $0 < a < 1$; y decreases as x increases.

exponential function A function in which the independent variable is used as an exponent such that $f(x) = a^x$, where $0 < a < 1$.

exponential growth The description of a function in the form $y = a^x$, where $a > 1$; y increases as x increases.

exponentiation An operation of arithmetic where the base (a number or variable) is raised to an exponent (power).

extrapolation A procedure used to predict values of a variable in an unobserved interval (outside the interval) from observed values inside the interval.

Fahrenheit temperature scale A scale calibrated at which water boils at 212° and freezes at 32°.

first quartile The median of the "first half" of a data set; the median of the data that is less than the median of the entire data set.

five-number summary The minimum, first quartile, median, third quartile, and maximum numbers of a set of numerical data.

forecasting A procedure used to predict future events such as sales, the weather, etc., based on known data.

frequency The number of times a value appears in a data set.

function Any process or rule that assigns to each element of a first set, the domain, exactly one element from a second set, the range.

function composition The process or operation on one function by another, so that the images of the second function are in the domain of the first function.

graph A pictorial representation of a set of points in a coordinate system.

greatest integer function (int) The function that matches each real number with the largest integer that is less than or equal to that real number.

growth function An exponential function such that $f(x) = a^x$, where $a > 1$; as x increases, $f(x)$ increases.

Published by IT'S ABOUT TIME, Inc. © 2000 MATHconx, LLC

G-3

histogram A graphical display of measurement data that uses rectangles to show the frequency of data items in successive numerical intervals of equal size.

image (of an element under a function) The element in a range assigned by the function rule to the given element of the domain.

independent variable The variable that represents the domain of a function; the variable, the values of which are not affected by a second variable to which it is related.

inequality An algebraic statement that says that two numbers or expressions representing numbers are *not* equal.

int An abreviation for the greatest integer function.

interpolation A procedure used to estimate values of a variable between two known values.

interquartile range The numerical difference between the first and third quartiles of a data set.

intersection (of sets) The set of elements common to two or more sets.

intuition Insight to a situation based largely on feelings and beliefs.

Kelvin temperature scale (absolute temperature scale) A scale calibrated where water boils at 373° and freezes at 273°. The scale starts at absolute zero and has the same-size degrees as the Celsius scale.

kiloWatt One thousand Watts of electrical power.

kiloWatt-hour (kWh) The amount of electrical energy used in one hour.

label data Category data; data that are not numerical.

Laws governing equality If $a = b$, then $a + c = b + c$.
If $a = b$, then $a - c = b - c$.
If $a = b$, then $a \cdot c = b \cdot c$.
If $a = b$ and $c \neq 0$, then
$a \div c = b \div c$.

least-squares line A straight line that minimizes the sum of the squares of the vertical distances from the line to the points of a given data set in a coordinate plane.

Published by IT'S ABOUT TIME, Inc. © 2000 MATHconx, LLC

linear equation An equation that can be put in the form $y = ax + b$ or $x = k$.

linear interpolation A procedure used to estimate values of a variable between two given points in a scatterplot by using the values of the points that lie on a straight line joining the two given points.

mathematical law A statement that is true for all values for which it is defined.

mean The sum of a collection of numerical data divided by the number of data items.

mean absolute deviation The mean (average) of all the distances between the individual data items and the mean of a data set.

measurement data Data that are numbers being used to count or measure things.

median The middle value of a set of numerical data when the data are arranged in size order. If there is an even number of data items, the median is the mean of the two middle data items.

n The set of all counting numbers: the natural numbers.

Ohm's Law Voltage equals resistance times electrical current.

ordered pair Two variables or numbers in which the order matters.

origin The point of intersection of the axes of a coordinate system.

outlier A data item that does not fit in well with the rest of the data; for measurement data, often a number much larger or smaller than most of the other data.

perimeter The measure around the outside shape of a figure.

principle A basic rule that we accept and use to solve problems.

probability A measure of our belief that some event will occur.

quadrant Each of four regions that are formed by the perpendicular axes of a coordinate plane.

quartile One of three numbers (first, second and third quartiles) that separate an ordered set of numerical data into quarters.

Published by IT'S ABOUT TIME, Inc. © 2000 MATHconx, LLC

R An abbreviation for the set of all real numbers.

range (of a data set) The numerical difference between the largest and smallest data values.

range (of a function) The set of all the images of a function.

rectangular coordinate system A coordinate system in which the axes and all grid lines intersect at right angles.

sample space The set of all possible outcomes of an experiment.

scatterplot A geometric representation of two dimensional data in a coordinate plane obtained by plotting the data as points.

scientific notation A form in which numbers are expressed as a single digit number times ten to some integer power.

second quartile The median of a data set.

sequence A function that has the set of all counting (natural) numbers as its domain.

set A well-defined collection of objects or elements.

set-builder notation A way to represent sets by specifying the form of a typical element and the conditions such an element must satisfy. Its structure is "{[form of element] $\mid$ [conditions]}."

simple interest Interest paid on the original principal only.

simulate To copy or replicate an activity as closely as possible without actually performing the activity.

slope The ratio $\frac{\text{change in vertical coordinates}}{\text{change in horizontal coordinates}}$ between any two points on the line.

slope-intercept form $y = mx + b$ is the form for a linear equation, where m is the slope and b *is* the y-intercept.

solution (solution set) The set of value(s) for which an equation or inequality is true or the correct answer(s) to a problem.

solving a system of equations Finding the solutions that make all the equations in the system true.

spreadsheet (electronic) A computer or calculator program that allows the user to organize, display and perform operations on data and information stored in a rectangular array (matrix) of locations (cells).

Published by IT'S ABOUT TIME, Inc. © 2000 MATHconx, LLC

square (of a number) The product of a number and itself.

square root (of a number) The factor of a number that when squared is the number.

standard deviation The number that is the square root of the variance of a set of data.

stem-and-leaf plot A graphical method of displaying numerical data by grouping items that agree in all but (at most) their final digits.

step function A function that changes from one value to another in a regular pattern and stays at each value level for intervals of the domain. The graph appears as horizontal segments each having only one endpoint.

subset One set is a subset of another if every element of one set is also an element of the other set.

system of equations A set of two or more equations, the variables of which are related in some way.

term Each of the elements of a set listed in a sequence.

theory A careful study of a topic based on accepted ideas or formulas and how they relate to each other.

third quartile The median of the "second half" of a data set.

tree diagram A pictorial representation of events frequently used for counting purposes.

union (of sets) The set of elements belonging to one or more of the sets involved; or the operation of determining which elements belong to one or more of the sets.

values Numbers that a variable represents.

variable A letter or other symbol that represents any one of a collection of numbers or things.

variance The mean of the squares of all the deviations of a data set.

Venn diagram A pictorial representation of sets usually using circles and/or rectangles.

Voltage Electric potential expressed in Volts.

Watt A unit of electrical power.

Published by IT'S ABOUT TIME, Inc. © 2000 MATHconx, LLC

Glossary I.a. and I.b.

x-intercept The x value of the point where a line or curve intersects the x-axis; i.e., where $y = 0$.

y-intercept The point at which a line or curve intersects the y-axis; i.e., where $x = 0$.

Published by IT'S ABOUT TIME, Inc. © 2000 MATHconx, LLC

Index   I.b.

A

$A (r) = \pi r^2$, 379

About Words
   compose, 401
   composer, 401
   composition, 401

compound, 387
   domain, 331
   function, 330
   function composition, 401
   intersection, 425
   recurs, 348
   union, 428

Algorithm, 275-280, 282-286

Analysis, 399

Arrangement, 414

Axis
   horizontal, 300
   vertical, 300

B

Bacteria, 313-315

Biased, 477

Binary
   bits, 416
   digits, 416
   string, 449

Bits, 416

Book on Games of Chance, The, 471

Branch, 439-441
   complete, 444

Break-even point, 326

C

Calculator, 375, 376, 379, 486-489

Cardano, Girolamo, 471

Celsius, 373-376

Chance, 453, 454, 472
   probability, 454-465

Circle, 337
   area of, 337, 379

Code, 415
   arrangement, 414

pattern, 418

Commutative Law, 317

Complement, 469, 470

Complete branch, 444

Composite, 401, 406
   function, 401, 402

Compound, 318, 387
   continuous, 393, 394
   formula, 394
   interest, 318, 391-393
   population, 394-396

Compounds, 399

Computer, 414, 486

Continuous compounding, 393, 394

Counting (natural) numbers, 421

D

Defined on function, 364

deMere, Chevalier, 471

Dependent variable, 300, 321, 336-339

deSantine, Gabriel, 475

Die (dice), 461

Difference of, 426

Disjoint sets ($\varnothing$), 431, 432

Distributive Law, 317

Domain, 330-336, 343-344, 351, 358, 372
   image, 331, 336, 372

Doubling function, 359, 360

E

e (natural logarithms), 393

Economist, 307

Edison, Thomas, 416

Electric rates, 282-284

Element of a set, 420

Ellipsis (...), 348

Empty set, 422

Equal functions, 350, 351

Equally likely, 462, 463, 467, 469
   fair, 463

Equations
   algebraic, 379

linear, 301
   solution to, 420
   solving, 292, 304

Estimating techniques, 275, 458

Event, 456, 469
   certain, 454
   equally likely, 462, 467, 469
   impossible, 454

Experiment, 457
   biased, 477
   sample space, 467, 469, 470
   simulate, 478

Exploration probabilities, 476

Exponential function, 390

Extrapolate, 309

F

Factor, 357, 359

Fahrenheit, 373-376

Fair, 463

FBI, 329

Fermat, Pierre, 471

Fey, Charles, 466

Fifth root, 286

Fingerprint, 329

Formula, 394

Fraction of occurrences, 482

Function, 330-337, 343-348, 350, 356, 372, 377-379, 389, 399, 404-407
   analysis, 399
   composite, 401
   composition, 399, 401, 402
   continuous
   compounding formula, 393, 394
   conversion of F to C, 376
   defined on, 364
   domain of, 330-336, 343-344, 351, 358, 372

Published by IT'S ABOUT TIME, Inc. © 2000 MATHconx, LLC

I-1

Published by IT'S ABOUT TIME, Inc. © 2000 MATHconx, LLC

Published by IT'S ABOUT TIME, Inc. © 2000 MATHconx, LLC

NOTES

NOTES

NOTES